EPITOMIC WRITING IN LATE ANTIQUITY AND BEYOND

sera tela: Studies in Late Antique Literature and Its Reception

Series Editor: Marco Formisano, Ghent University, Belgium

This new series challenges existing paradigms of subordinating late-antique texts to classical literature: instead, it places late-antique literature at the centre of inquiry, and its title plays on the ambiguity of *tela*, evoking both the drawing of weapons and the building of a web. Late antique literature becomes a vantage point for looking both forward to its reception and transformation in subsequent ages, and backward, by engaging in the new and exciting experiment of viewing classical literature through the lens of late antiquity. Each volume is animated by interpretive enthusiasm and experimentalism aiming at highlighting what is new, unique, and unprecedented, rather than focussing on relationships with the classical past.

Coming soon:
A Late Antique Poetics? The Jeweled Style Revisited, edited by Joshua Hartman and Helen Kaufmann

EPITOMIC WRITING IN LATE ANTIQUITY AND BEYOND: FORMS OF UNABRIDGED WRITING

Edited by Paolo Felice Sacchi and Marco Formisano

BLOOMSBURY ACADEMIC
LONDON • NEW YORK • OXFORD • NEW DELHI • SYDNEY

BLOOMSBURY ACADEMIC
Bloomsbury Publishing Plc
50 Bedford Square, London, WC1B 3DP, UK
1385 Broadway, New York, NY 10018, USA
29 Earlsfort Terrace, Dublin 2, Ireland

BLOOMSBURY, BLOOMSBURY ACADEMIC and the Diana logo are trademarks of Bloomsbury Publishing Plc

First published in Great Britain 2023
Paperback edition published 2024

Cover design: Graham Robert Ward

A catalogue record for this book is available from the British Library.

Library of Congress Cataloging-in-Publication Data
Names: Sacchi, Paolo Felice, editor. | Formisano, Marco, editor. | Academia Belgica (Rome, Italy), host institution.
Title: Epitomic writing in late antiquity and beyond : forms of unabridged writing / edited by Paolo Felice Sacchi and Marco Formisano.
Other titles: Sera tela – studies in late antique literature and its reception.
Description: London ; New York : Bloomsbury Academic, 2022. | Series: Sera tela: studies in late antique literature and its reception | Selection of papers from a conference entitled "Unabridged. Epitome from fragmentation to recomposition (and back again)", held 5–6 June 2018 at the Academia Belgica in Rome. | Includes bibliographical references.
Identifiers: LCCN 2022021821 | ISBN 9781350281936 (hardback) | ISBN 9781350281974 (paperback) | ISBN 9781350281943 (ebook) | ISBN 9781350281950 (epub) | ISBN 9781350281967
Subjects: LCSH: Classical literature–History and criticism–Congresses. | Christian literature, Early–History and criticism–Congresses. | French literature–20th century–Congresses. | Comparative literature–Congresses. | Condensed books–History and criticism–Congresses. | LCGFT: Conference papers and proceedings.
Classification: LCC PA3001 .E65 2022 | DDC 880.09—dc23/eng/20220525
LC record available at https://lccn.loc.gov/2022021821

ISBN: HB: 978-1-3502-8193-6
PB: 978-1-3502-8197-4
ePDF: 978-1-3502-8194-3
eBook: 978-1-3502-8195-0

Series: sera tela: Studies in Late Antique Literature and Its Reception

Typeset by RefineCatch Limited, Bungay, Suffolk

To find out more about our authors and books visit www.bloomsbury.com and sign up for our newsletters.

CONTENTS

List of Illustrations vii
Notes on Contributors x
Series Editor Preface xiii
Preface xv

Introduction: Unabridged *Marco Formisano and Paolo Felice Sacchi* 1

Part I Epitomic Dimensions

1 **Pascal Quignard's *Petits traités*: (Anti-)modern Epitomes?** *Irena Kristeva* 23

2 **Ausonius Epitomizer: Encyclopaedism and Ordering Knowledge in Late Antique Gaul** *Brian P. Sowers* 34

3 **Cato *Capitulatim*: Nepos the Censor** *Jared Hudson* 55

4 **Epitome and Its Surroundings: Between Written and Figural Domains** *Paolo Liverani* 73

5 ***Sarcinatorem esse summum*: Nonius Marcellus and the Modern Editor as Textual Frankensteins** *Matthew Payne* 82

Part II From the Whole to the Fragments?

6 **Dismembering the Truth: Pentheus' Dismemberment as an Image of the Epitomizing Dynamic in Clement of Alexandria's *Stromateis*** *Antoine Paris* 115

7 **Barthes's Dream at the Collège de France: From Critical Fragments to Literary Recompositions** *Mohammad Reza Fallah Nejad* 129

Part III Silence and Enigma

8 **Epitomizing Silence: The *Apophthegmata Patrum* as an Impossible Encyclopaedia of Unknowing** *Jesús Hernández Lobato* 141

9 **Dionysius' Imaginary Library** *Virginia Burrus* 168

10 **The Kaleidoscopic World of Symphosius' *Aenigmata*** *Philip Hardie* 177

Part IV Materiality

11 **'Disfigured' Writing? The Case of Antonin Artaud's 503 Notebooks** *Ana Kiffer* 193

12 **Visual Epitome in Late Antique Art** *Jaś Elsner* 202

Part V From the Fragments to the Whole?

13 **The *Aeneid* More or Less: The Verse *Argumenta* of the So-called 'Twelve Wise Men'** *Scott McGill* 233

14 **A Persistent 'Chronophobia': Composition, Time and Memory in Pliny the Younger's *Epistulae* and Vladimir Nabokov's *Speak, Memory*** *Tim Noens* 248

Index Nominum 277

ILLUSTRATIONS

Figures

Chapter 4

Figure 1: *Tabula iliaca*, Musei Capitolini, Rome 75

Chapter 5

Figure 1: Excerpt of a ninth-century manuscript of Nonius Marcellus' *De compendiosa doctrina* (128r) 99

Figure 2: Excerpt from E. W. Warmington's *Remains of Old Latin* (1936), featuring fragments of Naevius' *Lycurgus* (pp. 132–3) 100

Plates

Chapter 12

Figure 1: Wall painting of Ganymede (in the same form and posture as Endymion, Narcissus or Cyparissus) with Zeus as an Eagle led to him by a Cupid. From the Casa di Meleagro, Pompeii (VI.9.2); now Museo Archeologico Nazionale in Naples, no. 9547. Third quarter of the first century AD

Figure 2: Marble sarcophagus of Endymion asleep among winged putti; recut with a male portrait head from an earlier image of sleeping Ariadne. From Italy; now British Museum 1947,0714.8. Mid third century AD

Figure 3: Marble sarcophagus showing Jonah and the whale, a female orant, a reading philosopher figure (these two figures with unfinished heads), the good shepherd, the baptism of Christ. End of the third century AD. Made in Italy; from the Church of Sta Maria Antiqua, Rome

Figure 4: The Roman Vergil (BAV, MS Vat. lat. 3867) fol. 3v. Prefatory portrait to Vergil's Second Eclogue. Pigments on velum. Late fifth or sixth century, probably made in Italy. Now in the Vatican Library

Figure 5: The Roman Vergil (BAV, MS Vat. lat. 3867) fol. 14r. Prefatory portrait to Vergil's Sixth Eclogue. Pigments on velum. Late fifth or sixth century, probably made in Italy. Now in the Vatican Library

Figure 6: The Roman Vergil (BAV, MS Vat. lat. 3867) fol. 1r. Prefatory image to Vergil's First Eclogue, showing Tityrus playing his pipes to Meliboeus. Pigments on velum. Late fifth or sixth century, probably made in Italy. Now in the Vatican Library

Figure 7: The Roman Vergil (BAV, MS Vat. lat. 3867) fol. 16v. Prefatory image to Vergil's Seventh Eclogue, showing Meliboeus judging the poetic competition between Corydon and Thyrsis. Pigments on velum. Late fifth or sixth century, probably made in Italy. Now in the Vatican Library

Figure 8a and b: The Roman Vergil (BAV, MS Vat. lat. 3867) fols. 44v. and 45r. Double-page frontispiece to Vergil's Third Georgic. Pigments on velum. Late fifth or sixth century, probably made in Italy. Now in the Vatican Library

Figure 9a and b: The Roman Vergil (BAV, MS Vat. lat. 3867) fols. 100v. and 101r. Double-page frontispiece to the Second Book of Vergil's *Aeneid*. Pigments on velum. Late fifth or sixth century, probably made in Italy. Now in the Vatican Library

Figure 10: The Roman Vergil (BAV, MS Vat. lat. 3867) fol. 188v. Left-hand folio from a double-page frontispiece, perhaps to the Twelfth Book of Vergil's *Aeneid*, showing battle between the Trojans and the Rutulians. Pigments on velum. Late fifth or sixth century, probably made in Italy. Now in the Vatican Library

Figure 11: The Vatican Terence (BAV, MS Vat. lat. 3868) fol. 2r. Prefatory image for the whole codex with a portrait of the author in an imago clipeata held by two figures in actors' masks. Pigments on velum. Ninth-century copy (*c*. 825 AD) of an Italian original of the fifth century, perhaps made in Gaul. Now in the Vatican Library

Figure 12: The Vatican Terence (BAV, MS Vat. lat. 3868) fol. 77r. Prefatory image for the play *Phormio*, showing an arched aedicule with conch-filled tympanum flanked by vases holding thirteen actors' masks (for the speaking parts). Pigments on velum. Ninth-century copy (*c*. 825 AD) of an Italian original of the fifth century, perhaps made in Gaul. Now in the Vatican Library

Figure 13: The Vatican Terence (BAV, MS Vat. lat. 3868) fol. 4v. Prefatory image for the first scene of Act 1 of *Andria* (from line 28), placed between this and the last lines of the prologue (21–27, at the top of the page). The illumination with all figures in actors' masks shows precisely the action of line 28, the first in the scene: Simo orders two unidentified slaves to take provisions into the house and addresses his freedman Sosia (both named characters are labelled in red). Pigments on velum. Ninth-century copy (*c*. 825 AD) of an Italian original of the fifth century, perhaps made in Gaul. Now in the Vatican Library

Figure 14: Syriac Bible in Paris (BnF, MS syr. 341) fol. 178r. Prefatory portrait to the Book of Obadiah. Pigments on velum. Sixth or early seventh century, made in Syria, now in the Bibliothèque nationale, Paris

Figure 15: Syriac Bible in Paris (BnF, MS syr. 341) fol. 8r. Prefatory image to the Book of Exodus showing Moses and Aaron before Pharaoh and his attendants. Pigments on velum. Sixth or early seventh century, made in Syria, now in the Bibliothèque nationale, Paris

Figure 16: Syriac Bible in Paris (BnF, MS syr. 341) fol. 118r. Prefatory image to the Book of Proverbs showing the Virgin and Child between Solomon and Ecclesia or perhaps a personification of Wisdom. Pigments on velum. Sixth or early seventh century, made in Syria, now in the Bibliothèque nationale, Paris

Figure 17: The Rossano Gospels (Ms Σ, 042, Cathedral Library, Rossano, Italy) fol. 121r. Mark the Evangelist writing the gospel accompanied by a female figure with halo, perhaps a personification of Wisdom, perhaps the Virgin. His scroll bears the words in Greek 'the beginning of the Gospel of Jesus Christ, Son of God'. Pigments on purple-dyed velum. Sixth century, probably from the eastern Mediterranean, now in the Diocesan Museum, Rossano

Figure 18: The Rossano Gospels (Ms Σ, 042, Cathedral Library Rossano, Italy) fol. 7v. The Parable of the Good Samaritan. Pigments and silver ink on purple-dyed velum. Sixth century, probably from the eastern Mediterranean, now in the Diocesan Museum, Rossano

CONTRIBUTORS

Virginia Burrus is the Bishop W. Earl Ledden Professor of Religion at Syracuse University. A specialist in the literary and cultural history of Christianity in late antiquity, her research interests focus on gender, sexuality and the body; ecopoetics; martyrdom and ascetism; theology. Her most recent books are: *Earthquakes and Gardens: Saint Hilarion's Cyprus* (forthcoming); *Byzantine Tree Life: Christianity and the Arboreal Imagination* (2021, co-author); *The Lives of Saint Constantina* (2020, co-author) and *Ancient Christian Ecopoetics: Cosmologies, Saints, Things* (2019).

Jaś Elsner is Professor of Late Antique Art at Oxford and Visiting Professor of Art and Religion at the University of Chicago. He works on all areas of ancient Mediterranean and early Christian art and their receptions, in particular on questions of art and text as well as problems of comparative art history across Eurasia. His most recent books are *Landscape and Space: Comparative Perspectives from Chinese, Mesoamerican, Ancient Greek and Roman Art* (2022, editor) and *Eurocentric and Beyond: Art History, the Global Turn, and the Possibilities of Comparativism* (2022).

Mohammad Reza Fallah Nejad teaches French literature at Shahid Chamran University of Ahvaz. His research interests focus on Roland Barthes and twentieth-century French literature.

Marco Formisano is Professor of Latin literature at Ghent University (Belgium). He published extensively on late antique literature, both prose and poetry as well as early Christian martyr acts (in particular Perpetua and Polycarp). Other research interests include ancient technical texts (architecture, agriculture, art of war, medicine), Ovid's *Metamorphoses* and reception studies. He is the editor of the series '*sera tela.* Studies in Late Antique Literature and Its Reception' (Bloomsbury) and 'The Library of the Other Antiquity' (Universitätsverlag Winter, Heidelberg).

Philip Hardie is Senior Research Fellow and Honorary Professor of Latin at Trinity College, Cambridge. A renowned specialist in Lucretius, Virgil and Ovid, he has published extensively on diverse aspects of Latin literature and its reception. Among his books are: *Lucretian Receptions: History, the Sublime, Knowledge* (2009); *Rumour and Renown: Representations of Fama in Western Literature* (2012) and *The Last Trojan Hero: A Cultural History of Virgil's* Aeneid (2014).

Jesús Hernández Lobato is Associate Professor of Latin Language and Literature at the University of Salamanca. An expert on Sidonius Apollinaris, he has published extensively on late antique aesthetics and its reception. Among his books are: *Vel Apolline muto: estética y poética de la Antigüedad tardía* (2012); *The Poetics of Late Antique*

Literature (2017, editor) and *Literature Squared: Self-Reflexivity in Late Antique Literature* (2020, editor).

Jared Hudson is an associate professor of Classics at Harvard University. He teaches and writes about Latin texts and their contexts, especially prose from the late Roman republic and early principate. He has written about epitome in Florus and is the author of *The Rhetoric of Roman Transportation: Vehicles in Latin Literature* (2021).

Ana Kiffer is a writer, professor at the Pontifícia Universidade Católica do Rio de Janeiro, and columnist. A specialist in French writer Antonin Artaud, for many years she has been developing an investigation into the different modes of relationship between bodies and writing. Among her books are: *Antonin Artaud* (2016); *Tíraspola/Desaparecimentos* (2016); *Todo Mar* (2018); *Ódios políticos e politica do ódio* (with G. Giorgi, 2019) and *Las vueltas del odio* (with G. Giorgi, 2020).

Irena Kristeva is a professor at Sofia University in the Department of Romance Studies. She holds a PhD in Semiotics from Paris Diderot University and a DSc in Translation Studies from Sofia University. Her research interests focus on Translation Studies and French Literature. She has published several books, including *Pascal Quignard: la fascination du fragmentaire* (2008), *Pour comprendre la traduction* (2009), *Hermes Metamorphosis* (2015) and *Détours de Babel* (2017).

Paolo Liverani was Curator for Classical Antiquities at the Vatican Museum and is now Professor at the University of Florence in the Department of History, Archaeology, Geography, Fine and Performing Arts. His research interests focus on the topography of ancient Rome, Roman official art, polychromy of ancient sculpture, and the relation between word and image in late antiquity. He is the author of eight books, including *The Vatican Necropoleis* (2010).

Scott McGill is Deedee McMurtry Professor at Rice University. His research interests focus on Latin poetry, Roman history and the reception of Classical Antiquity. An expert on Vergil and on the Latin poetry of late antiquity, he has extensively published on late antique centos, ancient forgery and plagiarism. Among his most recent books are: *Plagiarism in Latin Literature* (2012); *Juvencus' Four Books of the Gospels* (2016) and *Virgil, Aeneid 11: A Commentary* (2020).

Tim Noens holds a PhD from Ghent University. His has worked on Latin literature, comparative literature and literary theory, with a focus on Flavian literature and Modernism.

Antoine Paris is Teaching Assistant in Greek at the Université Bordeaux Montaigne. He defended in 2021 a PhD thesis in ancient Greek (Sorbonne Université) and Biblical studies (Université de Montréal), in which, through a comparatist analysis of the *Gospel according to Mark*, the *Apocryphal Letter by James* and Clement of Alexandria's *Stromateis*, he suggests a model of the text as always oscillating between a raw material and an organized entity. He published several articles and chapters in collective books about

Bernard Quiriny, John R. R. Tolkien, Pier Paolo Pasolini, Palladius of Helenopolis, Hesychius of Jerusalem and Theodor of Heraclea.

Matthew Payne received his PhD from the University of St Andrews in 2018. He is currently a post-doctoral researcher at Leiden University.

Paolo Felice Sacchi received his PhD form Ghent University in 2020 with a thesis on late Latin epitomes. His research interests include late Latin poetry, literary theory and comparative literature.

Brian P. Sowers is an assistant professor of Classics at Brooklyn College of the City University of New York. His diverse research interests focus on early Christianity, late antique literature, Black studies and gender studies. He has published on late Latin reading communities, early Christian female martyrs, saints, and poets and on the use of ancient literature to resist systemic racism and white supremacy in the US. His first book, *In Her Own Words: The Life and Poetry of Aelia Eudocia* (2020) examines the poetry of Aelia Eudocia, one of antiquity's best surviving female authors.

SERIES EDITOR PREFACE

In recent years, the Greek and Latin literature of late antiquity has become the object of significant rediscovery, in line with heightened interest in the history and arts of the Mediterranean at a crucial period in the history of the Roman Empire. And yet, as the very term suggests, *late* antique texts are still often considered an appendix to classical literature and interpreted in relation to that literature, which provides the aesthetic standard by default. This new series aims at challenging such paradigms by placing late antique literature at the centre of inquiry, and its title joins the Latin *sera* ('late') with the ambiguous *tela*, evoking both the drawing of weapons and the building of a web. Late antique literature becomes a vantage point for looking both forward to its reception and transformation in subsequent ages, and backward, by engaging in the new and exciting experiment of viewing classical literature through the lens of late antiquity.

sera tela offers a laboratory for new ideas animated by interpretive enthusiasm and experimentalism aiming at highlighting what is new, unique, and unprecedented, rather than focussing on relationships with the classical past, and embracing new sets of theoretical approaches and hermeneutic tools deriving from cultural studies, psychoanalysis, cultural materialism, and ecocriticism, as well as post-human, queer, and media studies, among others. This series is a home for literary studies but is also a transdisciplinary adventure that focuses on the novelty and radical otherness of late antique literature and culture, denaturalizing 'lateness' and highlighting instead a productive sense of anachronicity and belatedness that characterizes literary works of this period. Finally, *sera tela* makes of late antiquity *another* antiquity in which contemporary readers might see reflected their own cultural anxieties around otherness.

Epitomic Writing in Late Antiquity and Beyond: Forms of Unabridged Writing is an especially appropriate inaugural volume in the series. It approaches epitomic writing as a typical product of late antique literary production: while epitomes certainly existed previously, they assumed a specific and new relevance and symbolic value in the late antique context. Epitomic writing perfectly embodies late antiquity as an age marked by the quality of 'untimeliness' inherent in its characteristic sense of belatedness; this volume shows that epitomic writing is characterized by the impossibility of being defined as a genre, a literary form, or a discourse. As this volume shows, explicitly and implicitly, from the introduction to its last chapter, epitomic writing is characterized by the impossibility of being defined as a genre, a literary form, or a specific discourse; it is here approached as a textual dimension rather than a fixed genre. Epitomic texts can exist in relationship with virtually any other kind of text, from epic poetry to historiography to theology to epigram to technical treatises to biography. Moreover, any writing which presents itself as an epitome shows an inherent anachronicity, reflecting the characteristic quality of late antiquity as an epoch that never belongs to itself and is marked by a deep disjunction from its own time.

This volume thus explores the epitomic as an aesthetic quality, both textual and visual, and invites readers to consider epitomes as texts *au premier degré,* and to take them seriously as 'replacements' of their originals. As a whole, the volume is meant as an invitation to a *kind* reader to accept the nature of this form of writing by de-contextualizing, re-configuring, and ultimately coping with the absence of the original epitomized texts. Finally, a major achievement of this volume is to identify, albeit *ex negativo*, the epitomic as an exquisitely late antique quality, shaped through comparison and conceptual interaction with visual artifacts as well as with texts written both before and after late antiquity. Thus this period becomes a unique paradigm marked by its own untimeliness.

Marco Formisano
Ghent University
May 2022

PREFACE

The papers collected in this volume are a selection of those that were presented at the conference 'Unabridged: Epitome from Fragmentation to Recomposition (and back again)' held on 5 and 6 June 2018, at the Academia Belgica in Rome and generously funded by FWO Research Foundation – Flanders. This conference was one outcome of a research project on the epitome in Late Latin literature led by Marco Formisano at Ghent University (Special Research Fund, 2015–19). Collaborating on the project, Paolo Felice Sacchi produced a doctoral dissertation entitled 'Vertigo, Paradox, and Thorns: Epitomic Writing in Virgilius Grammaticus, Solinus, Fulgentius' (2020). A few papers at the 2018 conference were devoted to proper epitomes, i.e. texts that present themselves as such. In order to focus on what we define the *epitomic* rather than epitomes themselves, and to avoid the usual – and perhaps avoidable – hermeneutic practice that systematically focuses on an epitome's relationship with a primary text, we decided not to include those papers in this volume; but we would like to express our warm gratitude to those speakers for their important contributions to the conference.

The papers collected here have been thoroughly revised since the conference, and are now tesserae in the kind of epitome that this volume, in its own way, represents. We have arranged the chapters in an order that we hope illustrates the 'epitomic movement' described in the Introduction, but we trust that readers will find their own individual ways to make use of *this* epitome.

Our warm thanks go to Vicente Flores Militello for his work on the index.

INTRODUCTION: UNABRIDGED

Marco Formisano and Paolo Felice Sacchi[*]

1. Obscure objects

> A rock crystal: a transparent stone enclosing a drop of water – an ice block with a melted core.
>
> A spool of thread that can run, laugh, and, more than anything else, can obsess a family man, drawing him to gloomy despair.

Both these objects share an uncannily haunting nature; both these objects are, in their own way, we shall argue, *epitomic*. And of course, they both belong in the literary discourse. To the fascinating paradox of the crystal rock is devoted a series of seven epigrams nestled at the heart of Claudian's (fourth- to fifth-century CE) *Carmina minora* (C.m. 33–39); the 'living' spool of thread is Odradek, the elusive protagonist of one of Kafka's most famous short stories, *The Cares of a Family Man*. Both the rock crystal and Odradek are presented, from the very beginning, as a challenge to the perceptive faculties of the observer. They are obscure objects, subtly ungraspable, and their elusiveness has something to do with their contradictory materiality and blurred ontology.

The rock crystal is solid and liquid at the same time: it is stone and water all at once. Claudian's first epigram in the series, just two elegiac couples, perfectly condenses the epistemological paradox embodied by the crystal:

> Possedit glacies naturae signa prioris
>   et fit parte lapis, frigora parte negat.
> sollers lusit hiems, inperfectoque rigore
>   nobilior vivis gemma tumescit aquis.
>
> *c.m. 33*

> This piece of ice still shows traces of its original nature: part of it has become stone, part resisted the cold. It is a freak of winter's, more precious by reason of its incomplete crystallization, for that the jewel contains within itself living water.[1]

This is an enigma, a riddle poem; a given *thing*, which, we know from the title, is *analysed*, that is, a grid is projected onto it. More precisely, the grid is a polarized one, based on conceptual dichotomies – past/present, opacity/transparency, solidity/liquidity. The thing has become a *dialectical* object, something captured in between polarities and crisscrossed by opposite forces; the poem is what stems from the friction between the *thing* and a binary *code*.

As for Odradek, a kind of epistemological anxiety is staged in the very first sentences of Kafka's short story:

> Some say the word Odradek is of Slavonic origin, and try to account for it on that basis. Others again believe it to be of German origin, only influenced by Slavonic. The uncertainty of both interpretations allows one to assume with justice that neither is accurate, especially as neither of them provides an intelligent meaning of the word.[2]

The name 'Odradek' falls out of the domain of etymology; the reader will soon find out that also the *res* designated by this *verbum* is hardly conceptualizable: Odradek is an 'impossible thing', apparently inorganic but provided with conscience, ubiquitous and arguably immortal. Odradek cannot be described as a unitary whole – it lacks definition because it lacks any *essence*:

> At first glance it looks like a flat star-shaped spool for thread, and indeed it does seem to have thread wound upon it; to be sure, they are only old, broken-off bits of thread, knotted and tangled together, of the most varied sorts and colors. But it is not only a spool, for a small wooden crossbar sticks out of the middle of the star, and another small rod is joined to that at a right angle. By means of this latter rod on one side and one of the points of the star on the other, the whole thing can stand upright as if on two legs.

Odradek might be referred to, however inaccurately, as an *assemblage*:[3] we can somehow recognize some of its components, but we cannot play them down to systemic synthesis. Odradek is exceeding and lacking at once, it could be a conglomerate of disparate fragments as well as the disfigured remnant of some former totality:

> One is tempted to believe that the creature once had some sort of intelligible shape and is now only a broken-down remnant. Yet this does not seem to be the case; at least there is no sign of it; nowhere is there an unfinished or unbroken surface to suggest anything of the kind; the whole thing looks senseless enough, but in its own way perfectly finished.

Both the rock crystal and Odradek, despite their provocative evidence, stand out as blind spots before the observer/interpreter: they constitute an epistemological scandal, they are opaque points that exert an irreducible recalcitrance to investigation – while, at the same time, and not surprisingly, they trigger interpretation.

Dialectically speaking, the rock crystal and Odradek are receptacles of *negativity*; or, if one wants to reject the dialectical model, they might be said to embody difference and point to a fissure in our conceptual and experiential continuum.[4]

2. Dissections: Derivativeness, dialectics and obtuseness

In what follows, the adjective *epitomic* will be employed to refer to such a negativity. It is clearly no chance that we have started discussing the epitomic by focusing on two objects and not only on the texts that, somehow, *picture* these very objects: this volume is meant as an attempt to account for a series of formal phenomena whose range encompasses potentially all media and semiotic systems (although here textual specimens will be privileged). In our use of the term *epitomic*, the stress will not lie so much on the most common meaning of 'shortened' as on the *being-fissured* of the epitomic object, on its conjuring up ideas of *shift*, *gap*, *interruption*.

We do not aim to completely discard the traditional meaning, but we would like to suggest looking at it (i.e. at the 'shortened text', at the 'summary') as only one of the possible outcomes of an epitomic process, based on *fragmentation* and *re-composition*. It might be objected that 'traditional epitomes', even more than by fragmentation and re-composition, are characterized by *selection*, since summarizing is, first and foremost, a selective procedure. In accordance with this view, the most distinctive aspect of 'epitomes-making' would then lie in selection-making, and our critical efforts should consist in investigating analytically such a process: what has been chosen? what left out? why? etc.

Indeed, the fact that summarizing is an interpretative practice is nowadays hardly a disputable assumption, just like the idea that epitomizers/summarizers can be studied as skilful authors.[5] The problem remains whether such functionalist approaches – that is, approaches that seek to read 'epitomes' strictly in the light of their *purpose* – may not lead us to ignore, at least to a certain degree, some formal qualities of the work under examination. Significantly enough, historian Hervé Inglebert has claimed that: 'While dealing with an epitome the most important question to be answered is not *What*, since this is provided by the model, but *When*, which is essential to the very comprehension of the epitome and sums up all of the other questions, *Why*, *For whom*, and *How*'.[6] One could hardly find a fitter formulation to express the reduction of the *what* to the *when*, of a text to its context. To delve into the epitomic will mean here, on the contrary, to investigate the friction between the textual object and its purported context as well as to cope with problematic approaches to temporality.

In the first place, our conception of the *epitomic* calls for a reconfiguration of the relationship between the original and the epitomized text. While it would be preposterous to argue for a complete dismissal of the notion of *derivativeness* – the epitomizing process has to be applied to a given material, therefore, in a sense, cannot but come 'after' and produce a derivative outcome – we invite the reader to problematize the linearity of such a process. In fact, even taken in the strictest sense of *summary*, the result of an epitomic gesture keeps modifying and, in a way, producing, not only re-producing, its own original. The selective process on which any summary is grounded can be interpreted as a dynamic tending to limit and stabilize the meaning of the so-called original, to circumscribe a set of finite readings. As a consequence, the reading of the epitomized object cannot but affect any subsequent reading of the primary object. This move is well-known to anyone who has ever faced the problems posed by reception and hermeneutics:

any interpretative movement is inherently bi-directional.[7] In some cases, epitomes explicitly undermine the *primary meaning* (that is, the apparent meaning of the *primary object*).[8] 'Derivativeness' simply comes down, in the end, to an indication of material commonality: 'primary' and 'secondary' objects show a common material ground, they are made of the same stuff; the 'primary' object is such only thanks to its chronological priority. And yet, our working hypothesis is precisely that one should try to limit the definitory relevance of chronology: an epitomic object as such, we argue, is less defined by its collocation within the chronological continuum than by its morphology, by its being a *trace* of some previous dismemberment (and subsequent re-composition). In this sense, depending on the level on which we decide to look for a disruptive/constructive process, epitomic features might be detected in any member of a series: even in the 'primary'. To give an example, Solinus' *Collectanea rerum memorabilium*, a third- to fourth-century CE geographical/encyclopaedical treatise with an enormous medieval *Fortleben*, has been commonly deemed to be a patchwork of geographical and naturalistic information found in Pliny's *Naturalis Historia* (and to a lesser extent in Pomponius Mela's *Chorographia*); in other terms, Solinus' work ought to be read as an epitome of Pliny's vaster achievement. But: can we imagine anything more 'epitomic' than the first book of the *Naturalis Historia*, a veritable *table des matières*? Or again, isn't the whole *Naturalis Historia* crisscrossed by epitomic dynamics? This holds true both if we look at the epitomic as a force leading to re-composition (let's think, among others, of the ambition to catalogue knowledge in a unitary, 'imperialistic' conceptual space),[9] or as a drive to dismemberment (the parcelling that knowledge has to undergo in order to fit into Pliny's agenda).

In our understanding, a *cento* is no less epitomic than the abridgement of a medical treatise; Virbius[10] and Frankenstein's creature are epitomic, as well as early modern emblems, Walt Disney's *Fantasia*, Borges's Chinese encyclopaedia – indeed, every conceivable encyclopaedia might be said to be epitomic. All these examples entail the disjunction of an 'original' set (be it a physical body, a semiotic code, any form of cultural heritage) and its displacement into a new constellation – strictly speaking, no selection is required, the scrambling of components being instead the fundamental moment (let's call it the *anagrammatic quality* of epitome).[11] We are of course aware that by so broadening the applicability of the term one runs the risk of losing its specificity – since, in the end, if fragmentation and re-composition are taken as the only definitory principle, any hermeneutical gesture, any act we call 'reading' or 'interpretation' would turn out to be epitomic. Even more: any cognitive or creative process. What if fragmentation and re-composition were nothing but less pretentious names for *analysis* and *synthesis*? Or again, do not they mirror the spiral movement of *thesis*, *antithesis*, and *synthesis*? Is maybe *the epitomic* nothing more than the umpteenth avatar of what Western philosophy has tried to conceptualize as the *dialectic*?

And yet, the fact is, *epitomic* would precisely designate objects resistant to dialecticization. The epitomic object is no synthetic object; it does not move 'beyond' the 'original', since there is no 'beyond' towards which one should move. We are compelled to try to think of a process that allows the negative moment (in Hegelian terms, the *antithesis*) without engendering any movement – to put it paradoxically, *epitomization* could be conceptualized as dialectics without dialectical movement.

We are now attempting to approach our topic by resorting to the category of process, or even by substantializing it as 'the epitomic'. Both approximations cannot but fall short in accounting for an 'object' that, as we have just seen, is meant to run against a certain idea of movement (or dialectical transformation) no less than against any idea of stable substance. Thus, 'epitomic' seems to come down to hardly more, or no less, than a textual-literary avatar of the (anti-)metaphysical speculations popularized by the so-called Continental Philosophy over the second half of the twentieth century. Given such a background, it is small wonder that we are confronted with an intimidating series of paradoxes and contradictions as soon as we try to stabilize 'the epitomic' as a definable concept – i.e, as a concept *tout court*. Therefore, this volume will consciously tread a dangerous path: it will seek to investigate the 'morphology' not of a *form* (a term to be taken in its broadest meaning), but, rather, of the gap, of the discontinuity that makes any form recognizable as such.

We started these few pages by looking at two 'objects' – although somehow connected to the verbal medium – precisely because of their *obtuseness*, of their exorbitance with respect to our interpretative efforts.[12] The domain of 'the epitomic' encompasses the negativity disclosed by any gesture of fragmentation, re-ordering and/or dis-ordering as well as the irreducible being-cut-off of the 'object' from our critical gaze. And since this 'object' is a textual one, to investigate 'the epitomic' will mean to investigate the text in its *exceedance*, in what escapes 'reading'. Even so, we would warn against the risk of making epitomic obtuseness overlap with any kind of intellectual unutterability, with what 'goes beyond reason'.[13]

We shall now look a little deeper into how epitomic writing destabilized the literary critical discourse.

3. Deferring the object: History

As will soon become clear, our insistence on speaking of 'objects' under investigation is probably, also, an unconscious attempt to compensate for the elusive nature of the epitomic phenomenon. *Epitome* can be satisfactorily defined only as a word; we can outline the story of its usage, determine its etymology, list its occurrences with reference to literary products – but it remains at best problematic to pin down its real referent. *Epitome* has no format, let alone a genre. We shall soon see that it might be useful to broaden the concept to encompass some very general cultural mechanisms connected to the creation, preservation and transmission of information; however, for the time being, the interesting thing is that several histories of this non-genre have already been written.[14]

Defined by what has become the most accepted meaning – as summaries of previous, more extended works, or as companions (*compendia*) to a given subject – epitomes owe a lot to, and are victims of, the most mature season of nineteenth-century positivistic philology.[15] Theodor Mommsen, Heinrich Keil, Alexander Riese and many others contributed to the re-edition and systematization of a great deal of works that could be dubbed as epitomic.[16] Nonetheless, they also consolidated a series of critical stereotypes surrounding epitomes, namely that:

1. Epitomes, being inherently derivative, are inevitably inferior to original texts;
2. Epitomes are symptoms of a certain decline in creativity;
3. Epitomes testify, at their best, to periods of cultural systematization, but not of cultural production;
4. Epitomes are most typical of late antiquity;
5. Although deprived of any intrinsic interest, epitomes represent a valuable source of fragments of lost works and textual variants.

This last point has often served as an apologetic argument for any scholars brave enough to undertake the thankless job of editing such uninteresting material. It would be illuminating to carry out a fully-fledged study on the 'rhetoric of self-sacrifice' that permeates late-nineteenth- and early-twentieth-century scholarly production, a highly telling compromise between two cultural *idola*: on the one hand the positivistic cult of unbiased science, on the other, the post-romantic celebration of 'novelty' as a criterion for establishing aesthetic hierarchies. This attitude, it should be noted, did not necessarily affect the quality of the philological achievements of the time. Ever since Wölfflin's articles in *Archiv für Lateinische Lexicographie*, scholars seem to have been primarily concerned with constructing a history of the term 'epitome'. Heinrich Bott opened his dissertation *De epitomis antiquis* (1920) with a reflection on the alleged distinction between *epitome* and *breviarium*, an approach echoed a few years later by Marco Galdi in his thorough monograph devoted to epitomes in Latin literature, *L'epitome nella letteratura latina* (1922). Still partially present as an undertone in Ilona Opelt's article in *Reallexikon für Antike und Christentum* (1962), the distinction re-emerged in Rosalind MacLachlan's unpublished dissertation *Epitomes in Ancient Literary Culture* (2004).[17]

Galdi's book is, in many respects, highly representative of such positivistic attitudes, in both its qualities and its limits.[18] Next to a rich collection of carefully (and chronologically) arranged material, Galdi makes several derogatory remarks about the low intellectual value of the works he has been analysing, exemplified in the very first lines of the introduction: 'Overall, the tendency to excerpt and summarize larger works is tightly connected with the political and moral decay of a nation.'[19] Resorting to the 'decadence' paradigm, Galdi produces an argument commonly employed to support pseudo-historicist claims. This is far from unexpected, and the same might be said for the strong nationalistic and idealistic undertones of statements such as the following:

> In ages characterized by thriving literary activity – when the production is original and capable of mirroring, to a large extent, the flourishing material and spiritual conditions of a population marching forward on the path of civilization, and when only one single concern seems to loom over writers, that of contributing to the greatness of one's own country or of celebrating one's own ancestry – summarizing someone else's works would be held to be a pointless chore.

> . . .
>
> It has already been observed that summaries usually turn out being detrimental to works of art. Indeed, an *opus integrum*, once summarized, is disfigured, since it loses those traces of freshness and immediacy, if not of organicity, that were its own.[20]

If today these claims sound grotesque, or even, in the light of the subsequent European history, utterly ominous (Galdi's nationalistic vocabulary might well remind us of the incipient Fascist era),[21] it is only because we have somehow *displaced* the same longing for coherent historical reconstruction that influenced the Italian philologist in the 1920s. Indeed, one can find many intuitions scattered throughout *L'epitome* that need only be properly relocated to appear as the basis of current historicist discussions on *epitome*.

In the wake of Birt and Bott, Galdi stressed the relevance of the introduction of the codex to the success of epitome from the fourth century onward, thus pointing to technological innovation as a fundamental component of cultural production.[22] This perspective would become central in the works of Ann Blair. Although devoted to an entirely different historical period (the Early Modern Age), Blair's studies engage with the problem of ordering and disseminating knowledge in times marked by a widespread feeling of information overload.[23] The theme of 'too much knowledge' might actually, at least partially, help us to rethink the flourishing of epitomic works in, for example, late antiquity as a phenomenon connected to an increased demand for information-storage technologies rather than to a simple decay in the capacity of readers to master long works.[24] Similarly, Galdi was well aware that epitomized texts were privileged in schools, but we had to wait for Rita Lizzi's considerations on 'selective memory' and Kaster's thorough survey on grammarians for late antique schools to lose any reductive connotations as receptacles of 'rudimentary culture' and be acknowledged as essential triggers of cultural development.[25] Finally, Galdi speaks poignantly of a true 'compendium industry'.[26] No one, of course, would be so naive as to confuse Galdi's use of 'industry' with the meaning that this word would assume in Critical Theory, nor presume that Galdi meant to oppose it, in a typically idealistic way,[27] to the more spiritually elevated 'work of art'; nonetheless, the intuition of a *cultural industry* is already present, almost foreshadowing Santo Mazzarino's path-breaking formula of the late antique 'democratization of culture'.[28]

This is not to say that *L'epitome* anticipated all the scholarly trends that would crop up in later decades: rather that, given the set of data we have, when looking at epitomes from a certain vantage point, the results can hardly be expected to undergo radical alterations. Ever since Birt, the *object* of scholarly observation has been epitomes as the product of a socio-historical constellation, precisely not our *object* here.

4. Deferring the object: Redemption

By looking at the same object as Galdi and his contemporaries and forerunners, one is likely to fall into a *redemptive mood*, equal and opposite to their disparaging attitude. In short, the most adopted strategy has become to deny the exclusively derivative nature of epitomes and to stress, instead, the many different ways in which the original text is fragmented, recombined, and transformed. In other words, critics and philologists started laying claim to the *authoriality* of the epitomizer. The apology of the text is hence substantiated through the introduction of a new persona: the *worthy, skilful author*. Even today the critical pendulum swings between two poles: on the one side, theories that hold that it is impossible to analyse and evaluate epitomes without making reference to their purportedly primary sources; on the other hand, the attempt to consider epitomes in their own right as self-sufficient literary objects, as the products of creative gestures and authorial self-confidence.

This former standpoint is, for instance, lucidly represented by Hervé Inglebert's 'contextual approach' we mentioned above:[29] according to this view, epitomes are functions, in mathematical terms, of previous texts, and the only way to predicate anything on them is to know the argument of the function, the input variable: *the original*.

The most systematic *functionalist interpretation* of this kind has probably been provided by Markus Dubischar under the concept of the *auxiliary*.[30] To put it in as a few words as possible, epitomes, like commentaries, translations, and many other kinds of *derivative literature*, help to make other texts understandable, that is, readable: '[Auxiliary texts] render service and help, as it were, to a primary text or corpus that needs or deserves this kind of service and help. [. . .] Since the fundamental purpose of a text is to be read and understood, texts are in difficulty when they find fewer and fewer readers, and perhaps even fail to find readers at all.'[31] Drawing mostly on Paul Grice's theory of conversation and Niklas Luhmann's analysis of sociological systems, Dubischar points out that 'all communication is based on, and made possible by, reducing complexity. Moreover, real communication is initiated by the recipient.'[32] Epitomes aim to give birth to a new audience for unheard texts by reducing the distance between the cultural system in which primary texts were produced and that of the current audience: 'Auxiliary texts could be viewed as "gate-keepers" placed at a system's boundaries, securing but also controlling the supply with information from the environment.'[33] But what about the intrinsic opacity of any textual object? How can we determine the borders of the pretended original readability? When do texts really start to 'need or deserve' help to be understood? How thin can the boundaries between two cultural systems be?

In a discussion on Vegetius' *Epitoma rei militaris* (fourth to fifth century), one of the most widely read Latin texts during the Middle Ages, it has been shown how epitomes can effectively *establish*, not only adapt, translate or preserve, a cultural system, by engaging in a complex, dynamic relationship with the past and tradition – in this particular case, even by founding a peculiar textuality:

> In fact, I would argue that the *Epitoma rei militaris* is more interesting for literary than for technical reasons. It aims to reintroduce to the contemporary system the ancient rules applied in Rome during the first stage of empire [. . .] Even the title *Epitoma rei militaris*, which might best be translated into modern languages as 'The Roman art of war' or 'The ancient art of war' [. . .] is a reminder of the close

> relationship the author wishes to have with the past. Vegetius' logic is circular: he begins from writing, substantiates actions with exempla that also derive from a world of books, only to return inexorably to writing. His work inherits, justifies, and sets up a system of profound interaction between 'literary' past and present action, which becomes the axiom of the art of war for the future.[34]

Actually, trying to connect the pragmatic of the auxiliary with the ambiguous field disclosed by such concepts as intertextuality, intratextuality and transtextuality, may turn out to be quite a challenge. Not surprisingly, these ideas constitute the basis for the other critical pole mentioned above, the one interested in reasserting the creative potential of epitomes. One need only look back at Gérard Genette's classical work *Palimpsestes* to find out that: 'no reduction, since it cannot be *simply* a reduction, is completely transparent, meaningless – innocent'.[35] It would suffice to select random passages from prefaces to late antique Latin and Greek epitomes to discover that their authors were proud to show what a difficult task it had been to sum up all of that information, to structure it, to make it, as it were, *useful*.[36] They seem to be well aware of the fact that they can lay claim to a certain degree of *ingenium*. Thus, when Markus Mülke, in his essay entitled *Epitome – Das Bessere Original?* ('Epitome – A better original?'), highlights the sophisticated expertise that a 'true epitomator' (*ein richtiger Epitomator*) had to display, he resumes a long-established motif (at least in late antiquity).[37]

5. Deferring the object: Subversion

Some scholars have taken further steps in the direction of establishing a more accentuated textual autonomy for epitomes, adopting other, more radical models of cultural transmission. In the sociological scheme proposed by Itamar Even-Zohar, goods – material or semiotic – having trespassed systemic borders can undergo a process he names *cultural transfer*: the imported goods cease to be perceived as external and are wholly integrated in the new economical/cultural repertoire.[38] If this osmotic dynamic is fully fulfilled (Even-Zohar gives it the name of *interference*), then 'the question of source/origin is no longer relevant. For the majority of the members of a community, once introduced into their repertoire, the fortune of an item in terms of success or failure becomes a domestic matter'.[39] This is to say that once texts have undergone *interference*, once, for example, texts have been epitomized in order to fit the requirements of a new reading audience, their former status must take second place: the extreme consequence of the auxiliary – and anyone dealing with the remnants of ancient literature should agree – is, paradoxically, the complete erasure of the source, its replacement.

In his influential book on rewriting, André Lefevere argues for an overtly dialectical interpretation of how cultural systems function.[40] His axiom is that they 'develop according to the principle of polarity, which holds that every system eventually evolves in its own countersystem'.[41] The point is instrumental in positing the possibility of subversive effects achieved through apparently non-subversive procedures: even *repetitive textual acts* such as translating or summarizing are likely to trigger a process of semantic shifting that will eventually lead from the original signifying set to its very opposite.

Subversion, if regarded from the perspective of a *redemptive* reading of epitomes, might be a very convenient tool, and has actually been used as such. Wolfgang Raible has drawn attention to different examples of *Reduktionsformen*, an umbrella concept under which he gathers epitomes, *compendia ad usum delphini*, registers, Japanese haikai, and more.[42] Grouping epitomes and registers (not to speak of haikai) under the same label may sound a little questionable, even without resorting to Genette's meticulous distinction between abridgement and condensed text, summary and digest.[43] We are nonetheless persuaded that Raible's attempt to find a common ground for practices of textual fragmentation and re-assemblage may be of use to extending our idea of epitomization. Raible argues that there is something in common between 'summaries' and, let's say, Raymond Quenau's rewriting of Mallarmé sonnets (which Queneau rewrote by picking up only the last word of each line): in dismembering a text and putting it together again, an ironical, subversive mechanism is taking place.

Two well-known late antique Latin works have been interpreted in this 'subversive' light. Aude Doody presents us with the strong clash between authority and authorship that she detects in the so-called *Medicina Plinii*.[44] The *Medicina Plinii*, which is thought to have been composed in the fourth century, belongs to a tradition of late antique medical compendia that tried to condense classical medical authorities into more accessible forms. It draws its material mainly from Pliny the Elder's *Naturalis Historia* and most of the manuscripts refer to its author as *Plinius Secundus Iunior*. Doody rightly points out that although medicine can be considered the focus of Pliny's books 20–32, Pliny's own position towards physicians (namely, Greek physicians) is relatively disapproving: no small a part of his ideological project consisted in opposing the intellectualistic and, according to him, suspicious Greek medical science to natural, reliable, traditional Roman medicine. As a consequence, as Doody puts it, 'while the *Medicina Plinii* is dependent on Pliny's name and Pliny's text for some of its authority, its radical reworking of the *Naturalis Historia*'s approach to medicine could be seen as an implicit critique of Pliny's organising strategies: the book of extracts aims both to co-opt and to supplant the authority of the source-text'.[45] An antagonistic attitude thus comes to light: reshaping the original, the epitomizer exerts an act of appropriation, whose violence is the *conditio sine qua non* for the emergence of his/her own textual identity.

The implications of such an antagonistic model were brilliantly exposed by Jeffrey T. Schnapp in his essay on Proba's famous *Cento vergilianus de laudibus Christi*.[46] Approximatively dated to the second half of the fourth century CE, this 694 hexameter-long patchwork of Virgilian lines makes 'the greatest poet' of Rome sing the history of Christian salvation. To describe what's going on here, Schnapp turns to the Situationist concept of *détournement*, that is, in the words of Guy Debord, the *appropriation*, *critical deflection* and *historicization* of the meanings of pre-existing artefacts without effacing them. In Debord's definition we can track the same dialectical tension between preservation and obliteration, continuity and discontinuity found in Even-Zohar's idea of *interference*, now slightly nuanced by the awareness that what was before referred to as 'replacement' is probably better defined as 'erasure': not effacement exactly, but a sort of *preservation through obliteration*.

In line with this approach, but with a broader perspective, it has been repeatedly argued that epitomes traditionally intended – *florilegia*, *centones*, but also grammatical commentaries, technical treatises, encyclopaedic compilation, etc. – can all be reduced to the series of common cognitive and textual procedures we mentioned further above, namely to *fragmentation*, *dislocation* and *replacement*:[47] '[that is] mechanisms of recollecting past textual traditions, fragmenting and dislocating their content and giving them a new form – like Hippolytus' body after the mythical *sparagmós*'.[48] An *epitomic dimension* would thus appear to underlie the entirety of late antiquity, consisting in the parcelling and displacement of earlier classical culture.[49] It has also been accordingly stressed the role played by *allegory* in late antiquity: not only is *allegory* a tool that implements the *détournement* of Antiquity, it affects late antique textuality more generally, a textuality constantly 'détourning' itself.[50]

Although subversive readings doubtlessly help to free epitomes from interpretations that tend to dissolve them into their sources (the obsession, in the last instance, of much *Quellenforschung*, and in many respects the dominant hermeneutical paradigm in the study of epitomes), they seem to be no less reductionist than their polemical target. By constantly looking for subversive patterns we run the risk of substituting a teleology oriented to *the original* with a teleology projected toward *the anti-original*. Exchanging one fetishism for another does not really seem to be a fruitful way to account for the complexity and semiotic richness involved in any writing or re-writing process. The very idea of 'subversion' is trapped in a dichotomy that opposes apparent meaning to concealed meaning; moreover, before turning something upside down you have to *crystallize the object of the subversion*, which means to *stabilize* it, to make it the *origin* of the whole process. In their redemptive efforts, scholars arguing for this *geometrical* reversal not only fail *to get rid of the original*, but, in the worst of cases, they fall victim to the temptation they reproach in more traditional analyses: they act *systematically* to get rid of it, exchanging the redemption of one textual constellation for the condemnation of another. Epitomes give rise, instead, to a state of inexhaustible and dynamic tension, of *perpetual self-projection toward perpetually absent objects*. Once again, an apologetic gesture has turned into an act of hermeneutical violence.

We are not suggesting that we completely delete what, in post-Hegelian terms, we should call the *negative movement* of the dialectical process. We take it to be undeniable that the *Medicina Plinii* destabilizes Pliny's text, and, more generally speaking, we continue to be convinced that we can hardly dismiss binary patterns of analysis: what we hesitate to do is to arrest this dynamic and to fix it into an oppositional *macro-system*. We would prefer, instead, to track a series of *multiple micro-systemic negativities*, of infinitesimal shifts, whose final sum does not necessarily result in the reversal of the previous configuration; it can, but it does not have to. Epitomes as results of *epitomic writing* – thanks to their status as *erasing texts*, to their being a *textual embodiment of absence*, at once preserving and negating a previous textuality – give us the opportunity to study interesting phenomena of what we may define as *pervasive negativity*, which cannot be reduced to the static scheme of dialectical reversals or subversion.

6. *This* epitome

Perhaps like any other collection of papers, the volume you hold in your hands is itself an epitome. The contributions to *this* epitome responded to an invitation by the editors to consider and take seriously the 'negativity' of any epitomic text in the sense described above by focusing on absence and interruption as inherent qualities of this particular . . . form? genre? discourse? Indeed, the epitome cannot be satisfactorily defined only as a word. By moving away from the chronological order that is usually followed in interpretations of an epitomic text – *from* the primary source *to* the secondary product – this volume aims at mimetically reproducing and in a way accompanying the process of epitomization as 'dialectics without dialectical movement' (see above). The epitomic, a quality that this volume aims to establish as a hermeneutic category, seems then to enlighten late antiquity as the age of negativity, i.e. as an historical phase, which by definition cannot be defined in itself, yet constantly constructs its distance from Classical Antiquity. As argued in a previous study,[51] to think of late antiquity means to think of an epoch in negative terms as inherently untimely, a period that never belongs to itself and that exists only in disjunction with its own time. Most discussions of late antique literature and culture nonetheless tend to reproduce a chronological line, aiming to show how what is late emanated from a previous age and thereby, whether explicitly or implicitly, introducing both an aesthetical hierarchy and a genealogical relationship.

This volume, the first of the new series *sera tela*, takes another move: while acknowledging the particular relationship between the epitomic and late antiquity, it considers epitomic texts not only in late antiquity but also in earlier periods – as well as in the twentieth century, the post-modern *time* that has been characterized precisely by its belatedness.

This epitome is organized into five sections that are meaningful both by themselves and in their sequence. The first of these, ***Epitomic Dimensions***, displays the richness, variety, and complexity of the 'epitomic' by touching upon many of the domains that will recur throughout the volume: postmodern literature, classical and late antique literature, semiotics, philology, and cultural memory studies. In the second section, ***From the Whole to the Fragments?***, readers are invited to focus on *dismemberment* as a highly productive literary strategy, moving from *cutting* as a t(r)opos in classical literature, to the role it played in scriptural exegesis, up to Roland Barthes's dismembered subject. After this exploration of dismemberment, the third section, ***Silence and Enigma*** dives even more deeply into the 'productive negativity' of the epitomic by investigating its relationship to apophatic aesthetics, mysticism and infinity; the epitomic is shown to be a useful tool for investigating the very borders and paradoxes of language. Departing from the epitomic as an impulse to the dissolution of language, the fourth section, ***Materiality***, interrogates the material implications of such a dissolution: what are the tenets of a philology that has to confront dismembered texts? How are (materially) different semiotic codes impacted by the epitomic? The fifth and final section, ***From the Fragments to the Whole?***, tackles the opposite of the textual/conceptual movement that was investigated in the second section; re-composition is here shown as a problematic concept – integrity and totality (be it of the existential subject, of memory, or of a cultural *monumentum* such as the *Aeneid*) are themselves *dismembering* agents.

This epitome is marked not only by the sequence of the individual chapters, but also by various associations linking them all. We invite readers not only to follow the straight path traced by the five sections but also to wander around, back and forth, identifying recurring themes and reflections. Irena Kristeva's chapter on Pascal Quignard represents the perfect opening for this venture, since it handles at one and the same time many of the aspects that will reappear in the following chapters. It focuses on an epitomic text, the *Petits traités* by Quignard, and what can be aptly defined as a 'critique of the epitomic' per se: Quignard's untimely relationship to the past, in particular to the classical tradition. The theme of reconstruction of the past in biographical terms returns as a wave investing the central Chapter 7 by Mohammad Reza Fallah Nejad, on Roland Barthes's autobiographical 'dream' at the end of his own life, as well as the final Chapter 14 by Tim Noens, on Pliny the Younger's and Vladimir Nabokov's differing narrative strategies for re-telling their lives. A true biographical snapshot is represented by the epitomized *Life of Cato the Elder* by Cornelius Nepos as discussed by Jared Hudson in Chapter 3, where the Republican hero is associated precisely with the writing of time, historiography. As a supreme act of miniaturization of a great man, Hudson's discussion finds an echo in Scott McGill's Chapter 13, devoted to the compression of the entire Virgilian corpus in the so-called *Argumenta* of the Twelve Wise Men contained in the *Anthologia Latina*.

The other direction opened up by Kristeva's discussion is the *via negationis* and the difficulty raised by any systematic approach to primary texts, inherent to epitomic processes. A radical manifestation of this negation is represented by the *Apophthegmata Patrum*, defined by Jesús Hernández Lobato (Chapter 8) as an epitome of what literally cannot be spoken: silence. Another sort of negation is represented by the methodological reflection offered in Chapter 4 by Paolo Liverani, who reminds us of the impossibility of transferring the semiotic system of language into visual material. But, as Ana Kiffer shows in Chapter 11 on the cahiers written and drawn by Antonin Artaud, the materiality emerging from the tactile and visual aspects of Artaud's diaries cooperates with writing in the production of a meaning continuously destabilized by an anti-linear notion of text. The relationship of text and image is extensively treated by Jaś Elsner in Chapter 12, who advocates – perhaps in tension with Liverani's discussion in Chapter 4 – for the centrality of pictures within the late antique codex as 'epitomic paratextuality.' The list, too, can be counted as a material aspect, since it is not directly thematized in words and yet heavily influences reading. The late Latin poet Ausonius, as described by Brian Sowers in Chapter 2, is undoubtedly the master of lists, a literary device usually perceived as secondary or marginal, but which, by means of attracting the reader's attention to the sequence itself, undoes previous hierarchic orders and genealogies, and linearity itself. Another way of celebrating a *cumulus* that is both textual and material is the collection of epigrams entitled *Aenigmata* by the late antique poet Symphosius; here, as argued by Philip Hardie in Chapter 10, the device of fragmentation is associated with the life of things, represented 'under the sign of paradox'.

Finally, Kristeva's discussion of Quignard's *Little Treatises* as an unconventional assemblage of short forms points to the fundamental act of unbinding between the signifier and the referent. Similar textual and discursive mechanisms can be detected in the late antique grammarian Nonius Marcellus, compared by Matthew Payne in Chapter 5 with the modern editor of fragments, busy with the dislocation and dismemberment, but also the consequential reuniting of several parts. In a similar vein, Clement of Alexandria's *Stromateis*, discussed by Antoine Paris in Chapter 6, represents an exemplary *mise-en-abyme* of the very dynamics of the act of epitomizing in its two fundamental aspects: cutting and re-uniting. But what if fragments and parts do not actually stem from any existing work? This is the complement added by Virginia Burrus in Chapter 9, on the virtual or imaginary library by an author called Dionysios. This peculiar situation evokes and sustains a desire for textual integrity that necessarily will remain elusive. Burrus's discussion represents (potentially) the ideal close to this volume, since it takes its readers to the extreme situation of an epitome of non-existent texts.

Notes

* Parts 1 to 5 of this Introduction are by Paolo Felice Sacchi, part 6 by Marco Formisano.

1. The English translation is taken from the old Loeb edition by Platnauer 1922.
2. Kafka 1971.
3. Bennett 2010: 6–10.
4. By this term we are referring to the concept as it was intensively discussed from both critical and literary perspectives particularly in the 1970s and 1980s. A thorough investigation can still be usefully read in Kristeva 1974: 101–50 . See also Agamben 1992: xii: 'The question that gives rise to this research [the connection between language and death] must necessarily assume the form of a question interrogating the place and structure of negativity. Our attempt to respond to this question has led us [. . .] to an examination of the problem of Voice and of its "grammar" as a fundamental metaphysical problem, and, at the same time, as an originary structure of negativity'.
5. This idea is central to many recent editions/studies of ancient and late antique epitomes: see for example Formisano 2003 (Vegetius); Fele 2009 (Festus); Bordone and Gasti 2014 (Eutropius); Bleckmann and Gross 2018 (Eutropius); Borgna 2018 (Iustinus); Borgna 2020 (Iustinus). An important theoretical framework is provided by the collective volume Horster and Reitz 2010. See further Dusil et al. 2016; Horster and Reitz 2018.
6. Inglebert 2010: 514: 'La question la plus importante pour un épitomé n'est pas le "quoi?", qui est donné par le modèle, mais le "quand?" qui est seule essentielle pour comprendre l'existence même de l'épitomé, et qui concentre les questions "pourquoi/ pour qui/ comment?"'
7. See Böhme et al. 2011.
8. For late antique specimens of such subversions see Schnapp 1992, Doody 2009 and below.

9. On 'imperialistic' forms of knowledge in the ancient world see at least Murphy 2004 and König and Whitmarsh 2007.
10. For Virbius' myth as a metaphor for late antiquity see Formisano 2001: 154–61.
11. We are referring to the disruptive power of *anagrams* and *paragrams* as illustrated by Starobinsky 1971.
12. *Obtuseness* as a hermeneutical concept was popularized by Roland Barthes's essay *The Third Meaning* originally published in the *Cahiers du cinema*, (*Le troisième sens*, 1970), on which see Oxman 2010.
13. For a critical stand against theories of ineffability and the risks they imply, see Meillassoux 2006.
14. See Galdi 1922 for Latin literature; Bott 1920 and MacLachlan 2004 for both Greek and Latin.
15. Drawing on Bott 1920, Opelt 1962, col. 945 distinguishes between *epitoma auctoris* and *epitoma rei tractatae* respectively.
16. We refer to Theodor Mommsen's edition of Solinus' *Collectanea rerum memorabilium* (1895), Heinrich Keil's *Grammatici Latini* (1855–1880), Alexander Riese's *Geographi Latini Minores* (1878).
17. See Wölfflin 1902a, 1902b, 1902c, 1904, 1906; Galdi 1922: 18–22; MacLachlan 2004: 3–14. Rosalind MacLachlan 2004: 24, though, cannot but admit that: 'The range and variety of epitomes argue against there being a neat definition and a simple answer. They seem not to be joined by a common form or to compose a genre with prescribed characteristics'.
18. Cf. MacLachlan 2004: 14–7 for a critical assessment of Galdi's theoretical tenets.
19. Galdi 1922: 1: 'In generale, la tendenza a fare estratti e compendi di opera di maggiore mole è strettamente connessa al fenomeno del decadimento politico e morale di un popolo'.
20. Galdi 1922 : 1: 'Nei secoli di ricca fioritura letteraria, quando la produzione è originale e rispecchia in larga parte le floride condizioni di ambiente e lo stato d'animo di un popolo che imprime le sue orme sul cammino della civilità, e quando una sola preoccupazione pare che incomba sugli scrittori, di nulla trattare che non contribuisca alla grandezza del proprio paese od alla celebrazione della propria stirpe, si reputerebbe vana fatica l'industriarsi a ridurre opera altrui'; Ibid.: 3: 'Si è già detto che il compendio, di solito, torna a detrimento dell'opera d'arte. E nel vero, un *opus integrum*, compendiato, si sfigura, perdendo quell'impronta di freschezza e d'immediatezza, se non di organicità, che gli era propria'.
21. Cf., for instance, Galdi 1922: 2: '[. . .] opere immortali e dove è impresso il genio della propria razza' – epitomes are not, of course, such works.
22. See Galdi 1922: IV. Cf. Birt 1907 and Bott 1920. For an overview of late antique librarian production see Cavallo 1975.
23. See Blair 2010: 14–22 on 'information management in antiquity'.
24. See Blair 2003, 2007.
25. See Lizzi 1990 and Kaster 1988. Indeed, 'school' has been an emblematic word for late antiquity ever since Henri-Iréné Marrou's groundbreaking work on Augustine's education (Marrou 1938). For a classic view on the socio-political impact of rhetorical education, see Brown 1992.
26. Galdi 1922: 2.
27. 'Idealistic' in the sense of Italian philosopher Benedetto Croce, whose extremely influential *Poesia e non poesia* was to be published just one year after Galdi's monograph, in 1923.

28. See Mazzarino ([1960] 1974). For an assessment and history of Mazzarino's controversial formula, see Carrié 2001 and the special issue of *Antiquité tardive* in which it is published. On how a new conception of rhetoric and literariness impacted on late antique textual production (*Fachliteratur*, commentaries, exegesis etc.), see Formisano 2012: 512–20.
29. Cf. *supra* note 6.
30. See Dubischar 2010: 41 ff.
31. Dubishar 2010: 42.
32. Dubischar 2010: 61. Cf. Grice 1975 and Luhmann 1984, 1997.
33. Dubischar 2010: 62 n. 53.
34. Formisano 2012: 525.
35. Genette ([1982] 2003): 349: 'aucune reduction, n'étant jamais simple réduction, ne peut être transparente, insignifiante – innocente'.
36. This is what Opelt 1962, col. 959, analysing the most common *topoi* in the prefaces of epitomes, dubs *Nutzen-* or *Zweckenformel*, that is, formulas pointing to the 'use' that could be made of the epitome.
37. Mülke 2010: 87.
38. Even-Zohar ([2005] 2010): 70–6.
39. Even-Zohar ([2005] 2010): 53.
40. See Lefevere 1992.
41. Lefevere 1992: 38.
42. See Raible 1995.
43. Genette ([1982] 2003): 341 ff.
44. See Doody 2009.
45. Doody 2009: 95.
46. See Schnapp 1992. For an in-depth study of the cento, see Schottenius Cullhed 2015.
47. See Formisano 2001: 154–61, 2012: 522–7.
48. Formisano 2012: 526.
49. This dialectic somehow also impacts on the status of late antiquity within the Western academy. See Formisano 2019: 119–25.
50. See Formisano 2017.
51. See Formisano 2020.

Works cited

Agamben, G. (1992), *Language and Death: The Place of Negativity*, trans. K. E. Pinkus and M. Hardt, Minneapolis: University of Minnesota Press.

Bennett, J. (2010), *Vibrant Matter: A political ecology of things*, Durham, NC: Duke University Press.

Birt, T. (1907), *Die Buchrolle in der Kunst: Archäologisch-antiquarische Untersuchungen zum antiken Buchwesen*, Leipzig: Teubner.

Blair, A. M. (2003), 'Reading Methods for Coping with Information Overload, ca. 1550–1700', *Journal of the History of Ideas* 64: 11–28.

Blair, A. M. (2007), 'Organizations of Knowledge', in J. Hankins (ed.), *Cambridge Companion to Renaissance Philosohpy*, 287–303, Cambridge: Cambridge University Press.
Blair, A. M. (2010), *Too Much to Know: Managing Scholarly Information Before the Modern Age*, New Haven, CT: Yale University Press.
Bleckmann, B. and J. Gross, eds (2018), *Eutropius. Breviarium ab urbe condita*. Paderborn: Schöningh.
Böhme H., Bergemann L., Dönike M., Schirrmeister A., Toepfer G., Walter M. and J. Weitbrecht, eds (2011), *Transformation: Ein Konzept zur Erforschung kulturellen Wandels*, Munich: Wilhelm Fink.
Bordone, F. and F. Gasti (2014), *Eutropio. Storia di Roma*, Santarcangelo di Romagna: Rusconi.
Borgna, A. (2018), *Ripensare la storia universale: Giustino e l'*Epitome *delle* Storie Filippiche *di Pompeo Trogo*, Hildesheim: Olms.
Borgna, A. (2020), *Giustino. Storie Filippicche. Florilegio da Pompeo Trogo*, Santarcangelo di Romagna: Rusconi.
Bott, H. (1920), *De epitomis antiquis*, Marburg: Hamel.
Brown, P. (1992), *Power and Persuasion in Late Antiquity: Towards a Christian Empire*, Madison: University of Wisconsin Press.
Carrié, J.-M. (2001), 'Antiquité tardive et 'démocratisation de la culture': un paradigme à géométrie variable', *Antiquité tardive* 9, special issue: *La 'démocratisation de la culture' dans l'antiquité tardive*: 7–46.
Cavallo, G. (1975), 'Libro e pubblico alla fine del mondo antico', in G. Cavallo (ed.), *Libri, editori e pubblico nel mondo antico. Guida storica e critica*, 83–132, Bari: Editori Laterza.
Doody, A. (2009), 'Authority and Authorship in the Medicina Plinii', in A. Doody (ed.), *Authorial Voices in Graeco-Roman Technical Writing*, 93–105, Trier: Wissenschaftlicher Verlag Trier.
Dubischar, M. (2010), 'Survival of the Most Condensed? Auxiliary Texts, Communication Theory, and Condensation of Knowledge', in M. Horster and C. Reitz (eds), *Condensing Texts – Condensed Texts*, 39–67, Stuttgart: Franz Steiner Verlag.
Dusil, S., Schwedler G. and Schwitter R., eds (2016), *Exzerpieren – Kompilieren – Tradieren: Transformationen des Wissens zwischen Spätantike und Frühmittelalter*, Berlin: De Gruyter.
Even-Zohar, Itamar ([2005] 2010), *Papers in Culture Research,* Tel Aviv: Unit of Culture Research University of Tel Aviv [electronic version].
Fele, M. L. (2009), *Il* Breviarium *di Rufio Festo*, Hildesheim: Weidmann.
Formisano, M. (2001), *Tecnica e scrittura: Le letterature tecnico-scientifiche nello spazio letterario tardoantico*, Rome: Carocci.
Formisano, M. (2003), *P. Vegezio Renato. L'arte della guerra romana*, Milan: Rizzoli.
Formisano, M. (2012), 'Late Antiquity, New Departures', in R. Hexter and D. Townsend (eds), *The Oxford Handbook of Medieval Latin Literature*, 510–534, Oxford: Oxford University Press.
Formisano, M. (2017), 'Displacing Tradition: A New-Allegorical Reading of Ausonius, Claudian, and Rutilius Namatianus', in J. Elsner and J. Hernández Lobato (eds), *The Poetics of Late Latin Literature*, 207–35, New-York: Oxford University Press.
Formisano, M. (2019), 'In nome dell'altro: lo studio della letteratura latina antica tra intertestualità e alterità', in C. Cappelletto (ed.), *In cattedra. Il docente universitario in otto autoritratti*, Milano: Raffaello Cortina Editore.
Formisano, M. (2020), 'Il tardo antico come contemporaneo? Identificazione e alterità di un'età non classica', *ClassicoContemporaneo* 6: 60–6.
Galdi, M. (1922), *L'epitome nella letteratura latina*, Naples: P. Federico & G. Ardia.
Genette, G. ([1982] 2003), *Palimpsestes: La littérature au second degré*, Paris: Seuil.
Grice, H. P. (1975), 'Logic and Conversation', in P. Cole and J. L. Morgan (eds), *Syntax and Semantics, Vol. 3: Speech Acts*, 41–58, New York: Academic Press.
Horster, M. and C. Reitz, eds (2010), *Condensing Texts – Condensed Texts,* Stuttgart: Franz Steiner Verlag.

Horster, M., and C. Reitz (2018), 'Handbooks, Epitomes, and Florilegia' in S. McGill and E. Watts (eds), *A Companion to Late Antique Literature*, 431–50, Malden, MA: John Wiley & Sons.
Inglebert, H. (2010), 'Lactance abréviateur de lui-même. Des Institutions divines à l'Epitomé des Institutions divines: l'exemple de l'histoire des religions', in M. Horster and C. Reitz (eds), *Condensing Texts – Condensed Texts*, 491–15, Stuttgart: Franz Steiner Verlag.
Kafka, F. (1971), 'The Cares of a Family Man', in *The Complete Short Stories*, trans. W. and. E. Muir, 469–70, New-York: Schocken Books.
Kaster, R. A. (1988), *Guardians of Language: The Grammarian and Society in Late Antiquity*, Berkeley: University of California Press.
Keil, H. ed. (1855–1880), *Grammatici Latini*, I-VII (+ Supplementum), Leipzig: Teubner.
König, J and T. Whitmarsh, eds (2007), *Ordering Knowledge in the Roman Empire*, Cambridge: Cambridge University Press.
Kristeva, J. (1974), *La révolution du langage poétique: L'avant-garde à la fin du XIX*[e] *siècle: Lautréamont et Mallarmé*, Paris: Seuil.
Lefevere, A. (1992), *Translation, Rewriting, and the Manipulation of Literary Fame*, London: Routledge.
Lizzi, R. (1990), 'La memoria selettiva', in G. Cavallo, P. Fedeli and A. Giardina (eds), *Lo spazio letterario di Roma antica*, vol. 3: *La ricezione del testo*, 647–76, Rome: Salerno.
Luhmann, N. (1984), *Soziale Systeme*, Frankfurt am Main: Suhrkamp.
Luhmann, N. (1997), *Die Gesellschaft der Gesellschaft*, Frankfurt am Main: Suhrkamp.
MacLachlan, R. F. (2004), *Epitomes in Ancient Literary Culture*, PhD diss., St John's College, University of Cambridge, Cambridge.
Marrou, H-I. (1938), *Saint Augustin et la fin de la Culture antique*, Paris: Éditions de Boccard.
Mazzarino, S. ([1960] 1974), 'La democratizzazione della cultura nel 'basso impero'', in Id. *Antico, tardoantico ed èra costantiniana*, 74–98, Bari: Dedalo.
Meillassoux, Q. (2006), *Après la finitude: Essai sur la nécessité de la contingence*, Paris: Seuil.
Mommsen, T. ed. ([1895] 1958), *C. Iulii Solini, Collectanea rerum memorabilium*, iterum recensuit Th. Mommsen, Berlin: Weidmann.
Mülke, M. (2010), 'Die Epitome – Das bessere Original?', in M. Horster and C. Reitz (eds), *Condensing Texts – Condensed Texts*, 69–89, Stuttgart: Franz Steiner Verlag.
Murphy, T. (2004), *Pliny the Elder's Natural History: The Empire in the Encyclopaedia*, Oxford: Oxford University Press.
Opelt, I. (1962), 'Epitome', in *Reallexicon für Antike und Christentum* 5: 944–73, Stuttgart: Hiersemann.
Oxman, E. (2010), 'Sensing the Image: Roland Barthes and the Affect of the Visual', *SubStance* 39: 71–90.
Platnauer (1922), *Claudian*. Vol. II, Loeb Classical Library, Cambridge, MA: Harvard University Press.
Raible, W. (1995), 'Arten des Kommentierens – Arten der Sinnbildung – Arten des Verstehens', in J. Assmann and B. Gladigow (eds), *Text und Kommentar*, 52–73, München: Wilhelm Fink Verlag.
Riese, A. ed. (1878), *Geographi latini minores*, Heilbronn: Henninger.
Schnapp, J. T. (1992), 'Reading Lessons: Augustine, Proba, and the Christian Détournement of Antiquity', *Stanford Literary Review* 9 (2): 99–123.
Schottenius Cullhed, S. (2015), *Proba the Prophet: The Christian Virgilian Cento of Faltonia Betitia Proba*, Leiden – Boston: Brill.
Starobinsky, J. (1971), *Les mots sous les mots: Les anagrammes de Ferdinand de Saussure*, Paris: Gallimard.
Wölfflin, E. (1902a), 'Die neue *Epitoma Alexandri*', *Archiv für Lateinische Lexicographie* 12: 187–96.
Wölfflin, E. (1902b), 'Epitome', *Archiv für Lateinische Lexicographie* 12: 333–44.

Wölfflin, E. (1902c), 'Zur Latinität der *Epitome Caesarum*', *Archiv für Lateinische Lexicographie* 12: 445–53.

Wölfflin, E. (1904), 'Das *Breviarium* des Festus', *Archiv für Lateinische Lexicographie* 13: 64–97; 172–99.

Wölfflin, E. (1906), 'Zum Chronikon Livianum von Oxyrhynchus', *Archiv für Lateinische Lexicographie* 14: 221–32.

PART I
EPITOMIC DIMENSIONS

CHAPTER 1
PASCAL QUIGNARD'S *PETITS TRAITÉS*: (ANTI-)MODERN EPITOMES?

Irena Kristeva

To revalorize the 'bewitching background'[1] of an enigmatic and fascinating Antiquity, which he re-elaborates from its scattered and fragmented remains, Pascal Quignard proposes an *aggiornamento* of ancient literary genres such as 'l'aphorisme, l'adage, le proverbe, la sentence, le dicton, la devinette, l'apophtegme, la formulation gnomique, l'énoncé paradoxal, le haïku, le précepte, l'énigme, l'épigramme à Paris au XVIIe siècle, le trait d'esprit à Rome au Ier siècle'.[2] Among those, we could classify the epitome, intended, in this case, as a concise reprise of a story of ancient times.

The *Petits traités* (Little Treatises) represent, indeed, an unconventional assemblage of short forms that condense the reflection, by endowing it with the sparkliness and fugacity of fireworks; that search for the deep meaning, by playing with the latent connotations of discourse; that translate the stream of thought, by fractioning the storytelling. The reflection opens an abyss concretized in several distances. The theoretical distance: the incommensurable estrangement from the Platonic world of *logos* and *graphé* of Ambrose's and Augustine's reading, carried out in the intimate and silent space of the soul. The cultural distance: the break between the culture of *mythos* and the civilization of *liber*. The ethical distance: the Nietzschean conflict between the Apollonian *ethos* and the Dionysian *pathos*, resolved in the *augmentum*.[3] The aesthetic distance: the breach between the postmodern vision of art and the baroque aesthetic of detail, fragmentation and affect. The poetic distance: the rupture of the great narrative and its crumbling into fragments.

The question that arises at this point is the following: will the interpretative process be sufficient to cross this abyss and absorb the original content through the quasi-magical transmutation of the signifier or is it not rather a question of an unbinding[4] between the signifier and its referent? However, we cannot speak of an ontological or non-referential unbinding, because the feeling of radical strangeness triggered by these 'heretical' treatises does not come from the absence of referents but from the distorted relation to the referent, from the twist, from the contamination, from the mutual perversion of the primary text and the treatment that their author reserves to it.

The (anti-)modernity of the little treatise

J'espère être lu en 1640.[5]

This astonishing desire for a baroque, and therefore anti-modern, reception is also revealed in an expressiveness that evokes baroque expressiveness. The *Petits traités* contain the characteristics of a baroque work: instability, mobility, metamorphosis, rupture, reconstruction. Moreover, since their publication,[6] the literary criticism has emphasized Quignard's attachment to the detail and its expansion; the finesse of his reflection; the raw explosiveness of his language.[7] Difficult to assimilate to the established genres of the literary canon, they evade any classification purpose. The attempt to suggest a definition covering them as a whole, including *per viam negationis*, turns out to be quite problematic, given that they constantly confront us with the systematic entanglement of the narration and the commentary, which translates the double intention and the double ambition of their author: man of letters and thinker.

This erudite prose juxtaposes the most diverse references concerning the texts of classical heritage (Heraclitus, Lucretius, Vergilius, Marcus Aurelius); the writings of the moralists of Port Royal (Esprit, Nicole, La Rochefoucauld); the pamphlets of the honest men (Saint-Evremond and La Bruyère); the critique of modernity (Adorno and Michelstaedter). It seems then legitimate to ask if the *Petits traités* are not modelled on the ancient *moralia* that are situated between philosophical reflection and fiction. All the more so since the thirty pages of *moralia* that end the *Rhétorique speculative* (Speculative Rhetoric) are accompanied by a micrological gaze *à la* Benjamin or *à la* Adorno.[8] The work, however, should not be viewed as an educational portfolio of preconceived ideas. Its narrative process is autonomous. Far from being reduced to predictable reasonings and easy rationalizations, it turns into free meditation where the spontaneous and the speculative intersect.

The opinions of Quignard's exegetes are well divided with regard to the generic autonomy of his little treatise. For some, this does not constitute a literary genre strictly speaking: 'Proche de l'essai, du fragment, du récit, de la note érudite, de la leçon, de la fable, il joue, telle une 'suite baroque' improvisée, sur tous les registres, sur tous les tons'.[9] Others are prone to attributing to it the status of a genre in its own right in spite of its problematicity and singularity: 'Inspiré de Pierre Nicole, le traité est un genre imprécis, qui trouve ici une forme particulière – étrange, parfois déroutante: ces traités sont à peu près tous composés de ce que notre époque appelle, faute de mieux, des *fragments*'.[10] Quignard's position remains quite ambiguous. He gives the little treatise the value of genre without this preventing it from shattering both its structural rigidity and its logical sequence. His understanding of the treatise as a derivative of 'trait' refers to the Latin verb *trahere, traho, traxï, tractum* meaning to drag, to draw, to advance.[11]

The 'little' is established as one of the two essential formal elements of the Quignardian work, the other being the 'treatise'. This tiny element manages to pierce the surface of everyday life, to tear apart its superficial entirety, to reveal the abyss of its own nameless and identityless being. The taste of the Modern Times for the short form is furthermore elicited by the confrontation with the two expressions of terror: original and modern. The little thus becomes the counterpoint to an imminent peril, an 'original figure of resistance'.[12] This explains the fascination it exerts on twentieth-century thinkers of the stature of Adorno, Benjamin or Kafka.

The 'choice of the little', to use the expression coined by Miguel Abensour to designate the tendency that has arisen within modernity as a result of the demand to 'se tourner vers ce qui a été délaissé, négligé, exclu',[13] imposes itself as one of the distinctive features of Pascal Quignard's essays. The motivation that conditions this choice can be supplemented by a few personal reasons: the critical attitude towards modernity and its forms; the anti-philosophical reaction of a rebellious thinker against the Cartesian expression; the rejection of the *grandeur* of what claims universality; the desire to return to the primitive, the unfinished, the savage, the *rudis*; the interest in what seems insignificant; the refusal to freeze the language. Moreover, the enhancement of the little attests to a deep reflection that digs to the bottom of things said or written, that goes beyond the perceptible.

The generic transversality of the *Petits traités* corresponds to the diversity and richness of their content.[14] The abundance of subjects and the specificity of their assemblage would hardly find an analogy in modern French literature with the exception, perhaps, of the work of Georges Perec. Pascal Quignard stands against the analytical and formal line that belongs to the structuralism and to the New Novel. Intrigued by the passage into other spaces, he opposes the concern for objectivity, the positivist coldness, the fixation of what lends itself to control in art. Its fragments therefore do not reflect the cosmic harmony of yore, but the chaos that modern man believes to be able to dominate. So, if the works of Antiquity 'nous étaient parvenus à l'état de fragments, les œuvres des modernes cherchaient à épouser en naissance cet état, imputant la fascination qu'elles exercent à la fragmentation et estimant que ces morceaux, qui évoquaient des touts indicibles et absents, par le désir qu'ils en laissaient, accroissaient l'émotion'.[15]

The interest in subjects such as the terror, the *tædium vitae* and the plunging into the abyss pushes the author of the *Petits traités* to take a regressive approach. If he sees writing as an 'interworld', he sees the fragment as a trace and negation of a particular memory, deposited by the retrospective movement of thought. Side by side with the generic transversality and the passion for the original, the Graecisms (*anagnôsis*, *noèsis*, *sarx*, *etc.*) and the Latinisms (*augmentum*, *fascinus*, *sordidissima*, *etc.*), to which he systematically resorts to extract staggering semantic effects, reveal an anti-modern attitude. At the same time, these anachronistic effects distinguish a writer who is conscious of his modernity because, as he observes in his essay *Une gêne technique à l'égard des fragments* (A technical discomfiture regarding fragments): 'Du moins dans l'art moderne l'effet de discontinu s'est substitué à l'effet de liaison'.[16] This unbinding signals the break between the oral world (Antiquity) and the written world (Modernity). The resulting fragmentation denotes the ruin of speech.

The fascination of the fragmentary

> Les mots latins de fragmen, de fragmentum viennent de frango, briser, rompre, fracasser, mettre en pièces, en poudre, en miettes, anéantir. En grec le fragment, c'est le klasma, l'apoklasma, l'apospasma, le morceau détaché par fracture, l'extrait,

> quelque chose d'arraché, de tiré violemment. Le spasmos vient de là: convulsion, attaque nerveuse qui tire, arrache, disloque.[17]

Starting from the Greek etymon *klasma*, Quignard underlines the destructive essence of the fragment by a confrontation between the *iconoclaste*, the *phonoclaste* and the *logoclaste*. In other words, he addresses the possibility of visual, acoustic and linguistic fragmentation that evokes the violence inherent in the production of fragments. The 'infirmity' of the fragments that stem from the fractionation, causes a spectrum of effects ranging from disgust to enjoyment: 'Des morceaux de membres partout, des déchets, des fragments de peau partout et des cicatrices partout qui les suturent mais qui brusquement, on ne sait pourquoi, saignent comme la lance du conte'.[18] Overwhelmed by the subjugating aggressiveness of an imaginary – palpable in its intrusive power – the reader of the *Petits traités* is carried away in this whirlwind of bodily elements, which fascinates with its unreality.

The corporeality of the fragment was noticed by Pierre Nicole, one of Pascal Quignard's master thinkers:

> Comme les corps ne se joignent presque jamais si parfaitement qu'il n'y ait toujours entre eux quelques petits intervalles remplis d'air qui les séparent, on ne sauroit aussi faire un tissu si continu de ses actions qu'il n'y reste quelques petits vuides, et ces vuides qui sont quelquefois nécessaires pour le délassement de l'esprit pourroient estre utilement remplis de quelques prières qui n'obligeassent pas à une grande contention.[19]

Philippe Lacoue-Labarthe and Jean-Luc Nancy note its immanent destructuring: 'Si le fragment est bien une fraction, il ne met pas d'abord, ni exclusivement, l'accent sur la fracture qui l'a produit. A tout le moins, il désigne autant, si l'on peut dire, les bords de la fracture comme une forme autonome que comme l'informité ou la difformité de la déchirure'.[20] Maurice Blanchot insists on its discontinuity, 'puisque les fragments, destinés en partie au blanc qui les sépare, trouvent en cet écart non pas ce qui les termine, mais ce qui les prolonge, ou les met en attente de ce qui les prolongera, les a déjà prolongés, les faisant persister de par leur inachèvement'.[21] And given that the creation of an overall image supposes the recourse to the accumulation of fragments that do not oppose but position themselves side by side, the 'Fragment word'[22] becomes the 'Word as Archipelago'.[23] As for Pascal Quignard, he definitely prefers the textual fragmentation to the assembly of fragments. The linguistic cleavage operated by his fragments reproduces the discursive destructuring. Paradoxically, the 'fragment trahit plus de circularité, d'autonomie et d'unité que le discours suivi qui masque vainement ses ruptures'.[24] It doesn't represent at all a part of a whole that can be reconstructed by a mechanical reassembly, but a little, well finished unit, despite its apparent imperfection: 'petit tout', 'petit morceau blotti et enveloppé sur lui-même'.[25]

Thus, breaking the image, the voice and the language, the fragment cuts up the *Petits traités*, punctuates their narrative, envelops the traces of yore that need to be unfolded. Its ruiniform nature unearths the past in order to transmit the image of a fragmented

Antiquity that fascinates precisely by what is lacking, and to reconstruct its irreparably lost objects: its art and its thought. In this impulse to return to the origin, the fragment establishes the absence that reveals the impossibility to fill the void, to escape nothingness, to lure death as the organizing principle of the essays. Sharpening the nostalgia intrinsic to all writing, it contains the repressed death drive, since all desire is a 'death principle',[26] including the desire to write.

The Quignardian fragments hammer the narration like the *tarabust*[27] that accompanies us throughout life. Their concise, very little modalized sentences pierce like an obsessive buzz. Their jerky brevity punctuates the saturation of a discourse that has nothing to do with empty word. And even though they are 'volontiers liés entre eux souvent par l'effet d'écho et de retour, l'entretissage des mots et des phrases qui reviennent',[28] this cyclical return is not monotonous, but rich in variations. It is conditioned by the retrospective quest for the thing that is at the origin: the Latin *res*, whose accusative *rem* gave *rien* (little thing; nothing) in French. On the other hand, the Quignardian fragments always contain the unnamed, conceal a secret and reserve a surprise. Like papyrus scrolls they have two sides: external and internal, *ēso* and *ēxo*, esoteric and exoteric. In any case, the fascination they exert does not stem from a sublime and poetic style, but from a language that distrusts any embellishment, given that:

> [...] le plus grand mystère ne naît pas de ce qu'on utilise des fragments de langue étroite, expressive et rythmée, d'une temporalité courte, aisément mémorables, intensément corporels, mécaniquement symétriques, compulsivement répétés et d'une syntaxe elle-même nécessairement pauvre et simple. Le plus grand mystère tient à ce que la forme poétique s'éloigne un beau jour d'elle-même, se sépare de ses chevilles, de ses pieds et de ses fredons, devienne plus complexe, d'un rythme plus sourd, d'une syntaxe plus riche et plus rigoureuse, d'une expression plus insidieuse, d'une signification plus habile et plus précise, d'une efficace moins émotive, d'une rétention impossible – bref que la langue poétique débouche sur la prose, puis sur la prose écrite, imprononçable, des livres.[29]

The decision to write the *Petits traités* in this short form is undoubtedly conditioned by the rhetorical expressiveness of the fragment that Quignard highlights by calling it in turn 'petit spasme rhétorique', 'noyau de pensée', 'plénitude essentielle, idéale, platonicienne, autarcique, limée, fourbie', 'bout de reste', 'détritus', 'singularité', 'minuscule catastrophe, minuscule épave, et minuscule solitude'.[30] The fragment catches the eye, focuses the mental activity on the page, and centres the attention on the effect produced by its brevity. The circularity, the autonomy and the unity are some of its strengths. The fragmentary, for its part, 'promet le désarroi, le désarrangement',[31] implies 'le désastre, ruine de parole, défaillance par l'écriture, rumeur qui murmure: ce qui reste sans reste'.[32] His 'caractère un peu ruiniforme, dépressif'[33] awakens an uncanny feeling, triggers anguish, by reintroducing the melancholy of loss, and at the same time fascinates as a testimony to a vanished world.

The fragment could then be defined as the trace of a quest, the mark of a pursuit of meaning. It turns out to be the most appropriate genre to reflect the mythical thought, the instantaneous verbal gesture, the manifestations of the heterogeneous, the arguments that raise questions, the re-use of already exploited motifs, treated from a different angle, alongside other units. From this perspective, the Quignard's essays represent a shaping of *grámmata* that are well suited to develop and envelop. The writer remains nevertheless aware of the fact that the abyss, which separates Antiquity and Modernity, would not be filled by scattered motley elements: scraps of myths or fragments of ideas, pieces of texts stitched together or reproduced works of art. The recurring cyclical reprise in his work aims in particular to structure the apparently chaotic succession of fragments.

The epitome revisited

> Ni Jean de La Fontaine ni Claude Lévi-Strauss ne se sont astreints à recopier servilement les textes sources des contes qu'ils multipliaient. Ni, à strictement parler, ils ne les ont traduits. Ils ont procuré une forme plus pure aux histoires qu'ils avaient recensées et qu'ils aimaient.[34]

Joining this lineage, Pascal Quignard tells, in his *Petits traités*, stories that happened yore and elsewhere, usually accompanied by a not directly related extra-narrative commentary. This comment, however, remains intra-textual, since it makes perceivable the effect produced by these stories on the narrator. The writer therefore takes up fragments of myths or literary works that he disarticulates and then rearticulates as other myths or texts, associating them freely with third-party myths or texts that carry their own symbolism or condense his ideas. The hyphenation and the moments of rupture, which are abundant in his succinct and often unfinished narratives, render it possible to establish transversal links between the different parts of the treatise.

The predilection for the *narratio brevis* takes into account its selective, explanatory and imaginative character. The brief narration sets up a secondary narration, by adopting the technique of the reprise. It fits well with the fragment as it violates the whole story and interrupts its continuity:

> *Résumer* un texte, c'est procéder simultanément à l'effritement des délires du héros, de l'auteur et du lecteur. C'est briser la complicité d'un texte continu qui dissimule par sa cohérence même qu'il est énigmatique. *Démembrer* le texte, c'est faire apparaître ses lacunes, l'absence de liens entre certains événements ou la substitution de liens fictifs aux liens réels. *Déconstruire* le texte est l'étape préalable nécessaire pour reconstruire un autre texte, en tissant entre les événements d'autres liens [. . .] *Résumer*, c'est séparer les différents éléments de la trame dans lesquels ils sont pris pour les tresser ensemble dans un autre tissu.[35]

Quignard tells concise and condensed stories. The condensation, apart from the fact that the fragment supposes it, penetrates right to its elocution: portmanteau words, keywords, symbols. Thus, the interpretation of the *blason* in the treatise 'Femmes fragmentées en 1535' transforms it into a condensed symbol of the female body. The emphasis on concentrating the whole in a part potentiates its meaning. In fact, the *blason* (the symbol) constitutes, in relation to the symbolized thing (the female body), 'un ensemble dont les éléments sont autres que ceux présents dans la chose, mais entre lesquels existent les mêmes relations'.[36] The writer tends to emphasize the metaphorical and disproportionate nature of the condensation that Freud defined as a process extended until the arrival in the region of perceptions.[37] The excess and the fragment intersect in the narrative or pictorial *augmentum*, which can be understood as a kind of condensation of the dramatism in a temporal point: the moment that precedes death (Narcissus) or the passage to the act (Medea). On the other hand, the Roman frescoes relate condensed myths: the plunging into the abyss from the Tomb of the Diver in Paestum indicates the dynamics of the passage into the other world; the assaulting bull from the Tomb of the Bulls in Tarquinia evokes the moment just before the assassination of Troilus ambushed by Achilles.

The *aggiornamento* of the primary text, undertaken by Pascal Quignard, rules out the possibility of offering a faithful copy or translation. The *epitome*, namely the condensed reprise of a story already told, goes hand in hand with the *ekphrasis*, namely the meticulous description embedded in the narrative. Their interference would at first glance seem paradoxical, given the fragmentary writing, if one does not consider the fact that being 'dans son principe synecdoctique et fragmentaire [. . .], l'*ekphrasis* suscite, à partir d'un organe isolé et découpé, le corps fantasmé'.[38]

Let us observe, for example, the detailed description of the assassination of Concino Concini, Conte della Penna, Marquis d'Ancre, Marshal of France:

> Le lundi 24 avril 1617 Concini fut tué. Vêtu de hauts-de-chausses de velours gris brun à grandes bandes de Milan; un pourpoint de toile noire brodée d'or; un manteau de velours noir à passementeries italiennes, il franchit la porte du Louvre, lisant une lettre. Après qu'il eut franchi la porte de Bourbon, on referma la porte derrière lui aussitôt sur le pont dormant. Cinq coups de feu furent tirés.
>
> Une balle entre les deux yeux; une à la joue droite; une à la gorge.
>
> Sarroque piqua son épée dans le flanc. Taraud planta la sienne dans le cou.
>
> Tous accourent, s'acharnent. Du Buisson arrache la bague où brille le diamant de six mille écus. La face de Concini tournée vers le pont est noire de poudre et du sang qui a déjà séché. La fraise est rouge et brûlée.
>
> On enveloppe le corps dans un drap de cinquante sols et on l'enterre à minuit dans l'église de Saint-Germain-l'Auxerrois sous les orgues.
>
> Le mardi 25 avril, le jour se levant, la foule s'attroupe sous l'orgue, crache sur les dalles. On gratte avec les ongles autour des pierres. On met à nu les pieds du corps. On attache les pieds avec la corde des cloches, et on arrache tout le cadavre. [. . .]
>
> On tire Concini hors de l'église Saint-Germain. [. . .] Alors on traîne le corps jusqu'au Pont-Neuf et on le pend par les chevilles à une des potences que le mort y avait fait mettre. On lui crève les yeux. On lui coupe le nez. On tranche les oreilles. On dénoue l'aiguillette, on rit, on arrache le sexe et les couilles avec la main.

> On coupe les mains. On dépèce les bras. On tranche la tête. A chaque quartier de Paris est attribué un morceau du corps de Concini.[39]

The reprise of the incident of the death of Marie de Medici's favourite, narrated in 1618,[40] is rather representative for the Quignardian storytelling. Short and sharp, the impersonal sentences announce the dismemberment of the corpse. The description stands out with its meticulousness with regard to the dynamic of the unfolding of the events, the physical aspect of the victim (clothes, accessories, colours, materials and gestures), the names and subsequent acts of the assassins. The phantasmatic presentation of the details seems quite real: as if the narrator has witnessed the murder. Part of a whole, detail is by definition fragmentary. The *ekphrasis*, characterized by excessive violence, inevitably leads to the 'lambeaux éclatants' that blow up the narrative. In addition, the declaration that 'le culte des reliques [. . .] est la même chose que le culte des fragments'[41] puts on the same level the dismemberment of the human body, which is at the origin of the relics, and the fragmentation of the text, which is at the origin of the fragments. The mutilated body indirectly refers to the disarticulation of the text. Therefore, one can perceive the epitome of Concini's assassination as an allegory of the writing method, which consists in textual cutting.

Quignard's strategy concretizes itself in a correlation between the marginal and the sublime. The confrontation of heterogeneous subjects aims at their reciprocal elucidation. All the more so since, instead of trying to reconcile 'high' and 'low' literature, the writer seeks to move them into new spaces and to combine them in an unusual way, by operating the intellectual 'bricolage',[42] symptomatic of the mythical thought. This metaphorical tinkering requires the disarticulation, the disjunction, the fragmentation, the tearing and the dismemberment of the body. Its 'bewitching background' involves both transformational and regenerative power. In short, the author of the *Petits traités* tinkers together a puzzle of reminiscences, remains of memories, bits of reflections that lead to the world of drives – a raw and primitive world, as fragmentary as dazzling, the world of *Bruta fulmina et vana*,[43] in other words, the world of 'foudres qui tombent au hasard'.[44]

Conclusion

The *Petits traités* surprise with the audacity of the literary invention. Their objective is to focus on the moment, seen as the knot of the world. Their object focalizes on what interrupts the usual course of things. Their narration, which is neither reduced to predictable reasonings nor easy rationalizations, can be determined as an (anti-)modern epitome. Their reading gives the sensation of constantly crossing the space between Scylla (the lazy renunciation of meaning) and Charybdis (the ideological confinement in ourselves) of our own convictions and pre-established knowledge.

The fragmentary form of this narration, which wanders through ages, contexts and literary genres, corresponds to a vision of the world as a fragmented space and of writing as a discontinuous and unfinished discourse. The fragmentary writing materializes

Quignard's conception of language as a partial object that has to be metaphorized. It fills the space of the 'interworld', which separates the original world incompletely reached by the fragment and the imaginary world incompletely created by the fragment. It can be envisaged as stunning (that strikes by the effect of the unexpected), desiring (that desires and enjoys its object) and fascinating writing (that seduces and frightens).

Notes

1. Quignard 1997c: 73.
2. Quignard 1986: 38.
3. The *augmentum* marks the crucial or ethical moment of the story told. It indicates the paroxysm of suffering, passion, and sacrificial passivity.
4. Cf. Green 1998: 20: 'L'analyste, à partir des traces qui demeurent offertes à son regard-écoute, ne lit pas le texte, il le *délie*'.
5. Quignard 1997: 282. 1640 is the year of Rubens' death, the beginning of the Portuguese Restoration War, the *Corpus de Sang* riot in Barcelona. According to Quignard, 'la fragmentation volontaire dans la prose française' dates from around the same time (Quignard 1986: 37).
6. Written from 1977 to 1980, the *Petits traités* were published in their entirety in 1990 by Maeght Editeur in limited edition, and re-published in two pocket volumes in Gallimard's 'Folio' collection in 1997.
7. Jean-Pierre Richard (1990: 48) highlights his 'attachement maniaque (le dirons-nous fétichiste?) au détail, à la petitesse'. Dominique Viart (2000: 61) notes the 'thoroughness' of his thought.
8. Dominique Viart (2000: 71) hears in the *Petits traités* 'l'écho des *Minima Moralia*: comme Adorno, Quignard livre des "réflexions petites, minimes, relatives aux mœurs, à la vie endommagée", dans des "fragments erratiques, décentrés, lacunaires", selon la formule que Miguel Abensour utilise pour Adorno'.
9. Wybrands 1997: 91.
10. Millet 1991: 129.
11. Semerano 2002: 592.
12. Abensour 1991: 234.
13. Abensour 1991: 234.
14. The 56 little treatises are divided into 8 volumes according to an intertextual logic. They revolve around a few thematic cores: volume I contains 8 treatises that address the problem of voice and silence; volume II – 6 treatises that revolve around the notion of language; volume III – 4 treatises that touch on the problematic of the book; volume IV – 6 treatises gathered around the divine word; volume V – 7 treatises that raise the question of silent reading; volume VI – 9 treatises that deal with the relationship between reading and listening; volume VII – 8 treatises that deal with the relationship between death and art; volume VIII – 8 treatises that examine the stakes of poetic creation. We should add the 6 treatises of *Rhétorique spéculative* (Speculative Rhetoric), the 10 treatises of *La haine de la musique* (The Hatred of Music), the 'Petit traité sur Méduse' ("Little treatise on Medusa"), and the 'Traité sur l'esprit' ("Treatise on the Spirit").

15. Quignard 1986: 45–6.
16. Quignard 1986: 20.
17. Quignard 1986: 33.
18. Quignard 1997b: 419.
19. Nicole 1714: 367–68.
20. Lacoue-Labarthe and Nancy 1978: 62.
21. Blanchot 1980: 96.
22. Blanchot 1969: 451.
23. Char 1986.
24. Quignard 1986: 43.
25. Quignard 1986: 43.
26. Quignard 1997a: 255.
27. Pascal Quignard forges, or rather updates, this concept to concretize the idea of a harassing rhythm. The *tarabust* would be the place of origin of the acoustic desire; the uncontrollable background noise coming from the pre-linguistic world; a sort of rhythmic, insane and instinctual background that constantly haunts the individual.
28. Viart 2000: 72.
29. Quignard 1997a: 593–4.
30. Quignard 1986: 26, 38, 45.
31. Blanchot 1980: 17.
32. Blanchot 1980: 58.
33. Quignard 1986: 44.
34. Quignard 2005: 32.
35. Kofman 1973: 109.
36. Lévi-Strauss 1993: 158.
37. Freud 1979: 159.
38. Lestringant 2000: 155.
39. Quignard 1997: 405–6.
40. Mathieu and Thévenin 1618.
41. Quignard 1997b: 407.
42. Lévi-Strauss 1962: 26.
43. Plinius Senior 1848–1850: XLIII, 3.
44. Quignard 1997a: 27.

Works cited

Abensour, M. (1991), 'Le choix du petit', in T. W. Adorno, *Minima Moralia: Réflexions sur la vie mutilée*, E. Kaufholz and J.-R. Ladmiral (eds), 231–43, Paris: Payot.

Blanchot, M. (1969), *L'entretien infini*, Paris: Gallimard.

Blanchot, M. (1980), *L'écriture du désastre*, Paris: Gallimard.

Char, R. (1986), *La Parole en archipel*, Paris: Gallimard.
Freud, S. (1979), *Jokes and Their Relation to the Unconscious*, trans. J. Crick, London: Penguin Classics.
Green, A. (1998), *La Déliaison*, Paris: Hachette.
Kofman, S. (1973), *Quatre romans analytiques*, Paris: Galilée.
Lacoue-Labarthe, P. and Nancy, J.-L. (1978), *L'absolu littéraire*, Paris: Seuil.
Lestringant, F. (2000), 'De Louis Cordesse et de quelques procédés rhétoriques à la Renaissance', in D. Lyotard (ed.), *Pascal Quignard, Revue des sciences humaines*, 260: 151–66.
Lévi-Strauss, Cl. (1962), *La Pensée sauvage*, Paris: Plon.
Lévi-Strauss, Cl. (1993), *Regarder, écouter, lire*, Paris: Plon.
Mathieu, P. and Thévenin, M. (1618), *La conjuration de Conchine*, Paris: Pierre Rocolet.
Millet, R. (1991), *Accompagnement: Lectures*, Paris: POL.
Nicole, P. (1714), *Essais de morale*, I-IV, Paris: chez Guillaume Desprez et Jean Dessartz.
Plinius Senior (1848–1850), *Histoire naturelle*, Livre II, édition d'Emile Littré, Paris: Dubochet.
Quignard, P. (1986), *Une gêne technique à l'égard des fragments*, Montpellier: Fata Morgana.
Quignard, P. (1997a), *Petits traités* I, Paris: Gallimard.
Quignard, P. (1997b), *Petits traités* II, Paris: Gallimard.
Quignard, P. (1997c), *Rhétorique spéculative*, Paris: Gallimard.
Quignard, P. (1997d), *La haine de la musique*, Paris: Gallimard.
Quignard, P. (2005), *Les Paradisiaques. Dernier royaume IV*, Paris: Grasset.
Richard, J.-P. (1990), *L'état des choses: Etats sur huit écrivains d'aujourd'hui*, Paris: Gallimard.
Semerano, G. (2002), *Le origini della cultura europea*, vol. II, Firenze: Leo S. Olschki Editore.
Viart, D. (2000), 'Le moindre mot. Pascal Quignard et l'éthique de la minutie', in D. Lyotard (ed.), *Pascal Quignard, Revue des sciences humaines*, 260: 61–75.
Wybrands, F. (1997), 'Un trouble au pays de l'écriture. Les *Petits traités* de Quignard', *Études*, 386: 91–4.

CHAPTER 2
AUSONIUS EPITOMIZER: ENCYCLOPAEDISM AND ORDERING KNOWLEDGE IN LATE ANTIQUE GAUL

Brian P. Sowers

Introduction

The extensive and much discussed correspondence between Decimus Magnus Ausonius and Pontius Meropius Anicius Paulinus – popularly known as Ausonius of Bordeaux and Paulinus of Nola, respectively – begins with an epistle, dating to the mid 380s, in which Ausonius thanks Paulinus for his newest poem, a now lost verse epitome of Suetonius' equally lost *De regibus*:[1]

> his longe iucundissimum poema subdideras, quod de tribus Suetonii libris, quos ille de regibus dedit, in epitomen coegisti tanta elegantia, solus ut mihi videare adsecutus, quod contra rerum naturam est, brevitas ut obscura non esset.

> Together with this letter you sent an extremely delightful poem wherein you have epitomized the three books of Suetonius, which he devotes to the kings, so gracefully that I regard you as having alone achieved what is contrary to the ordinary course of things – brevity without obscurity.[2]

This letter between Paulinus and Ausonius presents a snapshot of late fourth-century elite *amicitia*, characterized by a shared preference for pastoral *otium* over urban *negotium*, an exchange of material gifts ranging from figpeckers (*ficedulae*) and shellfish (*testae*) to oil (*oleum*) and fish sauce (*muria*), and a regular circulation of literary texts, ideally poetry but, failing that, letters.[3] Since late antique literary *amicitia* requires mutual participation, Ausonius responds to Paulinus' original letter and accompanying verse epitome with his own hexameter epistle along with an additional request for more poetry. In the ensuing years, they would exchange and critique each other's work using a highly stylized and carefully curated language of affectation that blends mutual warmth and support with critical acumen and analysis. After Paulinus left Aquitaine yet before he finally settled in Campania, the reciprocity that defined his friendship with Ausonius broke down and eventually led to a silence between them. Despite Ausonius' multiple overtures to revitalize the exchange, this silence continued until his death in the mid 390s.[4]

Consistent with his epistolary etiquette with other literary *amici*, in this letter Ausonius complements Paulinus and provides erudite judgement and critical feedback about his epitome. His assessment can be read as a specific response to Paulinus' poem and as a theoretical model for late antique epitomes more generally. According to Ausonius, Paulinus has composed an unusually accomplished epitome, which strikes that rare balance between abbreviating (*brevitas*) its model without obscuring (*obscura*) its content. To support this assessment, Ausonius cites nine lines of the epitome, the only section of it to survive antiquity. Since the Suetonian original is also no longer extant, it is impossible to measure the accuracy of Ausonius' evaluation of it. That said, there is no hint in his language of a general disdain for epitomes nor anything to suggest that epitomical poetry was unsuitable for the attention of his coterie. Rather, by excerpting Paulinus' poem, Ausonius fragments and appropriates it in miniature, in effect epitomizing an epitome within a theoretical critique on epitomes. Such (hyper)allusive play is a consistent feature of Ausonius' metaliterary moments with members of his coterie, especially when he describes their shared literary etiquette.[5]

More to the point, Paulinus' Suetonian epitome is precisely the sort of poem encouraged and expected of Ausonius' circle; it is also the type of poem he himself, quite literally, composed. For that reason, this brief epistolary exchange between Ausonius and Paulinus, despite its possible relevance for reconstructing Ausonius' broader poetic habits and literary programme, is an equally instructive starting point for a more focused critical treatment of Ausonius' epitomical interests. The poetic corpus of Ausonius abounds with abbreviated miniatures – compiled collections of knowledge or arcana, fragmented from their original literary contexts and reconstituted into new, sometimes shockingly original, wholes. Careful attention to these epitomes reveals two underlying features of Ausonius' authorial mode – fragmentation and recomposition – that centre the critical approach adopted in my analysis of Ausonius' wider literary programme in this chapter.[6] After summarizing Ausonius' epitomizing habit and tracing those compositional techniques and aesthetics that unite his seemingly disparate poetic collection (or series of collections), I focus on his *Epitaphia Heroum* and *Caesares* as two illustrative examples of his tessellated mini-poems, each a condensed bricolage or literary pastiche of the classical/textual past.

Condensing twenty-six heroic deaths into twenty-four poems, the *Epitaphia Heroum* captures select epic moments, extracted from the *Iliad* and elsewhere and recomposed into two groups of twelve epitaphs: one dedicated exclusively to the Greek contingent, the other to the Trojan. Thematically distinct, these two units of twelve poetic miniatures are united into a single composition of twenty-four heroes, an epyllion that gestures simultaneously to both Homeric and Virgilian traditions. Each epitaph, an epyllion in itself, is an even further miniaturized and curated Trojan review compiled within, yet entirely distinct from, the larger collection. My analysis of the *Epitaphia Heroum* highlights how Ausonius as re-composer of the epic past, structures his new narrative against its ur-texts, simultaneously borrowing and deviating from them. As an intertextual paradox, the *Epitaphia Heroum* necessitates multiple readings which, on the one hand, reconcile it with its Homeric/Vergilian models and, on the other, engage it on its own terms.

Ausonius' *Caesares* – in reality two sets of twenty-seven poems divided by separate paratextual introductions – is similarly arranged by meticulous selection and summary.

The first set contains three, twelve-line poems that summarize Suetonius' imperial biographies, organized by sequential order (*de ordine*), length of reign (*de aetate imperii*), and death (*de obitu*). Each of the twelve Caesars receives a single line per stanza, in effect, creating three distinct Suetonian synopses focused on a specific aspect of their reigns. The second set consists of twenty-four tetrastichs, each dedicated to a single emperor, beginning with Julius Caesar and ending with Elagabalus. Ausonius divides these tetrastichs into two subcategories: the first twelve Caesars – in effect creating a fourth Suetonian epitome – followed by the next twelve.[7] This method of organization mirrors the *Epitaphia Heroum* and forms a single, 'epic length' digest of twenty-four individual poems.

This chapter, therefore, demonstrates how Ausonius orients his epitomizing programme – as evinced in the *Caesares* and *Epitaphia Heroum* – around encyclopaedic knowledge reconstituted into original verse through meticulous selection, abbreviation, expansion, and repetition. I am primarily interested in Ausonius' epitomatory dimension as evinced in his method of literary compilation and re-organization, with only a secondary interest in his classical sources. For that reason, I limit my engagement with this classical material to those moments when he invites his addressee/reader to consider his sources or when, in my view, such a reading directly elucidates his unique, late antique compositional style. This approach, I believe, helps contextualize the *Caesares* and *Epitaphia Heroum* within Ausonius' wider encyclopaedic enterprise, which, in turn, further clarifies the role of epitome within his overall literary programme.

Ausonius' epitomizing programme

Ausonius' poetic diversity is abundantly evident after even a quick glance at his extant writings.[8] In terms of metrical and generic range, he demonstrates a nearly unrivalled proficiency in over two dozen metres spanning traditional and hybrid generic lines on nearly every conceivable topic, as well as a few inconceivable ones.[9] Such literary breadth gives his poetry the illusion of being somewhat heterogeneous, with each individual poem appearing disconnected and dissimilar from each other 'oddity'.[10] Seeing Ausonius' poetry as dissociated products written because of his copious *otium* and overactive imagination tacitly preserves the now dated view that his corpus is ephemeral and ridiculous, not to be read seriously – a view ironically championed by Ausonius himself in his many prefaces and paratextual reflections. A different, yet equally distorting interpretative strategy attempts to preserve the *gravitas* of Ausonius' poetic programme by subdividing it by thematic type (personal, descriptive/documentary, and gymnastic).[11] Unfortunately, these categories ignore those metrical/generic boundaries Ausonius intentionally blurred and those organizational units articulated by Ausonius himself, such as the *Epitaphia Heroum*, *Parentalia*, and *Commemoratio Professorum Burdigalensium*, three poetic assemblages linguistically and thematically linked by Ausonius but containing both personal and descriptive/documentary material. Creating too rigid boundaries between ludic and serious poetry or between commemorative and didactic topics reflects modern literary values, not those advanced by Ausonius and his *amici*.

That said, a few stylistic features recur frequently enough throughout Ausonius' corpus that they bring a sense of unity and cohesion to his seemingly heterogeneous poems. Foremost of these unifying features is his use of exhaustive or encyclopaedic knowledge creatively compiled and transformed, albeit in radically divergent ways and in equally divergent forms, into brief, 'pocket-sized' poems.[12] These poetic miniatures are occasionally further organized into collections of similar types as encyclopaedic repositories or catalogues, with their constitutive subtopics set off by section headings. When viewed as a whole, these carefully curated poetic assemblages fit into what we might call Ausonius' epitomizing programme.

Some of these poetic compilations, such as the *Griphus* and *Technopaegnion* – literary catalogues on the number three and Latin monosyllables – rework classical arcana to showcase Ausonius' encyclopaedism. The *Technopaegnion*, a work comprising twelve miniature poems totalling 164 lines, contains nearly every Latin monosyllable (except for *daps*, *gryps*, *lynx*, *par*, *splen*, *vas*, and *frons*) which end each line.[13] Ausonius organizes his monosyllables by type or topic (*De cibis*, *De dis*, *De membris*, *Grammaticomastix*, etc.) marked as subject headings at the start of each miniature poem. This organizational method gives the *Technopaegnion* a thematic unity oriented around a nearly exhaustive catalogue of monosyllables, while also allowing Ausonius to showcase various 'subspecialties,' as it were, on everything ranging from types of food to grammatical trivia. It also facilitates reading the *Technopaegnion* as a poetic unit from beginning to end or individually as a poetic collection on various topics. In other words, the reader is free to engage Ausonius' organization and miniaturization of single syllable words in various ways, with divergent interpretive trajectories.[14]

Whereas in the various prefaces to the *Technopaegnion* Ausonius never mentions that he has omitted some monosyllables, in his preface to the *Griphus*, he defends his work against the criticism that there are many instances of the number three not catalogued within the ninety-line poem.[15] His defense takes the form of a preemptive catalogue of additional fields intentionally excluded from the *Griphus*, including metrics, grammar, musicology, medicine, among others. Despite this selectivity, the *Griphus* bursts at the seams with an array of classical erudition and catalogues examples of the number three drawn from mythology, physics, mathematics, law, oratory, cosmology, history, and, in a deeply ironic final line, the Christian trinity.[16] While some of his exempla are easily recognizable, such as the three Graces, the three Fates, or three types of triangles, other exempla assume a more learned disposition, such as the 'fact' that crows live twenty-seven (3x3x3) human lifetimes or that stags live thirty-six (3x3x3+3+3+3) human lifetimes. Requiring deeper explanation – which the poet rarely proffers – these more erudite exempla spoliated from earlier classical authors gesture to the equally encyclopaedic disposition assumed of Ausonius' coterie and his wider readership.

Elsewhere, Ausonius catalogues and reworks historical and cultural material, most notably his three epitomes of Suetonius' biographies in his *Caesares* and his hierarchy of the major cities of the Roman empire in his *Ordo Urbium Nobilium*.[17] As I argue in more detail in the final section of this chapter, in the *Caesares* Ausonius extracts thematic details from each imperial *vita* and stiches them together, in brief, to make multiple, original poetic units offset by individual subject headings. Compositionally analogous to the *Griphus*, the *Caesares* highlights Ausonius' active and creative reuse of the classical past, a recurring literary feature that distinguishes him as, perhaps, the most late antique of all late antique authors.[18] If in his *Caesares* he maintains Suetonius' original order of emperors while creatively reworking his biographical programme, in the *Ordo Urbium Nobilium* his catalogue of major cities creatively decentres the imperial world from Rome by re-centring it around his hometown of Bordeaux. He accomplishes this geographical reorientation in at least two essential ways. First, the *Ordo Urbium* is structured as a poetic catalogue of fourteen miniature poems that moves the reader from Rome (the first poem of a single line) throughout the empire toward Bordeaux (the fourteenth poem of forty-one lines). After opening with Rome and rapidly covering the eastern cities of Constantinople, Antioch, Alexandria, and Athens, Ausonius sets his attention on the west where he praises Carthage, Trier, Milan, Capua, Aquileia, Arles, Seville, Cordova, Tarragona, Braga, Catana, Syracuse, Toulouse, Narbonne, and Bordeaux. Such disparity in coverage makes his final stop in Bordeaux more remarkable, especially because, second, he provides so much more detail about southern Gaul and Bordeaux than elsewhere. His three poems for Toulouse, Narbonne, and Bordeaux make up seventy-one of the total 168 lines, roughly forty per cent of the collection. The miniature poem about Bordeaux, if it deserves the description miniature, runs forty-one lines, approximately twenty-five per cent of the entire assemblage.

Ausonius' penchant for catalogues or encyclopaedic lists of brief poems can be found in his more personal works, such as the *Parentalia* and *Commemoratio Professorum Burdigalensium*, in which he commemorates his deceased family members and colleagues from Bordeaux, each of whom receives their own verse summary of their accomplishments.[19] Similarly, in his *Ludus Septem Sapientum*, Ausonius reworks the wisdom of the seven sages, Solon, Chilon, Cleobulus, Thales, Bias, Pittacus, and Periander, into seven theatrical speeches, each performed by a sage, who summarizes his most famous anecdotes and maxims.[20] Elsewhere, in his *Eclogues* Ausonius demonstrates his exhaustive knowledge of calendrical and astronomic erudition, which he organizes, again, by topic (days of the week, Roman festivals, etc.). Despite their metric and thematic diversity, these compilatory poems, comprising stitched together fragments of cultural information, share similar and unifying compositional methods.

Ausonius' carefully curated encyclopaedic disposition is evident even in the *Moselle* – his most celebrated poem – with its catalogue of indigenous fish (lines 75–149) and list of Gallic rivers (lines 448–68) that transport his reader from the Moselle south and west toward Bordeaux where the poem concludes, a geographic parallel to the structure of his *Ordo Urbium Nobilium*. At least one member of Ausonius' coterie responded to the *Moselle* with an equally erudite assessment of its encyclopaedic moments; Ausonius responded to this critical evaluation by sending his friend the *Griphus*, an even more encyclopaedically erudite tour de force.[21]

The *Cento Nuptialis* – literally comprising fragmented Vergilian lines and hemistiches – stands preeminent as Ausonius' most metapoetically representative piece, both in terms of his broader compositional style and the erudition he expects of members of his coterie.[22] In addition to being composed out of reconstituted line segments, the *Cento Nuptialis* contains an equally compilatory narrative structure with its seven isolated wedding scenes offset by distinct section headings. Its unique mode of composition notwithstanding, the *Cento Nuptialis* is structurally similar to Ausonius' other epitomizing poems and fits within his wider agenda of reorganizing information in miniature.

Based on these representative examples, to which many more could be added, it is possible to situate Ausonius' *Epitaphia Heroum* and *Caesares* within his wider poetic programme, in particular his habit of composing literary miniatures from fragmented pieces of the cultural past. In other words, these two poems should not be considered outliers, either in content or literary mode. Rather, through a more detailed reading of them, Ausonius' epitomizing programme comes into sharper focus. It is in this direction that the next two sections of this chapter turn.

The *Epitaphia Heroum*

As it is currently preserved in the manuscript tradition, Ausonius' *Epitaphia Heroum* is situated as the final part of a tripartite epitome project, paired with his *Parentalia* and *Commemoratio Professorum Burdigalensium*.[23] It is possible that Ausonius had originally composed and circulated the *Epitaphia Heroum*, the *Parentalia*, and the *Commemoratio Professorum* as individual poetic assemblages, and only united them as an interrelated series at some later date by adding those prefaces that still introduce them. Since these prefaces thematically unify the three poems, my discussion about the *Epitaphia Heroum* begins by situating it, however briefly, within this tripartite anthology.

An assemblage of thirty honorific poems about Ausonius' deceased relatives, the *Parentalia* opens with two prefaces, one in prose, the other in verse, followed by the collection proper, mostly in elegiacs, divided by section/title headings.[24] In these two prefaces, Ausonius explains that the collection is a poetic vestige of the Roman *Parentalia*, a festival established by the legendary king Numa to commemorate deceased ancestors. Since he conceptualizes his *Parentalia* as a retrospective set, Ausonius repeatedly uses language of memory and recollection throughout both prefaces and across the thirty poems.

As its title suggests, the *Commemoratio Professorum* is a collection of twenty-six poems, mostly in elegiacs and Sapphics, to memorialize Bordeaux's deceased teachers.[25] Similar to the *Parentalia*, Ausonius introduces the *Commemoratio Professorum* with a verse preface and uses section/title headings to set each poem apart from the next. In addition to mirroring the *Parentalia* structurally, Ausonius explicitly pairs these two poems in his preface to the *Commemoratio Professorum* when he echoes the *Parentalia*'s programmatic imagery of memory and recollection, which he develops further over the remaining twenty-five poems. As paired assemblages, the *Parentalia* and *Commemoratio Professorum* memorialize Ausonius' familial and professional networks through his act of gathering and succinctly versifying details of their lives and compiling these pocket-sized poems within his poetry book.

Structurally parallel to the *Parentalia* and *Commemoratio Professorum*, the *Epitaphia Heroum* opens with a prefatory epistle, in prose, addressed to the reader, followed by twenty-four (or twenty-six) epitomized poems of various lengths commemorating some of the heroes who had participated in the Trojan War. Each pocket-sized epitaph is set off from the wider assemblage by its own section heading indicating which hero(es) it commemorates. Within this prefatory epistle, Ausonius informs his reader that the *Epitaphia* is linked to the *Commemoratio Professorum* by their shared and well-suited (*congruentis*) subject matter (*materiae*), presumably their honorific recollection of the deceased. As is his habit when paratextually reflecting on his poetry to readers and friends, Ausonius underscores how trivial the *Epitaphia* is; his use of *vanum opusculum* situates this poem within his wider ludic programme and links it quite explicitly to the prose preface for the *Parentalia*.[26] Considering how closely Ausonius unites these three epitomizing poetic collections and considering their shared language of commemoration and memory, it is tempting to read the *Epitaphia*'s engagement with the epic (especially the Homeric) preoccupation with funerary rites and the pursuit of eternal *kleos* as a way to augment Ausonius' honorific tributes for his colleagues and family. Despite his ironic insistence that these poems are bankrupt, by the end of the tripartite collection Ausonius has placed his immediate professional and familial circles alongside some of the most famous heroes of the classical past.

That said, the *Epitaphia* is a markedly different poetic assemblage than the *Parentalia* and *Commemoratio Professorum*. As a commemorative collection for mythological figures, it lacks the emotive force of the *Parentalia* and the personal flourishes found within the *Commemoratio Professorum*. It is also uniquely and metapoetically linked to its ur-texts, a textual monument in miniature that simultaneously elides over and gestures toward the burials and memorializing found within the epic tradition. By including heroes alive at the end of the *Iliad* (and *Odyssey*), the collection has a temporal exhaustiveness unrivalled by Homer himself, while maintaining an abbreviated form and rigid selectivity: only twenty-four or twenty-six heroes make the cut. In other words, the *Epitaphia* is explicitly intertextual in ways the *Parentalia* and *Commemoratio Professorum* are not.

Viewed as a whole, the *Parentalia, Commemoratio Professorum*, and *Epitaphia Heroum* provide distinct yet complementary perspectives into Ausonius' epitomizing disposition. Each collection assumes a careful ordering of poetic subjects, whether deceased relatives, former colleagues, or mythological heroes. Moreover, the material included in each poem necessitates an equally meticulous selectivity. In the case of the *Epitaphia Heroum*, Ausonius has access to a nearly unlimited supply of heroes, well beyond those able to be included within twenty-four (twenty-six) epitaphs. For the most part, the epic material available on each hero could also easily exceed the limited space Ausonius allocates to them – no epitaph is longer than eight lines. In the case of Odysseus/Ulysses, Ausonius has, quite literally, an entire epic worth of material from which to draw. For that reason, the *Epitaphia Heroum*, along with the *Parentalia* and *Commemoratio Professorum*, is a monument, as it were, of Ausonius' ability to organize and reconfigure exhaustive, nearly encyclopaedic information into manageable miniatures. This programme of exhaustive knowledge writ small demands, in Ausonius' own words, brevity without obscuring his subject.

Unlike the other two parts of the tripartite collection, in the preface to the *Epitaphia Heroum* Ausonius adopts the persona of translator.[27] He claims to have found an ancient original (since identified as pseudo-Aristotle's *Peplos*) which he has loosely (*libere*) translated from Greek into Latin.[28] If certain parts of the *Epitaphia Heroum* depend on the *Peplos* – and both Roger Greek and Katherine Gutzwiller identify other possible models in addition to it – then Ausonius must have supplemented the Greek original with his own epitaphs since the collection as it survives includes a number of epitaphs not found in the *Peplos*. Indeed, Florian Lepetit highlights Ausonius's active hand as redactor/ translator/ compiler and sees the *Epitaphia* as Ausonius' revision of the Trojan war.[29] Following Lepetit, my approach emphasizes Ausonius' active control of his source texts, particularly the way he organizes and abbreviates the information available to him, including, but not limited to the *Peplos* and the Homeric epics.

As an epitomizer of epic material, Ausonius organizes his epitaphic assemblage on clear Homeric models: twelve epitaphs dedicated to Greek heroes, followed by twelve about Trojan ones.[30] This sense of Homeric completeness is undermined, however, by two additional epitaphs, both to Trojan women, an inconcinnity that destabilizes the seemingly balanced Greek and Trojan halves and also draws attention to the disproportionate attention given to male characters at the expense of their woefully underrepresented female counterparts. That the *Epitaphia* concludes with Polyxena – a character whose story is absent from the *Iliad* but expanded on in the wider Trojan cycle – gestures to the ways the collection actively participates in the epic tradition, despite Ausonius' ostensible claim that he is simply translating these miniature heroic moments.

Ausonius' active hand in the *Epitaphia* begins with his somewhat odd selection of which heroes to include. The twelve Greek heroes commemorated are (1) Agamemnon, (2) Menelaus, (3) Ajax, (4) Achilles, (5) Odysseus/Ulysses, (6) Diomedes, (7) Antilochus, (8) Nestor, (9) Pyrrhus, (10) Euryalus, (11) Guneus, and (12) Protesilaus. That Patroclus and the lesser Ajax are absent but Euryalus and Guneus are included suggests that Ausonius is doing more than simply selecting the most famous heroes. The Trojan side is similarly remarkable. Because three epitaphs commemorate two heroes each, there are fourteen male heroes represented: (13) Deiphobus, (14) Hector, (15) Astyanax, (16) Sarpedon, (17) Nastes and Amphimachus, (18) Troilus, (19) Polydorus, (20) Euphemus, (21) Hippothous and Pyleus, (22) Ennomus and Chromius, (23) Priam, (24) Priam and Hector, (25) Hecuba, (26) Polyxena. Some of these characters, Polydorus and Euphemus in particular, have rich mythological traditions outside the *Iliad*, even if they play a negligible role in Homer's account.[31] Hippothous, Pyleus, Ennomus, and Chromius, in contrast, are ancillary characters, little more than cannon-fodder to advance the narrative or to augment a Greek hero's *arete*. The somewhat remarkable absence of Paris, Aeneas, Glaucus, among others, parallels the omission of Patroclus and the lesser Ajax on the Greek side. Therefore, the *Epitaphia* is not a straightforward who's who of the Trojan war but, rather, a reflection of Ausonius' meticulous selectivity, which gives his collection of epitaphic miniatures an originality despite its popular content.

That said, certain epitaphs appear at first glance to be little more than direct translations from Homer or pastiches of Vergilian lines, quite literally epic writ small. Consider the epitaph for Nastes and Amphimachus (17):

> Nastes Amphimachusque, Nomionis inclita proles,
> ductores quondam, pulvis et umbra sumus.

> Nastes and Amphimachus, Nomion's famous seed,
> Formerly leaders, we are dust and shades.

Nastes and Amphimachus appear only in the Trojan catalogue, where they lead the Carian contingent (*Iliad* 2.867–75). One of them (the Greek is ambiguous) rather famously fought wearing golden ornamentation and was killed by Achilles during the battle in the Scamander.[32] The Homeric narrator characterizes this gold-wearing hero in effeminate terms, perhaps like Euphorbus who wore silver and gold brooches in his hair, thereby tarnishing his role in the war and anticipating his death at the hands of Achilles.[33] Ausonius elides over this material with a bare-bones (epitomized) account of Nastes and Amphimachus in two lines. Most of this couplet borrows directly from the *Iliad*; the first line is a literal, word for word translation of *Il.* 2.871 (Νάστης Ἀμφίμαχός τε Νομίονος ἀγλαὰ τέκνα). Such meticulous attention to the Greek down to its post-positive conjunction highlights the degree to which Ausonius actively engages the Homeric original.

At first glance, the second line of this couplet appears more original or at least less Homeric, which, for the most part, it is. The *ductores*, however, indirectly gestures to the final word of the previous Iliadic line, ἡγησάσθην (*Il.* 2.870). But here, Ausonius has elected to render the Homeric verb – in its original context about the Carians – as a noun without any direct reference to those soldiers whom Nastes and Amphimachus actually led. This subtle modification in word choice from verb to noun and in word order from end to beginning of the line suggests a meticulous engagement with the Homeric ur-text beyond mere translation. This leaves *pulvis et umbra sumus* as the epitaph's only non-Homeric material. As a direct quote from Horace, *Ode* 4.7, *pulvis et umbra sumus* is still intertextually charged, especially considering the ode's emphasis on human morality and each person's inevitable death. The fate of Nastes and Amphimachus, therefore, is hardly exceptional – it is the same fate shared by all humans.

Although most of the epitaph is a close, literal translation from the Trojan catalogue, it also engages with its Homeric model through an omission of details, especially details that could be potentially distracting or embarrassing. The Greek is ambiguous about whether it was Nastes or Amphimachus whom Achilles killed in the Scamander, so including any specific details about their deaths demanded an interpretative choice, one that divided ancient readers. Moreover, the golden ornamentation worn by Nastes or Amphimachus is doubly difficult because it tarnished its wearer's honour, essentially disqualifying them from any catalogue of 'real' heroes. Rhetorically, through his meticulous rearrangement of Homeric material and his omission of potentially unsuitable details, Ausonius preserves Nastes and Amphimachus' reputation and provides for them a reconstituted and revisionist heroic identity that simultaneously departs from and adheres to their Homeric roots. If, as Ausonius insists to Paulinus, the ideal epitome abbreviates without obscuring its subject, Epitaph 17 successfully contracts its Homeric model, clarifies (through deletion) originally indeterminate material, and gives the fate of Nastes and Amphimachus an Horatian universality/ inevitability.

If Epitaph 17 demonstrates Ausonius' creative/ critical adherence to or avoidance of previous epic material, the commemorative poem for Troilus (18) underscores how he deploys Vergilian material to enrich his subject:

Hectore prostrato nec dis nec viribus aequis
  congressus saevo Troilus Aeacidae,
raptatus bigis fratris coniungor honori,
  cuius ob exemplum nec mihi poena gravis.

Though Hector was laid low, and though in strength of arm and heavenly aid ill-matched,
  I, Troilus, met the fierce son of Aeacus face to face,
And, dragged to death by my own steeds, am linked in glory with my brother,
  Whose example made my suffering light.

Troilus plays a fairly insignificant role in the *Iliad*, although his death at the hands of Achilles was well-established early in antiquity, perhaps early enough for its inclusion in the Epic Cycle. In the *Aeneid*, his fateful encounter with Achilles is briefly depicted on the doors of Juno's Carthaginian temple (*A*. 1.474–78). Itself an ekphrastic epitome of the Trojan war meant to honour Juno and commemorate the heroic dead, these doors are the (con/inter)textual foundation upon which Ausonius' epitaphic epitome of Troilus' death is built. In fact, the second line of the epitaph likely gestures to *Aeneid* 1.475 (*infelix puer atque impar congressus Achilli*). This allusive connection to the doors of Juno's temple allows Epitaph 18 to be read as a miniature of an artistic miniature, a recursive epitome of an epitome.

At the same time, Epitaph 18 closely borrows from other Vergilian material. The second half of the first line comes directly from *Aen*. 5.809 (*congressum Aenean nec dis nec viribus aequis*) and the third line borrows from *Aen*. 2.272 (*raptatus bigis, ut quondam aterque cruento*). Since these passages are about heroes other than Troilus, they enrich this poem with an intertextual complexity that effectively conflates Troilus' death with the fate of other heroes. For instance, in *Aen*. 5.809, Jupiter recounts how he had once intervened during an encounter between Achilles and Aeneas, which he describes as an uneven contest that would have led to Aeneas' death, had he not enveloped Aeneas in a protective cloud and preserved the Trojan people. In *Aen*. 2.272 Aeneas describes his encounter with Hector's ghost, recognized by his body desecrated by Achilles' chariot. In the context of Aeneas' attempted escape from Troy, Hector's ghost fulfils a comparable purpose as Jupiter's protective cloud; both preserve Aeneas' life from certain death by removing him from an uneven and inevitably losing conflict.

These intertextual vectors charge the epitaph with interpretive expectations, however unresolved they might remain, about divine assistance and the preservation of life, in stark contrast to the death that opens the poem. The *raptatus bigis* of *Aen.* 2.272, on the other hand, underscores how Troilus explicitly and intertextually serves as a 'body double' for Hector. In other words, Ausonius weaves a scene about Troilus and Hector's shared death by using Vergilian words about Hector to describe Troilus. On the other hand, despite their shared death, Troilus' fate is only fully realized after or, perhaps, because of Hector's death, explicitly so through the heavily circumstantial *Hectore prostrato* of line 1. Similar to Hector yet unlike Aeneas, the epitaphic Troilus will not experience divine intervention. Jupiter will send no protective cloud. Achilles will kill him.

The implicit opposition between Aeneas' frequently preserved life and the death of Troilus makes Aeneas' repeated presence remarkable; that Aeneas, not given his own epitaph, repeatedly appears over the course of the assemblage is doubly curious. In fact, he lurks in the shadows of this entire poem, subtly present in those images gesturing to the doors of Juno's temple and his encounter with Achilles. As the speaker in *Aen.* 2.272, Aeneas is transformed within the epitaph's intertextual context(s) into a type of narrator who coopts Troilus' mouth to recount Troilus' death using imagery about Hector. That Aeneas' life is preserved twice in this epitaph highlights his survival of the Trojan war and anticipates his apotheosis. For that reason, Aeneas not receiving his own epitaph can be viewed as part of the *Epitaphia*'s subtle, intertextually rich interpretive programme.

Aeneas' active role as narrator is further evinced in the next poem commemorating Polydorus (19):

> cede procul myrtumque istam fuge, nescius hospes:
>   telorum seges est sanguine adulta meo.
> confixus iaculis et ab ipsa caede sepultus
>   condor in hoc tumulo bis Polydorus ego.
> scit pius Aeneas et tu, rex impie, quod me
>   Thracia poena premit, Troia cura tegit.

> Begone far hence, unconscious stranger, and avoid that myrtle tree:
>   'Tis grown from darts and nourished with my blood.
> Pierced through with spears and almost buried in my very slaying,
>   I, Polydorus, lie twice interred beneath this mound.
> Pious Aeneas knows my story, and you also, impious king; for as it was
>   Thracian cruelty that crushed me, so it was Trojan piety that buried me.

The multiple accounts of Polydorus' death is described by various ancient authors beginning with Homer. In *Il.* 20.407–18, Achilles sees Polydorus, still too young for Priam to send into combat, running among the Trojan ranks. Taking aim with his spear, Achilles kills him. Angered over Polydorus' death, Hector decides to confront Achilles, a decision that directly leads to his own death. By the classical period and continuing into the Roman era, Polydorus was said to have been sent to Thrace, typically but not always as a hostage, to live with the Thracian king Polymestor who killed him after the fall of Troy and the death of Priam. Vergil builds on this tradition in *Aen.* 3.22–68 where Aeneas inadvertently (dis/un)covers Polydorus' body buried by those very Thracian weapons used to kill him.

The narrative similarities between Epitaph 19 and Vergil's account of Polydorus' death are readily apparent; for that reason, Vergil's Aeneas plays multiple, polyvalent roles within Ausonius' epitaph. First, he indirectly appears as the *nescius hospes* in the opening line. Contextually addressing any passerby – a well-known epitaphic feature – the *nescius hospes* also gestures to Aeneas' accidental unearthing of Polydorus in *Aeneid* 3, a reading strengthened by the *fuge* in line 1, which parallels Polydorus' words to Aeneas (*Aen.* 3.44). Read alongside or against the *Aeneid*, the epitaph's addressee – that passerby who might, once again, disrupt Polydorus' final burial – is, within the poem's allusive register, an Aeneas redux. The potential for rediscovery is doubly heightened since the entire original event is reactivated through a proliferation of echoes back to the *Aeneid* (e.g., *myrtum, Aen.* 3.23; *tumulo, Aen.* 3.22, 63; *telorum seges, Aen.* 3.46; *Polydorus ego, Aen.* 3.45; *confixus iaculis, Aen.* 3.45–46), this despite the fact that Aeneas' chance discovery of Polydorus' corpse and its makeshift grave brought some closure to Polydorus' violent death.

Second, according to this reading, Aeneas is responsible for building commemorative monuments to the dead; he is not, in other words, the commemorated hero housed in monumental tombs. More specifically, he is the authority in Epitaph 19 responsible for knowing, remembering, and promulgating Polydorus' story (*scit pius Aeneas*). Considering that Aeneas serves as secondary narrator for most of the embedded story that makes up book 3 of the *Aeneid*, Epitaph 19's repeated gestures to *Aen.* 3.22–68 underscores Aeneas' role as narrator/commemorator of Polydorus' fate. On the one hand, this proliferation of Vergilian allusions transforms Epitaph 19 into an abbreviated retelling of Aeneas' own abbreviated account. For instance, Ausonius' *in hoc tumulo bis* of line 4 plays on the double use of *tumulus* in *Aeneid* 3, one that opens Aeneas' account (*A.* 3.22), and another that brings it to a close (*A.* 3.63). Through *tumulo bis* Ausonius orients his hyper-miniaturized (six-line) account of Polydorus' death and two-fold burials within the larger framework of Aeneas' own summary of his journey from Troy to Carthage, which itself takes the form of an abbreviated Odyssean-style nostos. Such allusive play by Ausonius allows Epitaph 19 to be read as a doubly miniaturized epyllion with added metapoetic potential. Considering the central role that memory and knowledge play in the *Epitaphia*, *Commemoratio Professorum*, and *Parentalia* as a tripartite assemblage, Aeneas as original commemorator of the heroic dead here serves as intertextual and narrative double for Ausonius.

The *Epitaphia* engages the epic cycle in more subtle ways than (inter)textually. For instance, Ausonius closes his Greek material with Protesilaus (12), the first Greek hero to die, a fact twice explicitly mentioned in the poem (lines 2 and 8). By organizing the Greek half to conclude with Protesilaus, Ausonius undermines a straightforward chronological order to his assemblage and ends with a gesture to the beginning of the war. Epitaph 12 frequently juxtaposes the war's beginning and end, as in lines 3–5 that focus on Odysseus' deception (*Lartiadae insidiis*), contextually about Odysseus' feigned jump to shore. It was this trick that convinced Protesilaus to leap from his ship and directly lead to his death. Any reference to *Lartiadae insidiisi* also alludes, however obliquely, to the Trojan horse and the end of the war. In other words, once the deception of the Greeks has come full circle, as it were, the collection shifts to the Trojan review.

Finally, at eight lines, Epitaph 12 is the longest of the collection, remarkably longer than some poems dedicated to characters with a more expansive role in the war, such as Agamemnon (four lines), Menelaus (six lines), Ajax (six lines), Achilles (four lines), or Odysseus (two lines). From a narrative perspective, that hero whose participation in the war was most abridged has received from Ausonius his most extended treatment, even if still in abbreviated form. These subtle interpretive consequences emerging from the assemblage's order and length reflect Ausonius' meticulous hand as epic epitomizer.

Hector plays a comparably unifying role. The epitaphs about him bookend the Trojan assemblage around the well-known association linking his death and the fall of Troy. This association shared between Hector and Troy likely predates the *Iliad* and is hardly remarkable in itself. What is remarkable, for the purposes of this chapter, is how Ausonius structures his epitomized pocket-sized poems around this theme. Hector's death is mentioned in two pairs of epitaphs, #14 and #15 (for Hector and Astyanax) and #23 and #24 (for Priam and Priam/Hector), approximately at the beginning and end of the Trojan epitaphs.[34] In Epitaphs 14 and 15, the deaths of Hector and Astyanax are explicitly linked with Troy and Asia; Troy itself is found buried inside Hector's tomb (*sua Troia sepulta est*), whereas Astyanax is described as the flower of Asia (*flos Asiae*). This imagery links father and son as representatives for their city/state, made more explicit when the death of Astyanax is described as crueller than the dragging of Hector's body (*crudelius Hectore tracto*). The penultimate epitaph (23), dedicated to Priam, returns back to Hector's body, where Priam had fled for refuge. In this sepulcher, Priam discovers Hector buried alongside Troy and Asia (*illic et natos Troiamque Asiamque sepultam inveni*), an intratextual gesture to both Epitaphs 14 and 15. This theme comes full circle in the final epitaph of the collection (24) in which Priam is again commemorated at the site of Hector's tomb. Here again, Hector's body is equated with the symbolic death of the homeland (*Hectore et patriae simul est commune sepulcrum*). This tripartite repetition gives the Trojan assemblage a thematic unity around the death of Hector and the fall of Troy/Asia. In this regard at least, the Trojan half of the *Epitaphia* parallels the *Iliad* and anticipates the *Aeneid*, albeit in an abbreviated and focalized form.

Throughout the *Epitaphia*, Ausonius frequently intimates that his epitomes can be read as miniaturizations of the Homeric and Vergilian epics. In *Epitaph* 5, one of the briefest in the collection, dedicated to Odysseus, Ausonius makes this intimation explicit:

> Conditur hoc tumulo Laeta natus Ulixes:
> Perlege Odyssean omnia nosse volens.
>
> Beneath this mount lies buried Laertes' son, Ulysses.
> If you would learn all his story, read through the *Odyssey*.

By directing his reader to the *Odyssey*, Ausonius effectively summarizes Odysseus' life and death within a single couplet and, in so doing, embeds an epic in miniature within one of his most abbreviated poems. This epitome within an epitome, a mise en abyme of the *Epitaphia* as a whole, adds recursive force to Ausonius' poetic programme.[35] On the other hand, by invoking the *Odyssey* Ausonius also expands the epigram's narrative scope and opens a larger narrative within an epic miniature. Both *perlege* and *omnia* suggest a comprehensive engagement with the *Odyssey* – this is no quick skim of the epic – that results in exhaustive knowledge (*omnia nosse*). Read metapoetically, Epitaph 5 perfectly encapsulates (summarizes, epitomizes) Ausonius' literary etiquette even as it conflicts with the *Epitaphia*'s overt claim of abbreviation. This rhetorical paradox that initially forced Ausonius' readers within his literary world of epitome, dependent on him as epic bard, has here ejected the reader out of its artificial and authorially controlled landscape back into the book world of the Homeric tradition, one which Ausonius does not control.[36]

The *Caesares*

Similar to the *Epitaphia Heroum*, *Parentalia*, and *Commemoratio Professorum*, Ausonius introduces his *Caesares* with a prefatory epistle, here in hexameters, addressed to his son, Hesperius:

> Caesareos proceres, in quorum regna secundis
> consulibus dudum Romana potentia cessit,
> accipe bis senos, sua quemque monosticha signant,
> quorum per plenam seriem Suetonius olim
> nomina, res gestas vitamque obitumque peregit.
>
> Here take the twice six Caesars into whose sovereignty
> the sway of Rome passed long ago, leaving the consuls second in authority.
> A single verse here records each of those emperors
> of whom through all their array Suetonius once detailed
> the names, the deeds, the lives and deaths.

In this rather brief preface, Ausonius uses language consistent with his wider programme of circulating poetry to his *amici*, although he eschews that characteristic self-deprecation and ludic jocularity found in many of his other paratextual reflections. This preface introduces the first section of the *Caesares*, namely three twelve-line poems, which according to Ausonius consists of single verses (*monosticha*) focused on specific themes related to Suetonius' twelve Caesars: the succession of their reigns (*de ordine imperatorum*), the duration of their reigns (*de aetate imperii eorum*), and the method of their deaths (*de obitu*).[37] These three poems are marked off by thematic section headings with each emperor receiving a single line (*monosticha*) in each poem. That this is an abbreviated – epitomized – selection from Suetonius is obvious, yet here marked by a double brevity. On the one hand, Ausonius condenses hundreds of pages into only thirty-six lines; by drawing attention to those *monosticha* that comprise his three epitomes, Ausonius implies, quite ironically, that he has epitomized each *vita* in just a single line. On the other hand, Ausonius explicitly abbreviates Suetonius' content. Within the preface Ausonius states that Suetonius' *Vitae* contains the names (*nomina*), deeds (*res gestae*), lives (*vitam*), and deaths (*obitum*) of the twelve Caesars, whereas his epitomized *Caesares* only includes their names in order (*ordine*), the length of their reigns (*aetate*), and their deaths (*obitu*), a literary mirror of the three fates (beginning, duration, end). Ausonius' selectivity compels his readers to step outside the Suetonian original they might be familiar with, but, if they wish to learn more about Rome's emperors, Ausonius' rigid brevity demands that they return once again to Suetonius. In other words, although it contains three pocket-sized miniatures of Suetonius' *Vitae*, Ausonius' *Caesares* does not and cannot replace the book world from which he drew. For that reason, Suetonius is explicitly mentioned in the preface.

That said, we should not take Ausonius' insistence that he is retelling Suetonius at face value, even if we might recognize spoliated Suetonian lines (alongside gestures to other imperial authors) reused within the *Caesares*. Rather, Ausonius has reorganized this Suetonian material to such an extent that it is no longer truly Suetonian. He has not, of course, altered the facts regarding the first twelve Augusti, but, by writing three poems dedicated to unique features of their reigns, he has made substantial generic changes to Suetonius' biographical agenda. From twelve thematically organized biographies each dedicated to a single emperor, Ausonius has composed three thematically organized epitomes of Suetonius' entire biographical programme that read more like digests or catalogues than biographies. By writing verse digests emphasizing the deaths of the twelve Caesars – which includes information about the length of their reigns – Ausonius' imperial catalogues are generically comparable to his other funerary poems, from the *Parentalia* and *Commemoratio Professorum* to his *Epitaphia*. Unlike these three assemblages, particularly the *Epitaphia*, which allow Ausonius to showcase his encyclopaedic and epitomary disposition through meticulous selectivity, the *Caesares* – or at least the first set of three mini-epitomes – necessitates a different type of exhaustive knowledge ordering. All twelve emperors, in other words, must be included in a rigid order.

After these three thematically organized epitomes, Ausonius turns to the second part of his epitome project, twenty-four tetrastichs, each dedicated to a Caesar.[38] By way of introduction to this material, he again interjects his own authorial voice into the collection with a second prefatory poem, though not one overtly in epistolary form. Like the biographical epitomes themselves, this preface is also a tetrastich:

> nunc et praedictos et regni sorte sequentes
>   expediam, series quos tenet imperii,
> incipiam ab divo percurramque ordine cunctos,
>   novi Romanae quos memor historiae.

> Now I will tell both of those already mentioned and of those who, following
>   them upon the throne fill up the list of empire.
> I will begin with the divine and run in sequence over all those princes
>   whom I know, mindful of Roman history.

With *nunc* and *praedictos*, Ausonius connects these twenty-four pocket-sized biographic poems to his previous three and gestures to his reader that she should see both epitomary assemblages as a unified whole. Yet, the force of *nunc* and the *prae* of *praedictos* implies that the following set diverges from the previous one. And, in fact, it does. Beginning with Julius Caesar and ending with Elagabalus, Ausonius' twenty-four tetrastichs each focus on a single emperor and are set apart with section headings. Moreover, this preface abounds in first-person verbs which were noticeably absent from his preface to the first collection. Through these first-person verbs, Ausonius draws attention to his active hand as epitomizer, a rhetorical decision that subtly overshadows Suetonius and his biographical book world. To underscore his authorial agency, Ausonius invokes his memory as a type of authority, not those classical texts on which he still obviously depends. Such claims to knowledge and recollection further link Ausonius' mini-biographies with his epitaphic projects and their repeated claims to memory and recollection.

At first glance, however, Ausonius' memory seems to have failed him – his imperial catalogue runs only to Elagabalus (d. 222 CE), well short of a complete, exhaustive list down to his own day.[39] That said, the assemblage's twenty-four pocket-sized poems parallel Ausonius' organizational method elsewhere, as in the *Epitaphia Heroum*, imbuing the entire collection with Homeric *gravitas*, and a sense of completeness, despite the fact that it ends abruptly in the middle of the Severan dynasty. When read against the first set of epitomary poems, this second set is, in effect, a fourth Suetonian epitome, from Julius Caesar to Domitian, followed by a complementary collection of twelve subsequent emperors, from Nerva to Elagabalus.

How then should we make sense of Ausonius' somewhat odd claim that this second set of epitomes represents everything he remembers about Roman history (*novi Romanae quos memor historiae*)? As suggested above, imagery of knowledge and memory, alongside associated claims of exhaustiveness or completeness, can frequently be found whenever Ausonius proffers metaliterary reflections about his epitaphic or compilatory poetry. By thematically unifying his seemingly disparate poetic projects, Ausonius helps orient his coterie around certain shared values or interests. Approaching Ausonius' corpus in this way clarifies how the *Caesares* advances his broader interest in knowledge ordering and encyclopaedism and, for that reason, fits within his wider poetic programme. On the other hand, it is equally constructive to interpret this specific claim of exhaustive knowledge as a subtle, self-effacing gesture aimed at Hesperius, who is expected to catch Ausonius' obviously incomplete catalogue. Ausonius puts other literary recipients in similarly ironic/impossible positions elsewhere. For instance, in the preface to the *Cento Nuptialis*, Ausonius 'informs' his recipient Paulus that one indicator of an inept cento is its use of sequential Vergilian lines, a practice he himself engages in three times over the course of his 131-line cento. Such elaborate, self-deprecating traps are only effective if Ausonius' coterie is expected to engage his pocket-sized poems with an encyclopaedic and pedantic disposition equal that of their author.

Conclusion

By way of conclusion, I would like to return to Ausonius' epistle to Paulinus that opened this chapter. As suggested earlier, Paulinus' epitome of Suetonius represents the ideal literary project for members of Ausonius' circle because such projects demand of their authors and readers a nearly exhaustive knowledge of the classical past. By showcasing their encyclopaedic expertise, often through fragmenting and re-composing texts, Ausonius and his friends position themselves as exemplars of late Roman literary culture. Fragmentation and recomposition are, in fact, central features of Ausonius' entire literary output, ranging from those ludic games that have historically bemused readers, such as the *Griphus*, *Technopaegnion*, and *Cento Nuptialis*, to those poems more closely aligned with classical genres, including his epigrams, *Moselle*, *Parentalia* and *Commemoratio Professorum*. Following his own literary etiquette, Ausonius provides Paulinus with critical feedback about and unqualified praise for his epitome, which, he claims, struck the perfect (and rare) balance of abbreviating its content without obscuring his material. Playing along with Paulinus' fragmentation of Suetonius, Ausonius extracts a brief selection from the poem and cites it within his letter. This quote is itself part of the cycle of selection, fragmentation, and abbreviation inherent to the type of literary games shared by members of the coterie, transformed in this epistle into an epitome of an epitome inserted within a critical discussion about epitomes.

My brief analysis of two representative examples from Ausonius' various epitomizing projects clarifies the relationship between these poems and Paulinus' biographical epitome. Foremost among these projects is his own epitome of Suetonius' *Vitae*. Even if it is impossible to know which of these Suetonian epitomes, Paulinus' or Ausonius', was composed first, it is fairly safe to say that they emerge from a literary etiquette shared by like-minded encyclopaedist-poets. At the same time, themes common to Ausonius' *Epitaphia* and *Caesares* provide a unifying order to his poetic programme. We have seen how memory and commemoration, explicitly central to Ausonius' *Epitaphia*, *Parentalia*, and *Commemoratio Professorum* play equally important roles in Ausonius' metaliterary reflections on his multiple Suetonian epitomes.

If we read Ausonius' epitome of Suetonius' *Vitae* alongside Paulinus' epitome of Suetonius' *De regibus*, it is possible to perceive an added layer of playful engagement on Ausonius' part. Whereas Paulinus creates brevity without obscuring his subject, Ausonius attempts to go one further by claiming an exhaustiveness beyond Suetonius' original project. His collection epitomizes Suetonius' *Caesares* as well as all subsequent ones, in effect surpassing both his model and, at least obliquely, Paulinus who only epitomized the *De regibus*. Ironically, or perhaps humorously, Ausonius' fails to accomplish this very goal, leaving Hesperius with the impression that Ausonius' memory of Roman history ended somewhere near the end of the Severan dynasty.

Notes

1. Paul. ad Aus. 17 (Green 1991: 215–16; Evelyn-White 1919: 81–7). See also Roberts 1843: 580–2; and Trout 1999: 30. For the correspondence between Ausonius and Paulinus, see Green 1980; Knight 2005; Fielding 2017: 22–51; Rücker 2012; Hardie 2019: 6–43.
2. Unless otherwise noted, all translations are adapted from Evelyn-White 1919.

3. Paul. *carm.* 1 and 2; Aus. *ep.* 19a.13–14; Evelyn-White *ep.* 25; Trout 1999: 56–7.
4. Witke 1971: 3–65; Conybeare 2000: 147–60; Knight 2005; Hardie 2019: 6–43.
5. A more complete treatment on Ausonius' reading community can be found in Sowers 2016.
6. My approach is here influenced by Formisano 2013. This theme of fragmentation is further developed in this volume within Irena Kristeva's chapter on Pascal Quignard's *Petits traités*.
7. Green 1991: 558–9 points out that, while the first twelve poems in the collection depend on Suetonius' lives, there is no evidence that the second half of the collection borrows from those sources used in the *Historia Augusta*.
8. The standard editions/commentary for Ausonius are Prete 1978; Green 1991; and Green 1999. In addition to Green 1991, Joseph Pucci provides an excellent introduction to Ausonius in Warren 2017. For more on the wider socio-historical contexts of late antique Gaul, see Matthews 1975; Booth 1982; Sivan 1993; and Frye 2003. Readers interested in late antique poetry are directed to Pelttari 2014; McGill and Pucci 2016; Elsner and Lobato 2017; and Hardie 2019.
9. Green 1991: xv.
10. Bright 1984: 80.
11. Green 1991: xv.
12. On classical and late antique encyclopaedism, see König and Whitmarsh 2007; Formisano 2013; and König and Woolf 2013.
13. Green 1991: 583. In some ways, the *Technopaegnion* has a similar organizational structure to Nonius Marcellus' lexicon, discussed by Matthew Payne in this volume.
14. Compare Pelttari 2014: 67–9, 73–114.
15. Green 1991: 111–12.
16. See the various interpretive strategies advanced by Ruggini 1989; Lobato 2007; and Lowe 2012.
17. Green 1991: 169–75; Spahlinger 2004.
18. For more on Ausonius as the prototypical late antique poet, see Formisano 2007. For more on the different ways late antique and classical poets related to the literary past, see Pelttari 2014: 115–60.
19. Booth 1978; Green 1985; and Pucci 2002.
20. Cazzuffi 2014.
21. Symmachus *Epistle* 1.14 (Salzman and Roberts 2011:43–7); Ausonius' epistle to Symmachus (Green 1991: 111–12). See Ruggini 1989 and Sowers 2020.
22. Bright 1984; McGill 2005; and Formisano and Sogno 2010. Paolo Liverani briefly addresses centos as part of his discussion of spoliation in this volume.
23. Green 1991: 25–65; Lepetit 2014: 2.
24. Only six poems are not in elegiacs (*Par.* 13, 17, 25–28). On the somewhat complicated metrics of these poems, see Green 1991: 316, 319, 325–7.
25. Technically, not all of the professors taught in Bordeaux; some received their education there before taking up posts elsewhere.
26. For a more complete discussion on Ausonius' ludic program, see Sowers 2016.
27. By circulating a text maintained to be a recent translation of an earlier Greek source about the Trojan War, Ausonius is here participant in a wider literary tradition with parallels to those accounts associated with Dictys Cretensis and Dares Phrygius, among others.

28. The non-Homeric epitaphs, which is to say those epitaphs not about Homeric heroes, occasionally included with the *Epitaphia* were likely added by an anonymous editor at a later date and, for that reason, are not included in my discussion here.

29. Green 1991: 369; Gutzwiller 2016: 222; and Lepetit 2014: 1.

30. In this regard, Ausonius' *Epitaphia* are literary parallels to the visual epitomes discussed by Paolo Liverani in his chapter to this volume.

31. Consider Polydorus's role in Euripides' *Hecuba* and Ovid's *Metamorphosis* (13.429–80) and Euphemus' role in Apollonius' *Argonautica* and Pindar's Pythian 4.

32. The debate over which of the two leaders wore golden objects and what specifically he wore began in antiquity. Aristarchus, it seems, interpreted this passage to be about Amphimachus; Simonides, in contrast, took it to be about Nastes. Simonides also interpreted the gold as golden armour. See Kirk 1985: 261.

33. Cf. *Iliad* 17.51–60.

34. The fact that Epitaph 24 is frequently divided into and printed as two separate poems dedicated to Priam and Hector can be misleading, particularly because Hector's name is not given its own original poetic heading. Considering Ausonius' preference for section/poetic headings in the *Epitaphia Heroum*, the *Parentalia*, and the *Commemoratio Professorum*, Epitaph 24 should be treated as a single poem that brings the entire *Epitaphia*, or at least the Trojan half, to a thematic conclusion. Compare Green 1991: 374.

35. Within his wider analysis of Nepos' epitome on the life of Cato in this volume, Jared Hudson points out a similar recursive feature to Nepos' epitomic approach.

36. For a somewhat different reading of this epitaph, see Pelttari 2014: 152.

37. Green 1991: 161–3.

38. Green 1991: 163–8.

39. On the various ways this issue has been resolved, see Green 1991: 557–8.

Works cited

Booth, A. D. (1978), 'Notes on Ausonius' *Professores*', *Phoenix*, 32: 235–49.

Booth, A. D. (1982), 'The Academic Career of Ausonius', *Phoenix*, 36: 329–43.

Bright, D. F. (1984), 'Theory and Practice in the Vergilian Cento', *Illinois Classical Studies*, 9: 79–90.

Cazzuffi, E., ed. (2014), *Decimi Magni Ausonii Ludus septem sapientum*, Hildesheim: Olms.

Conybeare, C. (2000), *Paulinus Noster: Self and Symbols in the Letters of Paulinus of Nola*, Oxford: Oxford University Press.

Elsner, J. and J. Hernández Lobato, eds (2017), *The Poetics of Late Latin Literature*, New York: Oxford University Press.

Evelyn-White, H. G. (1919), *Ausonius*. 2 vols, Cambridge, MA: Harvard University Press.

Fielding, I. (2017), *Transformations of Ovid in Late Antiquity*, Cambridge: Cambridge University Press.

Formisano, M. (2007), 'Towards an Aesthetic Paradigm of Late Antiquity', *Antiquité Tardive*, 15: 277–84.

Formisano, M. (2013), 'Late Latin Encyclopaedism: Towards a New Paradigm of Practical Knowledge', in J. König and G. Woolf (eds), *Encyclopaedism from Antiquity to the Renaissance*, 197–215, Cambridge: Cambridge University Press.

Formisano, M. and C. Sogno (2010), 'Petite Poésie Portable: The Latin Cento in its Late Antique Context', in M. Horster and C. Reitz (eds), *Condensing Texts - Condensed Texts*, 375–92, Stuttgart: Franz Steiner Verlag.

Frye, D. (2003) 'Aristocratic Responses to Late Roman Urban Change: The Examples of Ausonius and Sidonius in Gaul', *Classical World*, 96: 185–96.

Green, R. P. H. (1980), 'The Correspondence of Ausonius', *L'Antiquité Classique*, 49: 191–211.

Green, R. P. H. (1985), 'Still Waters Run Deep: A New Study of the *Professores* of Bordeaux', *Classical Quarterly*, 35: 491–506.

Green, R. P. H., ed. (1991), *The Works of Ausonius*, Oxford: Clarendon.

Green, R. P. H., ed. (1999), *Decimi Magni Ausonii Opera*, Oxford: Oxford University Press.

Gutzwiller, K. (2016), 'Heroic Epitaphs of the Classical Age: The Aristotelian Peplos and Beyond', in M. Baumbach, A. Petrovic, and I. Petrovic (eds), *Archaic and Classical Greek Epigram*, 219–49, Cambridge: Cambridge University Press.

Hardie, P. (2019), *Classicism and Christianity in Late Antique Latin Poetry*, Oakland: University of California Press.

Kirk, G. S. (1985), *The Iliad: A Commentary. Volume 1: Books 1–4*, Cambridge: Cambridge University Press.

Knight, G. (2005), 'Friendship and Erotics in the Late Antique Verse Epistle: Ausonius to Paulinus Revisited', *Rheinisches Museum für Philologie*, 148: 361–403.

König, J and T. Whitmarsh, eds (2007), *Ordering Knowledge in the Roman World*, Cambridge: Cambridge University Press.

König, J. and G. Woolf, eds (2013), *Encyclopaedism from Antiquity to the Renaissance*, Cambridge: Cambridge University Press.

Lepetit, F. (2014), 'Les *Epitaphia Heroum* d'Ausone, une vision mortuaire de la guerre de Troie', *Atlantide*, 2: 1–16.

Lobato, J. H. (2007), 'Ausonio ante el enigma del número tres: Política y poética en el *Griphus*', in C. C. Merino, G. H. Andrés, and J. C. F. Corte (eds), *Munus quaesitum meritis*, 455–62, Salamanca: Ediciones Universidad de Salamanca.

Lowe, D. (2012), 'Triple Tipple: Ausonius' *Griphus Ternarii Numeri*', in J. Kwapisz, M. Szymanski, and D. Petrain (eds), *The Muse at Play: Riddles and Wordplay in Greek and Latin Poetry*, 333–50, Berlin: De Gruyter.

Matthews, J. F. (1975), *Western Aristocracies and Imperial Court A.D. 364–425*, Oxford: Oxford University Press.

McGill, S. (2005), *Virgil Recomposed: The Mythological and Secular Centos in Antiquity*, Oxford: Oxford University Press.

McGill, S. and J. Pucci, eds (2016), *Classics Renewed: Reception and Innovation in the Latin Poetry of Late Antiquity*, Heidelberg: Universitätsverlag Winter.

Pelttari, P. (2014), *The Space that Remains: Reading Latin Poetry in Late Antiquity*, Ithaca, NY: Cornell University Press.

Prete, S. (1978), *Decimi Magni Ausonii Burdigalensis Opuscula*, Leipzig: Teubner.

Pucci, J. (2002), 'A Reading of Ausonius, *Professores* 1', in G. Bakewell (ed.), *Gestures: Essays in Ancient History, Literature, and Philosophy for A.L. Boegehold*, 87–101. Oxford: Oxbow.

Roberts, W. (1843), *History of Letter-writing from the Earliest Period to the Fifth Century*, London: William Pickering.

Rücker, N., ed. (2012), *Ausonius an Paulinus von Nola: Textgeschichte und literarische Form der Briefgedichte 21 und 22 des Decimus Magnus Ausonius*, Göttingen: Vandenhoeck and Ruprecht.

Ruggini, L. C. (1989), 'Simmaco, Ausonio e l'enigma del numero tre', in S. Costanza (ed), *Polyanthema: Studi di letteratura cristiana antica offerti a Salvatore Costanza*, 167–76, Messina: Sicania.

Salzman, M. R. and M. Roberts, eds (2011), *The Letters of Symmachus: Book 1*, Atlanta: Society of Biblical Literature.

Sivan, H. (1993), *Ausonius of Bordeaux: Genesis of a Gallic Aristocracy*, London: Routledge.

Sowers, B. P. (2016), '*Amicitia* and Late Antique *Nugae*: Reading Ausonius' Reading Community', *American Journal of Philology*, 137: 511–40.

Sowers, B. P. (2020), 'Caught in Ausonius' Net: Self-Reflection and Poetic Circulation in Late Antiquity', in J. Hernández Lobato and O. Prieto Domínguez (eds), *Literature Squared: Self-Reflexivity in Late Antique Literature*, 255–75, Turnhout: Brepols.

Spahlinger, L. (2004), 'Zur Struktur und Ordnung von Ausonius' "Ordo urbium nobilium"', *Gymnasium*, 111: 169–90.

Trout, D. E. (1999), *Paulinus of Nola: Life, Letters, and Poems*, Berkeley: University of California Press.

Warren, D. (2017), *Ausonius: Moselle, Epigrams, and Other Poems*, London: Routledge.

Witke, C. (1971), *Numen Litterarum: The Old and the New in Latin Poetry from Constantine to Gregory the Great*, Leiden: Brill.

CHAPTER 3
CATO *CAPITULATIM*: NEPOS THE CENSOR

Jared Hudson

Quod uix credendum sit tantas res tam breuiter potuisse declarari. 'It is hardly believable that such great achievements could be shown forth so concisely'. Thus Cornelius Nepos sums up Atticus' summary verse portraits of stand-out Romans, ones who surpassed the rest in the 'grandeur' of their deeds (*rerum . . . gestarum amplitudine*): he managed to capture them in just a few lines – *no more* (*non amplius*).[1] Nepos himself is of course notably complimented by Catullus for a comparable, and daring, act of compression, his synoptic *Chronica*: 'all time' in three learned-and-effortful volumes.[2] And Atticus himself composed a similar history-wringing work, in which, says Nepos, he exhibited (*exposuerit* 18.1 ~ *exposuit* 18.6) 'all antiquity' in a sole volume, his *Liber annalis*.[3] Singular feats of systematic culling and cramming in the Republic's eleventh hour: the vast sprawl of history – *Graeco-Roman* – synchronized and synthesized (*Chronica*, *Liber annalis*); larger-than-life figures pressed into lapidary headings (both sets of *Imagines*, *De illustribus uiris*); even a concentrated extract of morally teachable moments (Nepos' cutting-edge *Exempla*). These dots, however faint, connect to outline a distinctive intellectual sub-culture, and a fitting prose aesthetic, of late republican epitome. Signature miniature collections; personalized thumbnail galleries. At play no doubt was the sheer challenge of panoramic condensation. But this was also the work of variously marginal scholars concerned that the vital points of the Roman past might get lost in the shuffle, if not carefully lined up and boiled down – *by them*.[4]

In order to begin to grasp Nepos' *De uiris illustribus* as not only a significant (if still underrated) stage in the development of ancient political biography, but also as a rich specimen of late republican epitome, this chapter unpacks his slimmest of bios of one of Rome's 'greats', Cato the Elder.[5] Nepos' tiny (extant) version of his own (lost) volume-length *Cato* reads almost as a modern book-jacket blurb, complete with succinct paraphrase, glimpses of scenes from the Censor's illustrious career as commander, politician, orator, and historian, and even a pithy sign-off advertising the lengthier separate edition (3.5) – in short, easy to disregard. A one-off survival, it would seem, valuable only for the historical content it mostly mutilates, and (*maybe*) for the lost original it barely attests. But despite Horsfall's dismissive account of this diminutive *vita* in his 1989 commentary – much in line with that scholar's earlier belittling, and influential, epitome of Nepos ('an intellectual pygmy') – this chapter argues that a concerted aesthetic of concision underlies Nepos' slender portrait, however understated it may seem, and that such a technique of representation is pointedly suited to its portraitist's subject.[6] An etched (mini-)study in 'life'-compression – that of his own (*Cato*), and Cato's. Key to Nepos' surviving sketch (of his lost sketch) of Cato is his identification of his subject as, not merely an orator, or a general, but an *author* (thus classed in his *De Latinis Historicis*). This in part accounts for his mise-en-abyme overview of *Origines* (3.3–4) that reads as the biographical synopsis's point: both an aetiology of Latin prose and the essence of the man in the distillate of his written words. For Nepos reconstitutes Cato's action-packed life in this miniature work through a careful re-writing of actual Catonian words, and thus updates Rome's first true orator's taut precept disavowing oratory (*rem tene, uerba sequentur*): now *Nepos'* words follow from cleaving to Cato's 'content' (i.e., words).[7] The chapter suggests that the motivations for such a tight rendering of the strict Censor's legacy are political – plausibly deniable in its extreme concision, but quietly defiant in its backward-looking nostalgia.[8] On the brink of the Principate, Nepos thus sums up the life of the old – *republican* – morality, and its inextricable tie to historiography, in a diminutive, and unassailable, *Cato*.

Origins, early days

> M. Cato, ortus municipio Tusculo, adulescentulus, priusquam honoribus operam daret, uersatus est in Sabinis, quod ibi heredium a patre relictum habebat. inde hortatu L. Valerii Flacci, quem in consulatu censuraque habuit collegam, ut M. Perpenna censorius narrare solitus est, Romam demigrauit in foroque esse coepit. primum stipendium meruit annorum decem septemque. Q. Fabio M. Claudio consulibus tribunus militum in Sicilia fuit. inde ut rediit, castra secutus est C. Claudii Neronis, magnique opera eius existimata est in proelio apud Senam, quo cecidit Hasdrubal, frater Hannibalis. quaestor obtigit P. Africano consuli, cum quo non pro sortis necessitudine uixit: namque ab eo perpetua dissensit uita. aedilis plebi factus est cum C. Heluio. praetor prouinciam obtinuit Sardiniam, ex qua quaestor superiore tempore ex Africa decedens Q. Ennium poetam deduxerat, quod non minoris aestimamus quam quemlibet amplissimum Sardiniensem triumphum.[9]

> Marcus Cato, originating from the town of Tusculum, as a young man, before devoting his energies to public distinctions, lived in Sabine lands, because there he had an estate left him by his father. From there, at the urging of Lucius Valerius Flaccus, whom he had as a colleague in the consulship and the censorship (as Marcus Perpenna the ex-censor used to relate), he moved to Rome and started a public career. He served on his first campaign at seventeen. In the consulship of Quintus Fabius and Marcus Claudius, he was military tribune in Sicily. When he returned from there, he joined the staff of Gaius Claudius Nero and his action in the battle of Sena, where Hasdrubal, the brother of Hannibal, was killed, were highly valued. As quaestor he was assigned by lot to the consul Publius Africanus, with whom he did not live according to the connection of that allotment: for he disagreed with him for his whole life. He was made plebeian aedile with Gaius Helvius. As praetor he was allotted the province of Sardinia, from which, when as

> a quaestor at an earlier time he was departing from Africa, he had brought back with him Quintus Ennius the poet – something which we value no less than the grandest triumph in Sardinia.

Nepos' Cato starts out small. Even his name receives abbreviation.[10] Cato's local Tusculan origins (*ortus municipio Tusculano*) pin him down to a modestly sized Latin town, but say a great deal.[11] Right away, they read as forecasting his late-life's work in digesting, among other topics, 'every' Italian city's roots (*ortus* 1.1 ~ *unde quaeque ciuitas orta sit Italica* 3.3): two books of his history (*Origines*), second and third out of seven, which he had, notes Nepos, epitomize the whole (*ob quam rem omnes Origines uidetur appellasse* 3.3). Cato, apparently founding father in Nepos' line of *historici Latini*, worked as a kind of ethnographic proto-epitomator – a *Latin* one. Here, at the very start, Nepos picks up where Cato left off: tracing the roots of a man – first in a prolific series – who wrapped up his life's work in tracing roots.[12]

Behind the succinctness lurks the well-known exchange between 'Atticus' and 'Marcus' in Cicero's *De Legibus*, on the fundamental duality of Roman identity (2.5). There Cato is made *the* exemplary model for this doubleness: a special, authoritative case, given Tusculum's status as the first Latin community to receive Roman citizenship (back in 381) – his place of birth literally entitled him to membership in two communities – but also an eloquent figure for the broader notion of a Roman 'double *patria*'.[13] Cato's Tusculan 'Latinity' is crucial to authorizing Roman historiography, and Latin prose (he is a *Latin* historian in two senses). Nepos, himself from a more novel margin, Cisalpine Gaul (*Padi accola* Plin. *H.N.* 3.126), represents an updated version of Cato's 'Roman' authorship, forging *his* identity through the writing of Latin historical prose, the first to write biography in Latin.[14]

The bare marker *municipio Tusculo* also quietly passes over, and so points up, the town's contemporary resonances, what it has come to stand for by Nepos' lifetime, as well as its (then) already magnificent backstory. Far from being mean and 'unapproachable', Tusculum now spells wealthy leisure, probably more than anywhere else in first-century extra-urban Latium: L. Crassus, L. Sulla, M. Scaurus, Cicero, brother Quintus, Pompey, Lucullus, Gabinius, Lentulus, Varro, Brutus, and Hirtius all had extensive estates here.[15] By tacit contrast, then, we can detect in Cato's (ultimate) descent from Tusculum a quiet signal of a broader moral descent. Nepos' fragments reveal him as particularly prone to moralizing, noting down Roman culture's 'first adopters' of luxurious products, like a *censor* with a very long memory.[16] Of course, says Nepos, in his heyday Cato would try to check the luxury that was already starting to sprout up (2.3; see below).

If latter-day Tusculum could connote grandees' mansions, it also suggests a location for philosophy. For Cicero, of course, this place more than any other, especially in the 40s, means *philosophical otium*. A contrast between what Tusculum is now used, and known, for (*disputationes*) and what it produced back then (*the* Censor) could underlie Nepos' concision. A sole fragment from Nepos' letters, from one addressed to Cicero, has the biographer asserting to Roman philosophy's founding-father that Philosophia cannot be an adequate guide to life.[17] We are left to wonder if what Cicero tells Atticus (with some joshing) that Nepos wasn't keen on in Cicero's work was its philosophical content – in the midst of Cicero's ambitious writing-plan, including the *Tusculanae*.[18] Some have suggested mild disapproval written into Nepos' full-length (lost) life of Cicero, and we can ask if the extant epitome of Cato rubs out any contrasts, however implicit, between the habits of these two archetypal *noui homines*, even passing details such as their respective relationship to a special site like Tusculum. All of which is to say that the apparently passing Tusculum is marked, especially given Cato's close associations with Sabine country.

For, the Sabina frames Nepos' next phase of life-writing (conventional, cued by the curt heading *adulescentulus*), where he will not let readers forget that the ground was prepared for Cato's subsequent public career by hard labour. Nor would Cato, whose hammering, heaped-up boast to his opponent L. Thermus lies behind Nepos' tidy, cleaned-up paraphrase (*adulescentulus . . . uersatus est in Sabinis*): *ego iam a principio in parsimonia atque in duritia atque industria* [~ *industria Cato* 3.1, 3.4] *omnem adulescentiam meam abstinui agro colendo, saxis Sabinis, silicibus repastinandis atque conserendis* ('I from the very beginning kept my whole youth in thrift and toughness and hard work, by farming, by Sabine stones, digging up and planting').[19] The all-but invisibly idiomatic, and metaphorical, *operam daret* is set off against the abstract *uersatus est in Sabinis*, grounding its meaning in good, old-fashioned effort.[20] Indeed, Cato's *opera* in battle will shortly be valued highly (1.2): the preliminary time spent on the farm helps make it so.[21] That this fieldwork was an ongoing project is conveyed by the imperfect *habebat*: working that piece of land passed on by his father would help define his whole strenuous life (*in omnibus rebus singulari fuit industria* 3.1).[22] Whether it made it into the full volume or not, there was much more Nepos could record about Cato *in Sabinis*.

After all, *Cicero's* Cato (*senex*) is given the space to describe his own exemplary gaze upon the nearby villa of his Sabine neighbour, Manius Curius Dentatus, marvelling at the man's 'restraint' (*continentia*), and the old ways.[23] Plutarch's treatment (*Cato* 2.1–3) fleshes out the scene, and has Cato continuously tramping over to Curius' place to wonder at its 'slenderness' (τὴν μικρότητα) and the house's 'plainness' (τὸ λιτόν). He would ponder a man who became 'greatest' (μέγιστος) still hoeing that little place (τὸ χωρίδιον) himself. Here, a few turnips had trumped heaps of Samnite gold. Cato, fired up, would then take the lesson home, conduct a kind of household census, and redouble his own efforts, pruning back expenses.[24] Greatness begins (and ends) at home – in small spaces, by getting rid of excess. Plutarch's vignette is (*finely*) embellished, but '[i]t is a good guess that this came from Cato's writings'.[25] Nepos must know it, and prunes *it* out, for readers to supply. Already his (restrained) style makes the man.

Nepos' portrait of the Elder as a young man receiving career-defining advice from an older colleague-to-be (*hortatu L. Valerii Flacci*) prefigures the guidance *he* has received from his own senior associate in antiquarianism (*rogatu T. Pomponii Attici* 3.5), that he write *Cato*. Likewise, naming and phrasing both pave the way for ring composition (*L. Valerii Flacci, quem in consulatu censuraque habuit collegam* ~ *consulatum gessit cum L. Valerio Flacco* 2.1 . . . *censor cum eodem Flacco factus* 2.3). But beyond analogy, and formal arrangement, Nepos literally (if tacitly) links himself into the chain of transmission, by citing the report *he* apparently (habitually, *solitus est*) received from the remarkably long-lived M. Perpenna – one more *censor* whose memory stretches far back, and who does not forget. Cato accordingly sets off for the big city, and goes public. Nepos once made for Rome too (where, he says, he heard Cicero speak *Pro Cornelio* in 65), but would skip to the last stage of Cato's life for what to emulate.[26]

Briefly flagging his next biographical heading, Nepos limns Cato's first military service (*primum stipendum meruit annorum decem septemque*), perhaps recalling the Censor's own words, when (later) defending his conduct of his Spanish campaign as consul: *quid mihi fieret, si non ego stipendia [in ordine] omnia ordinarius meruissem semper?*[27] Even late in his career, he could harp on these early days of service. The rare numerical expression *decem septemque*, and the fact that Plutarch flags the point as straight from the horse's mouth (φησὶ γὰρ αὐτὸς ἑπτακαίδεκα γεγονὼς ἔτη τὴν πρώτην στρατεύσασθαι στρατείαν *Cat. Mai.* 1.8), suggest that Nepos may in fact distil a different embattled reminiscence of Cato's.[28] He may have chopped off a surviving fragment of Cato's speech *De Achaeis* (*cumque Hannibal terram Italiam laceraret atque uexaret* Gell. 2.6.7=Malcovati 187), given how Plutarch finishes the sentence (περὶ ὃν Ἀννίβας χρόνον εὐτυχῶν ἐπέφλεγε τὴν Ἰταλίαν) – so Hannibal only enters *this* life obliquely (1.2). Used nowhere else in Nepos' brief bio, the consular dating formula (*Q. Fabio M. Claudio consulibus*, 214) marking out Cato's precocious military tribunate in Sicily (*under Marcellus*, and, edited out, in Campania *under Fabius*), takes on added significance for the future chronicler of the Second Punic War (~ *in quinto secundum* 3.3) – he wrote up what he lived, making Roman history – and for the author of *Chronica*.

The narrative then covers ground fast as Cato gets back from his first tour in Sicily only to join (contextually, almost 'chase after') the staff of legendarily quick C. Claudius Nero rushing to reinforce co-consul M. Livius Salinator. Nepos' 'Battle of *Sena*' could pointedly pin down the more widespread 'Metaurus', a small town for a principal river (though cf. *Senensi proelio* Cic. *Brut.* 74), but the real thrust is to have a glimpse of Cato's exertion figure in the reckoning of that battle's outsize effect. Metaurus was a decisive victory, of course, but in the logic of anecdote it was the message sent by a chopped scrap (a terse synecdoche) that truly won the day. When Hasdrubal's severed head was flown back south to brother Hannibal by the speedy consul, then the general foresaw the destiny of Carthage.[29] In all this young Cato's *opera* was worth a great deal – was *reckoned* so (*magni . . . existimata est*), by his superiors, we could infer. Or even perhaps by *Origines* 5: Cato, notes Livy, was no depreciator of his own praises (*haud sane detractator laudum suarum* 34.15.9). But Nepos cuts the detail out, forcing a curt comment to simply make Cato's pains-taking rate highly.[30]

A string of rapid-fire magistracies (sentence-heading *quaestor . . . aedilis plebi . . . praetor*) sees Cato speeding through the *cursus honorum*, with condensed takeaways nesting this phase tightly into the *Life* to come. Cato quaestor's defiance of convention, in failing to hit it off with his lot-appointed consul, Scipio (*not-yet*) Africanus, gets a relative flourish, forecasting how young independence would help forge an entire lifestyle (*uixit:* ~ *perpetua . . . uita.*) of contrariness (*non pro sortis necessitudine* ~ *ab eo . . . dissensit*).[31] The set-piece crisis, the bio's narrative climax, will bring these consuls' tension to a boil

(2.1–2), or perhaps Nepos' biographer's nose for sniffing out behavioural origins prefabricates the early friction.[32] The glimpse of Cato's aedileship prunes out any notice of his and colleague C. Helvius' (scheming?) repetition of the Plebeian games, or bonus ones for the *Epulum Iouis* – which might clash with the later image of the austere Censor (3.3–4) – though the immediate jump to *praetor* in the succeeding sentence suggests the venture worked.[33] Nepos makes no mention of the praetor's legendary self-sufficiency, shrinking expenses, making his way throughout Sardinia on foot with a staff of one. The memorable portraits of Livy (33.27.2) and Plutarch (*Cato Mai.* 6.2–4) may go back to Cato's own words, perhaps taken for granted by Nepos, who clips the detail out in order to pivot back pointedly to the tense quaestorship (*Sardiniam, ex qua quaestor superiore tempore* [i.e., six or seven years prior – in the previous sentence]) so he can extract a valuable takeaway from Cato's lead-up to maturity, the first paragraph.

The doubling back is revealing. Cato had returned from service (*ut inde rediit* 1.2) only to set out to have the worth of his martial effort proved, and he has now (i.e., then, when finishing up as quaestor) come back from Africa (via Sardinia) bringing the treasure that is . . . Ennius. Whether he also brought back Greek lessons from the poet (or would one day receive them), Nepos won't say, but plants the seeds for Cato's later learning (3.2).[34] Military conquest, however theoretical, is not what Nepos would value of Cato's governorship (*praetor*) in Sardinia any more than his acquisition of the first national poet – a tidy template for this life.[35] It is a thing *we* (i.e., the concentrated compound *ego Nepos-nos Romani*) value no less than any grand triumph from Sardinia.[36] What (Nepos takes away from what) Cato extracts from his tour (*poetam deduxerat*) is deliberately set against any triumph he could have celebrated – and the one, as consul, he promptly did (*triumphum deportauit* 2.1).[37] The figure thus makes a pivotal place in Cato's life-story. Almost by way of correction (*magni . . . opera eius existimata est ~ quod non minoris aestimamus quam quamlibet amplissimum . . . triumphum*), the epitome's thematic of volume vs. value is sharpened, accentuating a claim that underwrites this economical *Life*. Here less *is* more, in terms of both 'content' and 'style': conventionally smaller acts of *otium* can count at least as much as (and even outweigh) grand achievements, and stripped-down *breuitas* can paradoxically magnify an already great subject.

Growth, and curbing growth

> Consulatum gessit cum L. Valerio Flacco, sorte prouinciam nactus Hispaniam citeriorem, exque ea triumphum deportauit. ibi cum diutius moraretur, P. Scipio Africanus consul iterum, cuius in priori consulatu quaestor fuerat, uoluit eum de prouincia depellere et ipse ei succedere, neque hoc per senatum efficere potuit, cum quidem Scipio principatum in ciuitate obtineret, quod tum non potentia, sed iure res publica administrabatur. qua ex re iratus senatui <consulatu> peracto priuatus in urbe mansit. at Cato, censor cum eodem Flacco factus, seuere praefuit ei potestati. nam et in complures nobiles animaduertit et multas res nouas in

> edictum addidit, qua re luxuria reprimeretur, quae iam tum incipiebat pullulare. circiter annos octoginta, usque ad extremam aetatem ab adulescentia, rei publicae causa suscipere inimicitias non destitit. a multis tentatus non modo nullum detrimentum existimationis fecit, sed, quoad uixit, uirtutum laude creuit.[38]
>
> The consulship he held with Lucius Valerius Flaccus, receiving by lot the province of Hither Spain, and brought back a triumph from it. When he remained there too long, Publius Scipio Africanus, then consul for the second time (in whose previous consulship he had been quaestor), wanted to expel him from the province and take his place personally; but he was not able to bring this about through the senate, even though Scipio did hold the leading position in the state, because at that period the government was administered not by power, but by law. As a result of this he was angry at the senate and once his consulship was ended he remained in the city without holding office. But Cato, having been made censor with Flaccus once again, led that position with severity. For he both punished numerous nobles and added many new provisions to the edict, whereby luxury could be repressed, for it was already at that time beginning to sprout. For some eighty years, from youth until the end of his life, he never ceased taking on feuds for the sake of the republic. Although attacked by many he not only underwent no loss of reputation, but, as long as he lived, grew in the praise of his virtues.

The peak phase is marked by the headlining *consulatum*, which Cato held together with his old backer Valerius Flaccus, with whom he would also be censor (~ 1.1, 2.3): the high point of a *public* career. Civic activities (*leges Porciae*, opposition to the repeal of the *lex Oppia*) go without saying, perhaps. And Nepos all but skips over Cato's Spanish campaign, picking out his allotment of the province, perhaps to summon up his chance falling in with Scipio as quaestor (*pro sortis necessitudine* ~ *sorte prouinciam nactus*) in order to make way for their imminent clash, but also to evoke Cato's ability to outgrow whatever fortune throws at him. The gap between allotment and triumphant return could have been filled by Cato's own ample words of self-praise, but in structure and phrasing it reads as if Nepos' concern is more with the contrast between the virtual spoils represented by his winning Ennius (1.4) and the real (but symbolic) triumph he brings back from Hither Spain.[39] For the gently marked *triumphum deportauit* turns out to dredge up a Ciceronian idea (or idée fixe) on the relative worth of triumphs and home-front exertions: without the latter, victory has no place to which to come home.[40]

A miniaturized scene of civic stability tested by imposing personalities is precisely what Nepos stages next, lingering on an episode with loaded significance for the extraordinary (and conflicted) commands of his own lifetime.[41] While Plutarch makes Cato's conquest of the Lacetani an act of super-strenuous defiance when Scipio arrives in person to take over command, having Cato derisively play the *nouus homo* card in answer to Scipio's objections (*Cat. mai.* 11), Nepos' interest is in the senate's resolution of the conflict by law rather than by personal influence, or force.[42] He sums up Cato's act as, if not actually a breach of his customary restraint, then a bit of uncharacteristic foot-dragging (*ibi cum diutius moraretur*), which is seized on by Scipio (now *properly*) Africanus as an opportunity to one-up his formerly difficult underling.[43] Such dawdling jars somewhat with what Cato himself (is said to have) said of his conquest – in his speech *De consulatu suo*, perhaps, or else in *Origines* – that he took more cities in Spain than he spent days here (Plut. *Cat. mai.* 10.3), or with his famously expedient ploy, strategically disarming a slew of cities with a single act of coordinated epistolography.[44]

Nepos is instead concerned to bring other features into relief. For such a laconic account, his flashback sounds redundant (*P. Scipio Africanus consul iterum, cuius in priori consulatu quaestor fuerat*), but the takeaway is that neither Africanus nor Nepos will let that old *inimicitia* die. He wanted to eject Cato and take over personally, but couldn't do so through the senate. This sentence, *Cato*'s longest, may not be pretty (or periodic), but its ad hoc structure – after the *cum*- and relative clauses a string of seeming add-ons: *uoluit . . . neque . . . potuit, cum quidem . . . obtineret, quod . . . non . . . sed . . . administrabatur* – reveal Nepos, for a moment, almost letting his guard down, just barely opening up to deliver a moralizing, political critique. His strikingly current, but studiously unspecific lament for the times (*quod tum non potentia, sed iure res publica administrabatur*) fixes on the dangers of excessive individual power by showing how it once was structurally impotent: *potentia*, that catchword of late republican politics, here 'illegitimate power', was simply powerless to trump the senate and the laws (*neque hoc . . . potuit . . . quod tum non potentia*).[45]

Also tucked into this sentence of atypical prolixity is another potential barb aimed at the shifted (and still shifting) meaning of *principatus* (*cum quidem Scipio principatum in ciuitate obtineret*). The mildly emphatic concessive *cum quidem* says much ('though he did in fact hold . . .'), prefiguring the clash between then and now – the point of the sentence. *Obtineret* quietly glosses Scipio's position of *princeps senatus* as legitimate, akin to state procedure like Cato's acquisition of Sardinia as his province (*obtinuit* 1.3), and so limited.[46] With striking economy, Nepos stages how a potential struggle between magnates could be arbitrated by the state, rather than spin off into civil war, or *another* kind of *principatus* (a sense which he here eerily anticipates). Even, that is, if one party would be left fuming (*iratus*) at the senate: but he would remain a private citizen in the city – no further offices and, crucially, no legions at his beck and call, to sic on foes. Nepos' articulation happens to chime with a sentiment already latent in Cato: *iure, lege, libertate, re publica communiter uti oportet: gloria atque honore, quomodo sibi quisque struxit.* ('we must employ law, right, liberty, and state in common; glory and rank, as each individual has achieved for himself').[47] The terms are somewhat different – Cato's (orphan) fragment is usually read as a fierce assertion of the ethic of *nouitas* – but the division between shared, public right and individual sway is evocative. It may be that Nepos pits Ur-*nouus homo* against super-*nobilis* in part to demonstrate how the threat of excessive power from *either* can be neutralized. *Could have been.* Nepos' miniature portrait of Cato *consul* is, then, rather surprisingly, not really about him: it is (and was) articulated around an understated σύγκρισις of these two grandees, but his bigger point is to insist that their showdown could be successfully managed by *res publica*.

With *at Cato, censor* (2.3) the Elder truly comes into his own (and assumes his moniker), and Nepos wraps up a public career. *At* carries on the contrast with Scipio (*consulatu peracto priuatus*) – no sulking for relentless Cato – and almost mimes this contrarian calling his rival(s) out. The circle is at last complete (*cum L. Valerio Flacco* ~ *cum eodem Flacco*), with the pair of old associates now occupying the morally highest ground, but this time with erstwhile patron turned sidekick (*Cato* ... *praefuit*). *Seuere*, connoting a trickier business in the social habits of Nepos' day, is how Cato runs the censorship, *potestati* ('legitimate position, office') in pointed contrast with dangerous *potentia*.[48] The sequence *seuere praefuit ei potestati* thus focalizes a potential difficulty, only to account for it: Cato does his job only too well. There may even be undertones of Cato's own use of the term (*potestas*) in his speech *Pro Rhodiensibus* (reiterated by him in *Origines* 5), where it means (*Roman*) 'self-control'.[49] In his institution of moral correction, Cato cuts nobles no breaks (and the σύγκρισις lives on . . .), a single magistrate (*cum Flacco*) writing up 'very many' for their sins. He expands the censors' edict, adding many *res nouas*, in order to restrain luxury, which is proliferating. Cato's censorship grows for and through its reduction of immoral growth. Nepos' nostalgic moralizing cuts both ways here, to make *Cato* timely. This was an era, his slim style says, that was deeply like and unlike today. *Res nouae, then*, could mean new, legitimate measures contributing to the war on vice – nothing like the 'revolution' decried by his contemporaries (especially Cicero).[50] But it was, also, an age when *luxuria* had already (*iam tum*) taken root. In putting this pointed agricultural metaphor (*pullulare*, 'sprout up') to work here, Nepos – in the steps of the *agricola sollers* (3.1) himself? – cuts a complex, societal epidemic down to a simple task of weeding.[51]

Restraint and growth are played out thematically in the conclusion of Cato's career. Nepos' Censor won't back down from personal rivalries, but shoulders the burden of them (*suscipere*) for the sake of the commonwealth – once more in tacit but pointed contrast to the *inimicitiae* that rocked the *res publica* throughout Nepos' life. Readers have seized on Nepos' erroneous accounting here, which appears to impute a career's worth of feuding (his [long] adulthood, *usque ad extremam aetatem ab adulescentia*) to Cato's entire lifetime (*circiter annos octoginta*).[52] The shift does seem careless: he is mistaken (and thinks Cato lived considerably longer than eighty years), or exaggerating (and *circiter* covers a *large* margin). But it seems to be pressed out of Nepos' tendency towards a thematic of 'economizing'. His underlying concern with reduced parts standing in for larger wholes leads him to make this faintly rhetorical substitution: thus Cato's years of controversy (from adolescence to advanced age) easily represent a whole 'life' of altercation. For it is in the related framework of growth (and diminution) that Nepos sums up Cato's civic career. Despite personal attacks by many (and, of course, his own litigiousness), he not only suffered 'no reduction in estimation' (*detrimentum existimationis* ~ *magni* . . . *existimata est* 1.2 ~ *non minoris aestimamus* 1.4), but by the praise of his excellence actually 'grew' (*creuit*).[53] This last stage recapitulates the moral dissent of his youth (*quoad uixit* ~ *uixit* . . . *perpetua dissensit uita* 1.3). The agricultural metaphor figuring his activity as censor (*reprimeretur* . . . *pullulare*) carries over, and

Cato paradoxically grows even in his 'declining' years. His attacks on immoral excess aim at restraint, and effect his estimation's increase (like *Cato*).

Summing up

> In omnibus rebus singulari fuit industria: nam et agricola sollers et peritus iuris consultus et magnus imperator et probabilis orator et cupidissimus litterarum fuit. quarum studium etsi senior arripuerat, tamen tantum progressum fecit, ut non facile reperiri possit neque de Graecis neque de Italicis rebus, quod ei fuerit incognitum. ab adulescentia confecit orationes. senex historias scribere instituit. earum sunt libri septem. primus continet res gestas regum populi Romani, secundus et tertius unde quaeque ciuitas orta sit Italica, ob quam rem omnes Origines uidetur appellasse. in quarto autem bellum Poenicum est primum, in quinto secundum. atque haec omnia capitulatim sunt dicta. reliquaque bella pari modo persecutus est usque ad praeturam Seruii Galbae, qui diripuit Lusitanos: atque horum bellorum duces non nominauit, sed sine nominibus res notauit. in eisdem exposuit, quae in Italia Hispaniisque aut fierent aut uiderentur admiranda: in quibus multa industria et diligentia comparet, nulla doctrina.[54]
>
> In all respects he was a man of outstanding exertion: for he was an able farmer, expert lawyer, great commander, compelling orator, and very avid about literature. Although he took up the pursuit of literature as an older man, still he made such progress, that it is not easy to find anything in Greek or Italian affairs with which he was unfamiliar. From his youth he composed speeches. As an old man he began to write histories. Of these there are seven books. The first contains the achievements of the kings of the Roman people, the second and third an account of where each Italian city has come from; for this reason he seems to have called the entire work *Origins*. Then in the fourth is the first Punic war, in the fifth, the second. All this is recounted summarily. And the remaining wars he set forth in like manner up to the praetorship of Servius Galba, who ravaged the Lusitanians: he did not name the generals of these wars, but recorded events without names. In the same work he exhibited, remarkable occurrences and sights in Italy and the Spains. Therein is much effort and diligence, but no learning.

Cato. How to take him all in? Nepos tries to sum him up in a word: *industria*. It was there from the start, and will cap off his life's work (~ *operam* 1.1 ~ *opera* 1.2 ~ *industria* 3.4). A man of unique exertion, in all aspects, and in all his activities. Nepos' deadpan *accumulatio* – no other extended, paratactic lists like this in *Cato* – points to a contrast between this singular man and his plurality of engagements (*omnibus . . . singulari*): Cato the Farmer, the Lawyer, the General, the Orator – the Man of Letters (. . .?).[55] So many guises, but *industria* can encompass all. He said it himself, after all, once giving a defiant account of his conduct, emphasizing the risks involved in energetic public service, in his (*edited*) speech on his consulship (*egoque iam pridem cognoui atque intellexi atque arbitror rem publicam curare industrie summum periculum*).[56] And his writing carries on from his public career (even epitomizes it).

Nepos is trying to smooth over the transition from 'life' to 'writing' (i.e., the gap between *Cato* 2 and 3). He does this by moving towards a reckoning of Cato's *otium*, (again) pointedly taking him at his word: the first Latin Historian had written the justification of *otium* right into the start of his *Origines* (*clarorum uirorum atque magnorum non minus otii quam negotii rationem exstare oportere*) – a call to 'political' biography if ever there was one.[57] So *In omnibus rebus* also, by its emphatic position, and by contrast with the final term in the catalogue (*cupidissimus litterarum* – the predicate adjective stands out after the run of modified predicate nouns), invites comparison with *words* (i.e., not simply 'in all respects', but 'in all his *activities*').[58] On closer inspection, each of these real-life parts of Cato can be seen to have taken shape in his variegated writings: *De agri cultura* (*agricola sollers*), *Commentarii iuris ciuilis* (*peritus iuris consultus*), *De re militari* (*magnus imperator*), and *Orationes* (*probabilis orator*). These Nepos is now (ch. 3) cramming into a species of 'literary' biography (to settle on *Origines*), and it is the Elder's range that has special significance for Nepos the synthesizer.

Nepos' list of Cato's real-life roles of course also helps prepare the idea, taken up by *quarum studium . . . senior arripuerat*, that Cato took up these literary interests late, his life so elegantly enacting that very *Greek* concept (ὀψιμαθής). After such a bustling, strenuous life he at last turns to literature and then writes it all up (*everything* – *non facile reperiri possit . . . quod ei fuerit incognitum*) in short order. Cicero's mad dash to get as much of philosophy down in Latin as he could in these years – *his* last – makes its way into Nepos' brief account, and the second sentence (*quarum studium . . . fuerit incognitum* 3.2) sounds much like Cicero on study.[59] By indefatigable *industria*, it would seem, he makes up for lost time, and Nepos runs us through his career again in ultra fast-forward, this time in writing (in fact, just two stages, taken up from his actual life: *ab adulescentia* ~ *adulescentulus* 1.1 *ab adulescentia* 2.4; *senex* ~ *ad extremam aetatem* 3.4). *Confecit* reveals that he had in fact been engaged in composition (speech-writing) all along, and there is perhaps a pointed contrast between that form of writing and his mature pursuits, historiography.

Now comes Nepos' final act of accounting. Rather than painting a picture of simple assembly or cataloguing, we see him miming his subject's technique of compressing large tracts into smaller chunks, thereby making them worth more. Cato's final years convert to seven history books. The first packs in the history of the Roman people's kings (i.e., *Roman* origins), the second and third the roots of Italian cities (~ *de Graecis . . . de* Italicis *rebus* 3.2) – all of them in one place, accounted for, and thus more meaningful. He made, by managed restructuring, the name for *that* content (seemingly 2, 3, *and* 1) stand in for the whole set (*Origines*). The Punic War, the first, fits in the fourth, the second in the fifth. But in each case thus far, *Nepos'* recapitulation is emphatically tight: Book One appears to include material that predates Aeneas and stretches past the kings, Two and Three contain more than merely cities' origins, Four features material from the time of the *Second* Punic War, and Five goes well beyond the Second.[60] For a reader with any inkling of such pointed reduction, *atque haec omnia capitulatim sunt dicta* reads as a pointed description of Nepos' own account *here*.[61] But his reference is of course to Cato's epitomizing historiography, which, he continues, recounts 'the rest of the wars' (up to Servius Galba) in an equal fashion (*pari modo*), i.e., equally *capitulatim*. The first *atque* had quietly announced Nepos' synthesizing bullet point (*capitulatim*) and the second accordingly extracts another nugget: Cato apparently avoided naming generals, but recorded content without names – another (idiosyncratic) means of stripping his account down, however reliable Nepos' picture may be.[62] Even Cato's *admiranda* can resemble a form of digest: he 'sets out' (*exposuit*) a selection of sights and occurrences, just as Atticus 'set out' all antiquity in his one volume (*ut eam totam in eo uolumine exposuerit Att.* 18.1) and 'set out' his portraits of outstanding men in verse (*exposuit* 18.6): scarcely believable that such great affairs could be set forth so briefly.[63] But Cato doesn't entirely achieve the ideal of slimmed-down writing Nepos would appear to aim at, despite, that is, his astonishing industry (*in quibus multa industria et diligentia comparet, nulla doctrina*). Nepos' likewise eulogizes Cato's life in a highly incomplete and fragmented portrait. Absence makes the heart grow fonder.

In the preface to his *De excellentibus ducibus exterarum gentium*, Nepos cuts his intro narrative of Graeco-Roman *mores* short to get the point (8): *sed hic plura persequi cum magnitudo uoluminis prohibet, tum festinatio, ut ea explicem, quae exorsus sum. quare ad propositum ueniemus et in hoc exponemus libro de uita excellentium imperatorum* ('But here both the magnitude of the volume and my haste to unfold what I have undertaken prevent me from recounting further examples. Therefore let me come to the point and set out in this book an account of the lives of outstanding generals.'). He has scores of miniatures to delineate – no time to waste. This affirmation of economy, while conventional in Latin prose prefaces and so easy to undervalue, rather than a mere pretext, reveals Nepos' distinct perspective of epitome. In the case of *Cato*, Nepos, with extreme concision, figures Cato as an early version of the author he is in the process of becoming: moralizing, 'Roman' (with Italian sensitivities), even universally synthesizing – but of course inimitable. Nepos' sign-off, advertising his previously published full edition, reads as nearly mock-apologetic, accounting for its length in Atticus' request: *Huius de uita et moribus plura in eo libro persecuti sumus, quem separatim de eo fecimus rogatu T. Pomponii Attici. quare studiosos Catonis ad illud uolumen delegamus.* ('I have set out more about this man's life and character in the work I produced about him separately, at the request of Titus Pompius Atticus. Thus I refer those interested in Cato to that volume.')[64] Nepos' account of his earlier work here (*plura in eo libro persecuti sumus* ~ *hic plura persequi*) imitates that of Cato's *Origines* (*persecutus est* 3.4) just previously, which, we must not forget, famously featured himself, and his speeches, at crucial junctures. *That* was how a Roman legend wrote – above all, by summing up a life (*his*). But through the opposition between referring back to *his own* previous lengthier volume (3.5) and his preface that now renounces going on at great length, Nepos adumbrates an image of authorial maturation that takes shape by contrast with *Cato's* model of authorship. As the latter is simply no longer available to an outsider such as Nepos, he will go on etching out rows of miniature *Lives*. In helping to sharpen the meaning of this gap, says Nepos, the value of the life of Cato *historicus* – however neat his *Cato* might be – is not aesthetic, but moral, and political.

Notes

1. Nep. *Att.* 18.6: *namque uersibus, qui honore rerumque gestarum amplitudine ceteros Romani populi praestiterunt, exposuit ita, ut sub singulorum imaginibus facta magistratusque eorum non amplius quaternis quinisque uersibus descripserit.* The Latin text is Marshall 1977; the English version is by me. Varro's *Imagines* would do a similar job of packing vast paper-trails of lives into tidy portraits, and tight epigrams (a not so tidy 700 of them, vs. Nepos' 400-odd lives); cf. Plin. *H.N.* 35.11.
2. Catul. 1.5–7: ... *cum ausus es unus Italorum | omne aeuum tribus explicare cartis | doctis, Iuppiter, et laboriosis* (~ Nepos *Praef.* 8: *ut ea explicem, quae exorsus sum*; *Hann.* 13.4: *sed nos tempus est huius libri facere finem et Romanorum explicare imperatores*). See below on the analogous pairing that Nepos (*Cato* 3.4) extracts from Cato's *Origines* (*industria et diligentia* ... nulla *doctrina* ~ *doctis* ... *et laboriosis*). On this much studied question, see, e.g., Cairns 1969: 153–4; Wiseman 1979: 141–82; Geiger 1985b: 68, 71; and now the helpful overview of Stem 2012: 1–11.
3. *Att.* 18.1: *moris etiam maiorum summus imitator fuit antiquitatisque amator, quam adeo diligenter* (~ *diligentia Cato* 3.4) *habuit cognitam, ut eam totam in eo uolumine exposuerit, quo magistratus ordinauit* ... And cf. Nepos' own opening (*Praef.* 8): *in hoc exponemus libro de uita excellentium imperatorum.* On the *Liber annalis*, see Douglas 1966: lii–iv.
4. For background, see Rawson 1985: esp. 103 and 230–10; also Millar 1988.
5. In addition to Momigliano 1993: 96–9 and Geiger 1985b (whose thesis – Nepos invented that genre – is challenged by J. Moles 1989, but accepted by Wiseman 1987), see, most recently, the study of Stem 2012; cf. the valuable discussion of epitome by Woodman 1975 (286 on Nepos and contemporaries).
6. Horsfall 1989: 3–4; Horsfall 1982: 290; the latter is summed up by the former in terms both unyielding ('My description of N. as an 'intellectual pygmy' attracted a good deal of amused opprobrium: without doubt, though, he was the social and intellectual inferior of Varro, Atticus, and Cicero', p. xvi) and softening ('My own discussion in *CHCL* ii was in part hasty and uninformed [~ 'hasty and unverified', p. 4 of Nepos' epitome]', p. 13; 'close study has greatly increased my respect for N. since my survey of 1982', p. 8). Cf. the incisive review by Moles 1992 ('*something* of a palinode' [emphasis mine], p. 314); also, Titchener 2003 and Moles 1993. For broader comparison, see Sowers's chapter in this volume for a sensitive account of late antique aesthetics of epitome in Ausonius.
7. Iul. Vict. *Rhet.* 197 (Orell.), almost too good to be true.
8. See below, on *studiosos Catonis* 3.5.
9. *Cato* 1.
10. Horsfall 1989: 47 notes 'the non-significant omission of the *nomen* or *gentilicium* (Porcius)', but there could be something in marking out a typically shortened 'big name' such as Cato's, right here; *Atticus* starts out *T. Pomponius Atticus* ...
11. Cf. Astin 1978: 2, on the 'very restricted territory of Tusculum itself ... only about 50 square kilometers in total' and Horsfall 1989: 47, 'There was little room for expansion at Tusculum': the great man literally grows out of a small hometown, to move on to the Sabina (see below).
12. 'The fact that [Nepos] can be seen as representatively "Roman" is however itself a reflection of that well-known process by which the greatest age of Roman literature, and with it our conceptions of "Rome", were the product of people of non-Roman origin' (Millar 1988: 41).
13. *Ego mehercule et illi* [sc. *Catoni*] *et omnibus municipibus duas esse censeo patrias, unam naturae, alteram ciuitatis: ut ille Cato, quom esset Tusculi natus, in populi Romani ciuitatem*

susceptus est, ita, quom ortu Tusculanus esset, ciuitate Romanus, habuit alteram loci patriam, alteram iuris. Cf. Dench 2005: 132.

14. Nepos was perhaps from Mediolanum (see Millar 1988: 40 and p. 54 n. 6), or Hostilia.

15. Fest. 355L: *Tusculum . . . quod aditum difficilem habeat, id est,* δύσκολον (so in origin not unlike its native son – far from cuddly; but its rugged terrain would prepare him for arduous campaigns: *asperrimo atque arduissimo aditu* Malcovati 19 [*De triumpho ad populum*]). Wiseman 1971: 191. Seaside Formiae must have been a close second (but not so illustrious).

16. Esp. in *Exempla*, e.g., Plin. *H.N.* 9.137 (fr. 27 Marshall) on purple; 10.60 (fr. 28), fowl; 33.146 (fr. 31), *triclinia*; 36.48 (fr. 33), marble; 36.59 (fr. 34), onyx amphorae. The dynamics of Nepos' moralizing are no doubt complex (and difficult to recover); cf. his preface to the *Foreign Generals*, where some see an anthropologist's perspective, or even moral relativism, e.g., M. Bettini 2000: 241ff. (also Bettini 2013: 13–20); F.-H. Mutschler 2000: 391–406.

17. Lactant. *Div. Inst.* 3.15.10: *tantum abest ut ego magistram putem esse uitae philosophiam beataeque uitae perfectricem ut nullis magis existimem opus esse magistros uiuendi quam plerisque qui in ea disputanda uersantur. uideo enim magnam partem eorum qui in schola de pudore <et> continentia praecipiant argutissime eosdem in omnium libidinum cupiditatibus uiuere.* Cf. Nepos on Atticus 'living' philosophical teachings, not using them for show (*Att.* 17.3).

18. Cic. *Att.* 16.5 (9 July, 44): *Nepotis epistulam exspecto. cupidus ille meorum, qui ea quibus maxime* γαυριῶ *legenda non putet? et ais* 'μετ' ἀμύμονα'. *tu vero* ἀμύμων, *ille quidem* ἄμβροτος. See J. Geiger 1985a: 261–70.

19. Malcovati 1955: 128 (*De suis uirtutibus contra <L.> Thermum post censuram*).

20. The articulation (*priusquam honoribus operam daret . . .*) makes for a striking contrast with the moralizing justification of Atticus' thoughtful bowing out (*Att.* 6.2): *honores non petiit, cum ei paterent propter uel gratiam uel dignitatem: quod neque peti more maiorum neque capi possent conseruatis legibus in tam effusi ambitus largitionibus neque <geri> e re republica sine periculo corruptis ciuitatis moribus* 6.2 (~ *quod tum non potentia, sed iure res publica administrabatur, Cato* 2.2, on which see below).

21. *Opera* may have a special Catonian ring: e.g., the military tribune Q. Caedicius of *Origines* 4, whose (relatively *under*-valued) efforts Cato would make proverbial (*operam reipublicae fortem atque strenuam perhibuit* Gell. 3.7.19=76 *FRH*); Cato says his enemies take pains that he be badmouthed (*ei rei dant operam, ut mihi falso maledicatur* Malcovati 1955: 23 [*Dierum dictarum de consulatu suo*]); when purchasing land, the farmer should spare no pains in inspecting it (*neue opera tua parcas uisere Agr.* 1.1); Justin (*praef.* 5) quotes Cato's assertion that one should take care that the account of one's leisure should add up (*ut et otii mei, cuius et Cato reddendam operam putat, apud te ratio constaret*); see below on *otium*-accounting.

22. Contrast Atticus' enormous inheritances (from father, 2 million, from uncle Caecilius, 10 million sesterces, *Att.* 5.2, 14.2), out of which Nepos paints a carefully constructed portrait of beneficence.

23. Cic. *Sen.* 55 (Cato speaking [in Rome]): *cuius* [sc. *M'. Curii*] *quidem ego uillam contemplans (abest enim non longe a me) admirari satis non possum uel hominis ipsius continentiam uel temporum disciplinam.* See J. G. F. Powell 1988: 218–19, on the anecdote's versions. Horsfall 1989: 48 seems to imply that Curius' home was at Tusculum.

24. *Cato* 2.3: ταῦθ' ὁ Κάτων ἐνθυμούμενος ἀπῄει, καὶ τὸν αὑτοῦ πάλιν οἶκον ἐφορῶν καὶ χωρία καὶ θεράποντας καὶ δίαιταν, ἐπέτεινε τὴν αὐτουργίαν καὶ περιέκοπτε τὴν πολυτέλειαν (~ τῇ περικοπῇ τῆς πολυτελείας 18.2, of Cato's actual censorship).

25. Powell 1988: 218. Cf. Astin 1978: 2. Plutarch clearly knows Cicero's *Cato* (e.g., 17.5), and perhaps Nepos' monograph version.

26. Hieron. *Contra Ioann. Ierosol.* 12.

27. Malcovati 1955: 129 (*Dierum dictarum de consulatu suo*).

28. Nipperdey 1849: 166 compares Tac. *Hist.* 5.11.

29. Livy 27.51.11–12; Hor. *Carm.* 4.4.50–77 has Hannibal wax tragic, at considerable length.

30. Cato's preface to *Agr.* strikingly foregrounds the language of reckoning value (*existimarint . . . existimare . . . existimabatur . . . existimo*).

31. Comparing Cic. *Diu. in Caec.* 61 on the special relationship between praetor and quaestor (perverted by Verres) we can imagine what kind of comment Nepos offered in his longer *Cato* about decadent *mores*.

32. Cf. Plutarch's account (*Cato Mai.* 3.5–7) fills out the picture (Scipio at odds with Fabius, with whom Cato sides; Cato outraged at Scipio's wasteful largesse).

33. Astin 1978: 19–20, citing Livy 32.7.13, and Sen. *Epist.* 86.10, who makes him a hands-on aedile (Cato the Plumber).

34. *De uir. ill.* 47.1: *in praetura Sardiniam subegit, ubi ab Ennio Graecis litteris institutus*. This 'reduction' of Sardinia is apparently imaginary (perhaps a misreading of Nepos?).

35. Nepos also quiets down any associations of poetry with *personal* panegyric (Cicero has Ennius praise Cato to heaven, *Arch.* 22), or its role in the cut and thrust of political rivalry (Cato attacked Nobilior for embedding Ennius in his Aetolian campaign, *Tusc.* 1.3). See also Gildenhard 2007: 136 n. 144, on Cato setting such poetry against 'native' feasting songs *de clarorum uirorum uirtutibus*.

36. Note the rare stylistic 'amplitude' in *quemlibet amplissimum Sardiniensem triumphum*.

37. Cf. Horsfall 1978: 50, 'an awkward flashback', as against Moles 1993: 76, 'no "awkward flashback" (H.), but a carefully contrived juxtaposition'.

38. *Cato* 2.

39. E.g., Malcovati 1955: 21–55 (*Dierum dictarum de consulatu suo*). Cf. Astin 1978: 52–3.

40. *Off.* 1.78: *mihi quidem certe uir abundans bellicis laudibus, Cn. Pompeius, multis audientibus, hoc tribuit, ut diceret frustra se <u>triumphum</u> tertium <u>deportaturum</u> fuisse, nisi meo in rem publicam beneficio ubi triumpharet esset habiturus. sunt igitur domesticae fortitudines non inferiores militaribus; in quibus plus etiam quam in his operae studiique ponendum est.* Cf. *Cat.* 4.21.

41. Cf. the penetrating reading of such themes in Nepos' *Foreign Generals* by Dionisotti 1988.

42. And Africanus probably never went (or wanted to go) to Spain at all: Nepos may have confused him with P. Cornelius Scipio Nasica. Cf. Astin 1978: 51–2.

43. Note *P. Scipio Africanus* here vs. *P. Africano* (1.3).

44. *De uir. ill.* 47.2–3 is tersest: *consul Celtiberos domuit et, ne rebellare possent, litteras ad singulas ciuitates misit, ut muros diruerent. cum unaquaeque sibi soli imperari putaret, fecerunt.* Cf. Livy 34.17.11, Frontin. *Strat.* 1.1.1, App. *Iber.* 41, etc. Plutarch (10.3) cites Polybius.

45. Horsfall 1989: 52 notes Cic. *Off.* 3.83 (Julius Caesar above the law) and *Phil.* 8.8 (Cicero and Romans defending the laws etc. against Antony), as well as Lepidus' speech against the tyranny of Sulla in Sall. *Hist.* 1.55.4: *nam quid a Pyrrho, Hannibale Philippoque et Antiocho defensum est aliud quam libertas et suae quoique sedes, neu quoi nisi legibus pareremus?*

46. Cf. Cic. *Rep.* 1.68 *ex nimia potentia principum*, noted by R. Syme 1939: 311. Also *Att.* 20.5, where Nepos sums up the struggle between Antony and Octavian (*cum se uterque principem non solum urbis Romae, sed orbis terrarum esse cuperet*).

47. Malcovati 1955: 252.

48. Moles 1993: 76: 'the key contrast between legal *potestas* and the illegitimate *potentia* of 2.2'.

49. *quo maiore opere dico suadeoque uti haec res aliquot dies proferatur, dum ex tanto gaudio in potestatem nostram redeamus* (Gell. 6.3.14=Malcovati 163=*FRH* 87).

50. E.g., Cic. *Cat.* 1.3 (*C. Seruilius Ahala Sp. Maelium nouuis rebus studentem manu sua occidit*).

51. Horsfall 1989: 52 ('arguably borrowed by N. from Cato himself'). Cf. Verg. *G.* 2.17 and attested in Columella.

52. Nipperdey 1849: 168–9; Horsfall 1989: 53 ('The facts are striking enough but N., innumerate, generalizes ineptly: Cato died at the age of 83, and the approximate life-span is transferred unthinkingly to the length of Cato's political activity.').

53. Behind this may also lurk Cato's famous comparison of human life to 'iron', by which he urged tireless exertion as a means of limiting 'loss' (Gell. 11.2.6, from his *Carmen de moribus*): *nam uita humana prope uti ferrum est. si exerceas, conteritur; si non exerceas, tamen rubigo interficit. item homines exercendo uidemus conteri; si nihil exerceas, inertia atque torpedo <u>plus detrimenti</u> facit quam exercitio.* Elsewhere, in his speech *Pro Rhodiensibus*, Cato links *crescere* with the increased pride that accompanies excessive prosperity (which his style nicely mimics!): *scio solere plerisque hominibus rebus secundis atque prolixis atque prosperis animum excellere atque superbiam atque ferociam augescere atque <u>crescere</u>* (Malcovati 163= *FRH* 87). His 'growth' in Nepos is an abstract one, which accompanies the praise for his excellence.

54. *Cato* 3.1–4.

55. Cf. Pliny's (*H.N.* 7.100) Cato the Three-for-One Deal: *Cato primus Porciae gentis tres summas in homine res praestitisse <u>existimatur</u>, ut esset optimus orator, optimus imperator, optimus senator*. For Nepos' *Life* thus far, *cupidissimus litterarum* comes as something of a surprise.

56. Malcovati 1955: 21 (a stance accordingly taken up by Sall. *Cat.* 3.3). Cf. Cato's boiled-down characterization (in *Orig.* 2) of 'most of' Gaul's twin (*energetic*) pursuits, fighting and speech: *pleraque Gallia duas res <u>industriosissime</u> persequitur, rem militarem et argute loqui* (*FRH* 33).

57. Cic. *Planc.* 66 (=*FRH* 2).

58. Nepos' *so awkward* use of forms of *res* in *Cato* (and Cato's *dictum*) almost suggests deeper consideration of the nature of words and content (let me count the *res*): *res publica* (next to the marked *non*-adverb *iure*) 2.1, *qua ex re* (i.e., because of the fact he wasn't able to replace Cato, but also, because the *res publica* was managed *iure*) 2.1, *res nouas* (literal 'new items', no euphemism) 2.3, *qua re* (i.e., by his addition of *res nouae* to the edict) 2.3, *rei publicae causa* (why Cato kept taking on litigation) 2.4, *in omnibus rebus* (in all respects and in all areas of life) 3.1, *neque de Graecis neque de Italicis rebus* (matters and writings) 3.2, *res gestas* (achievements and accounts of them) 3.3, *ob quam rem* (i.e., because Cato's history traced origins in books two and three, it was named *Origines* [this sequence only in Varro and Hyginus!]) 3.3, *sine nominibus res notauit* (content [in words]) 3.4.

59. For the notion of Cato learning in his last years ('amplified' by Cicero), see, e.g., Cic. *Sen.* 3: *qui* [sc. *Cato*] *si <u>eruditius</u> uidebitur disputare, quam consueuit ipse in suis libris, attribuito litteris Graecis, quarum constat eum <u>perstudiosum</u> fuisse in senectute* (cf. 26, 38). 'Ciceronian', e.g.: *arripuerat* ~ *quas* [sc. *Graecas litteras*] *quidem sic auide adripui, quasi diuturnam sitim explere cupiens Sen.* 26, *pueri . . . ita celeriter res innumerabiles arripiant Sen.* 78, *tantum progressum* ~ *in suis studiis tantos progressus Tusc. Disp.* 4.44, *tantos progressus habebat in Stoicis Nat. Deo.* 1.15; *non facile reperiri* ~ *facile reperientur De Orat.* 2.319, *certe istum uirum bonum non facile reperimus Off.* 3.64.

60. Cf. Horsfall 1989: 55–6.

61. On the meaning of *capitulatim*, see Badian 1966: 8 ('by subject matter') vs. Astin 1978: 218 ('"in summary fashion" or "outlining only the most important facts"').

62. This notice, as with each of Nepos' summary points (on the title, on *capitulatim*), has a limited reference when read strictly, but instead has a broader application: *ob quam rem* appears to refer to the content of 2 and 3 alone, but likely includes 1 also (and may refer more broadly to the later books); *captiulatim* appears only to refer back (*haec omnia*), but probably describes the whole; and *horum bellorum* refers to books 6 and 7, but seems to refer to a wider tendency.

63. *quod uix credendum sit tantas res tam breuiter potuisse declarari* (see above).

64. *Cato* 3.5.

Works cited

Astin, A. E. (1978), *Cato the Censor*, Oxford: Oxford University Press.

Badian, E. (1966), 'The Early Historians', in T. A. Dorey (ed.), *Latin Historians*, London: Routledge and K. Paul.

Bettini, M. (2000), *Le orecchie di Hermes*, Turin: Einaudi.

Bettini, M. (2013), 'Cornelio Nepote e un modo di pensare molto romano', in G. Solaro (ed.), *La Roma di Cornelio Nepote: studi*, 13–20, Rome: Aracne.

Cairns, F. (1969), '*Catullus I*', in *Mnemosyne*, 22: 153–4.

Dench, E. (2005), *Romulus' Asylum*, Oxford: Oxford University Press.

Dionisotti, A. C. (1988), 'Nepos and the Generals', in *Journal of Roman Studies*, 78: 35–49.

Douglas, A. E. (1966), *Cicero: Brutus*, Oxford: Oxford University Press.

Geiger, J. (1985a), 'Cicero and Nepos', in *Latomus*, 44: 261–70.

Geiger, J. (1985b), *Cornelius Nepos and Ancient Political Biography*, Stuttgart: Steiner Verlag.

Gildenhard, I. (2007), *Paideia Romana: Cicero's Tusculan Disputations*, Cambridge: Cambridge University Press.

Horsfall, N. (1989), *Cornelius Nepos: A Selection including the Lives of Cato and Atticus*, Oxford: Oxford University Press.

Horsfall, N, (1982), 'Cornelius Nepos', in E. J. Kenney and W. V. Clausen (eds), *Cambridge History of Classical Literature* II, 290–2, Cambridge: Cambridge University Press.

Malcovati, E. (1955), *Oratorum Romanorum fragmenta liberae rei publicae* (2nd edn), Turin: Paravia.

Marshall, P. K. (1977), *Cornelii Nepotis Vitae cum fragmentis*, Leipzig: Teubner.

Millar, F. (1988), 'Cornelius Nepos, "Atticus", and the Roman Revolution', *Greece & Rome*, 35: 40–55.

Moles, J. (1989), rev. of Geiger 1985, in *Classical Review*, 39: 229–33.

Moles, J. (1992), rev. of Horsfall 1989, in *Classical Review*, 42.2: 314–16.

Moles, J. (1993), 'On Reading Cornelius Nepos with Nicholas Horsfall', in *Liverpool Classical Monthly*, 18.5: 76–80.

Momigliano, A. (1993), *The Development of Greek Biography*, Cambridge, MA: Harvard University Press.

Mutschler, F.-H. (2000), *Moralischer Relativismus bei Nepos?*, in A Haltenhoff and F.-H. Mutschler (eds), *Hortus Litterarum Antiquarum: Festschrift für Hans Armin Gärtner zum 70. Geburtstag*, 391–406, Heidelberg: C. Winter.

Nipperdey, K. (1849), *Cornelius Nepos*, Leipzig: Weidmannsche Buchhandlung.

Powell, J. G. F. (1988), *Cicero: Cato Maior de Senectute*, Cambridge: Cambridge University Press.

Rawson, E. (1985), *Intellectual Culture in the Roman Republic*, London: Duckworth.

Stem, R. (2012), *The Political Biographies of Cornelius Nepos*, Ann Arbor: University of Michigan Press.

Syme, R. (1939), *The Roman Revolution*, Oxford: Oxford University Press.

Titchener, F. (2003), 'Cornelius Nepos and the Biographical Tradition', in *Greece & Rome*, 50.1: 92–7.
Wiseman, T. P. (1971), *New Men in the Roman Senate 139 B.C.–A.D. 14*, Oxford: Oxford University Press.
Wiseman, T. P. (1979), *Clio's Cosmetics*, Leicester: Leicester University Press.
Wiseman, T. P. (1987), rev. of Geiger 1985, in *Journal of Roman Studies*, 77: 250.
Woodman, A. J. (1975), 'Questions of Date, Genre, and Style in Velleius: Some Literary Answers', in *Classical Quarterly*, 25: 272–305.

CHAPTER 4
EPITOME AND ITS SURROUNDINGS: BETWEEN WRITTEN AND FIGURAL DOMAINS

Paolo Liverani[*]

In this paper I will try to establish how one might use the concept of epitomization to evaluate if and to what extent we can find common ground between written and figural texts.[1] I will start from a fairly well-known example: for some time, a parallel has been proposed between some literary practices and the archaeological phenomenon of the reuse of *spolia*. In a dense essay, Salvatore Settis[2] draws a parallel between citations and collections of *topoi* on one side and *spolia* on the other. The historical context to which Settis refers is that of the high Middle Ages within a quite broad yet no less rich discussion of the relationship between monuments and literature. In a general sense, we could compare paremiography, *florilegia* and collections of *gnomai/sententiae* with the reuse of *spolia* to show that, in both cases, fragments of a toppled or disappearing past are saved, giving them a new role and function.

It would be, to use a Wittgensteinian concept, a question of a 'family resemblance', that is to say a classification endowed with nuanced and flexible characters. Yet we know and must always keep in mind that family resemblances by definition cannot be specified beyond a certain limit. Today, however, some scholars try to give a more precise meaning to this parallel, proposing an equivalence between the literary *cento* of late antiquity and *spolia* starting in the fourth century AD.[3] Yet such a comparison can easily become too mechanical and cannot be accepted. To guard against this outcome, let us make a philological observation as a preliminary point: when we compare *centones* with *spolia*, we must remember that in antiquity neither in Latin nor in Greek does a precise word or definition exist for *spolia* in the modern archaeological meaning of the term,[4] nor for 'quotation'.[5] However, there are further and more serious obstacles.[6]

Whereas *spolia* are materially wrested from a pre-existing context, damaging or even destroying it, the citation replicates an expression considered to be authoritative. The original context of the citation not only remains untouched but, on the contrary, it is raised to classic status and enriched with new resonances. At least theoretically, we could verify a citation – or an allusion – by comparison with the original text, but by definition this cannot be done in the case of the reuse of physical material, as the source simply no longer exists after it has been reused.

A second and more radical observation raises further obstacles. Properly speaking, is the citation possible in a figural text? We could consider two features in order to recognize a citation: literalness and its delimitation.[7] The first criterion does not apply, by definition, to anything but a written text (and one written with alphabetic notation); the second can be satisfied only with difficulty in a figural text. For delimiting or 'closing' an image we can consider the frame[8] and similar devices. For example, in a relief or painting, a base below a figure signals that this figure is a statue and thus a meta-image different from the remaining figural field. Anyway, these features allow us to formally identify only a minor fraction of the possible occurrences of visual citations, at least as it has been considered so far. I cannot consider here the problem, common both to literal and figural citation, of the distinction between citation, copy, replica or plagiarism. Nor can I discuss the criteria to recognize a bond of derivation classifiable as an allusion, which is a particularly thorny question for ancient art.

In order to consider the issue in a more general way, it seems to me that the core of the problem lays in the difference between 'autograph' and 'allographic' works. Nelson Goodman[9] defines as 'autograph' works that exist in a single copy – such as a painting or a sculpture – whose exact replication is technically and theoretically impossible. Opposed to this are 'allographic' works of art, such as a symphony or a literary text. Here what counts is 'sameness of spelling', that is, the exact correspondence of a series of signs, in which each execution, every edition, or printing, is equally 'authentic' in the sense that it does not constitute an imitation, although it can be more or less accurate. If we accept these terms of the question, it is quite evident that, strictly speaking, citation is not possible in the figurative arts.[10] At most we could speak about a figural evocation of another image.[11]

Now that we have defined the theoretical framework of reference and proffered the necessary methodological cautions, let us seek out visual phenomena that have some analogues with the literary practice of epitomization. To do so, we will have to examine certain cycles of scenes that can be considered epitomes of larger visual narratives. Yet this consideration is far from simple because, unlike what happens with literary texts, we rarely know the precise source from which an image is derived. What is more, we know numerous cases of copies, derivations, and evocations of images – one might easily think of the masterpieces of Greek sculpture known to us only through Roman copies – but they are mostly isolated instances. In the case of larger figurative cycles, we can hardly ever identify the prototype, or the 'hypotext' to use the terminology of Gérard Genette,[12] to understand the extent to which the original has been abbreviated or revised.

Probably the best illustration of this phenomenon is that of the *Tabulae Iliacae*. As is known, this *corpus* consists of fragments of 22 different marble slabs finely decorated with miniature images and brief Greek inscriptions illustrating the Homeric poems and the Trojan cycle. The most complete plate is that of the Capitoline Museum (Figure 1), dating to the first century AD, preserved at a size three-quarters of the original. Today it measures 25 centimetres in height by 30 in width, but in its complete form would have reached approximately 40 centimetres in width. It currently features as many as 250 figures and, in its original form, included in its lower central panels all the essential scenes of the *Ilioupersis*, the *Aethiopis* and *Little Iliad*, alongside which there were illustrations of all 24 books of the *Iliad*. Unfortunately, only the last 12 friezes survive, just to the right side of the monumental pilaster.

Over fifty years ago, Weitzmann[13] posited that the *Tabula Capitolina* was the epitome of a Hellenistic cycle illustrated on papyrus, but this theory has been strongly (and rightly)

Figure 1 *Tabula iliaca*, Musei Capitolini, Rome. Credit: Wikicommons.

contested. Indeed, we have very few papyri with illustrations from the Hellenistic or the early imperial periods. Instead, we begin to find illustrated codices from the fifth century AD, such as the Vatican *Virgil*, the Ambrosian *Iliad*, or in the Christian context the fragment of the *Quedlinburg Itala*. More recent studies[14] have shown that the prototypes of the images in the *Tabula Capitolina* derive from very heterogeneous sources of different epochs and that they have thus been elaborated and put together expressly for this work, without depending on a single pre-existing model. Moreover, in several details the figures do not precisely match the texts to which they refer, but this should not be attributed to the errors, misunderstandings or ignorance of the sculptor but to the freedom with which the artist referred to the 'hypotext', the original source. We have to carefully consider that the culture of the time was an oral or at least 'aural' culture.[15]

It was normal for texts, especially poetic and dramatic ones, to have been disseminated and received through public or private recitations rather than through personal reading.[16] In any case, silent reading was not widespread and we know from anecdotal evidence that it was more common for the reader to voice the text as he read, even in the absence of listeners.[17] Accordingly, what we might call orality is not a technical or secondary aspect of a culture, but a widespread and all-encompassing phenomenon.[18] This means primarily that the artist would most likely have elaborated or interpreted a figural text from memory rather than from a written text physically present before his eyes.[19]

We can express the concept even more strongly by saying that the artist himself is part of this culture of orality. With this I do not want to equate sculptor's work (for example, a sarcophagus) to an oral text, but rather I mean that the figurative artist has considerable freedom in referring to the vibrant, fluid tradition, a tradition that forms a chain in which he is himself a link. In other words, the artist, like the bard, has on the one hand a traditionalist attitude towards his sources, but at the same time maintains a certain freedom. His originality does not consist in the creation of new narratives or iconographies, but rather in fashioning with intelligence and sensitivity traditional elements for the client and the viewing public, as appropriate to the new context.

Orality is characterized by typification, formulation, and the paradigmatic features of characters within apposite scenes; these features manifest themselves through repetition, compositional rhythms and traditional formulae, each of which evolves slowly.[20] All these characteristics are necessary for poems or songs that were performed orally, because, unlike in the case of private reading, the listener obviously cannot stop the performer and ask him to repeat a section in order that it be better understood.

Oral discourse must exploit stereotypes and easily recognizable *topoi* and a high level of redundancy, in order to overcome what communication theory defines as 'noise', i.e. all elements of the communication channel that confuse, distract, or negatively affect the passage of information. For example, in the case of a public performance, the distance from the speaker, the background noises of the environment, the distraction caused by other members of the public, etc.

These aspects of orality recall the phenomenon of the traditionalism of the compositional schemes and the iconographies of classical art, which are repeated with variations in the details while maintaining some fixed elements, so that a fundamental nucleus is always recognizable. Yet it could be objected that, unlike verbal discourse, in the face of a figural cycle, it is possible to return at will to the observation of a particular detail. This element would indeed bring figurative art closer to writing. It should however be noted that in many cases, and especially in the objects of the so-called minor arts, perception occurs in distraction and this is the reason why textual strategies analogous to those used in oral texts are necessary.

Let us now return to the epitome. In light of the arguments outlined above, we must conclude that the figural texts have a visual logic with certain affinities that bring them closer to orality than to literacy. In this case, therefore, we cannot speak of epitome in the strict sense, or rather we cannot speak of it in the same way we speak of the epitome of Dio Cassius, to take one example. The epitome of Xiphilinus and the text of Dio Cassius are both written, verbal texts and we can imagine that the epitomator compiled his synthesis while keeping the original text in front of his eyes. The *Tabula Capitolina*, conversely, would be an epitome in the strict sense only if Weitzmann was right and it depended on a larger figural cycle. Yet since it seems to depend directly on Stesichorus' *Ilioupersis*, the *Tabula Capitolina* is rather a figurative synthesis of a verbal text. In other words, there is a jump between two different semiotic systems, maybe even three if the knowledge of the text has passed through an oral reading. It is the difference that Roman Jakobson describes when he distinguishes the 'intralingual translation' (or 'rewording', that is 'an interpretation of verbal signs by means of other signs of the same language') from the 'intersemiotic translation' (or 'transmutation', that is 'an interpretation of verbal signs by means of signs of nonverbal sign systems').[21] Otherwise we could reformulate the same concept through the more articulated classification by Umberto Eco. For the Italian semiotician the first is a case of 'intralinguistic interpretation', the second an 'intersystemic interpretation with transmutation of continuum'.[22]

We might ask ourselves whether it is easier to find possible examples of an illustrated epitome in late antiquity, when the illustrated codices begin to appear, which could serve as a model. One area we can investigate is that of Christian art, and here I will limit myself to examining only two categories of works. We possess a rich output of sarcophagi decorated with scenes taken from the Old and New Testaments or from the apocryphal texts. The most ancient sarcophagi, beginning in the Constantinian age, are decorated with continuous friezes in which different scenes are juxtaposed without a clear separation between them. Later, columnar sarcophagi appear in which the individual scenes have a more or less elaborate architectural frame. In both cases, however, there is no correspondence between the chronological order with which the biblical stories or the miracles of the Gospels are narrated and that with which the corresponding scenes are depicted. On the contrary, the scenes are arranged mixing the Old and New Testament and even apocryphal texts. The sculptors have chosen a thematic order that varies from time to time depending on their client's needs and choices. It is in no way possible to recognize a standard order, so we can speak of the epitome neither narrowly nor broadly.

A second possibility of interpretation can be derived from the cycles of mosaics or frescoes in the early Christian basilicas. The most ancient cycles that are adequately preserved date back to the fifth century, as can be seen for example in the mosaics of the fifth-century basilica of S. Maria Maggiore in Rome (dating specifically to the age of Pope Sixtus III, 432–440), with stories of the Old and New Testament divided between the mosaic panels of the nave and the apsidal arch at the end of that same nave.[23] We can perhaps go back a little further in time thanks to some manuscripts, which preserve the seventeenth-century copies of now-lost frescoes that decorated the nave of Old St. Peter's on the Vatican hill and the Basilica of St. Paul on the via Ostiensis. Until a few years ago these frescoes were attributed to the pontificate of Pope Leo the Great (440–461), but they have recently been re-examined in a systematic manner with quite interesting results,[24] although obviously the evaluation of a fresco through later copies is difficult, due to the possible mistakes and misunderstandings of the copyist.

Also, in the Basilica of St. Paul some scenes underwent extensive restoration and repainting in the Middle Ages. It is clear, however, that the cycle with stories from the Old Testament in the Basilica of St. Paul depended on the Vatican model that must be older. A recent detailed and careful iconographic analysis by Cecilia Proverbio proposes to raise the dating of the Vatican cycle to the end of the fourth century,[25] but Hugo Brandenburg has proposed attributing these frescoes even to the Constantinian age.[26] Proverbio notes affinities with the iconographic tradition that later – at the end of the fifth century – merged into the Cotton Genesis codex, but also with that which produced the Vienna Genesis codex. The different iconographic traditions, however, are mixed without showing the prevalence of one or the other and further elements of different origins are added to them. It is therefore difficult to think that a monumental cycle of this size can be considered an epitome. Instead, it must be an original creation that combines elements drawn from multiple iconographic traditions.

In this regard we can also avail ourselves of an interesting written source: a passage from the *History of the Franks* related to the decoration of the St. Stephen's Basilica in Clermont. Gregory of Tours describes the wife of the bishop of that city, Namantius (446–462), as she chooses the subjects of the figural decoration of the basilica:[27]

> Cuius coniux basilicam sancti Stephani suburbano murorum aedificavit. Quam cum fucis colorum adornare velit, tenebat librum in sinum suum, legens historias actionis antiquae, pictoribus indicans, quae in parietibus fingere deberent.

> His wife built the church of Saint Stephen in the outskirts of the city. And wishing to adorn it with colours she used to carry a book in her bosom, reading the histories of ancient times and describing to the painters what they were to represent on the walls.

According to this text the source of the images is a book, but anyway the bishop's wife has 'read' it and given verbal directions to the painter. It was therefore the painter who had to choose the iconography useful to illustrate the events requested by the client on the basis of the written text. In this case also we can consider the decorative (lost) cycle of the Basilica of Clermont as an epitome in the broad sense, as it figuratively synthesized a written text that would have passed verbally through oral mediation.

We now come to one final point that still needs to be considered. So far, we have talked about written and figural texts of various kinds, but we have done so only in the abstract, without considering their use or their intended recipients and audience. The epitome of a verbal text generally serves a scholarly or educational use. Usually, it is used by a single person at a time or by a small group. In the case of the *Tabulae Iliacae* we could think of such scholarly use and a relatively limited audience.

But in the case of the cycles of frescoes of the early Christian basilicas the intended audience of the works is the whole people of God in a liturgical context. The clients, the recipients and the functions of the frescoes in a basilica are therefore very different from that of an illustrated codex or the epitome of a literary text. This means that the criteria with which it was developed must in fact differ significantly.

Let us now pull these seemingly disparate strands to a simple conclusion: the comparison between verbal and figural texts shows that the differences between the two semiotic systems are profound and structural. Moreover, the examples we possess have different functions and different audiences: accordingly, their horizon of expectations are different too. We must therefore be very cautious, as comparison between the two systems must be kept on a very general level, avoiding the pretension of transferring without careful adaptation in a specific field the concepts and terms that were developed distinctly for the other. That said, the relationship between image and figure can fruitfully be understood better when considered in the sense of complementarity and interaction than it would be merely in terms of duplication or imitation. We must resist the temptation to consider expressions such as the famous *bon mot* of Horace *ut pictura poësis*, or the definition of palaeochristian and early medieval figurative cycles as *biblia pauperum*, in too a mechanical manner, lacking the necessary qualifications.

Notes

* For help in the translation of my Italian text, I am deeply indebted to Alden Smith.

1. For the sake of clarity, I note here that I will use 'figural' as relating to human or animal figures and not as a synonym of 'metonymic'.
2. Settis 1986: 382–4; cf. Kinney 2006: 244–5.
3. Elsner 2000: 175–7; Fabricius Hansen 2003: 168–72; *contra* Liverani 2004: 386–9; Liverani 2011: 41–4; Liverani 2013: 354–5.
4. Kinney 1997: 119–22.
5. Compagnon 1979: 95–154; Svenbro 2004.
6. Liverani 2011.
7. Morawski 1970.
8. Goodman 1974: 299; Marin 1988; Groupe μ 1992: ch. 7; Stoichita 1997; Platt and Squire 2017; cf. Liverani 2018.
9. Goodman 1968.
10. Goodman 1974: 300 considers a figural quotation only in case of a photograph containing a duplicate of a second photograph, but this is precisely an allographic work.
11. Forero-Mendoza 2004: 25.
12. Genette 1997: 5-10.
13. Weitzmann 1947: 36–44; Weitzmann 1959: 31–62, especially 34–7.
14. Valenzuela Montenegro 2004; Squire 2011: 129–65.
15. Ong 1967: note 219; Liverani 2007.
16. Zumthor 1984: 36; Zumthor 1990: 25; Ong 1967. About the public readings of prose texts cf. Lizzi Testa 2004: 34–7 with further bibliography.
17. Knox 1968; Svenbro 1991: 161–87; Svenbro 1995.
18. Havelock 1983: 42–3, 109 ff, 162 ff; Zumthor 1984: 279–80; Ong 1986: 50, 59–65.
19. Small 2003: 156, 161.
20. Havelock 1983: 70, 73–4, 103, 138, 155, 106–7.
21. Jakobson 1959: 233.
22. Eco 2001: 75, 98, 106, 119.
23. Nestori and Bisconti 2000.
24. Proverbio 2016.
25. Ibid.
26. Brandenburg 2017: 95–101.
27. Gr. Tour., *Hist. Fr.* 2.17 (transl. E. Brehaut 1916).

Works cited

Brandenburg, H. (2017), *Die konstantinische Petersbasilika am Vatikan in Rom: Anmerkungen zu ihrer Chronologie, Architektur und Ausstattung*, Regensburg: Schnell & Steiner.

Brehaut, E. (1916), *History of the Franks by Gregory, Bishop of Tours* (Records of Civilization: Sources and Studies), New York: Columbia University Press.

Compagnon, A. (1979), *Le seconde main, ou le travail de la citation*, Paris: Seuil.

Eco, U. (2001), *Experiences in Translation*, Toronto: University of Toronto Press.

Elsner, J. (2000), 'From the Culture of Spolia to the Cult of Relics: The Arch of Constantine and the Genesis of Late Antique Forms', *Papers of the British School at Rome*, 68: 149–84.

Fabricius Hansen, M. (2003), *The Eloquence of Appropriation: Prolegomena to an Understanding of Spolia in Early Christian Rome, Analecta Romana Instituti Danici, Supplementa* 33, Rome.

Forero-Mendoza, S. (2004), 'De la citation dans l'art et dans la peinture en particulier', in P. Beylot (ed.), *Emprunts et citations dans le champ artistique*, 19–31, Paris: L'Harmattan.

Genette, G. (1997), *Palimpsests: Literature in the Second Degree*, trans. C. Newman and C. Doubinsky, Lincoln: University of Nebraska Press.

Goodman, N. (1968), *Languages of Art: An Approach to a Theory of Symbols*, Indianapolis, IN: Hackett Publishing.

Goodman, N. (1974), 'On Some Questions Concerning Quotation', *The Monist*, 58.2: 294–306.

Groupe μ (1992), (Edeline, F., Klinkenberg, J.-M. and Minguet, P.), *Traité du signe visuel : Pour une rhétorique de l'image*, Paris: Seuil.

Jakobson, R. (1959), 'On Linguistic Aspects of Translation', in R. A. Brower (ed.), *On Translation*, 232–9, Cambridge, MA: Harvard University Press.

Havelock, E. A. (1983), *Cultura orale e civiltà della scrittura: Da Omero a Platone*, trans. M. Capitella, Bari, Laterza.

Kinney, D. (1997), 'Spolia damnatio and renovatio memoriae', *Memoirs of the American Academy in Rome*, 42: 117–48.

Kinney, D. (2006), 'The concept of Spolia', in C. Rudolph (ed.), *A Companion to Medieval Art: Romanesque and Gothic in Northern Europe*, 233–52, Malden, MA: Wiley-Blackwell.

Knox, B. W. (1968), 'Silent Reading in Antiquity', *Greek, Roman and Byzantine Studies* 19: 421–35.

Liverani, P. (2004), 'Reimpiego senza ideologia. La lettura antica degli *spolia*, dall'Arco di Costantino all'età di Teodorico', *Mitteilungen des Deutschen Archäologischen Instituts. Römische Abteilung* 111: 383–434.

Liverani, P. (2007), 'Tradurre in immagini', in F. and T. Hölscher (eds), *Römische Bilderwelten: Von der Wirklichkeit zum Bild und zurück*, 13–26, Heidelberg: Verlag Archäologie und Geschichte.

Liverani, P. (2011), 'Reading Spolia in Late-Antiquity and Contemporary Perception', in R. Brilliant and D. Kinney (eds), *Reuse Value: Spolia and Appropriation in Art and Architecture, from Constantine to Sherrie Levine*, 33–51, Farnham: Ashgate.

Liverani, P. (2013), 'Il museo come «Spolienraum»', in S. Altekamp, C. Marcks-Jacobs and P. Seiler (eds), *Perspektiven der Spolienforschung 1. Spoliierung und Transposition* (Topoi 15), 351–66, Berlin-New York: De Gruyter.

Liverani, P. (2018), review of Platt and Squire 2017, *BMCR* 2018.06.25 http://bmcr.brynmawr.edu/2018/2018-06-25.html

Lizzi Testa, R. (2004), *Senatori, popolo, papi: Il governo a Roma al tempo dei Valentiniani*, Bari: Edipuglia.

Marin, L. (1988), 'Le cadre de la représentation et quelques-unes de ses figures', in *Art de voir; art de décrire II,* Les Cahiers du Musée national d'art moderne 24, 62–81, Paris.

Morawski, S. (1970), 'The Basic Functions of Quotation', in A. J. Greimas et al. (eds), *Sign, Language, Culture*, Janua Linguarum, Series major 1, 690–705, The Hague: Mouton.

Nestori, A. and F. Bisconti, (2000), *I mosaici paleocristiani di Santa Maria Maggiore negli acquerelli della collezione Wilpert*, Vatican City: Pontificio Istituto di Archeologia Cristiana.
Ong, W. J. (1967), *Presence of the Word*, New Haven, CT: Yale University Press.
Ong, W. J. (1986), *Hopkins, the Self, and God*, Toronto: University of Toronto Press.
Platt, V. and M. Squire, (2017), 'Framing the Visual in Greek and Roman Antiquity: An Introduction', in V. Platt and M. Squire (eds), *The Frame in Classical Art: A Cultural History*, 3–99, Cambridge: Cambridge University Press.
Proverbio, C. (2016), *I cicli affrescati paleocristiani di San Pietro in Vaticano e San Paolo Fuori le mura. Proposte di lettura*, Bibliothèque del l'Antiquité Tardive 33, Turnhout: Brepols.
Settis, S. (1986), 'Continuità, distanza, conoscenza. Tre usi dell'antico', in S. Settis (ed.), *Memoria dell'antico nell'arte italiana* III, Turin: Einaudi.
Small, J. P. (2003), *The Parallel Worlds of Classical Art and Text*, Cambridge, MA: Cambridge University Press.
Squire, M. (2011), *The Iliad in a Nutshell: Visualizing Epic on the* Tabulae Iliacae, Oxford New York: Oxford University Press.
Stoichita, V. I. (1997), *The Self-Aware Image: An Insight into Early Modern Meta-Painting*, Cambridge: Cambridge University Press.
Svenbro, J. (1991), *Storia della lettura nella Grecia antica*, trans. V. Laurenzi, Bari: Laterza.
Svenbro, J. (1995), 'La Grecia arcaica e classica. L'invenzione della lettura silenziosa', in G. Cavallo and R. Chartier (eds), *Storia della lettura*, 3–36, Bari: Laterza.
Svenbro, J. (2004), 'Façons grecques de dire «citer»', in C. Darbo Peschanski (ed.), *La citation dans l'antiquité*, 265–79, Grenoble: Million.
Valenzuela Montenegro, N. (2004), *Die* Tabulae Iliacae: *Mythos und Geschichte im Spiegel einer Gruppe frühkaiserzeitlicher Miniaturreliefs*, Berlin: dissertation.de.
Weitzmann, K. (1947), *Illustrations in Roll and Codex: A Study in Origin and Method of Text Illustration*, Studies in Manuscript Illumination 2, Princeton, NJ: Princeton University Press.
Weitzmann, K. (1959), *Ancient Book Illumination*, Cambridge, MA: Harvard University Press.
Zumthor, P. (1984), *La presenza della voce: Introduzione alla poesia orale*, trans. C. Di Girolamo, Bologna: Il Mulino.
Zumthor, P. (1990), *La lettera e la voce: Sulla «letteratura» medievale*, trans. M. Liborio, Bologna: Il Mulino.

CHAPTER 5
SARCINATOREM ESSE SUMMUM: NONIUS MARCELLUS AND THE MODERN EDITOR AS TEXTUAL FRANKENSTEINS

Matthew Payne

A lexicon consisting of thousands of quotations with only the briefest discussion may not seem to have much in common with epitomes at first glance, not least since epitomes usually consist of rewritten, concentrated summaries of material, whereas quotations are defined by the verbatim repetition of material. However, in this chapter I will be exploring how changing attitudes towards knowledge in the late antique period shaped the creation of both these kinds of texts.[1] The fragmentation of older texts in order to recombine them and reuse them for other purposes and to make comparison between them easier is a pattern shared by both epitomes and grammatical lexica, and reflects conceptions of time and cultural inheritance in late antiquity.[2] Yet the fragmentation created by these works and the posture that they adopt towards the texts they rework have also contributed towards modern scholarly attempts to reconstruct the texts these 'secondary' works adapt. In the case of Nonius Marcellus' lexicon, this is achieved by further fragmentation and recombination. My title comes from a fragment of Lucilius cited by Nonius; in their different ways Nonius and modern editors of editions of fragmentary works create by stitching the scraps of other works together, transforming them into new autonomous creations.[3] I will show how there are more parallels that result from this phenomenon of fragmentation between late antique grammatical writers and modern scholars than might be expected. I will start by providing a brief overview of this lexicon, *De Compendiosa Doctrina*, and how fragmentation is observed in the circumstances and nature of its composition, before considering what Nonius' relationship with the texts he quotes and the grammatical tradition he operates within indicates about the conceptualization of knowledge in the late antique period.[4]

The nature of Nonius' *De Compendiosa Doctrina*

Nonius Marcellus' *De Compendiosa Doctrina* is a twenty-book lexicon covering a variety of the grammatical and semantic aspects of words. What we know about its author is limited, but he seems to have come from the north African town of Thurbusicum Numidarum, and most likely he was alive during the early fourth century.[5] Although almost every entry begins with a keyword (a 'lemma') whose form or meaning is explicated, *De compendiosa doctrina* is not a dictionary, since Nonius is just as interested in morphological variants and grammatical gender as synonymy and definition. Another crucial feature significantly separates *De Compendiosa Doctrina* from the average glossary: his use of quotation. At least one quotation is found for almost every entry of the lexicon; usually there are multiple quotations. The words within quotations make up the vast majority of words in the lexicon.

It is not merely that quotations provide content in Nonius' work, but they also shape its structure. At the turn of the last century, Wallace M. Lindsay, building on the hypotheses of a number of earlier nineteenth-century scholars, divined the architecture of the lexicon.[6] Understanding how the work was constructed has been hugely important for understanding the lexicon, because so much about the work is opaque.[7] Nonius had drawn up forty-two lists of items to be discussed from his reading, which included many literary texts as well as some earlier grammatical and lexicographical works. For each book, Nonius worked through the lists in the same order, proceeding through the items that he had picked out, making each of these items a lemma in the lexicon. If this had been all Nonius had done, his working method would have been easier to reconstruct, but in addition to the quotation that first prompted the keyword for the lemma (the 'leading' quotation, to use Lindsay's terminology) Nonius would sometimes also supplement this with further quotations from other lists that also contained the keyword of the lemma.[8] By this method, Nonius worked from his texts to the lemmas, rather than devising his lemmas first and then illustrating them from quotations he found.

Past and present: Nonius on 'antiquity'

An important feature of Nonius' lexicon that is arguably characteristic of many late antique texts and other cultural objects is its conception of time. Nonius' only representation of chronology within his lexicon is a binary between then and now.[9] 'Then' is the period in which the texts he cites from were written, whose authors he calls the *ueteres* (literally, 'the old ones'). 'Now' is represented by contemporary usage, by the time in which the authorial 'we' occupies. 'Then' is a colossal time period spanning from Livius Andronicus and the beginnings of Latin literature to Augustan writers such as Virgil and Horace, a period of almost three hundred years.[10] 'Now' is not merely Nonius' present: previous writers in the grammatical tradition, such as Aulus Gellius, are also included, and Nonius often simply echoes these sources (*dicimus*, 'we say').[11] Aligned with this artificial then/now, past/present binary is the distinction drawn between *consuetudo* and *auctoritas*.[12] The terms themselves are familiar from Varro's enumeration of the four grounds to explain linguistic usage and norms: *natura*, *analogia*, *consuetudo* and *auctoritas*.[13] Nonius never mentions the first two terms and the concepts appear only rarely, but the last two are frequently used by Nonius, and operate as binary categories, although they can align.[14] A good example is the following lemma:

> MODICVM in consuetudine pausillum uolumus significare; modicum ueteres moderatum et cum modo dici uolunt.
>
> *Nonius 342.23–24 M = 541 L*

> We customarily intend *MODICVS* to mean 'very small', but the old authors intend it to mean 'moderate' and 'limited'.

Here the dichotomy between the first person plural 'we' and *consuetudo* on the one hand and the *ueteres* on the other is clear. While the *ueteres* can be spoken of in the literary present tense, other lemmata make the past / present distinction obvious:

> SQVALERE non sordium plenum esse tantummodo, ut nunc consuetudine persuasum est, sed et honesta re abundare et refertum esse ueteres honesta auctoritate posuerunt.
>
> *Nonius 452.18–20 M = 752 L*

> The old authors did not only use *SQVALERE* to mean 'full of dirt', as is now established in contemporary usage, but also, on good authority, to mean 'overflowing' or 'abounding with' something positive.

Here we can see the opposition between *nunc* and *consuetudo*, on the one hand, and the *ueteres* and their *auctoritas* on the other. Almost always it is only the *ueteres* who possess *auctoritas*; the few exceptions are revealing and I will discuss them later in this chapter. The reduction of several hundred years of very different works and authors into this one category of *ueteres* both eases and is supported by the fragmentation and paralleling of those texts. Nonius, when he assigns all the Republican and Augustan authors to this homogenous category, makes it easier to present linguistic evidence from any one of his authors for any grammatical point. At the same time, the fragmentation of texts into short quotes reduces consciousness of the extent of thematic, generic and temporal differences between these texts, as Nonius presents quotes from different authors as pertinent to the same grammatical question.[15] Yet this arrangement of quotations from different authors where a point of linguistic usage can be paralleled, speaks to the importance of synoptic reading, a trend that we can already detect in Gellius.[16]

The binaries present in Nonius' lexicon, between past and present, *auctoritas* and *consuetudo*, *ueteres* and 'we', are suggestive of the concept of anachronicity, developed by Nagel and Wood (2010) and already applied to late antiquity by Formisano (2017). In the grammatical text, like the Renaissance artworks that Nagel and Wood (2010) explore and the panegyric and historical texts considered by Formisano (2017), the artificial past and present are both opposed yet also placed in close dialogue. History is reshaped to maintain this: the *grammatici* belong to the authorial 'we', even if they are long dead and closer to the *ueteres* than Nonius' audience. But it is the few rare moments in which texts from long after the Augustan era, even Nonius' own literary efforts, appear as citations within Nonius' lexicon that make the anachronic a useful concept to apply to Nonius, for it is one way to make sense of these instances, which I explore further below.

The veneration Nonius displays towards *antiquitas* is on full display in his lemma *VETVSTAS* (184M): *uetustas et antiquitas uel felix uel sapiens uel mansueta est habita* ('the words *uetustas* and *antiquitas* were used to mean "happy" or "wise" or "affable"').[17] Very occasionally in Nonius' lexicon the usage of past and present can align, but usually it does not. The need to make sense of the past, to break down its vast edifice of texts into quotations, to translate forgotten words and meanings through other, contemporary words would seem to speak to a sense of distance.[18] The past can be comprehended, its knowledge analysed, but only in the particular. The comparison between the creation of centos and the phenomenon of spoliation has been pursued as a reflection of attitudes towards the past, but this could be broadened still further to include the treatment of classical literature by late antique grammatical texts such as Nonius.[19] Like Nonius' work, centos also extract material from the past to recontextualize in the present, and yet the obvious repurposing of verbatim material found in the *Cento Probae* is not quite the same as the reframing of verbatim material in Nonius' lexicon.[20] Moreover, as Sowers (Chapter 2) shows, for Nonius' (probable) contemporary Ausonius, the creative processes of fragmentation and recomposition extend across far more of Ausonius' works than just his *Cento Nuptialis*. So these creative processes of fragmentation and recomposition might be reflective of an attitude towards the past and found in a wide variety of late antique texts, objects and performances, which excerpt and reframe, isolating and translating.[21] (Liverani in Chapter 4 provides some examples from visual culture of similar processes.) To evaluate where Nonius' lexicon belongs on this hypothetical spectrum, and what dynamic it creates between past and present, it is necessary to scrutinize how Nonius regards these fragments of the past and the ways they come to him.

Quotation and epitomization

Nonius' quotations shape his work in a much more direct way than grammars, where larger overarching structures (e.g., parts of speech, or rhetorical topoi) provide the skeleton, even if the grammars, like Nonius' lexicon, are substantially aimed at the explication of literary texts. It is in this process of selecting material to reduce a text's size to something smaller that still serves the grammarian's purposes, that – I suggest – we can see a process of epitomization.[22] What separates Nonius' lexicon from texts we would conventionally identify as epitomes is that for an epitome, the content that interests the original author and the creator of the epitome is often taken to be the same. For Nonius, his interest in grammatical matters is at a different level from those of the quoted authors, who created their texts for literary, historiographic or other purposes. But the process of epitomization, if seen as a process of repackaging existing cultural knowledge in order to satisfy the new requirements of later readers, is at the heart of Nonius' project.[23]

The re-use of fragmented material is something Nonius and later scholars who work on Nonius have in common. Both take material and restructure it from the arrangement in which they find it according to their own organizational and thematic criteria. Both Nonius and modern scholars working on him note the origin of the fragmented material even as they separate it from that origin. Both Nonius and Nonian scholars also minimize the impact of their interventions, presenting themselves as engaged merely in the presentation of material, that their different kinds of glosses – lexical and reconstructive – are, to some extent, self-evident, readily apparent to every reader of these textual fragments.

Yet how fragments are combined and contextualized can affect what impressions and understandings are formed of them.[24] It is in the interest of the scholarly reconstructor to present Nonius as devoid of personality and agency, and in the process suggest that his intervention in the process of the formations of these fragments is limited solely to the reduction of wholeness to fragmentedness. This idea has been supported by Nonian scholars themselves. Back in 1902 Lindsay argued that Nonius' methodical working process fundamentally characterized him: 'this mechanical regularity is not inconsistent with what we can infer of Nonius' type of mind', and it is striking how often this sentence is quoted approvingly by subsequent scholars of Nonius.[25] On this point it is worth comparing the belittling of Cornelius Nepos by some modern scholars highlighted by Hudson in Chapter 3. But it is the idea of Nonius and his text as characteristically 'mechanical' that is so important for the rhetoric of the reconstructor, because it suggests that all that is needed to restore the text from the fragments is the equally mechanical undoing of the process of fragmentation.[26] In this respect, parallels can be observed with previous scholarly attitudes towards the epitomist, where scholars have sometimes, for their own interests, insufficiently recognized that 'they reflect the interests of the authors who cite or summarize lost works as much or more than the characteristics of the works concerned'.[27] At other times, however, when Nonius seems to have made a mistake, he is depicted as a dopey scribe, a copyist ignorant of what he is copying.[28] Aside from passages where Nonius is in error, where hope is often abandoned, reconstruction involves nothing more than a systematic reversal of Nonius' process of fragmentation – all the parts remain fundamentally unchanged and the machine's original function *qua* text can be restored – and the reconstructor is equally as mechanical as Nonius: an insult to Nonius' abilities rebounds to the credit of the reconstructor, because describing reconstruction as mechanical process – a careful stripping down of the parts of Nonius' dictionary, close examination and fitting back together into their respective original machines – presents it as far more objective, with right and wrong answers, than any alternative.

Nonian deconstruction in action: Nonius' use of Aulus Gellius' *Noctes Atticae*

One way in which we can observe greater agency for Nonius is the differences between the relationships that he establishes with his grammatical predecessors and with the authors he quotes. A difficulty in judging this is that while Nonius probably constructs some of his lists from grammatical works such as Verrius Flaccus' *De uerborum significatu*, such works are not among those that survive to us: we only have an impression of Verrius Flaccus' work from the incomplete work of the second-century writer Festus that was based on it, which was itself catastrophically damaged and for which we lean heavily on the epitome made of it by Paul the Deacon in the eighth century. In this tale of tattered remains, it is not surprising that it is difficult to evaluate what stance Nonius might have taken towards his grammarian ancestors. However, one author who offers a way to understand how Nonius positions himself in the grammatical tradition is Aulus Gellius.[29]

Nonius does not name Gellius once. Often Nonius attributes his quotation directly to the original author, with no indication that Gellius is the author who has passed it on, but since Gellius often omits the title of a work, Nonius must do so too, which means that such citations differ markedly from his lemmata for other lists. It is interesting, then, to see the different ways in which Nonius appropriates Gellius' material and adapts it for his own work. This is the application of the fragmentary process to material that has already been fragmented, as Gellius excerpts his own material from previous texts.

Aulus Gellius' *Noctes Atticae* is a highly discursive work, and critics are increasingly recognizing the role that narrative plays across Gellius' creation, both within chapters themselves that feature characters and stories and between books, through recurring characters, topics and themes, even if the episodes in contiguous chapters do not tend to exhibit narrative continuity.[30] Nonius' use of Gellius shows what occurs when narrative is stripped from the *Noctes Atticae* in an attempt to engage with the writings that Gellius is working with, or the writings Nonius thinks Gellius is working with. This is why it is worth moving away from the idea of Nonius 'plagiarizing' Gellius.[31] Rather, Nonius seeks to cut through Gellius to the authors whom Gellius refers to. At times Nonius does effectively lift Gellius' words written *in propria persona* – though at others Nonius rewords a statement or paraphrases it. When Gellius' words are lifted, it may be a question of efficiency, or a wariness that rewording could result in distortion. Nonius' priority is communicating the material that Gellius is transmitting. Here, again, we face the desire to minimize the role of a transmitting author and to maintain the façade that even if information can be altered in the mediation process the effects of that mediation can be later undone and the original information reconstructed and recorded.

Rethinking Nonian concerns over Gellian *auctoritas*

However, it is notable that whereas Nonius has some select writers to whom he attributes *auctoritas*, many of the entries sourced from Gellius express concerns about *auctoritas*. Previous scholars have suggested that these are directed at Gellius himself, that Gellius lacks *auctoritas*. But as we have already seen, even if Gellius predates Nonius by several hundred years, he belongs to some degree, like other grammatical writers, to the Nonian 'now', rather than the 'then' of the *ueteres*. As I will try to show, it is arguably not so much that Gellius lacks *auctoritas*, than it is that Nonius does not consider *auctoritas* the best dimension in which to measure Gellius: *auctoritas* can only and should only be assessed with regard to the *ueteres*. Perhaps Nonius simply is not concerned with whether Gellius as a grammatical writer has *auctoritas* or not; yet he is very much concerned with whether authors cited, discussed or mentioned by Gellius have *auctoritas* or not. But the situation is complex and merits detailed attention paid to the exact wording Nonius uses in any given instance.

For a start, there are plenty of entries drawn from Gellius where *auctoritas* is not mentioned at all and where Nonius presents definitions and citations without any comment, as though the works cited from, the works that were originally cited by Gellius, are ones to which Nonius himself has direct access, such as the sequence of lemmata *CISSIVM* to *COPIATVR* in Book 2:

> CISSIVM, uehiculi biroti genus. M. Tullius Philipp. libro II: 'delituit in quadam caupona atque ibi se occultans perpotum cisio domum uenit.'
>
> CELERATIM, celeriter. Sisenna *Historiarum* lib. VI: 'quo magis celeratim poterant, insidiis suos disponit.'
>
> COPIATVR, a copia, honeste positum, ut lignantur et pabulantur et aquantur. Coelius lib. I: 'armis et magno commeatu et praeda ingenti copiantur.' Vergilius *Georgicorum* lib. IV: 'sub moenibus urbis aquantur.'
>
> *Nonius 86.29–87.7 M = 123 L*

> CISSIVM, a kind of two-wheeled vehicle. Marcus Tullius Cicero in the second book of the *Philippics*: 'he skulked in some tavern, got drunk while hiding, then came home in a gig'.
>
> CELERATIM 'quickly'. Sisenna in the fourth book of his *Histories*: 'wherefore as quickly as they were able, he stationed his men in ambush'.
>
> COPIATVR, from 'possessions', used with good sense, like 'they fetched wood' or 'they pastured' or 'they watered'. Coelius in his first book: 'they take possession of many weapons and a large quantity of provisions and a great deal of booty'. Virgil in the fourth book of the *Georgics*: 'under the walls of the town they watered'.

Here all the lemmata are sourced from Gellius but the format does not differ from any of the other lists.[32] And in this list there is no indication that there is any other source for these citations than the quoted work itself. We might miss that these entries were indirectly sourced if the *Attic Nights* had not survived, even though Nonius has even lifted much of his definition directly from Gellius, although there is a clue in the switch from singular *copiatur* to the plurals.[33] This appropriation of Gellian material without comment is not the case for some lemmata, however, such as on *NOCTESCERE*:

> NOCTESCERE, caecari. Furius poematis, etsi est auctoritatis incertae: 'omnia noctescunt tenebris caliginis atrae'.
>
> *Nonius 145.9–11 M = 211 L*

> NOCTESCERE, to be obscured. Furius in his poems, although he is of uncertain authority: 'Everything becomes obscured in the murk of the black darkness'.

Here Nonius caveats the citation.[34] Nonius' estimations of Furius as a writer seem to be complicated by Nonius' awareness of his reliance on Gellius alone for information about Furius, when Gellius himself probably knew very little of the poet. In the relevant Gellian chapter, Gellius is writing about the opinion of Casellius Vindex about Furius Antias, noting the words that he took issue with and giving the lines those words appear in, as part of his objections to Casellius' treatment of Furius.[35] Gellius himself describes Furius as a *uetus* and praises him. Gellius offers no supporting material, such as other parallels in Furius, for his disagreement with Casellius' grammatical judgement, which would strongly suggest that Gellius has no access to Furius outside Casellius. Nonius may well have been able to draw this conclusion too. Nonius may be questioning Furius' authority not because of any qualitative judgement of Furius as a writer, but because Nonius is conscious that very little is now to be known of Furius.

Moreover, Furius' *auctoritas* is stated to be in question, not necessarily lacking. In contrast, for the lemmata above, Nonius himself makes use of Cicero's *Philippics* and the third and fourth books of Sisenna's *Histories*, which might offer an explanation why Nonius does not question their *auctoritas* when they appear in Gellius. Nonius never quotes anything that he says has no authority or lacks authority; but when he does quote from a work and make a reference to authority, all of the terms he uses when he does include a quotation could indicate epistemic uncertainty.[36] On the one hand, this may be purely coincidental, but, on the other, it may suggest that when Nonius is unsure whether to credit a source with good authority, he prefers to offer his readers the verbatim quotation, inform them of his own uncertainty, and let them judge for themselves.

In the last lemma in the *CISSIUM* sequence, *COPIATVR*, Nonius does not attribute the usage to Q. Claudius Quadrigarius, as Gellius does, but attributes it instead to Coelius. While this is usually seen as a mistake by Nonius it is worth reflecting that Nonius does this to four of Gellius' citations of Quadrigarius in this chapter. This could well be because Nonius has indeed made a mistake, but it could also be because he does not trust Gellius' attribution, perhaps due to some other authority – that Nonius trusted more – attributing these lines to Coelius (presumably, Nonius means L. Coelius Antipater, quoted by Nonius side-by-side with Quadrigarius elsewhere).[37] In the remaining lemma *DIVRNARE*, which features a quotation of Quadrigarius taken from the same Gellian chapter, Nonius does not mention either his name or the work, instead describing the citation as from 'a careful ancient writer of unrecognized authority' (*ueterem prudentem auctoritatis incognitae*). Here, the line appears at the end of the chapter, so we could ascribe this to Nonius' incompetence, that he forgot which writer was being discussed. But another alternative could be that whatever authority compelled Nonius to attribute the other lines to Coelius was lacking this line. In any case, I would argue that Nonius' phrase *ueterem prudentem auctoritatis incognitae* does not treat Gellius as a *uetus* or state anything directly about his *auctoritas* – rather it indicates that concerns are often triggered in Nonius about the *auctoritas* of a quoted author when *Attic Nights* is the source of such a quotation.[38] It is worth considering the intertwining of the concepts of 'authorship' and 'authority' in the term *auctoritas*: to be unsure of the authorship of a phrase containing a linguistic anomaly would naturally entail uncertainty over the authority of those words as a pattern for acceptable language.

With other citations drawn from Gellius, on closer inspection it seems more plausible that Nonius' parenthetical comments like *ueterem prudentem auctoritatis incognitae* apply principally to what Gellius is quoting, not Gellius himself directly. Nonius makes such comments about *auctoritas* even if the Gellian citation does not refer within Gellius to a literary text as such comparable with those Nonius uses as the base for his other lists. For instance, the lemma for *APLVDAS* is based on Gellius, but Nonius' parenthetical comment (*hoc in antiquis inuenitur, quorum in dubio auctoritas*) would seem to refer to the lawyer and the legal commentaries this lawyer consults within Gellius' narrative who introduces the quotations from the *ueteres*: it is this lawyer who does the 'finding' in Gellius' text. All of the other lemmata where we observe this phenomenon, I suggest, also exhibit the same characteristics.[39] What this hopefully shows is that, contrary to previous conclusions, plausibly there is no case in which Gellius is described as both *prudens* or *uetus* by Nonius and yet also of dubious authority.[40] Instead, it is whoever Nonius takes Gellius' source to be that is described in such a way, and because frequently these are anonymous figures like the lawyer, or figures whose names would probably be meaningless to Nonius, then by definition their authorship, and thus their authority, is frequently in question. This seems more plausible than combinations such as *uetus prudens auctoritatis incognitae* being wholly about Gellius, which is oxymoronic when the status of *uetus* is an indication of respect in all other instances in Nonius' work, and it also makes more sense of why Nonius can happily extract citations without caveat from Gellius on some occasions while expressing these concerns about *auctoritas* at other points.

What these different instances point to is that when Nonius mentions deficiencies of *auctoritas* in a lemma drawn from Gellius, Nonius may not be simply disparaging Gellius' *auctoritas* in contrast to a favourite author like Virgil, but rather that *auctoritas* is diminished when a mediating author must be relied upon, particularly if that mediating author does not present information in a way that can be easily and satisfactorily adjusted to Nonius' format to provide the fragmented quotation with a clear provenance. This would tally with Nonius' strenuous attempts to reach past Gellius to the texts that he uses. For example, in the lemma *FLAVISAS* (112.26–113.2 M = 161–62 L), Nonius alters Gellius' indirect discourse in which Gellius is apparently paraphrasing Varro into a direct quotation, but without changing its grammatical construction, leaving it as an accusative-infinitive construction and with its first-person plural voice.[41]

Mediation, mediator and the reader's trust

For many lemmata, for which Gellius yields citations in Nonius' preferred format, Nonius seems to simply ignore Gellius: Gellius' mediation leaving no trace.[42] This is not unusual but rather the standard practice for writers in the grammatical tradition – they leave earlier grammatical writers unnamed while naming the authors of the literary works they quote and discuss. Nonius can treat glossaries in the same way as he treats Gellius, for instance, in his lemma *CINIS*:[43]

> CINIS . . . feminino apud Caesarem et Catullum et Caluum lectum est, quorum uaccillat auctoritas: 'cum iam fulua cinis fueris'.
>
> *Nonius 198.13–15 M = 291 L*

> CINIS ... it is found in the feminine in the work of Caesar and Catullus and Calvus, whose authorship is unclear: 'when soon you will be tawny ash'.

These are authors contemporary with Cicero and prior to Virgil, and so Nonius seems to be flagging the ambiguity of authorship of the line, rather than the authority of these figures.[44] In this lemma it is unclear whether the citation should be attributed to Caesar, Catullus or Calvus, or to which work the line belongs: this must be due to how the glossary preserved the information, and obviously does not fit with Nonius' format for the lexicon.

Nonius effectively ignores Gellius as an author, is bothered by him as a mediator, and dispenses with him entirely where possible. And yet Nonius is also concerned not to wander too far from Gellius with respect to the material he preserves. This problematization of mediation and mediator seems to be a theme not only with Nonius, but also with Gellius and leads to something of a paradox. On the one hand, the ideal Nonius and Gellius propound is to read texts directly for oneself. On the other, Nonius and Gellius both create texts that extract the desired information from those texts, rendering direct engagement apparently redundant. With respect to this paradox, it is worth contrasting Ausonius' blunter claims to be superseding Suetonius in his verse epitome, as discussed by Sowers in Chapter 2. Gellius voices the paradox almost explicitly:

> Ego uero, cum illud Ephesii uiri summe nobilis verbum cordi haberem, quod profecto ita est πολυμαθίη νόον οὐ διδάσκει, ipse quidem uoluendis transeundisque multis admodum uoluminibus per omnia semper negotiorum interualla in quibus furari otium potui exercitus defessusque sum, sed modica ex his eaque sola accepi quae aut ingenia prompta expeditaque ad honestae eruditionis cupidinem utiliumque artium contemplationem celeri facilique compendio ducerent aut homines aliis iam uitae negotiis occupatos a turpi certe agrestique rerum atque uerborum imperitia uindicarent.
>
> *Gell.* NA *pr. 1.12*

> Indeed, since I took the well-known and noble sentiment of that old Ephesian to heart, that 'A great deal of learning does not an educated mind make', I busied myself to the point of exhaustion with opening and unrolling many a scroll whenever I had a break from business and I could steal a spare moment, but I selected a modest number and only those which could either lead prompt and ready minds to the desire for honest learning and the examination of useful skills by a quick and easy shortcut, or so that men already busy with all the other tasks of life could overcome a repulsive and moronic ignorance of literature and other matters.

Gellius does split his audience into two groups, those for whom his work might be a spur to their own reading, and those who may be too busy for anything other than reading his work. But then his description of his own busyness in the preceding sentence suggests that Gellius does not think this a good enough reason not to read for oneself. But the paradox is in the juxtaposition of 'the quick and easy short-cut', by which he means his work, and the desire for erudition, which he thinks everyone should strive to possess. Gellius is certainly not the first Latin author to be concerned about so-called shortcuts to knowledge: Seneca the Younger evinces suspicion of epitomic writing when he worries that his addressee Lucilius might neglect true engagement with the great philosophers in favour of abbreviations of their work.[45] Nothing about Gellius' efforts sounds particularly easy, but offering the results in the form of his work means that his reader does not need to match his efforts. It is noteworthy that the title of Nonius' work, *De compendiosa doctrina*, 'Abridged Erudition', not only echoes Gellius' words about his own work as a 'short-cut' (*compendium*), but also encapsulates this paradox shared by both epitomes and Nonius' work.[46]

Scavenging knowledge

This paradox similarly emerges with another of Nonius' lemmata based off Gellius:

> MENDICIMONIVM et MOECHIMONIVM Laberius in libro quem *Cophinum* inscripsit. in eo uerba haec inueniet, qui doctrinae studium putauerit adhibendum.
>
> *Nonius 140.31–33 M = 205 L*

> MENDICIMONIVM and MOECHIMONIVM Laberius in his book which is entitled *Cophinus*. In it whoever thinks that they should put effort into learning will find these words.

This is given in Nonius' second book of innovative coinages by writers. The lemma is based on a Gellian chapter devoted to many of Laberius' coinages in his mimes [farces that included spoken dialogue and songs], and in fact Gellius merely states the words *mendicimonium* and *moechimonium* in a general list as examples of new coinages, along with *adulterionum, depudicauit* and *abluium*, and then *Cophinum* is the first title that Gellius specifically mentions (for the use of *manuatus est* for 'he stole'). On a charitable, hypothetical interpretation, Nonius assumed that these words belonged to mimes in the same book that the mime *Cophinus* belonged to, and that *Cophinus* furnished the name for this collection of mimes, perhaps because it was the first mime in this collection.[47] This would require Nonius to know that Laberius wrote mimes and that mimes were gathered into collections.[48] All of this is a hypothetical proposal for what Nonius thought Gellius was doing, but if there is anything to this, it suggests that Nonius thought Gellius operated in a similar fashion to himself, reading through a scroll or codex and picking out lemmata from a series of works in order. And it shows Nonius trying to make the most out of his source: he was aware (on this charitable reading) that he did not have the title for the exact mime these words came from, but he made a logical leap, in order to avoid simply leaving it as 'from Laberius', as he must for five other lemmata.[49] Modern critics should perhaps have at least some sympathy for Nonius trying to make as much as he can of the fragmentary scraps a previous writer has bequeathed him. Yet at the same time, Nonius, while struggling with the difficulties of the fragmentary, also participates fully in the fragmentizing process, taking his own whole texts and abbreviating them into grammaticalized atoms for his successors.

While the *MENDICIMONIVM* lemma suggests that Nonius and the modern scholar working on him in fact share frustrations and approaches that are more similar than the latter might wish to acknowledge, the second half of the lemma, with its keyword *doctrina*, encapsulates the paradox at the heart of Nonius' work. Owing to the deficiencies (a favourite word of Nonius' own critics) of Gellius – Nonius' intermediating, fragmenting source – Nonius cannot offer his reader the quotation of Laberius that he wishes to. Instead, he advises anyone who thinks that they should exercise their zeal for learning to find it for themselves in Laberius' work. This is a good method for making the most out of a bad situation, but it points to a similar problem that underlies Gellius' work. If hunting down words in obscure texts demonstrates a love of learning, then all the rest of Nonius' quotations do not seem to encourage such reading. While Nonius' search for such quotations would demonstrate his *doctrina*, providing such quotations to his reader would seemingly remove any incentive or encouragement to cultivate their own *doctrina*. In the other lemma, based on the same Gellian chapter, Nonius issues such an encouragement:

> ADVLTERIONEM pro adultero Laberius *Cophino*. quem si quis legere uoluerit, ibi inueniet et fidem nostram sua diligentia adiuuabit.
>
> *Nonius 70.3–5 M = 97 L*

> ADVLTERIONEM for adultery, Laberius in *Cophinus*. Whoever wishes to read it will find this word there and through their scrupulousness they will endorse our trustworthiness.

Any reader who would chase down the quotation in Laberius' work would in fact be supporting Nonius' efforts to convince the reader to trust him as he passes on his knowledge to the reader. This goes even further in posing the problem that while Nonius seems to ascribe to the values of conducting one's own research, of reading texts for oneself, his work in a fundamental fashion renders that step superfluous.[50] Nonius' text is precisely addressed at the difficulty in finding the contexts for odd grammatical words, and yet, like Gellius' text, participates and drives the process that strips context from these words. This is not a soluble tension, and at base it exists because of a clash between distinguishing oneself as an individual, as an exemplary possessor of the values esteemed by the grammatical tradition, of knowledge and judgement, and also participating in the community that upholds and subscribes to those values.[51]

The remark that it is up to the reader to find the citation also admits something that is so often suppressed in Nonius' work: that all these quotations belong to works that the reader both is and is not reading. The reader is reading words that belong to these works, but in their snatched lines and disconnectedness, whatever their level of contextual knowledge, the reader is aware that much is missing. The reference to Nonius' confidence in the reader is also a reverse from the rest of the lexicon, where it is the reader who must place their trust in Nonius, even though Nonius himself has already shown how he is reluctant to place his own trust in other makers of glossaries. In several of the definitions of *fides*, Nonius gives a definition that something is as it seems (313.20 M = 489 L, 23.11–13 M = 35 L), and Nonius gives one definition of *credere* as *fidem habere dictis uel factis* (275.4 M = 421 L) ('to have faith in what is said or done'). The reader must have confidence that Nonius presents his citations truthfully. But the reverse is not true, except for *adulterio* and *mendicimonium*, that Nonius requires his reader to prove themselves worthy of Nonius' confidence: for all his other lemmata Nonius never places any burden on the reader that requires Nonius to trust the reader or that asks for any input or participation by his audience. Nonius' desired result is the production of apparently autonomous grammatical statements and proofs that require no interpretation or criticism by his audience. In this respect his position (to the extent we can infer it from such meagre scraps) is antithetical to Gellius' stated opinions, even if in practice, because of the fragmenting processes that they both adopt, the situations that they each bequeath the reader become, as time passes and the source texts lost, very similar. And yet even Gellius, while often extolling the merits of argument and discussion, tends towards a rhetoric of authoritative assertions and incontrovertible proofs framed as the self-evident statements of the *ueteres*. Perhaps this is the greatest problem for Nonius with Gellius: his mediation, his presence in between Nonius and the *ueteres* figures Nonius' textual encounter with them, recounted to his reader, not as privileged, fleeting encounter, but as merely another link in the chain of transmission. Gellius' presence speaks to continuity, to progression, which is opposed to the anachronic.[52]

Becoming *docti*

The references to inadequate *auctoritas* shown by other glossaries and the *auctoritas* that Nonius invests in the ancient authors combine to reflect on Nonius' own status as an author. By emphasizing that his grammatical points are underpinned by texts written by *auctores*, he bolsters his own work with their *auctoritas*. When, for instance, Nonius states *pauciens pro raro dici ueterum auctoritas docet*, he elides his own role of grammatical teacher into the authority of the *ueteres*. On one occasion, such an elision is made explicit, in his lemma on MERIDIEM, where Nonius offers a quotation from his own work alongside one from Varro:

> MERIDIEM mediam diei partem omnes putant solum esse dicendam, cum et noctis et aetatis partem doctorum auctoritas dixerit. Varro *Marcipore*: 'repente noctis circiter meridie, cum pictus aer feruidis late ignibus caeli chorean astricen ostenderet'. nos in epistulis quae inscribuntur a doctrinis de peregrinando: 'exuigila igitur aliquando et moracium cogitationum, priusquam aetas in meridie est, torpidinem pelle'.
>
> *Nonius 451.5–13 M = 723 L*

> MERIDIES: Everyone thinks that it should only be used for the mid-point of the day, although learned authorities use it of the night and the year. Varro in *Marcipor*: 'suddenly around the middle of the night, the sky coloured far and wide by burning fire showed the starry dance of the heavens'. And we ourselves in our letters which are entitled 'On Neglect of Study': 'so stay up a little while and banish the sluggishness of dithering thoughts, until you're middle-aged'.[53]

Here Nonius does not use his frequent phrase *ueterum auctoritas* but instead *doctorum auctoritas*, found only here in the lexicon.[54] The variation seems significant, aiding Nonius' attempt to give himself the same status as Varro and sharing his characteristics of learnedness and authority. Using fragmented quotations as the sole support for definitions throughout the lexicon supports the occasional violation of the overall principles that it is the *ueteres* whose linguistic usage is correct. A fragmented quotation from Nonius' own work can stand with Varro's, by virtue of it being selected as appropriate. The dynamic between fragmenter and fragmented here is evident: the knowledge of the *ueteres* authorizes Nonius as quoter and intermediary between them and his audience; inclusion by Nonius guarantees the authority of each fragment.[55] The trust vested in Nonius by his reader allows him the liberty of including a snippet of his own work, but also could operate to demonstrate that Nonius has already mastered the lessons he wants his son, and his other readers, to learn.

But Nonius is not so egotistical that he is the only writer after the Augustan period he deems worthy of being made an *auctor* to compare with the *ueteres*. Nonius quotes Apuleius in company with Lucilius and Varro.[56] Serenus is quoted twice on his own and twice in the company of Varro.[57] Nonius makes no statement as to the relative validity of a quotation from Serenus against one from Varro. We might wonder at the reason for their inclusion when Nonius is so selective, and perhaps the answer lies in the reputation of Serenus and Apuleius as *docti*. Both are consciously archaizing authors; Apuleius even directly appeals to the *doctus lector*.[58] Nonius may well have felt that they deserved to be quoted alongside *doctissimus* Varro, whose reputation for learnedness did not dim in late antiquity.[59] But it is the fragmentation of all his source texts that makes the insertion of quotations from these later authors much simpler, without disrupting the essential dichotomies at the heart of his work. By quoting them alongside the *auctores* Nonius renders Serenus and Apuleius *auctores*: the reader's capacity to judge and distinguish between Apuleius and Lucilius, Serenus and Varro, to divine any differences in usage, is hamstrung by the brevity of the lemma and the paralleling of quotations. Perhaps the best way to understand these citations of Apuleius, Serenus and Nonius himself is through the anachronic. These quotations substitute for – rather than represent or echo – the words of the *ueteres* themselves, that they *are* in some sense the words of the *ueteres*, suggesting that the reward and the true goal of *doctrina* is the fleeting transcendence through the text of that distance, the spatial juxtaposition momentarily effacing a temporal one, and the brief (re)performance of what is irrevocably gone.[60] It is worth comparing how Quignard's fragments highlight a somewhat similar abyss in his thought between Antiquity and Modernity, as discussed by Kristeva in Chapter 1.

The role of quotation in the grammatical tradition

Grammarians typically used quotations to support the arguments they were making, yet Nonius largely gets rid of the arguments and only includes the quotations. But these quotations still represent only those issues of grammar and vocabulary that required explanation. For instance, Nonius cites an instance where Virgil uses the active instead of the expected passive:

> FATIGARE positum pro fatigari. Vergilius lib. VIII: 'olli remigio noctemque diemque fatigant'. (*Aen.* 8.94)
>
> *Nonius 112.14–15 M = 161 L*

> 'To wear out' used in place of 'to be worn out'. Virgil in the fourth book of the *Aeneid*: 'they wear out the night and day with their rowing'.

Servius also gives a lemma on this line for exactly the same reason, but in an expanded form:

> noctemque diemque fatigant ut 'siluasque fatigant': pro 'ipsi fatigantur'. an deest 'se', ut sit 'fatigant se': an 'diem fatigant' pro 'occupant et consummant'?
>
> *Serv.* ad Aen. *8.94*

> 'They wear out the day and night' is used like 'and they wear out the woods': in place of 'they themselves are worn out'. But is the phrase omitting 'themselves', as though it were 'they wear out themselves', or is it more like 'they wear out the night', as though it is being used in place of 'spend and use up'?

Here what Servius adds are questions about whether Virgil's use of *fatigant* should be understood as a reflexive verb with the reflexive pronoun omitted or as a metaphorical extension of *fatigare*. Nonius' brief comment leaves no space for this kind of uncertainty on the part of the grammarian. Both of these lemmata show how focus on the *Aeneid* could be directed exclusively on grammatical matters. The primary function of Virgil's text, providing a narrative of a fictional event within the *Aeneid* (Aeneas sailing up the Tiber), has been lost as the grammatical has been elevated. In Servius' commentary, at least, because the lemmata run in order through the *Aeneid*, and are to be read alongside it, the usage of the line to illustrate a grammatical oddity does not supersede the narrative progression of the text. But in Nonius, the line fulfils no narrative function. Interestingly, Nonius includes this use of *fatigare* in his second book, on novel yet correct usages, and not in his seventh book, which is devoted to changed verb forms and includes many examples of reversed active and passive verbs. In that book Nonius includes an instance of a deponent, as we would term it, instead of an active verb from the *Aeneid*:

> BELLANTVR pro bellant. Vergilius lib. XI: 'et pictis bellantur Amazones armis'.
>
> *Nonius 472.7–8 M = 757 L*

> 'They make war' for 'they war'. Virgil in Book 9: 'the Amazons make war with their decorated arms'.

Servius' explanation is fuller, giving a parallel from the Georgics and also illustrating the reverse, active for deponent, with a line from the second book of the *Aeneid*:

> BELLANTVR pro 'bellant': nam solent uerba pro uerbis poni: unde nunc passiuam declinationem sub actiua posuit significatione, sicut in *Georgicis* 'et placidam paci nutritor oliuam' (*Georg.* 2.425) futurum tempus a passiuo posuit pro praesenti ab actiuo: nam 'nutritor' pro 'nutri' posuit. inde est econtra 'nox umida caelo praecipitat' (*Aen.* 2.8–9).
>
> *Serv.* ad Aen. *11.660*

> 'They make war' for 'they war': for some words are customarily used for other words: where now Virgil used the passive form with an active meaning, just as in his *Georgics* 'and tend the quiet olive of Peace' (*Georg.* 2.425) he used the future tense of the passive in place of the present tense of the active: for he used 'be tended!' in place of 'tend!'. There is also the opposite of this: 'the humid night rushes down from the sky' (*Aen.* 2.8–9).

Nonius' point is briefer than Servius', but it reflects the same approach. The same line is cited by Sacerdos, Diomedes, Priscian and Julianus Toletanus, never in fuller form than Nonius gives it, mostly shortening it to the three words *bellantur Amazones armis*. The original function of the Virgilian line, which is to provide a description of Hippolyta and her Amazons in a simile comparing her with Camilla, is lost.

As lines are excerpted to be used in the grammatical tradition, their function as linguistic corpora becomes the only way to evaluate them, and simultaneously their primary function within their original work – whether they served a narrative, didactic, descriptive, humorous or other role – is lost. Moreover, this excerpting can often distort. For instance, if the eleventh book of the *Aeneid* was lost to us, we might read this line and assume that the line served a narrative function, and that Amazons appeared in some battle, given that there is no indication from the line itself that it forms part of a simile.

The atomization that is the result of the process of 'grammaticalizing' texts such as the *Aeneid* means that restoring their original incarnations from within the text is impossible. Reconstructing the original functions means creating frames around the text that supply what has seemingly gone missing between the quotations, but the conceptualization of what has gone missing is based upon evidence from outside of those texts. In Nonius, one way a grammatical frame is created is by paralleling citations from texts of different genres and periods around a presumed linguistic similarity. In order to reconstruct a tragedy by Accius or a comedy by Naevius, these same citations are paralleled with full texts that are of the same genre but may also be of very different periods and contexts. The very fragmented nature of the citation encourages the search for literary (rather than grammatical) parallels, with which it can be reframed to provide agreement not on grammatical matters but rather those such as plot, theme and character. The degree to which fragments cohere with these paralleled texts is taken as confirmation of the reconstruction's validity. The conclusions drawn are not inherently invalid, but the process is a natural consequence of the fragmenting of text. Once performed, comparing fragments synoptically becomes one of the few ways to understand and process this material, whatever the desired function and purpose. Nonius and the modern scholar working on his lexicon in this respect use this fragmented material in similar fashion.

Nonius' refragmentation by modern scholarship

It is precisely the honing of quotes to illustrate the relevant grammatical point as briefly as possible that creates the difficulty of discovering a line's 'original' function. But as the *Aeneid* line shows, that function is not transparent in the line itself, nor is it recoverable from knowing what kind of literary work the line belongs to. Even genres like tragedy or comedy, which might entirely consist of speech by a fixed cast of characters can include embedded narratives, descriptions, similes and so on within monologues and dialogues.

The quotations that Nonius preserves have some particular grammatical concern or interest guiding their inclusion. Reconstructors, on the other hand, have somewhat less of a decision to make over what material to include but a similar latitude on how to frame the fragment. To conclude I will briefly give an example about how fragments in Nonius are recontextualized by modern scholars.

Figure 1 shows a page from an important ninth-century manuscript of Nonius' work. The following text is a transcribed section of the lemma *CONTENDERE* in Nonius, which can be found in the top left column in Figure 1:[61]

> Contendere significat conparare. plautus in uidularia: signum recte conparebat: huius contendi anulum. lucilius satyrarum: ut contendere possem thestiados ledae atque ixiones alcholocheo. idem libro VII: huncin ego umquam hyacintho hominem cortinipotentis deliciis contendi caecilius titthae: egon uitam meam attican contendam cum istac rusticana syra: licinius macer in epistula ad senatum: illi suam uitam mecum contendunt quorum in corpore ita crebra sunt uulnera uitae nouae cicatrici ut locus non sit **naeuius in lycurgo: caue sis tuam contendas iram contra cum ira liberi:** accius in tereo: uideo ego te mulier, more multarum utier, ut uim contendas tuam maiestatem uiri. uarro gnoti seauton: age nunc, contende alterum genus filothoreon, nequid ibi uiderit melius.
>
> *Nonius 258.38–259.1 = 395–96 L*

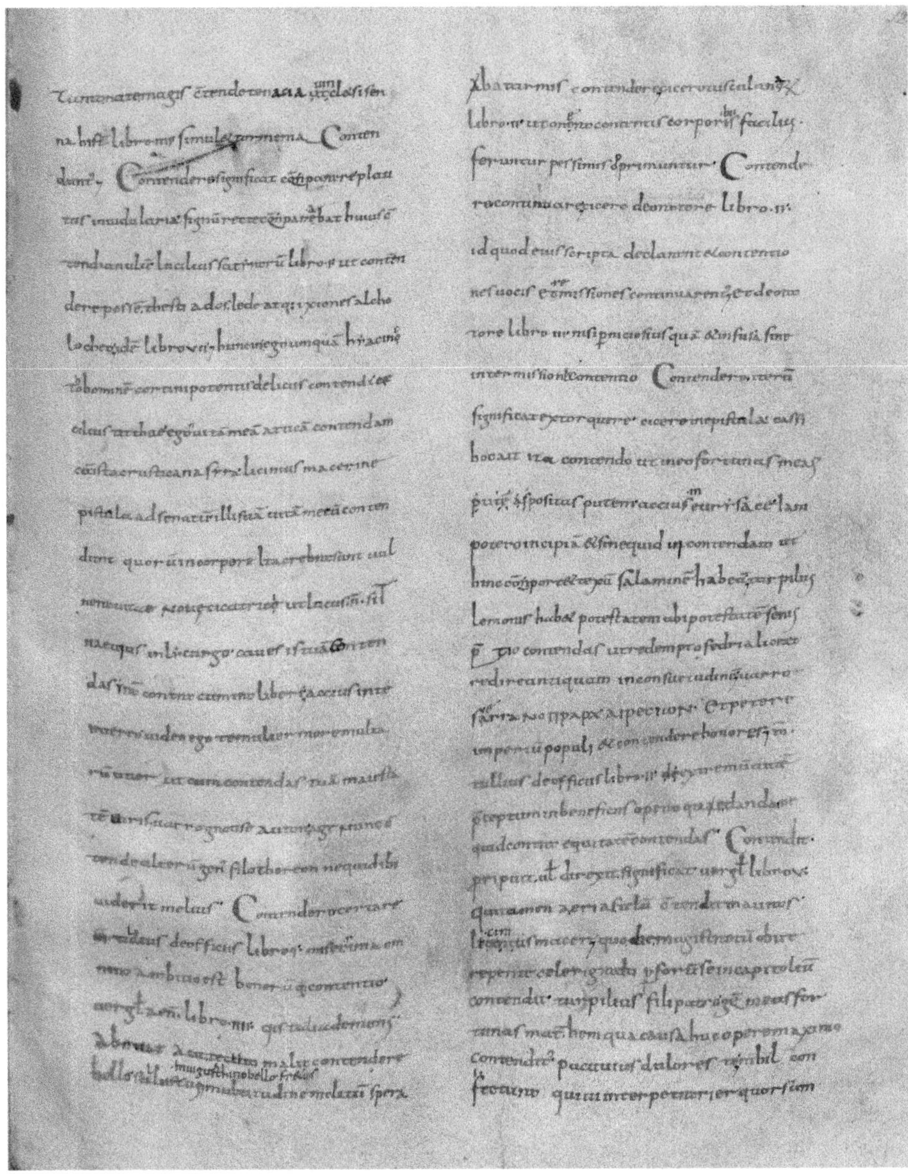

Figure 1 Excerpt of a ninth-century manuscript of Nonius Marcellus' *De compendiosa doctrina* (128r). Credit: Leiden University Libraries, VLF 73.

I want to highlight how the line from Naevius' Lycurgus found within this lemma has been treated in the second volume of E. W. Warmington's 1936 Loeb edition *Remains of Old Latin* (Figure 2). Here the excerpting and rearrangement of Nonius' text is manifest. The text highlighted in bold in the excerpt from the Nonian text is numbered 48, a product of Warmington's judgement of where it belongs in the plot of the *Lycurgus*. Warmington assigns the fragment to a speaker, the god Liber; he also interprets the line

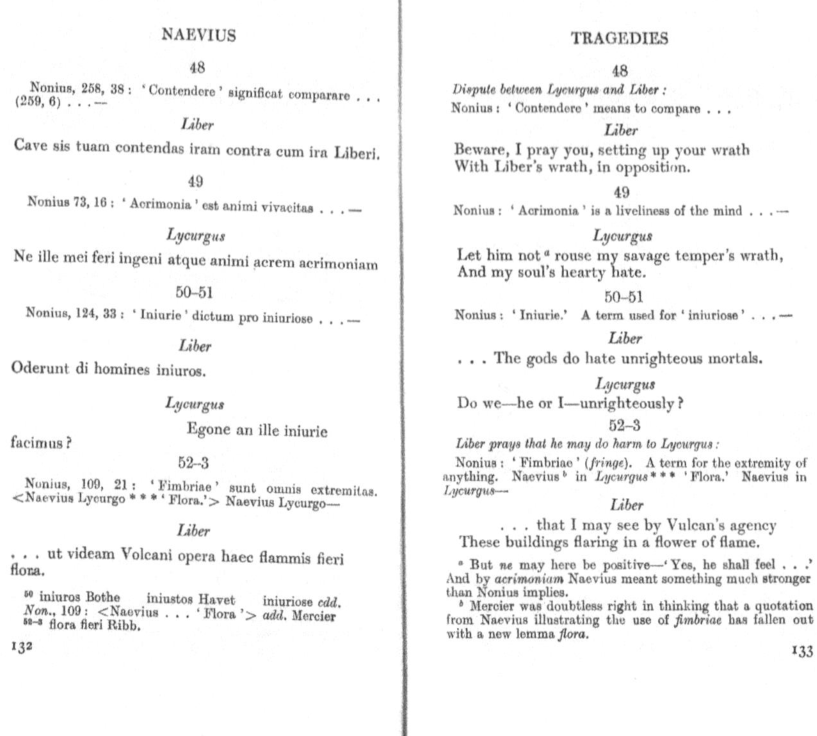

NAEVIUS

48

Nonius, 258, 38 : 'Contendere' significat comparare . . . (259, 6) . . .—

Liber

Cave sis tuam contendas iram contra cum ira Liberi.

49

Nonius 73, 16 : 'Acrimonia' est animi vivacitas . . .—

Lycurgus

Ne ille mei feri ingeni atque animi acrem acrimoniam

50–51

Nonius, 124, 33 : 'Iniurie' dictum pro iniuriose . . .—

Liber

Oderunt di homines iniuros.

Lycurgus

Egone an ille iniurie
facimus ?

52–3

Nonius, 109, 21 : 'Fimbriae' sunt omnis extremitas. <Naevius Lycurgo * * * 'Flora.'> Naevius Lycurgo—

Liber

. . . ut videam Volcani opera haec flammis fieri flora.

50 iniuros Bothe iniustos Havet iniuriose *cdd. Non.*, 109 : <Naevius . . . 'Flora'> *add.* Mercier 52–3 flora fieri Ribb.

132

TRAGEDIES

48

Dispute between Lycurgus and Liber :

Nonius : 'Contendere' means to compare . . .

Liber

Beware, I pray you, setting up your wrath
With Liber's wrath, in opposition.

49

Nonius : 'Acrimonia' is a liveliness of the mind . . .—

Lycurgus

Let him not[a] rouse my savage temper's wrath,
And my soul's hearty hate.

50–51

Nonius : 'Iniurie.' A term used for 'iniuriose' . . .—

Liber

. . . The gods do hate unrighteous mortals.

Lycurgus

Do we—he or I—unrighteously ?

52–3

Liber prays that he may do harm to Lycurgus :

Nonius : 'Fimbriae' (*fringe*). A term for the extremity of anything. Naevius[b] in *Lycurgus* * * * 'Flora.' Naevius in *Lycurgus*—

Liber

. . . that I may see by Vulcan's agency
These buildings flaring in a flower of flame.

[a] But *ne* may here be positive—'Yes, he shall feel . . .' And by *acrimoniam* Naevius meant something much stronger than Nonius implies.

[b] Mercier was doubtless right in thinking that a quotation from Naevius illustrating the use of *fimbriae* has fallen out with a new lemma *flora*.

133

Figure 2 Excerpt from E. W. Warmington's *Remains of Old Latin* (1936), featuring fragments of Naevius' *Lycurgus* (pp. 132–3). Credit: Harvard University Press.

as semantically complete. Warmington has, with the facing English translation, asserted a context for the fragment of an argument between protagonist and antagonist. Clearly none of these assumptions of the *dramatis personae* or the plot can be made from Nonius' presentation of the text, and yet they are crucial to how Warmington presents and uses the fragment. While Warmington does provide some information on where it is found in Nonius, once the line has been excerpted the temptation for subsequent editions to further separate this information from the fragment, or commentators to entirely dispense with it, increases substantially.[62]

Warmington's assumptions here substantially draw upon the work of Otto Ribbeck: his ordering of the fragments in this section mirrors Ribbeck's (1897) edition, and the context Warmington describes draws heavily on Ribbeck's (1875) reconstruction of Naevius' *Lycurgus*. While Ribbeck (1875: 57) states that 'Welchem grieschischen Vorbilde sich Naevius angeschlossen hat, ist unbekannt' ('Which Greek model Naevius has followed is unknown'), in crucial ways he suggests that Naevius modelled his play after Euripides' *Bacchae*. In describing the hypothetical scene in which the line above occurs, he states 'Es scheint, dass er (wie Pentheus bei Euripides) seinen Gefangen nicht für den

Gott selbst hielt' (Ribbeck 1875: 60). Ribbeck creates the context for this line by comparison with Euripides' play. Regardless of whether this is a valid conclusion to draw, the treatment of this fragment by Ribbeck and Warmington successfully extracts it from its Nonian context where it is being used to enumerate the different meanings of the word *contendere* and recontextualizes it, presenting it instead as an instance of the close relationship between Greek and Latin tragedy. Such successful recontextualization, just as Nonius practices, takes advantage of the brevity of the fragment and the ability to couple it with other fragments.[63] In Nonius this parallel presentation is used to persuade the reader of a grammatical commonality; in modern editions of fragments, the parallel presentation is usually deployed to persuade the reader of a shared narrative.[64] And just as the paratext and parallels of their editions and commentaries reveal how our modern critics are reading these fragments, so too could we use the paratext and parallels to shed more light on how Nonius is reading his citations.

Conclusion

I have attempted to show in this chapter how the very form of the fragment is key to the recontextualization and repurposing of knowledge, but also how those carrying out such fragmenting in late antiquity, such as Nonius, raise concerns over the mediation of fragments and the uncertainties they can create. However, the modern usage of Nonius' lexicon is in turn to refragment it, extract from it and rearrange these new fragments according to new criteria, and the nature of their Nonian origin to be minimized as far as possible. What I would hope to highlight is that Nonius carries out his fragmenting according to his own strategies of reading and interpretation. While I do not think that means, for instance, that Nonius' definitions are to be unquestioningly trusted, we can perhaps think of new ways to approach his lexicon that takes greater advantage of what we know about how Nonius read and worked, particularly using technological possibilities that did not exist a hundred years ago when Lindsay first systematically attempted to break down the structure of Nonius' text. For instance, with XML markup of all the quotations, we could better explore questions such as how Nonius moves between texts; which texts prompt repeated comparisons; and whether there are particular words in quotations that catch Nonius' eye. Ironically, digital technologies may be the key to recapturing Nonius the human reader from the prejudice of Nonius the machine. In a culture where the reading of texts is central to everything from conceptions of knowledge to self-definition, Nonius' lexicon has the potential to tell us so much more about that reader.

Notes

1. Compare Galen's comments in the preface to his *Synopsis librorum suorum sedecim de pulsibus*, where he seems to distinguish two kinds of condensing texts: one group condensing subject matter, the other condensing a text – see further Dubischar 2010: 63–4.

2. On fragmentation of material in order to create a new unity in late antique literature and art, see Roberts 1988: 181–95; Cox Miller 1998: 113–38; Formisano 2017; Squire 2017: 82–99.

3. *SARCINATOR Lucilius lib. XXVIII: sarcinatorem esse summum, suere centonem optume* (175.33–176.1 M = 258 L) ('to be the best tailor, to stitch up a patchwork brilliantly'). I cite throughout from Lindsay's (1903) edition of Nonius, unless specified, and references are to both the page numbers from Mercator's edition and to Lindsay's edition. The Mercator page numbers can also be found in Lindsay's edition. While I quote Lindsay's edition for the text of Nonius except where noted, I have made changes from his punctuation and indentation to bring it slightly closer to its appearance in the manuscripts, while attempting to maintain readability.

4. Chahoud's article (2007) on the relationship between *auctoritas* and *antiquitas* in Nonius has been an important contribution towards finding authorial voice in Nonius and also constitutes an excellent account of Nonius' lexicon, although I dispute some of Chahoud's conclusions, particularly on Nonius' use of Gellius, which I cover below.

5. See Chahoud 2007: 69–72 for what we can divine about Nonius' biography. Keyser 1994 argues for an earlier date of around 200 CE mainly based on the cluster of late second-century writers quoted by Nonius, but Deufert 2001 rightly raises concerns over such a dating, pointing to Nonius' apparent use of codices and his vocabulary, which Deufert believes makes a date of around 400 CE more probable.

6. Detailed in Lindsay 1901; he provided analysis of the 'secondary' quotations for the alphabetized books in Lindsay 1906. Questions were raised by Strzelecki 1932 but answered by White 1980 in a general endorsement of Lindsay 1901.

7. The work as it survives lacks a preface. On the survival of a Nonius *plenior*, a fuller text than the one that we possess now, into the Renaissance, which the humanist Niccolò Perotti may have utilized in his *Cornucopiae siue Latinae Commentarii*, as first suggested by Oliver 1947, see Bertini 1981 and 1986. But traces of Nonius' preface are unlikely to be found in Perotti's preface.

8. Nonius consulted the lists for the 'secondary' quotations, as Lindsay termed them, in the same order as he proceeded through his lists for the leading quotations. It is unclear to what extent Nonius found the parallel secondary quotations for himself or simply copied them from marginal comments on his texts consisting of observations by previous critics. However, given that Nonius found the leading quotations for himself through reading his texts, it is likely that the secondary quotations given for texts that contribute to his lists were also directly consulted by himself. In a couple of books, a limited alphabetization (by initial letter only) has added a further stage to the ordering of lemmas. Yet this has not totally disrupted the sequencing of lists, rather merely making it appear that Nonius has cycled through his lists much more rapidly. It seems more probable that it was done by Nonius himself than a subsequent editor, though we cannot be sure: see White 1980: 131–40. We also cannot know whether Nonius composed them alphabetically in the first place or alphabetized the lemmata at a subsequent stage, though White makes a case for the former.

9. Cf. Chin 2008 on the grammatical writers: 'Late ancient reading practice required a constant invocation of an imagined past and a constant reproduction of an abstract relationship between the reader and that past' (35).

10. Chahoud 2007: 84 notes that Nonius, like Servius, ignores the distinction of *auctores* from *ueteres* found in grammarians such as Charisius: see further Dionisotti 1984: 207.

11. See Keyser 1994: 383, who gives examples of Nonius repeating *dicimus* from Gellius and other glossaries. On Gellius' own notions of *auctoritas*, see Gunderson 2009: 62–8.

12. Barabino 2003: 83–108 provides a detailed survey of all the instances in which Nonius mentions *auctoritas*, and concludes 'sembra dunque che l'*auctoritas* sia il principio della *Latinitas* seguito come norma dal nostro grammatico' (107) ('it seems therefore that

auctoritas is the principle of Latinity followed as a norm by our grammarian'). However, Barabino, like Chahoud 2007: 81, treats all Nonius' non-positive statements about the *auctoritas* of writers as a kind: I argue for greater nuance in Nonius' stance below.

13. Diomedes (*GLK* 1.439.15–30) supplies us with Varro's fourfold scheme. For Varro *auctoritas* is the weakest justification for a grammatical point, a last resort (Varro's scheme is explained by Zetzel 2018: 53–5). Quintilian's four-way distinction between *ratio, uetustas, auctoritas* and *consuetudo* represents a shift from Varro, especially since for Quintilian *consuetudo* subsumes *ratio, uetustas* and *auctoritas* to some degree, but Quintilian's *consuetudo* is also explicitly restricted to the educated among the population (*Inst. Or.* 1.6.45). Nonius' scheme thus represents a development from the grammatical categories of earlier Roman writers and is far more like Augustine's threefold scheme of *auctoritas, consudetudo* and *ratio*, particularly in the way that on some points *consuetudo* and *auctoritas* can agree, but on others differ. On Augustine's scheme, see further Law 1990: 195–202.

14. *Ratio* in this sense is only mentioned explicitly in a lemma (51.18–21 M = 73 L) ultimately derived from P. Nigidius, who clearly maintained (see Gell. *NA* 10.4) that *ratio/natura* (which Nigidius connected) played the most important role in word-formation. Although Nonius' lemma appears to be sourced from Gellius, the actual phrase in which *ratio* appears, *ratione naturae modificatione quadam*, has no analogue in the Gellian passage (*NA* 10.2). But whether it derives from insightful reading of Gellius by Nonius or from comparison with one of his other glossarial sources that also furnishes Nonius with quotes from Nigidius, *ratio* and *natura* are not concepts that Nonius himself utilizes. Nonius often recycles a note from Nigidius concerning *analogia* without commenting on it, as with the lemma *EXPVLSIM*: *EXPVLSIM dictum a frequenti pulsum. Varro Serapi: recte purgatum scito, quom uidebis Romae in foro ante lanienas pueros pila expulsim ludere. Nigidius Commentariorum XX: cuiusmodi genus aduerbiorum, a uerbis motus quae ueniunt, ut expulsim, cursim* (104.28–33 = 149 L). Nonius is here interested in the unusual form and its meaning, rather than looking for any underlying linguistic principle. The same seems true even for the lemma *DISSENTANEVM*, even though at first glance it might seem a definition rooted in analogy: *DISSENTANEVM discors et dissentiens, ut consuentaneum contra. Nigidius: eum locum facit dissentaneum* (100.5–7 M = 142 L). Cf. Garcea 2019 on Nigidius' use of analogy.

15. See further Chin 2008: 18–19 on the dynamics of non-linearity and interchangeability utilized by the grammatical writers.

16. See Holford-Strevens 2003: 195–205 and Howley 2018: 190–201 on Gellius' comparative reading.

17. On this lemma and what it reveals about Nonius, see Chahoud 2007: 83–4. On *uetustas* in other grammatical writers, see particularly De Nonno 2017.

18. For a suggestion of how impossibility of unity was recognized and thematized in late antiquity through reaction to the classical past, see Formisano 2018: 45–6.

19. On the comparison of centos and *spolia*, cf. Elsner 2017: 203–4; on centos and grammatical texts, Formisano and Sogno 2010: 389. Somewhere on this spectrum could also be placed the late antique poetics of intertextuality, on which see further Pelttari 2014: 138–60.

20. Cf. Ausonius' description to Paulus of his *cento nuptialis* as a collection of scattered, mutilated parts: *centonem uocant, qui primi hac concinnatione luserunt. solae memoriae negotium sparsa colligere et integrare lacerata, quod ridere magis quam laudare possis* (*Pref.* 3–4).

21. Cf. Sternberg 1982: 145 on quotation: 'Whatever the units involved, to quote is to mediate, to mediate is to frame, and to frame is to interfere and to exploit'.

22. On epitomization, for an up-to-date overview and bibliography, see Horster and Reitz 2018: 431–50. Nonius' lexicon clearly bears more resemblance to those works covering a single topic

using multiple authors (*epitome rei tractatae*) than those covering a work by a single author (*epitome auctoris*) but the ancient terminology was various and inconsistent: see further Opelt 1962.

23. On the development of encyclopaedism in Classical Antiquity, see König and Woolf 2013, and particularly worth noting is their observation 'encyclopaedic works, such as those of Pliny, Solinus, Mela and Isidore assumed their real prominence only when their sources were no longer easily accessible' (ibid.: 63).

24. On this topic, see particularly Elliott's 2013 study of the transmission of the fragments of Ennius, particularly in her demonstration of how authors who include Ennian quotations while critiquing Virgil give a completely different impression of material than authors who are quoting for other purposes.

25. E.g., White 1980: 145: (of Nonius himself) 'a cumbersome, mechanical regularity linked with a limited intelligence'; (of his lexicon) 'a peculiar mixture of the mechanical with the slapdash'; both statements quoted approvingly by Zetzel 2018: 99.

26. On the way that the rhetoric of textual criticism can shape and influence the practice of textual criticism, see particularly Tarrant 2016: 30–48.

27. Brunt 1980: 494. Cf. Brunt's earlier comment that 'scholars have often been too precipitate in characterizing and evaluating lost histories on the basis of evidence that is irremediably insufficient' 1980: 477.

28. See Müller's repeated note *n. N.* (=*nugatur Nonius*) in the *apparatus criticus* of his 1888 edition (Müller 1888). Of course, Nonius does make mistakes, but there is typically little recognition that often these mistakes can be expected from a grammatical writer within Nonius' context – Chahoud 2007 is a welcome exception.

29. Hertz 1862: 705–26; *Id.* 779–99 deduced that Nonius had made use of Gellius for many of his lemmata, and Lindsay 1901 showed that Nonius devoted one of his word lists to Gellius' *Noctes Atticae*. Using Varro's *De lingua Latina* for this purpose is unfortunately not feasible. While Nonius gives hundreds of quotations from the Menippean satires and many from the first book of the *De Re Rustica*, from *De uita populi* Romani and *Catus uel de liberis educandis,* and almost certainly directly consulted all of these, there are only four citations from *De lingua Latina*, two from *De sermone Latino*, and one from *De proprietate scriptorium*, despite the fact that these works are occupied with exactly the sorts of lexicographical questions that interest Nonius. All of these references, however, come from the different glossaries. There is no other evidence that Nonius was directly acquainted with the *De lingua Latina.* For the interesting contrast in the works of Varro used by Nonius and those familiar to Augustine, see Marshall 2016.

30. On Gellian meta-narratives, see now particularly Howley 2018.

31. On the danger of applying the modern notion of plagiarism, see Daintree 1990: 71–2 on Donatus; cf. Elsner 2017: 178–81 on Ausonius' preface to his *cento nuptialis.*

32. This is not to say that Nonius preserves the Gellian material immaculately. Far from it. For instance, at some point, whether changed by Nonius himself or in the manuscript tradition, Gellius' *celatim* has been corrected to *celeratim*. The writer named as Claudius (Quadrigarius) in Gellius is referred to as Coelius by Nonius, see below. Nonius has found the quotation from the *Georgics* independently of Gellius.

33. *NA* 17.2.9: *'et Romani' inquit* [Claudius Quadrigarius] *'multis armis et magno commeatu praedaque ingenti copiantur'. uerbum castrense est, nec facile id reperias apud ciuilium causarum oratores, ex eademque figura est, qua 'lignantur' et 'pabulantur' et 'aquantur'* ('and the Romans,' he [Claudius Quadrigarius] says, 'take possession of many weapons and a large quantity of provisions and a great deal of booty'. It is soldier's talk, not easily found among the

orators of the law courts, and formed in the same fashion as 'they gather wood' or 'they forage' or 'they water').

34. In a later lemma, *LVTESCIT* (133.23–25 M = 194 L), which draws on the same Gellian chapter, the name Furius is lacking in the manuscript entirely, only *poematis* remaining. Again, Nonius adds a caveat to his citation, saying that *lutescit* is a legitimate form (*honeste dictum*), 'even though it may be of murky authority' (*tametsi auctoritatis sit ignobilis*). The omission of Furius' name here could be down to a slip on Nonius' part, which would be more easily made if Nonius was responsible for the alphabetization, or it could have dropped out at some point in the manuscript tradition.

35. Mazzacane 1986: 135–43 discusses other citations of Furius in Macrobius and argues that these refer to Furius Bibaculus. But since Nonius displays no awareness of Macrobius' comments, this would not seem to affect how to interpret Nonius' remarks.

36. The lemmata *CONTICINIVM* (62.20–22 M = 87 L), *NVNTIVS* (215.9–11 M = 317 L) and *PENVS* (219.30–220.1 M = 324–25 L) are the exceptions that prove the rule. Nonius gives his definition for *conticinium*, derived from one of his glossaries, but without citations, stating: *auctores sunt multi mihi, sed auctoritate deficiunt*. Of examples for *nuntius* treated as neuter, Nonius states *neutro aput aliquos non receptae auctoritatis lectum est, sed doctos*, derived from another of the unknown glossaries. In both of these cases, since we do not possess the original glossary text from which these lemmata were derived, it is difficult to say much more. With the lemma *PENVS* (219.30–220.1 M = 324–25 L), sourced from Gellius, Nonius writes *neutri etiam lectum est apud plurimos, quorum auctoritatis non probatur*, where 'authority is not proved' seems likelier than 'authority is not approved', since Gellius does not provide any citations, which is precisely what prompts Nonius' comment. For the other terms that do accompany citations, *obscurus*, *incertus*, *incognitus* can all refer to epistemological uncertainty, and the concessive clause in which *ignobilis* appears is in the subjunctive: *Furius, tametsi auctoritatis* **sit** *ignobilis* ('Furius in his poems, although he **may** be of murky authority'). Nonius himself gives one of his definitions of *obscurus* as *ignobilis*, citing Cic. *Off.* 1.116. And it is worth imagining what might have rendered Nonius certain about authors such as Furius: if Nonius had possessed Cicero's *Brutus* (he never cites it) would the reference that Cicero makes there to *A. Furium poetam* (*Brut.* 35) have caused Nonius to drop his questioning of Furius' *auctoritas*? In the lemma *CIMA* (195.3–6 M = 286 L), when Nonius refers to the 'lesser authority' of Celsus, *etsi minoris auctoritatis*, this is in comparison with Lucilius, to whom the preceding quotation belongs (cf. Maggiulli 1997: 190).

37. *PEDETEMTIM ET PEDEPRESSIM . . . Quadrigarius Annalibus: exercitu instructo pedetemtim milites ducere coepit. Coelius Annali VI: ipse cum cetera copia pedetemtim sequitur* (29.1–8 M = 42 L). These secondary quotations seem to originate from one of the other glossary lists. A possible reason is that Nonius' text of Gellius was corrupt in multiple passages and read Coelius instead of Claudius. But then the lemma for *DIVRNARE* (100.14–17 M = 143 L) poses problems – why did Nonius not attribute this to 'Coelius' as well? It is worth noting that the manuscripts of Nonius in some instances uniformly transmit Caelius, not Coelius, but this is a common enough textual corruption. See Cornell et al. 2013: 94.

38. Not that Nonius is necessarily consistent in raising his concerns: in the lemma for *OPVLISCERE* (148.15–16 M = 216 L), Nonius comments that it is *dictum decore*, and there is no discussion of *auctoritas*. Nonius could have prepared all the entries together, yet normally he has no qualms about repeating similar sentiments in close proximity.

39. Of the twenty-five instances where Nonius adds a parenthetical comment about authority or source but without referring to a specific author in a lemma drawn from Gellius, all but two have the information imparted within Gellius by an embedded authority such as an earlier author or an individual like Favorinus. This is the case for the following lemmata:

VICTVRVS (188.2–4 M = 276 L), *RECENTARI* (167.13–16 M = 246 L), *MEMORDI* (140.20–28 M = 204–05 L), *APLVDAS* (69.24–70.3 M = 97 L), *ATQVE* (530.1–9 M = 850 L), *FVRES* (50.9–15 M = 71 L), *PELICIS* (6.18–20 M = 10 L), *VENTORVM PROPRIETATES* (50.16–26 = 72 L), *PENI VEL PENORIS* (51.3–6 M = 72 L), *RVDENTES* (51.13–15 M = 73 L), *LICTOR* (51.26–28 M = 73 L), *SOROR* (52.1–4 = 73 L), *HVMANITATEM* (52.7–13 M = 73–74 L), *FACIEM* (52.20–27 M = 74 L), *VESTIBVLA* (53. 3–12 M = 75 L), *IVMENTVM* (54.25–55.2 = 77 L), *MORBVS ET VITIVM* (440.32–441.2 M = 708 L), *MATRONAE* (442.1–8 M = 709–10 L), *INLATEBRARE* (129.21–23 M = 188 L), *LVTESCIT* (133. 23–25 M = 194 L). These are analogous to the Furius lemmata.

One of the remaining two instances is the lemma *DIE QVARTE* (441.8–10 M = 708 L). Gellius names several authorities, Cato the Elder and Gnaeus Matius, but in the final definition, which Nonius bases his whole lemma on, Gellius uses the first-person plural when relating the information. Nonius' comment is that *hoc differre prudentis uolunt, quorum tamen auctoritas in obscuro est* . . . ('Some, whose authority is, however, unclear, wish to make this prudent distinction . . .'). First, it is worth noting that Nonius refuses to mention Gellius as in every instance. Second, that Nonius could assume that Gellius is drawing here upon other writers who go unnamed and it is these grammatical writers to whom he is referring. While Macrobius almost certainly uses Gellius for the opening words when Macrobius' character of Servius mentions this issue of *die quarto* (cf. Kaster 1980: 218–19), Charisius (*GLK* 1.102.25–3.4) also discusses it in a slightly different fashion, which might suggest that Gellius was not the first antiquarian to think the matter worth discussing (see Uría Varela 2006: 251–2). This is to say, Nonius might have used Gellius for the form of his lemma while being aware (albeit perhaps only dimly) that there had been other writers earlier who had written on the topic. The other lemma is *INTEMPERIA* (493.4–5 M = 791 L): this is based on a Gellian chapter (*NA* 1.17) on Socrates' behaviour towards his wife Xanthippe and Varro's Menippean satire *De officio mariti*. Nonius takes his words almost exactly from Gellius, except, crucially, that Nonius' lemma concerns *intemperia*, quoting *has eius intemperias in maritum*, where Gellius' text reads, as would be expected, *intemperies*. This lemma comes from Nonius' book devoted to rare forms of words belonging to different declensions than the expected form, in this case, a 1st declension form for the usual 3rd declension. The likeliest scenario is that Nonius' text of Gellius was wrong, but that Nonius believed this was a rare form. And given that Nonius believed that *intemperia* was indeed an antique form once in use, it seems much likelier that he believed Gellius had reused a word from some hypothetical word in which Gellius had found this account, than that Gellius is the *uetus* that he mentions (*apud ueterem auctoritatis obscurae*).

40. Latyon 2002: 489–522 explores one interesting instance of plagiarism in late antiquity in the accusations levelled at Jerome: he demonstrates that apparent ingratitude was the problem. If so, that would add a further reason why Nonius might be unlikely to directly disparage an author whose words he borrows.

41. Similarly, the lemma *DVRITVDO* (100.16–18 M = 143 L) is constructed as a typical Nonian direct citation, and yet Nonius has forgotten to remove Gellius' *inquit* ('Cato says . . .').

42. As Howley 2018: 174–90 demonstrates, Gellius has his own wrangles with mediators: 'The intermediating texts and authorities that link present to past are personified by Tiro, an inherently servile figure whose strengths and weaknesses as an individual . . . illustrate the strengths and limitations of the kind of secondary literature he wrote'.

43. See White 1980: 205, who observes that Gellius' *Noctes Atticae* effectively functions for Nonius like one of these glossaries, as a miscellany of quotations from a wide range of authors, as opposed to his other word-lists formed from a single author. For recent work on some of these glossaries (Lindsay's 'Gloss. iii', 'Alph. Verb' and 'Alph. Adverb'), see Walsh 2012, who suggests that these all derived from a single lexicographer 'who had access to and excerpted a

substantial collection of works of Republican drama and literature', much like Nonius himself, although unlike Nonius they were concerned with niceties such as quoting complete metrical units (Walsh 2012: 843–5).

44. Nonius seems to have quoted Catullus 63.49 for the lemma *MISERITER* (517M), although the text is damaged, the citation has dropped out and the line of Serenus that follows for the lemma *PROPERITER* is attributed to Catullus instead (i.e. *MISERITER pro misere. Laberius . . . PROPERITER Catullus: animula miserula properiter abiit*). But even with this textual confusion it does not seem probable that there was a concern raised with Catullus' *auctoritas* here – if the lemma had such a comment a scribal slip seems less likely. For the passage, cf. Zaffagno 1975: 260–1.

45. Seneca, *Ep.* 39.1: *Commentarios quos desideras, diligenter ordinatos et in angustum coactos, ego uero componam; sed uide ne plus profutura sit ratio ordinaria quam haec quae nunc uulgo breuiarium dicitur, olim cum latine loqueremur summarium uocabatur. Illa res discenti magis necessaria est, haec scienti; illa enim docet, haec admonet.* ('I will indeed prepare those notes you wanted, and I'll make them carefully and keep them short. But take care that you rely more on the usual methods, rather than what's called nowadays in common parlance a 'digest', although in the Latin we all once used to speak it was called a 'summary'. A proper course of reading is rather a necessity for learning philosophy, although summaries are useful for revision: for the former actually teaches, while the latter remind'.)

46. On *compendiosus*, see Chahoud 2007: 82. This paradox was also confronted by Galen in the preface to the epitome he wrote to his own sixteen-book work *On the Pulse*. Galen acknowledges that epitomes were being read as shortcuts but remonstrates that they ought to be read as introductions or to help recollection, rather than replacing the reading of the epitomized work. See further Dubischar 2010: 48–50.

47. On the less charitable interpretation, Nonius has indeed read Gellius carelessly as attributing these words to only the *Cophinus* mime. For this view, see Panayotakis 2010. Although the lemma for *ADVLTERIONEM* reads simply *Cophino*, before the alphabetization this lemma would have followed *MENDICIMONIVM* immediately, perhaps making the more specific note unnecessary – if so that would also suggest that Nonius' comments were then added.

48. We do not know ourselves that the latter is true for Laberius, but a scroll including thirteen mimes by the Greek writer Herondas (along with Aristotle's *Constitution of the Athenians*, some of Bacchylides' odes and Hyperides' orations) was found in 1890. It is hardly unreasonable to think that standard collections of Laberius' mimes could emerge, though this statement by Nonius would be our only evidence for this. More to the point, whether it was the case or not, it is not unreasonable to imagine that *Nonius* could think there were standard collections of Laberius. It is worth comparing with the situation for Plautus: Nonius uses a word-list of the twenty-one plays of Plautus deemed canonical by his period – these he presumably found in one codex, given that we know that there was a codex, from which our manuscripts descend, created in the same contemporary period as Nonius writes (Questa 1983: 23–129); Lucarini dates the edition of the twenty-one plays to the second century CE, given Gellius' evidence (Lucarini 2012: 260–91). But the alphabetization of the Plautine plays seems to go back to the time of Varro at least: Piras 2015: 67 finds traces of it in Book 7 of *De Lingua Latina*. What this suggests is that alphabetization might well have been a well-established way of organizing an author's works and Nonius might have applied that logic to this situation.

49. 74.15 M = 104.14 L; 100.8 M = 142.7 L; 122.7 M = 176.5 L; 490.20 M = 787.20 L; 517.2 M = 831.1 L.

50. Compare, on the Greek commentary tradition that emerged out of Alexandria, Sluiter 2000: 188: 'The legitimation of writing commentaries is based on two presuppositions, which are in

partial conflict. The first presupposition is that the source-text is valuable and should be made widely available and accessible. The second is that whatever is contained in the source-text is not optimally effective unless it is supplemented by the explanations of the commentator'.

51. Ibid.: 190: 'These commentators, qua intellectuals, formed part of one and the same 'network,' with a much lesser degree of scholarly compartmentalization than is familiar to us'.

52. Cf. Nagel and Wood 2010: 364: 'The substitutional system, which governed manuscript tradition just as much as it did artefacts, was a mechanism that allowed an original utterance to survive through a chain of iterations, *without difference* [Nagel's and Wood's italics]'.

53. Müller 1888 identified the title of Nonius' work as *Epistulae de Peregrinando a Doctrinis*, which Lindsay 1901 translates as 'On the Neglect of Study', although Mantero 1975: 167 interprets the title as 'allontanamento dall'attività di insegnamento' ('a departure from the activity of study'). Chahoud 2007: 73 n. 45, given the (albeit ambiguous) content of the fragment, notes the possibility that the title might perhaps 'be reconstructed as *Doctrinae de Peregrinando*, in the sense of περὶ ἀμελείας, 'Instructions on Negligence''. But it is also worth noting that late nights spent in study is also a repeated theme of Aulus Gellius' *Attic Nights* (cf. e.g., pr. 10, pr. 19, 1.7.5), so the fragment may instead be advocating for late nights spent in study, not away from them.

54. Nonius uses the phrase *ueterum auctoritate doctorum* in the lemma *SULCUS* (448.15–20 M = 719 L), where the quotation is also taken from a work of Varro. Here *doctorum* qualifies *ueterum* rather than being used substantively, unlike in the phrase *doctorum auctoritas*. *Doctorum* is also used for a group in the title of Nonius' twelth book, *De doctorum indagine*, 'On the research of the learned', and which generally focuses on the contrast between usage contemporary with Nonius and usage by Republican authors (for Nonius' specialized grammatical vocabulary found in his book titles and throughout his work, see Chahoud 2007: 82). Notes are (relatively) longer in this book and more discursive, and seem likely to reflect the opinions of other grammarians, not just Nonius.

55. On this reciprocality, see further Chin 2008: 15–16.

56. 68.20–69.1 M = 96 L.

57. On the basis of Serenus' unusual inclusion, Keyser 1984: 374–8 argues that Serenus and Nonius were contemporaries, but see further n.4 above. On the question of whether the poet Serenus Septimius is to be identified with the antiquarian Serenus Sammonicus, see Champlin 1981: 189–212, but the evidence is rather tenuous.

58. In his poetry Apuleius, like Serenus, used archaizing vocabulary, neologisms with old-fashioned suffixes, and antique metres: see further Courtney 1993: 371–4, 392–400, 406–18. Mattiacci 1986 discusses Apuleian archaizing in depth.

59. Aug. *De civ. D.* 6.2: *uir doctissimus undecumque Varro*.

60. Cf. Formisano 2017: 78 on Ammianus: 'Il testo di Ammiano diviene così anche anacronico, in grado cioè di eludere la propria storicità riallacciandosi ad un passato remoto che torna a rivivere, ma non come ricostruzione storica né come semplice analogia, piuttosto come il manifestarsi di una conoscenza lampeggiante che non conosce i confini stabiliti dalla temporalità storica' ('Ammianus' text thus also becomes anachronic, namely, able to evade its own historicity by reconnecting to a remote past which returns to life, not as a historical reconstruction or a simple analogy, but as the manifestation of a flash of knowledge which does not keep to the bounds of historical temporality').

61. The entries in Book IV, *De uaria significatione sermonum* ('On the different meanings of words'), in which this lemma appears, consist of lemmata for words such as *contendere* repeated for each different signification with appropriate synonyms. This disjunctive presentation creates a further fragmentation of a word into multiple different, mutually

exclusive meanings. I have presented this lemma closer to how it is found in our Nonian manuscripts (while keeping it easily readable) in order to show how even editions of Nonius such as Lindsay's begin a process of fragmentation through their graphical presentation of the lemmata.

62. For instance, Traglia's 1986 edition puts the Nonian citation in footnotes, and Boyle's 2006 *Roman Tragedy* places it in endnotes: Nonius' presence becomes more and more physically distanced on the page and within the book from the fragment.

63. On the general capacity of the quotation to recontextualize, see Sternberg 1982, particularly his identification of the 'representational bond, structural framing, communicative subordination, and perspectival montage or ambiguity' as 'the universals of quotation' (ibid.: 109).

64. Not that there was anything new in Nonius' use of such a strategy: Plutarch combines citational brevity with moral or ethical frameworks, which can even be incongruous with a citation's original context – see König 2007: 335–45.

Works cited

Barabino, G. (2003), 'Il tema dell'*auctoritas* in Nonio Marcello', *Prolegomena Noniana* 2: 81–108.

Bertini, F. (1981), 'Niccolò Perotti e il *De compendiosa doctrina* di Nonio Marcello', *Res Publica Litterarum* 4: 27–41.

Bertini, F. (1986), 'Ancora su Nonio e Perotti' in S. Prete (ed.), *Commemoratio: Studi di filologia in ricordo di Riccardo Ribuoli*, 7–12, Sassoferrato: Istituto Internazionale di Studi Piceni.

Boyle, A. (2006), *An Introduction to Roman Tragedy*, London: Routledge.

Brunt, P. A. (1980), 'On Historical Fragments and Epitomes', *Classic Quarterly* 30: 477–94.

Chahoud, A. (2007), 'Antiquity and Authority in Nonius Marcellus' in J. H. D. Scourfield (ed.), *Texts and Culture in Late Antiquity: Inheritance, Authority, and Change*, 69–96, Swansea: Classical Press of Wales.

Champlin, E. (1981), 'Serenus Sammonicus', *Harvard Studies in Classical Philology* 85: 189–212.

Chin, C. M. (2008), *Grammar and Christianity in the Late Roman World*, Philadelphia: University of Pennsylvania Press.

Cornell, T. J., E. Bispham, J. W. Rich and J. C. Smith, eds (2013), *The Fragments of the Roman Historians: in 3 volumes* (vol. 1), Oxford: Oxford University Press.

Courtney, E. (2003), *The Fragmentary Latin Poets*, Oxford: Oxford University Press.

Cox Miller, P. (1998), '"Differential Networks": Relics and Other Fragments in Late Antiquity', *Journal of Early Christian Studies* 6: 135–6.

Daintree, D. (1990), 'The Virgil Commentary of Aelius Donatus: "Black Hole" or "Éminence Grise"?', *Greece & Rome* 37: 65–79.

De Nonno, M. (2017), 'Grammatici latini', in S. Rocchi and C. Mussini (eds), *Imagines Antiquitatis: Representations, Concepts, Receptions of the Past in Roman Antiquity and the Early Italian Renaissance*, 213–48, Berlin: De Gruyter.

Deufert, M. (2001), 'Zur Datierung des Nonius Marcellus', *Philologus* 145: 137–49.

Dionisotti, A. C. (1984), 'Latin grammar for Greeks and Goths', *The Journal of Roman Studies* 74: 202–8.

Dubischar, M. (2010), 'Survival of the Most Condensed? Auxiliary Texts, Communications Theory, and Condensation of Knowledge' in M. Horster and C. Reitz (eds), *Condensing Texts – Condensed Texts*, 39–67, Stuttgart: Franz Steiner Verlag.

Elliott, J. (2013), *Ennius and the Architecture of the Annales*, Cambridge: Cambridge University Press.

Elsner, J. (2017), 'Late Narcissus: Classicism and Culture in a Late Roman Cento' in J. Elsner and J. Hernández Lobato (eds), *The Poetics of Late Latin Literature*, 176–206, Oxford: Oxford University Press.

Formisano, M. (2017), 'Tarda antichità anacronica. Tra storiografia e panegirico' in S. Rocchi and C. Mussini (eds), *Imagines Antiquitatis: Representations, Concepts, Receptions of the Past in Roman Antiquity and the Early Italian Renaissance*, 65–84, Berlin: De Gruyter.

Formisano, M. (2018), 'Fragments, Allegory, and Anachronicity: Walter Benjamin and Claudian' in S. Cullhed and M. Malm (eds), *Reading Late Antiquity*, 33–50, Heidelberg: Universitätsverlag Winter.

Formisano, M. and Sogno, C. (2010), 'Petite poésie portable' in M. Horster and C. Reitz (eds), *Condensing Texts – Condensed Texts*, 375–92, Stuttgart: Franz Steiner Verlag:.

Garcea, A. (2019), 'Grammar' in S. McGill and E. Watts (eds), *A Companion to Late Antique Literature*, 451–70, London: John Wiley.

Gunderson, E. (2009), *Nox philologiae: Aulus Gellius and the Fantasy of the Roman Library*, Madison: University of Wisconsin Press.

Hertz, M. (1862), 'A. Gellius und Nonius Marcellus', *Neue Jahrbücher für Philologie und Paedagogik* 85, 705–26.

Holford-Strevens, L. (2003), *Aulus Gellius: An Antonine Scholar and His Achievement*, Oxford: Oxford University Press.

Horster, M., and C. Reitz (2018), 'Handbooks, Epitomes, and Florilegia' in S. McGill and E. Watts (eds), *A Companion to Late Antique Literature*, 431–50, Malden, MA: John Wiley.

Howley, J. A. (2018), *Aulus Gellius and Roman Reading Culture*, Cambridge: Cambridge University Press.

Kaster, R. A. (1988), *Guardians of Language: The Grammarian and Society in Late Antiquity*, Berkeley: University of California Press.

Keyser, P. T. (1994), 'Late authors in Nonius Marcellus and other evidence of his date', *Harvard Studies in Classical Philology* 96: 369–89.

König, J. (2010), 'Conversation and Citational Brevity in Plutarch's *Sympotic Questions*' in M. Horster and C. Reitz (eds), *Condensing Texts – Condensed Texts*, 321–48, Stuttgart: Franz Steiner Verlag.

König, J., and G. Woolf (2013), 'Encyclopaedism in the Roman empire', in J. König and G. Woolf (eds), *Encyclopaedism from Antiquity to the Renaissance*, 23–63, Cambridge: Cambridge University Press.

Law, V. (1990), '*Auctoritas, consuetudo* and *ratio* in St Augustine's *Ars grammatica*' in G. Bursill-Hall, S. Ebbensen, E. Koerner (eds), *De Ortu Grammaticae: Studies in Medieval Grammar and Linguistic Theory in Memory of Jan Pinborg*, 191–208, Amsterdam: John Benjamins.

Layton, R. A. (2002), 'Plagiarism and Lay Patronage of Ascetic Scholarship: Jerome, Ambrose and Rufinus', *Journal of Early Christian Studies* 10: 489–522.

Lindsay, W. (1901), *Nonius Marcellus' Dictionary of Republican Latin*, Oxford: J. Parker.

Lindsay, W., ed. (1903), *Nonii Marcelli De Compendiosa Doctrina* (3 vols), Leipzig: Teubner.

Lucarini, C. M. (2012), 'Per la storia del testo di Plauto nell'antichità (e ancora sui due Sisenna)', *Philologus* 156: 260–91.

Mantero, T. (1975), 'La *Inscriptio* dei codici del *de Compendiosa Doctrina e Nonius Marcellus peripateticus Thubursicensis*', *Studi Noniani* 3, 123–88.

Marshall, R. (2016), '"Bi-Marcus?" The two Varrones of Augustine and Nonius Marcellus', *Res Publica Litterarum* 19: 180–203.

Mattiacci, S. (1986), 'Apuleio e i poeti latini arcaici' in Munus amicitiae: *Scritti in memoria di A. Ronconi*, Florence: F. Le Monnier: 159–200.

Mazzacane, F. (1986), '*Furii poemata* in Nonio'. *Studi Noniani* 9: 131–43.

Müller, L., ed. (1888), *Noni Marcelli Compendiosa doctrina*, Leipzig: Teubner.

Nagel, A. and C. S. Wood (2010), *Anachronic Renaissance*, New York: Zone Books.

Oliver, R. P. (1947), '"New Fragments" of Latin Authors in Perotti's *Cornucopiae*', *TAPhA* 78: 376–424.

Opelt, I. (1962), 'Epitome', in *Reallexikon für Antike und Christentum* 5: 944–73, Stuttgart: Hiersemann.

Panayotakis, C., ed. (2010), *Decimus Laberius: The Fragments*. Cambridge: Cambridge University Press.

Pelttari, A. (2014), *The Space that Remains: Reading Latin Poetry in Late Antiquity*, Ithaca, NY: Cornell University Press.

Piras, G. (2015), '*Cum poeticis multis uerbis magis delecter quam utar*: Poetic Citations and Etymological Enquiry in Varro's *De lingua Latina*' in D. J. Butterfield (ed.), *Varro Varius: The Polymath of the Roman World*, 51–70, Cambridge: Cambridge Philological Society.

Ribbeck, O. (1875), *Die Römische Tragödie im Zeitalter der Republik*, Leipzig: Teubner.

Ribbeck, O., ed. (1897), *Scaenicae Romanorvm poesis fragmenta tertiis cvris* (vol. 1), Leipzig: Teubner.

Roberts, M. (1988), 'The Treatment of Narrative in Late Antique Literature', *Philologus* 132: 181–95.

Sluiter, I. (2000), 'The Dialectics of Genre: Some Aspects of Secondary Literature and Genre in Antiquity' in M. Depew and D. Obbink (eds), *Matrices of Genre: Authors, Canons, and Society*, 183–205, Cambridge, MA: Harvard University Press.

Squire, M. (2017), 'POP Art: The Optical Poetics of Publilius Optatianus Porfyrius', in J. Elsner and J. Hernández Lobato (eds), *The Poetics of Late Latin literature*, 25–99, Oxford: Oxford University Press.

Sternberg, M. (1982), 'Proteus in Quotation-land: Mimesis and the Forms of Reported Discourse', *Poetics Today* 3: 107–56.

Strzelecki, L. (1932), *Quaestiones Verrianae*, Warsaw: Nakladem Towarzystwa Naukowego Warszawskiego.

Tarrant, R. J. (2016), *Texts, Editors, and Readers: Methods and Problems in Latin Textual Criticism*, Cambridge: Cambridge University Press.

Traglia, A. (1986), *Poeti latini arcaici, vol. I. Livio Andronico, Nevio, Ennio*, Torino: UTET.

Uría Varela, J. (2006), 'Charisiana I (Char. Gramm. P. 102.25–P. 103.4 Barwick)', *Exemplaria Classica: Revista de Filología Clásica* 10: 245–52.

Walsh, J. T. (2012), 'The Methods of Nonius Marcellus' Sources 26, 27 and 28', *The Classical Quarterly*, 62.2: 827–45.

Warmington, E. H., ed. (1936), *Remains of Old Latin* (vol. 2). Cambridge, MA: Harvard University Press.

White, D. (1980), 'The method of composition and sources of Nonius Marcellus', *Studi Noniani* 8: 111–211.

Zaffagno, E. (1975), 'Catullo in Nonio Marcello', *Studi Noniani* 3: 260–1.

Zetzel, J. E. (2018), *Critics, Compilers, and Commentators: An Introduction to Roman Philology, 200 BCE–800 CE*, Oxford: Oxford University Press.

PART II

FROM THE WHOLE TO THE FRAGMENTS?

CHAPTER 6
DISMEMBERING THE TRUTH: PENTHEUS' DISMEMBERMENT AS AN IMAGE OF THE EPITOMIZING DYNAMIC IN CLEMENT OF ALEXANDRIA'S *STROMATEIS*

Antoine Paris[*]

Introduction: The *epitome* as dynamics

The word ἐπιτομή, coming from the verb τέμνω 'to cut', appears in ancient Greek literature to qualify certain works, with two ambiguities.

The first one is the fact that an author rarely characterizes her or his own work as an *epitome*. This qualification is rather due to other writers, referring to some other author's work, or to copyists, who choose this word to entitle a work. The Pseudo-Scymnos exemplify the first case, to the extent that, at the beginning of his *Travel around the Earth in Comic Verses* (*Περίοδος γῆς ἐν κωμικῷ μετρῷ*),[1] he talks about the work of 'one among the genuine Attic philologists',[2] who composed 'an *epitome* of every facts which were told as a flood'.[3] The Pseudo-Scymnos intends to produce a similar work. However, he doesn't call it directly an *epitome*, but a 'detailed description' (διέξοδος).[4] We can also quote Dionysius of Halicarnassus, who describes the books about Roman history written in Greek before his own as 'summary and very short *epitomai*'[5] and the forty occurrences of ἐπιτομή in the tenth-century *Suda* to refer to authors that are referenced in it.[6] For the use of *epitome* by copyists, we can mention the so-called Byzantine *Zoological Encyclopaedia of Constantine VII*: never in the text does the word ἐπιτομή appear, but it is used in the title given by a copyist, who, in the *codex* P, describes the work as an '*epitome* by Aristophanes'.[7]

Nevertheless, in the same manuscript, another term is used to qualify the book, which at first seems diametrically opposed to *epitome*. According to the same *codex* P, the *Zoological Encyclopaedia* is, at the same time, a συλλογή, that is to say, a 'collection',[8] whereas the action of collecting seems opposite to the cutting process implied in the word *epitome*. As Arnaud Zucker precises it, a third qualification appears in another manuscript, which, like συλλογή, emphasizes the idea of uniting various data: συναγωγή 'gathering'.[9] In this way, the three titles emphasize two different and opposite dynamics that guided the composition of the *Zoological Encyclopaedia*: on the one hand, a dynamic of cutting from other books and, on the other, a dynamic of reuniting those various materials into a new work. These two dynamics appear also in the work by the Pseudo-Scymnos. He describes the poem that inspires him as an *epitome*, but also as a composition: its author '*gather[ed]* the main facts of the times'.[10] Similarly, the Pseudo-Scymnos' own work follows the model of this former *epitome* in the same two ways. Meaningfully, the author uses words with the same root as ἐπιτομή to describe his own text: 'from the scattered inquiries about some facts I have written ἐν ἐπιτομῇ', that is to say 'in brief'[11] or 'in an *epitome*'[12] and 'will expose [the facts] συντεμών', that is to say 'by cutting' or 'in a nutshell'.[13] But, at the time, he also describes it as the result of a reuniting process: as a σύνταξις, a 'composition'.[14]

Consequently, the *epitome* seems to be not only a process of cutting, but, as well, a process of reuniting. These two ambiguities lead us to three presuppositions concerning the definition of an *epitome*.

First, it seems difficult to define the *epitome* on the basis of a 'rhetoric' or a 'topic',[15] that is to say of 'conventions' or 'regulatory standards'[16] to which the *epitome*'s author would conform. To put it in other words, the *epitome* is not a 'genre',[17] in the sense of a set of static characteristics present in a work,[18] but a dynamic, which is the reason why we prefer to talk of an epitomizing dynamic.[19]

Second, if one accepts the idea of the *epitome* as a dynamic, it is more related to the text as a productivity than to the text as a finished product. We take up here an idea by Julia Kristeva, according to whom, from Greek Antiquity, the work and process leading to the creation of a text are concealed in favour of the conception of the text as a static object, and more precisely as a consumer object.[20] Defining a text as an *epitome* is – unavoidably – to consider this text as the process having led to it rather as the constituted object we are looking at. In other words, it means considering the *epitome* as a work, in the sense of an activity, rather than as a work, in the sense of an object,[21] which leads us not far from Roland Barthes's conception of literature according to Mohammad Reza Fallah Nejad in this same volume: 'not as a body or a series of works but as (. . .) a writing practice.'

The ambiguities we noted about the use of the word *epitome* lead us to our third point, which is a first hypothesis concerning the definition of *epitome* as a dynamic, participating in the productivity of certain texts. This dynamic is twofold: it couldn't be limited to a cutting process but is also, at the same time, a reuniting one. Consequently, defining the *epitome* means understanding the links between these two dynamics. The following study of the *Stromateis* by Clement of Alexandria as an *epitome* is based on this presupposition: what, in this work, is the relationship between a dynamic of cutting and a dynamic of reuniting?

After having analysed the use of the word ἐπιτομή by Clement of Alexandria in this text, we will focus on a metaliterary passage where a process of cutting and a process of reuniting are linked together before showing how this twofold dynamic is at work in the whole *Stromateis* and makes of this text a double *epitome*.

Clement's uses of the word ἐπιτομή

The qualification of a book as an *epitome* is not unknown to Clement. In *Stromateus*[22] 5, 14, 97, 7, he refers to the author of the Second book of the Maccabees as 'the one who put together the *epitome* (ἐπιτομή) of the Maccabees',[23] which echoes the indication we find in this biblical book: 'what was shown by Jason of Cyrene in five books, we tried to epitomize (ἐπιτεμεῖν) in one work'.[24]

Admittedly, Clement doesn't characterize his own work as an *epitome*. However, he uses two expressions with the word ἐπιτομή while writing about his *Stromateis*. In 1, 14, 64, 5, he concludes a sequence by saying 'And such is the succession of the Greek philosophers in *epitome* (ὡς ἐν ἐπιτομῇ).'[25] In the same way, in the beginning of *Stromateus* 4, one of the passages where he presents a (never fully realized) plan of his text, Clement announces an 'exposition of the Scriptures for the Jews according to an *epitome* (κατ' ἐπιτομήν)'.[26] Neither of these expressions could be convincingly used to characterize the *Stromateis* as an *epitome*: both are common ways of speaking of an abbreviating process without any reference to *epitome* as a literary genre.[27] Moreover, contrary to what was the case with the works we mentioned before, the process described by the expressions 'in *epitome*' (ὡς ἐν ἐπιτομῇ) and 'according to an *epitome*' (κατ' ἐπιτομήν)' isn't carried out from previous writings: Clement presents an abbreviated way of writing his own book.[28] This doesn't preclude that the author abbreviates also other works. On the contrary, Clement often states that he borrows from previous texts in a summary way. For example, he explains that, for composing two passages of *Stromateus* 5, the first one about faith, the second one about hope and love, he 'displayed (. . .) testimonies from the Greeks' writings'.[29] Indeed, in the section about faith he quotes Empedocles,[30] Heraclitus[31] and Plato[32] and in the one about hope and love, alludes to and quotes Plato,[33] Empedocles[34] and Parmenides.[35]

From these two observations – in the *Stromateis*, ἐπιτομή refers to a way of writing in summary, while other authors' books such as Clement's own work are subjected to it – we draw the conclusion that *epitome* in the *Stromateis* is not a set of static generic characteristics but a dynamic; something that characterizes not Clement's book as a finished product but Clement's act of writing. *Stromateus* 1, 13, which we understand as a metaliterary passage, shows more precisely what this epitomizing dynamic of writing could be.

Cutting and reuniting in *Stromateus* 1, 13

We begin by quoting and translating this section.

> 57 [1] Μιᾶς τοίνυν οὔσης τῆς ἀληθείας (τὸ γὰρ ψεῦδος μυρίας ἐκτροπὰς ἔχει), καθάπερ αἱ βάκχαι τὰ τοῦ Πενθέως διαφορήσασαι μέλη αἱ τῆς φιλοσοφίας τῆς τε βαρβάρου τῆς τε Ἑλληνικῆς αἱρέσεις, ἑκάστη ὅπερ ἔλαχεν ὡς πᾶσαν αὐχεῖ τὴν ἀλήθειαν· φωτὸς δ᾽, οἶμαι, ἀνατολῇ πάντα φωτίζεται. [2] Ξύμπαντες οὖν Ἕλληνές τε καὶ βάρβαροι, ὅσοι τἀληθοῦς ὠρέχθησαν, οἳ μὲν οὐκ ὀλίγα, οἳ δὲ μέρος τι, εἴπερ ἄρα, τοῦ τῆς ἀληθείας λόγου ἔχοντες ἀναδειχθεῖεν. [3] Ὁ γοῦν αἰὼν τοῦ χρόνου τὸ μέλλον καὶ τὸ ἐνεστός, ἀτὰρ δὴ καὶ τὸ παρῳχηκὸς ἀκαριαίως συνίστησι, πολὺ δὲ πλέον δυνατωτέρα τοῦ αἰῶνος ἡ ἀλήθεια συναγαγεῖν τὰ οἰκεῖα σπέρματα, κἂν εἰς τὴν ἀλλοδαπὴν ἐκπέσῃ γῆν. [4] Πάμπολλα γὰρ τῶν παρὰ ταῖς αἱρέσεσι

δοξαζομένων εὕροιμεν ἄν (ὅσαι μὴ τέλεον ἐκκεκώφηνται μηδὲ ἐξετμήθησαν τὴν φυσικὴν ἀκολουθίαν, καθάπερ τὸν ἄνδρα αἱ γυναικωνίτιδες ἀποκοψάμεναι τὸν χριστόν),[36] εἰ καὶ ἀλλήλοις ἀνόμοια εἶναι δοκεῖ, τῷ γένει γε καὶ ὅλῃ τῇ ἀληθείᾳ ὁμολογοῦντα· ἢ γὰρ ὡς μέλος ἢ ὡς μέρος ἢ ὡς εἶδος ἢ ὡς γένος εἰς ἓν συνάπτεται. [5] Ἤδη δὲ καὶ ἡ ὑπάτη ἐναντία τῇ νεάτῃ οὖσα, ἀλλ᾽ ἄμφω γε ἁρμονία μία, ἔν τε ἀριθμοῖς ὁ ἄρτιος τῷ περιττῷ διαφέρεται, ὁμολογοῦσι δὲ ἄμφω τῇ ἀριθμητικῇ, ὡς τῷ σχήματι ὁ κύκλος καὶ τὸ τρίγωνον καὶ τὸ τετράγωνον καὶ ὅσα τῶν σχημάτων ἀλλήλων διενήνοχεν. Ἀτὰρ καὶ ἐν τῷ κόσμῳ παντὶ τὰ μέρη σύμπαντα, κἂν διαφέρηται πρὸς ἄλληλα, τὴν πρὸς τὸ ὅλον οἰκειότητα διαφυλάττει. [6] Οὕτως οὖν ἥ τε βάρβαρος ἥ τε Ἑλληνικὴ φιλοσοφία τὴν ἀίδιον ἀλήθειαν σπαραγμόν τινα, οὐ τῆς Διονύσου μυθολογίας, τῆς δὲ τοῦ λόγου τοῦ ὄντος ἀεὶ θεολογίας πεποίηται. Ὁ δὲ τὰ διῃρημένα συνθεὶς αὖθις καὶ ἑνοποιήσας τέλειον τὸν λόγον ἀκινδύνως εὖ ἴσθ' ὅτι κατόψεται, τὴν ἀλήθειαν.

[1] But truth is one (because lie has thousand twists and turns), like the Bacchae who tore apart Pentheus' limbs, the schools of Greek and Barbarian philosophies, each one, what it got, it praised it as if it was the whole truth, but I think that, at the rise of light, everything is enlightened. [2] Thus, every Greeks and Barbarians who tried to reach the truth, if it is so, might have been shown as having, the ones not little, the others a part of the *logos*[37] of the truth. [3] Yet eternity gathers future, present and even past in one moment, and truth is far more able than eternity to bring together its own seeds, even if they fell on an alien ground. [4] Indeed an immense amount of the doctrines proclaimed by the schools, we can discover that (all of them which were not entirely made deaf nor mutilated themselves concerning the law of nature, by cutting up Christ, like the inhabitants of the gynoecium[38] cut up the man), even if they seem dissimilar to each other, agree for the genre and for the whole truth. Indeed, as limb, as part, as specie or as genre they link together to form a unity. [5] And also the high string is opposed to the low string, but both are an only chord,[39] and, among numbers, the even number differ from the odd, but both are similar because they belong to arithmetic, as, because they belong to geometric shapes, the circle, the triangle, the square and every other geometric shapes, while differing from each other. Moreover, in the whole universe, all the parts, even if they differ from each other, keep their common identity towards the whole. [6] Consequently, in the same way, the Greek and Barbarian philosophy made a dismemberment, not the one of Dionysius from the myth,[40] but of the Logos who exists forever from the theological story. But the one who will put together again the torn apart parts and who will make them one, be sure he will watch the *logos* in his/its[41] perfection, the truth.

Stromateus *1, 13, 57, 1–6*

After having shown how those lines reveal the *epitome* as an epistemological and theological issue for Clement, we'll see how they work as a metaliterary passage about the author's own use of *epitome*.

A first difficulty concerning the passage and its meaning ensues from the complex syntax of the first sentence, where it is difficult to know to which or whom Pentheus and the Bacchae are compared: to the truth defined as a unity, to the lie defined as a plurality of twists and turns or to the various Greek or Barbarian – 'Barbarian' meaning, as often by Clement, Jewish and Christian, with a paradoxical positive re-use of this adjective[42] – 'philosophical schools' (αἱρέσεις, para. 1). For the same reason it is also difficult to understand if those multiple schools should be likened to truth or to lie. Two reasons lead us to choose the first solution. First, αἵρεσις – which, in that context, has the meaning of 'choice' – is opposed to ἐκτροπή (the 'twist') in *Stromateus* 1, 18, 89, 2, which leads us to give a positive meaning to αἵρεσις. Therefore, even with the meaning of 'school', αἵρεσις could be here more akin to 'truth' than to the 'twists and turns' of 'lie'. Second, despite its confused and interlaced syntax, the beginning of the sentence is organized as a chiasm between two mentions of truth ('But truth is one… as if it was the whole truth', para. 1), before some kind of *clausula*. The sentence is consequently more about truth than about lie: despite every school's arrogance ('it praised it as if it was the whole truth', para. 1), each one possesses a part of truth. Clement's position here is thus a radical eclecticism: every school has got a part of truth and its only lie is to see this part as the whole truth.[43]

This theory about truth has theological aspects, as it appears in a veiled manner at the end of the same first sentence: φωτὸς δ', οἶμαι, ἀνατολῇ πάντα φωτίζεται 'at the rise of light, everything is enlightened' (para. 1). Indeed, in *Stromateus* 7, 7, 43, 6 the ἀνατολή, with the meaning of 'Orient' – the place where the sun rises – is seen as a symbol of Christ.[44] Other indications in the passage confirm that ἀνατολή should be linked with Christ in 1, 13 too. The first one is the polysemy of the word λόγος, which, for that reason, we kept unchanged in our translation. In the framework of a comparison between this *logos* and a man – Pentheus – (para. 1) λόγος could refer to another person, the Christ, an assimilation which the following lines make explicit, if one accepts, as we did, to not correct the text transmitted by the manuscript ('by cutting up Christ (χριστός)', para. 4). Moreover, the end of the passage switches from one dismemberment to another: 'the Greek and Barbarian philosophy made a dismemberment, not the one of Dionysius from the myth…' (para. 6). Here the comparison is not with Pentheus torn apart by the Bacchae anymore, but with a god, Dionysius, torn apart by the Titans, according to a myth recounted, among others, by Plutarch in *On Isis and Osiris*,[45] but also by Clement himself in his *Protrepticus*.[46] In a veiled manner, the *logos* is here at the same time Pentheus and Dionysius; at the same time a man and a god. In this way, Clement's hermeneutics of truth is also a Christology. What was divided between the philosophical schools is truth, but it is also Christ himself, even his very body.[47]

This presence of Christ is linked with a discreet idea of providence, when Clement mentions what each philosophical school 'got' (ὅπερ ἔλαχεν, para. 1). Indeed, among the various and contradictory explanations the author of the *Stromateis* gives for the origin of philosophy, this expression could be linked with the idea of philosophy as a gift by God.[48] But the whole passage could also fit the solution Clement often relies on for the problem of the origin of philosophy, *id est* the idea, common in the first centuries

Christianity, that the Greeks stole philosophy from the Hebrews.[49] To that extent, lines from *Stromateus* 5 present striking common points with 1, 13: Ὅθεν ἡ μὲν Ἑλληνικὴ φιλοσοφία τῇ ἐκ τῆς θρυαλλίδος ἔοικεν λαμπηδόνι, ἣν ἀνάπτουσιν ἄνθρωποι, παρ' ἡλίου κλέπτοντες ἐντέχνως τὸ φῶς · κηρυχθέντος δὲ τοῦ λόγου πᾶν ἐκεῖνο τὸ ἅγιον ἐξέλαμψεν φῶς. 'In this way Greek philosophy is similar to the wick humans lit by skilfully stealing the light from the sun. But when the *Logos* is proclaimed, this holy light shines entirely.' (*Stromateus* 5, 5, 29, 6) Such as the dispersion of truth will end with the rising of the light of Christ, revealing the dismembered truth as a unity (*Stromateus* 1, 13, 57, 1), the Greeks' theft will end with the proclamation of the *Logos*, revealing their weak and incomplete glow as the 'holy' and 'entir[e]' light.

It is possible to go a step further. Clement uses once the word ἐπιτομή to describe the Greek's theft: Αὐτίκα ἐπιτομὴν τῶν περὶ δικαιοσύνης εἰρημένων Μωυσεῖ ὁ Πυθαγόρας πεποίηται λέγων ζυγὸν μὴ ὑπερβαίνειν, τουτέστι μὴ παρέρχεσθαι τὸ πρὸς τὰς διανομὰς ἴσον, τιμῶντας τὴν δικαιοσύνην 'But Pythagoras made an *epitome* of the words of Moses about justice when he said: 'Don't go beyond the yoke', that is to say, honour justice by not transgressing the equality in distributions' (*Stromateus* 5, 5, 30, 1). By doing so, the supposed borrowings by the Greeks from the Scriptures are described as a process of epitomizing: the Greek philosophers cut out words and ideas in the Scriptures just as the Bacchae cut out Pentheus' limbs.

However, the word *logos* has another, more obvious meaning than 'Christ'. In 1, 13, it could also refer to a speech or a text, more precisely to the *logos* the reader is discovering, that is to say, to the *Stromateis*, '*Logos* of the truth' (cf. 1, 13, 57, 2) because they intend to speak the truth about God. Several arguments can support such a metaliterary reading of *Stromateus* 1, 13. First, the comparison with the Bacchae appears immediately after an evocation of the *Stromateis* at the end of 1, 12:

> Ἀλλ' ἔστι τῷ ὄντι ἡ τῶν ὑπομνημάτων ὑποτύπωσις † ὅσα διασποράδην καὶ διερριμμένως ἐγκατεσπαρμένην ἔχουσι τὴν ἀλήθειαν, ὅπως ἂν λάθοι τοὺς δίκην κολοιῶν σπερμολόγους. Ἐπὰν δὲ ἀγαθοῦ τύχῃ γεωργοῦ, ἐκφύσεται ἕκαστον αὐτῶν καὶ τὸν πυρὸν ἀναδείξει.
>
> But the form of those notes [the *Stromateis*] is truly this one: every word which comprehend the truth sown here and there and in all directions, to be hidden to those who peck the seeds as jays. But if a good grower gets them, each one of them will sprout and show the ear.
>
> Stromateus *1, 12, 56, 3*

Morevoer, this passage presents several precise common points with 1, 13. The danger of 'those who peck the seeds' (σπερμολόγοι) fits the agricultural image mingled with the dismemberment comparison: 'truth is far more able than eternity to bring together its own seeds (τὰ οἰκεῖα σπέρματα), even if they fell on an alien ground (εἰς τὴν ἀλλοδαπὴν ἐκπέσῃ γῆν)' (*Stromateus* 1, 13, 57, 3). Furthermore, the end of *Stromateus* 1, 12, 56, 3, with the sprouting, growing and sown seed as an image of the revelation of the hidden truth, looks like the end of 1, 13, 57, 1, with the rising of light, through which 'everything is enlightened'.

If we accept such an interpretation, Clement would here characterize his work itself as a dismembered text, similar to the dismembered bodies of Pentheus and Dionysius. Such a text is torn between various 'schools', that is between various texts and more precisely between Greek references and quotations of the Scriptures, a twofold nature of the *Stromateis* that the author often underlines.[50] To put it in different words, *Stromateus* 1, 13 would be a way to describe the *Stromateis* as an *epitome*. This hypothesis is all the more credible given that another metaliterary use of the comparison with Pentheus and the Bacchae exists in Greek literature. In the third century BCE, probably also in Alexandria, Theocritus concludes his *26th Idyll*, dedicated to the dismemberment of Pentheus, by qualifying this act as an ἔργον (. . .) οὐκ ἐπιμωματόν, an 'act (. . .) which shall not be blamed'.[51] This apparently pious affirmation towards Dionysius has also been interpreted as a way to defend, in the penultimate and last verses, the poetic 'act' of Theocritus itself.[52] To that extent, we would suggest that the text of the *26th Idyll* itself is likened to the dismembered Pentheus, which would be consistent with the divided structure of this text, which juxtaposes two parts separated by what Christophe Cusset calls 'a split of the focalization'.[53]

In the same way, *Stromateus* 1, 13 affirms the divided nature of the *Stromateis*. But, at the same time, since Clement puts an emphasis on the unity of truth and *logos*, it also emphasizes its unity. To put it in other words, this passage underlines and helps us to grasp the twofold nature of the epitomizing dynamic – cutting and reuniting – for the *Stromateis* themselves and, consequently, the double nature of the *Stromateis* as an *epitome*.

The *Stromateis* as a double *epitome*

In *Stromateus* 1, 13, 57, 6, who is 'the one who will put together again the torn apart parts and who will make them one'? And who is the 'good grower' able to make the seeds of the truth grow in *Stromateus* 1, 12, 56, 3? Because of his revelatory role in the first case, it is tempting to identify him with the risen light mentioned in 1, 13, 57, 1, that is to say with the *Logos*, the Christ. But in this passage, precisely, the person who 'will make' the dispersed parts 'one' will also be able to 'watch the *logos* in his perfection', which means he is not the *Logos* himself. Which leads us to two possible identities.

The person able to (re)unite the cut and dismembered parts into a new body could be Clement himself. Three arguments can support this hypothesis. First, on several occasions the author compares his activity to the one of a grower.[54] Second, in one of their first chapters, he compares the *Stromateis* to a body, similar to the one of Pentheus or Dionysius.[55] Third, it seems logical that the author of the *logos* that are the *Stromateis* would be able to 'watch' this *logos* 'in its perfection'.

But this person could also be the *Stromateis*' reader. Indeed, in at least one passage, he too is compared to a 'grower', more precisely to a grower able to create a new unity:

> [1] Ἐοίκασι δέ πως οἱ Στρωματεῖς οὐ παραδείσοις ἐξησκημένοις ἐκείνοις τοῖς ἐν στοίχῳ καταπεφυτευμένοις εἰς ἡδονὴν ὄψεως, ὄρει δὲ μᾶλλον συσκίῳ τινὶ καὶ δασεῖ κυπαρίσσοις καὶ πλατάνοις δάφνῃ τε καὶ κισσῷ, μηλέαις τε ὁμοῦ καὶ ἐλαίαις καὶ συκαῖς καταπεφυτευμένῳ, ἐξεπίτηδες ἀναμεμιγμένης τῆς φυτείας καρποφόρων τε ὁμοῦ καὶ ἀκάρπων δένδρων διὰ τοὺς ὑφαιρεῖσθαι καὶ κλέπτειν τολμῶντας τὰ ὥρια, ἐθελούσης λανθάνειν τῆς γραφῆς. [2] Ἐξ ὧν δὴ μεταμοσχεύσας καὶ μεταφυτεύσας ὁ γεωργὸς ὡραῖον κατακοσμήσει παράδεισον καὶ ἄλσος ἐπιτερπές. [3] Οὔτ' οὖν τῆς τάξεως οὔτε τῆς φράσεως στοχάζονται οἱ Στρωματεῖς, ὅπου γε ἐπίτηδες καὶ τὴν λέξιν οὐχ Ἕλληνες εἶναι βούλονται καὶ τὴν τῶν δογμάτων ἐγκατασπορὰν λεληθότως καὶ οὐ κατὰ τὴν ἀλήθειαν πεποίηνται, φιλοπόνους καὶ εὑρετικοὺς εἶναι τοὺς <ἀναγιγνώσκοντας> εἴ τινες τύχοιεν παρασκευάζοντες.
>
> [1] The *Stromateis* are in no way like those paradises, which are carefully arranged, planted in rows for the pleasure of the eyes, but rather like a shaded and wooded mountain, planted with cypresses and plane trees, laurel tree and ivy, apple trees with olive and fig trees, where the planting of fruit trees is intentionally mixed up with the one of trees without fruit because of those who dare to take and steal the seasonal fruits, because my writing wants to stay hidden. [2] Then, by picking out and transplanting from them, the grower will order a graceful paradise and a charming wood. [3] Therefore the *Stromateis* aim neither to a beautiful arrangement nor to a beautiful style, since, deliberately, they refuse to be Greek also according to the style and realized the sowing of doctrines in a hidden way and not according to the truth, making the <readers>, if they exist, effort-lovers and able to discover.
>
> Stromateus *7, 18, 111, 1–3*

Even if the 'readers' are not directly mentioned here,[56] it is indubitable that they are shown here as the 'grower' (*Stromateus* 7, 18, 111, 2) who, 'pricking out and transplanting' (ibid.) from the disordered 'paradises' (ibid., 1) of the *Stromateis*, is able to create a new ordered paradise (ibid., 2). If we read *Stromateus* 1, 13 parallel to these lines, the reader appears as the one able to reunite the body of truth and to 'watch', beyond Clement's text, 'the *logos* in his/its perfection' (*Stromateus* 1, 13, 57, 6).

Both identifications are possible because the *Stromateis* are in two different ways an *epitome*. On the one hand, they are built from Clement's abbreviated ideas and from Clement's short borrowings from various books and, consequently are themselves a new unity, thanks to the author's work.[57] But, at the same time, on the other hand, by Clement's own admission, they remain a dismembered body, which the reader can reunite. Consequently, the epitomizing dynamic isn't fully realized in the static object that would be Clement's book. The *Stromateis* stay dynamic. They are less a product than a productivity, less a book than an ongoing process of writing by (re)fragmenting and (re)composing.

Notes

* At the beginning of this article, I would like to express all my gratitude to Marco Formisano and Paolo Felice Sacchi for having accepted my proposition for the conference 'Epitome. From Fragmentation to Re-composition, and Back Again' and the paper I wrote afterwards and for having organized that meeting and the present volume despite such difficult times.

1. The Greek text of the work by the Pseudo-Scymnos was notably edited by Didier Marcotte in Marcotte 2000. As for every other texts in Greek, Latin or French, we give our own translations in English unless otherwise specified.
2. τῶν Ἀττικῶν τις γνησίων τε φιλολόγων (Pseudo-Scymnos, *Travel*, v. 19, in Marcotte 2000) This 'genuine Attic philologis[t]' is probably Apollodorus of Athens and the work that the Pseudo-Scymnos refers to, his *Chronicle* (cf. Marcotte 2000, 3).
3. πάντων ἐπιτομὴ τῶν χύδην εἰρημένων (Pseudo-Scymnos, *Travel*, v. 32 in Marcotte 2000).
4. Ibid., v. 90.
5. κεφαλαιώδεις ἐπιτομαὶ πάνυ βραχεῖαι (Dionysius of Halicarnassus, *Roman Antiquities*, 1, 5, 4). Cf. Dionysius of Halicarnassus 1961. One can also mention a passage where Plutarch relates how Brutus wrote an *epitome* of Polybius during the war between Pompey and Caesar (*Life of Brutus*, 4, 8). Cf. Plutarch 1918.
6. For example, the historian Barron, author of an '*epitome* (ἐπιτομή) of the things concerning Alexander of Macedon' (*Suda*, letter *beta*, entry 123).
7. Ἀριστοφάνους τῶν 'Αριστοτέλους περὶ ζῴων ἐπιτομή, ὑποτεθέντων ἑκάστῳ ζῴῳ καὶ τῶν Αἰλιανῷ καὶ Τιμοθέῳ καὶ ἑτέροις τισὶ περὶ αὐτῶν εἰρημένων '*Epitome* by Aristophanes of the accounts by Aristotle about the living things, concerning each living thing and of the words by Aelian, Timotheus and by others about them'. This title is quoted by Arnaud Zucker in Zucker 2012.
8. Συλλογὴ τῆς περὶ ζῴων ἱστορίας, χερσαίων πτηνῶν τε καὶ θαλαττίων, Κωνσταντίνῳ τῷ μεγάλῳ βασιλεῖ καὶ αὐτοκράτορι φιλοπονηθεῖσα. 'Labour-loving collection of the inquiry about the living things of the earth, the air and the sea, for Constantine the great king and absolute ruler' (ibid.).
9. συναγωγὴ περὶ ζῴων ἱστορίας χερσαίων θαλαττίων καὶ πτηνῶν πονηθεῖσα παρὰ βασιλέως Κωνσταντίνου τοῦ {deest Imperatoris cognomen spatio vacuo relicto} καὶ ἐκ διαφόρων βιβλίων ἐρανισθεῖσα 'Gathering of the inquiry about the earthly, marine and winged living beings elaborated as asked by the king Constantine {a space follows, for the emperor's *cognomen*, which is missing} and collected from various books' (ibid.).
10. κεφάλαια συναθροίσας χρόνων (Pseudo-Scymnos, *Travel*, v. 45 in Marcotte 2000).
11. The expression ἐν ἐπιτομῇ appears in the same way, without reference to the *epitome* as a literary concept, for example in the *Letter from Clement to James* (19, 2) (Clement of Rome [attributed to] 1847).
12. ἐκ τῶν σποράδην γὰρ ἱστορημένων τισὶν ἐν ἐπιτομῇ σοι γέγραφα (Pseudo-Scymnos, *Travel*, v. 65–6 in Marcotte 2000).
13. συντεμὼν ἐκθήσομαι (ibid., v. 70).
14. Ibid., v. 103 and 109. Turning our attention to Latin literature, the same two processes appear in Justin's preface to his compilation of passages from Gnaeus Pompeius Trogus' forty-four-books *Philippic Histories*. On the one hand, Justin 'excerpted (*excerpsi*) the passages which are the worthiest of being known'. On the other hand, he organized those excerpts to make a 'little book (*corpusculum*) like of flowers' (Justin 1985, *praefatio*: 4). Nevertheless, Justin doesn't use the Latin transliteration *epitome* or *epitoma* to characterize his book.

15. Both terms are used by Jean Schneider to pin down the Graeco-Latine letter as a literary genre (Schneider 2014: 14).
16. Jean-Marie Schaeffer uses those terms to define, for example, the ways to identify a sonnet in Schaeffer 1989, 159 for the first one and 171 for the second.
17. For example, János Jarecsni considers the *epitome* as a genre in Jarecsni 1997: 203.
18. It seems to us that 'genre' in general is not a useful concept to talk about ancient texts or about texts at all. At best, it is some kind of way to grasp, so to speak statistically, common characteristics from different texts but it fails, among other things, to seize the dynamic nature of any text.
19. To that extent, our perspective is close to Arnaud Zucker's, who, by analysing the *Zoological Encyclopaedia*, demonstrates that 'ancient *epitome* (. . .) seems to have never existed as a genre' (Zucker 2012, para. 13). The conception of *epitome* as a dynamic helps to understand why the *epitome* can be an abbreviation of a previous text (without any change of its order or wording) as well as a reformulation or a re-ordering of it (cf. ibid., para. 16).
20. Kristeva 1968: 59, and 1969.
21. It is our main point of disagreement with Arnaud Zucker, who considers that the word *epitome* 'doesn't refer to an 'operation' but to a 'product'' (Zucker 2012, para. 14). Yet is is striking that, parallel to passages where he speaks of the *epitome* as an 'abridged form' or a 'short version' (ibid.), the scholar describes it using dynamic terms: according to him, the word *epitome* refers to 'operations' (ibid., para. 13); in the *Epitome* by Aristophanes of Byzantium, one finds 'extraction and redistribution' (ibid., para. 15); what Arnaud Zucker defines as 'the AB regime' 'combines (stylistic) reformulating and (structural) reorganizing' (ibid., para. 16).
22. Following Clement's own habit (cf. for example 1, 29, 182, 3), we call each volume of the *Stromateis* a '*Stromateus*'. Except otherwise specified, for the Greek text of the *Stromateis*, we follow Otto Stählin in Clement of Alexandria 1906 and 1909.
23. ὁ συνταξάμενος τὴν τῶν Μακκαβαϊκῶν ἐπιτομήν (*Stromateus* 5, 14, 97, 7).
24. ὑπὸ Ἰάσωνος τοῦ Κυρηναίου δεδηλωμένα διὰ πέντε βιβλίων πειρασόμεθα δι ἑνὸς συντάγματος ἐπιτεμεῖν. We quote the text from the Septuagint. Cf. Anonymous 1976.
25. Καὶ ἡ μὲν διαδοχὴ τῶν παρ᾽Ἕλλησι φιλοσόφων ὡς ἐν ἐπιτομῇ ἥδε (*Stromateus* 1, 14, 64, 5).
26. ἡ πρὸς τοὺς Ἰουδαίους κατ᾽ ἐπιτομὴν τῶν γραφῶν ἔκθεσις (*Stromateus* 4, 1, 1, 3).
27. For ἐν ἐπιτομῇ, besides the example from the *Letter from Clement to James* we already referred to, we could quote the treatise *On Fate* by Plutarch (568 E–F) : Δυνάμει μὲν οὖν εἴρηται, ὁποῖα χρὴ λέγεσθαι περὶ τῆς κατ᾽ οὐσίαν εἱμαρμένης · καὶ γὰρ ἥτις ἐστὶ καὶ πόση τις καὶ ὁποία καὶ ὅπως τέτακται καὶ ὅπως ἔχει αὐτή τε πρὸς ἑαυτὴν καὶ δὴ καὶ πρὸς ἡμᾶς, *ὡς ἐν ἐπιτομῇ* εἴρηται· τὰ δὲ καθ᾽ ἕκαστα περὶ τούτων ὁ ἕτερος μῦθος ὁ ἐν τῇ Πολιτείᾳ μετρίως αἰνίττεται, καὶ ἡμεῖς εἰς δύναμίν σοι ταῦτ᾽ ἐπειράθημεν ἐξηγήσασθαι. 'Thus, we spoke as far as it was possible, as we should speak, of destiny according to its being and, indeed, about what it is, how big it is, how it is, how it is ordered, how it is to itself and, above all, to us; we spoke *in summary*, but the details about these things, the other myth in the *Republic* alludes to them and we ourselves, as far as possible, will try to explain them to you.' (Cf. Plutarch 1959.) The difference between the two developments about fate that Plutarch alludes to is not a distinction of genre but of content: the first one is a summary, whereas the second one is a detailed presentation. Among other occurrences, we find the expression κατ᾽ ἐπιτομήν also in Philo of Byzantium's treaty on artillery. (Cf. Philo of Byzantium 1693, 64.)
28. When, in the beginning of *Stromateus* 4, Clement announces an 'exposition of the Scriptures for the Jews according to an *epitome* (κατ᾽ ἐπιτομήν)', he doesn't talk of the *epitome* of the book by another author or by other authors – in that case, the Scriptures. What is abbreviated

is not the Scriptures themselves, but an ἔκθεσις, an 'exposition' about them by Clement himself. Therefore, the epitomizing process doesn't apply here to someone else's book but to Clement's own discourse.

29. Περὶ μὲν οὖν πίστεως ἱκανὰ μαρτύρια τῶν παρ' Ἕλλησι γραφῶν παρατεθείμεθα· ὡς δὲ μὴ ἐπὶ μήκιστον παρεξίωμεν καὶ περὶ τῆς ἐλπίδος καὶ τῆς ἀγάπης πλεῖστα φιλοτιμούμενοι συναγαγεῖν, ἀπόχρη μόνα ταῦτα εἰπεῖν. . . 'And about faith, we displayed enough testimonies from the Greeks' writings, but in order not to go on for a very long time about hope and about love in the desire of gathering very many of them, it is enough to tell those ones alone. . .' (*Stromateus* 5, 2, 14, 1). The section about faith goes from *Stromateus* 5, 1, 1, 1 to 5, 1, 13, 4 (the testimonies from the Greeks being given more precisely in 5, 1, 9) and the shorter one about hope and love goes from 5, 2, 14, 1 to 15, 4.

30. Empedocles, fragment 114, edited in Diels and Kranz 1960–1, quoted by Clement in *Stromateus* 5, 1, 9, 1, where Empedocles is referred to as ὁ Ἀκραγαντῖνος ποιητής 'the poet from Agrigento'.

31. Heraclitus, fragment 28 in Diels and Kranz 1960–1, quoted in *Stromateus* 5, 1, 9, 3, where Heraclitus is called ὁ Ἐφέσιος 'the Ephesian'.

32. Plato, *Timaeus*, 22 c 1–3, quoted in *Stromateus* 5, 1, 9, 5; 22 d 1–3, in 5, 1, 9, 6 and 22 d 7 – e 1, in 5, 1, 9, 7.

33. Plato, *Crito*, 48 b 5–6, quoted in 5, 2, 14, 1; *Phaedrus* 248 and 249, alluded to in 5, 2, 14, 2; *Symposium*, 206 c – 208 b, alluded to in 5, 2, 15, 1; *Theaetetus* 150 b–c, alluded to in 5, 2, 15, 2.

34. Empedocles, fragments 17 and 21 in Diels and Kranz 1960–1, quoted in *Stromateus* 5, 2, 15, 4.

35. Parmenides, fragment 4 in Diels and Kranz 1960–1, quoted in *Stromateus* 5, 2, 15, 5.

36. We keep here the text of the *Laurentianus* v, 3, the only manuscript of the *Stromateis* – the only other extant one, the *Parisinus Supplementum Graecum* 250, is a copy of the *Laurentianus* v, 3. Most editors replace here χριστόν with λόγον.

37. Because λόγος is polysemic in this passage, we choose to transliterate this Greek word.

38. Γυναικωνῖτις usually means 'women's apartments' (see for example Philo, *De somniis*, 2, 55, 4) but can also metonymically refer to 'women', such as in Plutarch, *Life of Cato the Younger*, 30, 819 d (cf. Philo 1968 and Plutarch 1919) or, later than Clement, in the Pseudo-Martyrius' *Funeral oration to John Chrysostom* (84, 7). Cf. Van Ommeslaeghe 1974.

39. The word ἁρμονία can refer to a chord, for example in Plato, *Symposium* 187 a–b. Cf. Plato 1989.

40. Among other books, in Clement's *Protrepticus*, μυθολογία refers not to 'mythology', that is to say to a group of tellings, but to one story, that is to say, to a 'myth', like, for example the telling of Pherephatta's abduction in *Protrepticus* 17. Cf. Clement of Alexandria 1905.

41. Due to the polysemic use of λόγος in this passage, it can be translated both as referring to an object and to a masculine individual.

42. Cf., for example, Stromateus 1, 3, 22, 1 – 'because they [malevolent Greek thinkers and orators] don't want to believe, they laugh about the truth worthy of a whole solemnity [the Christian one], making fun of its barbarian nature (τὸ βάρβαρον)' – and 1, 20, 99, 1 – 'the divine and barbarian (βάρβαρος) philosophy'. About this re-appropriation by Clement of the word 'barbarian', see, among others, Le Boulluec 1999.

43. Despite some contradictions if one considers the whole *Stromateis*, this eclecticism can be found elsewhere in the work, for example in 1, 7, 37.

44. Ἐπεὶ δὲ γενεθλίου ἡμέρας εἰκὼν ἡ ἀνατολὴ κἀκεῖθεν τὸ φῶς αὔξεται ἐκ σκότους λάμψαν τὸ πρῶτον, ἀλλὰ καὶ τοῖς ἐν ἀγνοίᾳ καλινδουμένοις ἀνέτειλεν γνώσεως ἀληθείας ἡμέρα κατὰ

λόγον τοῦ ἡλίου, πρὸς τὴν ἑωθινὴν ἀνατολὴν αἱ εὐχαί. 'And because the Orient is the image of the day of birth and because from here grows the first light that shines from the darkness, but because also, for those who dwelled in ignorance rose the day of the truth of knowledge, in the same way as the sun, the prayers are made to the Orient at morning.' (*Stromateus* 7, 7, 43, 6) The passage refers to Mt. 4.16 quoting Is. 9.2 ('the people sitting in the darkness has seen a great light and on those who sat in the land and in the shadow of death, a light has risen') and interpreting it as a prophecy about Jesus.

45. Plutarch, *On Isis and Osiris*, 28. Cf. Plutarch 1988.

46. Clement of Alexandria, *Protrepticus*, 17.

47. Because the *logos*, in this passage, is at the same time the text of the *Stromateis* and the body of Christ, Clement is able to do what, according to Mohammad Reza Fallah Nejad, is impossible for Roland Barthes. See his contribution in this same volume: 'Barthes believes, moreover, that he can do everything with the language, but not with the body'(p. 129). Nevertheless, the assimilation of a text and a (here both human and divine) being is not unlike the Barthesian idea that, in the words of Mohammad Reza Fallah Nejad, '[o]ur being melts and is found in the text' (p. 116).

48. This idea is expressed for example in *Stromateus* 1, 5, 28, 3: τάχα δὲ καὶ προηγουμένως τοῖς Ἕλλησιν ἐδόθη 'Maybe it [the philosophy] was given to the Greeks as a main principle'.

49. Cf., among others, Sanna 1989, 119–43, and Ridings 1995.

50. We can quote for example *Stromateus* 1, 1, 18, 1: Περιέξουσι δὲ οἱ Στρωματεῖς ἀναμεμιγμένην τὴν ἀλήθειαν τοῖς φιλοσοφίας δόγμασι, μᾶλλον δὲ ἐγκεκαλυμμένην καὶ ἐπικεκρυμμένην, καθάπερ τῷ λεπύρῳ τὸ ἐδώδιμον τοῦ καρύου 'My *Stromateis* contain the truth [the Christian one] mixed up with the ideas of philosophy [the Greek truth], or rather hidden and veiled through them like through the shell the edible part of the nut'.

51. Theocritus, *26th Idyll*, v. 37–38. We follow the Greek text edited by Christophe Cusset in Cusset 2001.

52. This hypothesis was among others put forward by Christophe Cusset (ibid., 29).

53. Ibid., 18. The image of the text as a dismembered then remembered body is not foreign to works seen as *epitomai*. For example, both Ausonius and Marcellus Empiricus compare, respectively, their *Cento nuptialis* (Ausonius 1919–21) and *De medicamentis* (Marcellus Empiricus 1916) to the cut out and reunited body of Virbius, whose story is, among other sources, told by Ovid in the *Metamorphoses* (xv, v. 479–546). We thank Marco Formisano for these two references.

54. See, among other passages, *Stromateus* 1, 1, 17, 4: Καθάπερ δ' οἱ γεωργοὶ προαρδεύσαντες τὴν γῆν, οὕτω δὴ καὶ ἡμεῖς τῷ ποτίμῳ τῶν παρ' Ἕλλησι λόγων προαρδεύομεν τὸ γεῶδες αὐτῶν, ὡς παραδέξασθαι τὸ καταβαλλόμενον σπέρμα πνευματικὸν καὶ τοῦτο εὐμαρῶς ἐκθρέψαι δύνασθαι. 'Like the growers, beforehand, water the earth, we too, beforehand, water their earthly part [of the readers] with what it is possible to drink in the Greek words, so that they can receive the spiritual seed fallen in them and easily make it grow.'

55. Σιωπῶ γὰρ ὅτι οἱ Στρωματεῖς τῇ πολυμαθίᾳ σωματοποιούμενοι κρύπτειν ἐντέχνως τὰ τῆς γνώσεως βούλονται σπέρματα. 'Because I stay silent about the fact that the *Stromateis*, made as a body through erudition, want to skilfully hide the seeds of knowledge.' (*Stromateus* 1, 2, 20, 4).

56. The word ἀναγιγνώσκοντες 'readers' doesn't appear here in the *Laurentianus* but is an addition by Otto Stählin.

57. I am very thankful to Marco Formisano for having fruitfully brought this aspect of *Stromateus* 1, 13 to my attention.

Works cited

Anonymous (1939), *Septuaginta. Vetus Testamentum Graecum. 14. Isaias*, J. Ziegler (ed.), Göttingen: Vandenhoeck & Ruprecht.
Anonymous (1976), *Septuaginta. Vetus Testamentum Graecum.* IX, *2, 2. Maccabeorum liber II*, W. Kappler and R. Hanhart (eds), Göttingen: Vandenhoeck & Ruprecht.
Ausonius (1919–21), *Cento nuptialis*, in *Ausonius*, ed. and trans. H. G. Evelyn-White, London: William Heinemann and G. P. Putnam.
Clement of Alexandria (1905), *Protrepticus*, in *Clemens Alexandrinus. Erster Band. Protrepticus und Paedagogus*, O. Stählin (ed.), Leipzig: J. C. Hinrichs.
Clement of Alexandria (1906), *Stromateis* I-VI, in *Clemens Alexandrinus. Zweiter Band. Stromata Buch I-VI*, O. Stählin (ed.), Leipzig: J. C. Hinrichs.
Clement of Alexandria (1909), *Stromateis* VII, in *Clemens Alexandrinus. Dritter Band. Stromata Buch VII-VIII. Excerpta ex Theodoto. Eclogae prophetica quis dives salvetur. Fragmente*, O. Stählin (ed.), Leipzig: J. C. Hinrichs.
Clement of Rome [attributed to] (1847), *Letter from Clement to James*, in A. Schwegler (ed.), *Clementis Romani Quae Feruntur Homiliae*, Stuttgart: Sumptibus A. Becheri.
Cusset, C. (2001), *Les Bacchantes de Théocrite. Texte, corps et morceaux. Édition, traduction et commentaire de l'*Idylle 26, Paris: L'Harmattan.
Diels, H. and W. Kranz (1960–1), *Die Fragmente der Vorsokratiker*, Berlin: Weidmann.
Dionysius of Halicarnassus (1961), *Roman Antiquities*, 1, E. Spelmans (ed.), Cambridge, MA: Harvard University Press.
Jarecsni, J. (1997), 'The "*Epitome*": an original work or a copy? An analysis of the first eleven chapters of the "*Epitome de Caesaribus*"', *Acta Classica Universitatis Scientiarum Debreceniensis* 33: 203–14.
Justin (1985), *Epitoma historiarum Philippicarum Pompei Trogi*, F. Rühl and O. Seel (eds), Stuttgart: Teubner.
Kristeva, J. (1968), 'La productivité dite texte', *Communications* 11: 59–83.
Kristeva, J. (1969), 'Le texte clos', in J. Kristeva, *Σημειωτική: Recherches pour une sémanalyse*, 113–42, Paris: Éditions du Seuil.
Le Boulluec, A. (1999), 'La rencontre de l'hellénisme et de la "philosophie barbare" selon Clément d'Alexandrie', in J. Leclant (ed.), *Alexandrie : une mégapole cosmopolite. Actes du 9ème colloque de la Villa Kérylos à Beaulieu-sur-Mer les 2 & 3 octobre 1998*, 175–88, Paris: Académie des Inscriptions et Belles-Lettres.
Marcellus Empiricus (1916), *De medicamentis*, M. Niedermann (ed.), Berlin: Teubner.
Marcotte, D. (2000), *Les Géographes grecs. Tome 1. Introduction générale. Pseudo-Scymnos*, Paris: Les Belles Lettres.
Matthew [attributed to] (2012), *Gospel according to Matthew*, in E. Nestle, E. Nestle, K. Aland and B. Aland (eds), *Novum Testamentum Graece*, 28th edn, Stuttgart: Deutsche Bibelgesellschaft.
Ovid (2008), *Metamorphoses*, trans. A. D. Melville, Oxford: Oxford University Press.
Philo (1968), *De somniis, in Philo. 5.*, Cambridge, MA and London: Harvard University Press and W. Heinemann.
Philo of Byzantium (1693), *Belopoieca* in M. Thévenot, J. Boivin and P. de La Hire (eds), *Veterum Mathematicorum Athenaei, Apollodori, Philonis, Bitonis, Heronis et aliorum Opera*, Paris.
Plato (1989), *Symposium*, in Plato, *Œuvres complètes. Tome IV, 2e partie : Le Banquet*, ed. and trans. P. Vicaire, Paris: Les Belles Lettres.
Plutarch (1918), *Life of Brutus*, in Plutarch, *Lives. VI. Dion and Brutus. Timoleon and Aemilius Paulus*, ed. C. Sintenis and I. Bekker, trans. B. Perrin, London and New York: William Heinemann and G. P. Putnam.

Plutarch (1919), *Life of Cato the Younger*, in Plutarch, *Lives.* *VIII. Sertorius and Eumenes. Phocion and Cato the Younger*, ed. C. Sintenis and I. Bekker, trans. B. Perrin, London and New York: William Heinemann and G. P. Putnam.

Plutarch (1959), *On Fate*, in Plutarch, *Moralia. Vol. VII*, ed. and trans. P. H. De Lacy and B. Einarson, Cambridge, MA: Harvard University Press.

Plutarch (1988), *Sur Isis et Osiris* in Plutarch, *Œuvres morales. Tome V, 2e partie*, ed. and trans. C. Froidefond, Paris: Les Belles Lettres.

Pseudo-Martyrius (1974), *Funeral oration to John Chrysostom*, in F. Van Ommeslaeghe, 'De lijkrede voor Johannes Chrysostomos toegeschreven aan Martyrius van Antiochie', PhD thesis, Catholic University of Louvain.

Pseudo-Scymnos (2000), *Circuit de la terre*, in D. Marcotte (ed.), *Les Géographes grecs. Tome 1. Introduction générale. Pseudo-Scymnos*, Paris: Les Belles Lettres.

Ridings, D. (1995), *The Attic Moses. The Dependency Theme in Some Early Christian Writers*, Göteborg: Acta Universitatis Gothoburgensis.

Sanna, I. (1989), 'L'argomento apologetico "Furta Graecorum"', in M. Bordoni (ed.), *Problemi attuali di filosofia – teologia – dirrito. Studio della Pontificia Università Lateranense per il 50. Della nuova sede*, 119–43, Rome : Libreria editrice lateranense.

Schaeffer, J.-M. (1989), *Qu'est-ce qu'un genre littéraire?* Paris : Seuil.

Schneider, J. (2014), 'Avant-propos', in J. Schneider (ed.), *La Lettre gréco-latine. Un genre littéraire?*, 9–23, Lyon : Maison de l'Orient et de la Méditerranée Jean Pouilloux.

Soudas [attributed to] (1928), *Lexicographi Graeci recogniti et apparatu critico instructi. 1. Suidae lexicon. Pars I*, ed. A. Adler, Leipzig : Teubner.

Theocritus (2001), *26th Idyll*, in C. Cusset (ed.), *Les Bacchantes de Théocrite. Texte, corps et morceaux. Édition, traduction et commentaire de l'*Idylle 26, Paris: L'Harmattan.

Zucker, A. (2012), 'Qu'est-ce qu'épitomiser? Étude des pratiques dans la *Syllogè* zoologique byzantine', *Rursus* 7. Available online: http://journals.openedition.org/rursus/961.

CHAPTER 7
BARTHES'S DREAM AT THE COLLÈGE DE FRANCE: FROM CRITICAL FRAGMENTS TO LITERARY RECOMPOSITIONS

Mohammad Reza Fallah Nejad

Introduction

The end of a writer's life is often not an easy one. They are indeed most of the time forced to overcome family hardships and endure the loss of loved ones. Twentieth-century writers are no exception, and we can cite the examples of A. Gide and M. Proust. Barthes is like Proust, he loses his mother and decides to 'change his life'. He now dreams of reviving her body, soul and memories: he thinks of his literary testament. His last course at the Collège de France, *La Préparation du roman*, concludes his work and expresses his theories in a 'romanticized' form. At the end of his career, Barthes wanted a *Vita Nova*[1] and proceeded, like Proust and Tolstoï, by steps.

In his last lectures, we can find the sketches of a theory: Barthes writes *himself* and recomposes his masterpiece. We will thus be able to observe how the creator of *The Death of the Author* now wishes to bring the fragments back to life in his lectures. Then we will examine a broken novelesque dream. Finally, we will study the wish of rewriting a text.

A fragmentary *corpus*

The final parts of a writer's work summarize his research and describe an intimate other-self. Most of the time, they correspond to new points of view expressed in his work. And they also manifest a whole different universe by describing certain parts of literary work as such. Barthes even imagines:

> To scrutinize the loved body for a long time (like the narrator before Albertine's sleep). To scrutinize means to search: I search the body of the other, as if I wanted to see what is inside [. . .]. Certain parts of the body are particularly peculiar to this observation: eyelashes, nails, hairline, very partial objects.[2]

Fragments, like the voice, make it possible to react against the inertia of language by using an 'impure, attenuated discontinuous' discourse.[3] Barthes believes, moreover, that he can do everything with the language, but not with the body, each image of the latter mingling with that one of the *other*. He speaks of figures of speech in the sense of 'gymnastics: scheme [. . .] gesture of action (athlete, orator, statue)'.[4] Writing is a neutral, composite element, from which our subject flees, where all identity is lost, starting with 'the very one of the body that writes'.[5] Moreover, *masterpieces* unify a coherent fictitious whole like those of Diderot.[6]

Barthes himself also redefines literature not as a body or series of works but as a 'profession'[7] or as a writing practice. He interchangeably associates 'literature, [writing] or [text]'.[8] The writing-*I* penetrates the body by passing in turn through 'sensation'.[9] The fragment is in the end like the haiku, the maxim, the thought or the piece of newspaper: 'a rhetorical genre'.[10] Barthes likes to talk about the division between genres and a varied theme, examples of which we find throughout his work: 'The miniatures, the rings, the brilliant details [. . .] the sight of the fields, the windows, the haiku, the line, the writing, the fragment, the photograph, the Italian scene, in short, whatever you want and all things articulated by the semanticist or all the material of the fetishist'.[11]

Rather than opposing the oral and the written, Barthes emphasizes the specificity of each mode of expression. In *De la parole à l'écriture* he wonders moreover about the transcription of an interview, about this common practice that he calls 'scription'.[12] Barthes is interested in all oral and written manifestations of the body. He wanted a rewriting that would occur in all the plastic arts, in music and even in other less 'noble' arts such as 'cooking, fashion and all the semiotics of the body'.[13] He thus throws on the written work, on the past corpus, a sort of '*patch-work*',[14] a rhapsodic cover resembling fragments of sewn tiles.

The writer seems also to aspire to a novel by recalling, for example, the photo of the *Winter Garden*[15] designated 'metonymically by the place'[16] and found at the heart of his *Chambre claire*.[17] This work, which was published in homage to his dead mother, can be considered as the most beautiful 'example'[18] of the Barthesian *third form* or: 'Novel by fragments, *a* Novel-Fragments. [. . .] *Perhaps there are novels which approach the novel-fragments*'.[19]

As with literature, a rebirth of being can also be seen through a photo,[20] while recreating and mortifying it at the same time: we see here a science of 'desirable or hateful' bodies.[21] Looking at a photo, it is the figure of the loved one that we see again. It is about stopping in time by observing the *noema* or the '*It was*' capturing the photographic rays emitted by the object. These rays last in time like fragments of reality[22] and produce an 'effect' on the reader. The photo reflects the past to the present, since time and space freeze next to each other. Such is the case with Barthes himself, eternalizing himself by his work among us. Actually, we still talk about his work and take a look at one of his photos. Just as he did for his mother who died on October 25, 1977. Her disappearance was also a stasis breaking up the couple formed with the mother:[23] 'Now, Freud says of the maternal body that "there is no other place of which one can say with comparable certainty that one has already been there"'.[24]

Photography, like any language, is a means of 'diverting' the orality in order to create another literary universe.[25] The coexistence of two *Barthes* can be observed: one writing the 'death of the author' and the other bringing the author back to life through the '*tableautins* of *Mythologies* and *L'Empire des signes*'[26] by bringing together, just like in a photo, the 'present and the past'.[27] To write a novel is to talk about the memory of those we have loved as well as about the aborted fragments that we can see in *another place*.

The broken dream

Time is a precious commodity and with age we gradually realize its value. This was also the case with writers such as Molière, Proust, Pascal and Barthes. Their last days were tinged with sadness and sickness. The death of relatives and in particular that of the mother pushed them to think about their own deaths. Barthes draws portraits by using words as photograms and expressing sorrow and memories: 'I can't wait [. . .] to get down to the book on the Photo, that is to say to integrate my grief into writing.'[28]

Pain drives you to create by taking you out of yourself: isn't that what suffering should bring? The writer discovers himself and, paradoxically enough, the disappearance of the loved ones such as the mother allows for a new life because literature protects against 'real death'. The author now has the power to transform books or images into *text*. Barthes dreams of his sadness and is inspired, just like Proust and Tolstoï, by maternal memory: 'June 9, 1978: This morning, passing through the Saint-Sulpice church, [. . .]: if only I could succeed in the Photo-Mam book. And then I notice [. . .] the Childish Desire. [. . .]'.[29]

He creates from what is frozen in time and passes then from *bio-graphy* or living-writing on to *photo-graphy* or writing-of-the-image, thus creating a perfect metaphor of the 'text-life'.[30] The *Chambre claire* thematizes this photographic revelation. Barthes's literature is no longer 'against the author' but refocuses on 'his person, his tastes, his passions'.[31] And we see him still wanting with his brother Michel the photos of the mother, of this 'particular soul'[32] causing a 'crisis of sorrow'[33] and tears. The relationship with these souvenir-portraits becomes emotional and the author takes pleasure in capturing them[34] just as when he chooses a catalog from a 'department store'.[35] And his very great bitterness does not prevent him from putting them away while being upset. He observes the photo: 'Where mam. little girl, gentle, discreet next to [her brother] Philippe Binger (Jardin d'Hiver de Chennevièvres, 1898)'.[36]

'*Preparing the novel*'[37] means bearing witness to the past of the 'impossible'.[38] Because it is necessary to go towards the text, in the quest of the *fantasme* which is already a story. Therefore, 'novel' is a nostalgic word preventing this 'death of literature'.[39] We must write the text like a dress that we assemble, weave or, in a word, *prepare*: 'Basically, the novelist's dream of housework (this will be my last fantasy) would be to be an in-house tailor.'[40]

This *preparation* for the *novelesque* unifies a life sewn up like the dress. For Barthes, this dress is as important as the imposing clothing of the 'Iranian clergy'.[41] The parts of our life are linked in time and form a literary unit because our 'biography' is also an 'autobiography' of the masterpiece. Our being melts and is located in the text, defining itself as the rewriting of a life or a *novel of matter*. Barthes broods about his book as well as about his mother's 'pink Uniprix . . .' nightgown.[42]

A bad dream experience may obscure the awakening. In front of the photo of the mother in the *Winter Garden*, Barthes turns into a 'bad dreamer'.[43] The other sleep, however, is 'utopian [. . .] without a dream'.[44] Like the Proustian sleeper-awake, nocturnal delirium makes time collapse and can also constitute a 'panorama'.[45] The writer exchanges space for time. Barthes also wants to create by drawing inspiration from the Orient and by referring to distant civilizations: 'Satori: kind of mental catastrophe that occurs all at once → experienced by the Buddha under the Bodhi tree = nirvana realized during earthly life.'[46]

The writer imagines, 'meditates' and feels like sitting down. He gets then to being a free spirit without a subject and does not even assert anything. Barthes states: 'Wang Ming: that is to say, losing awareness of the glory [. . .] in a way, losing awareness of the very name of the Tao [. . .]'.[47]

Barthes thinks all day long and forgets his 'request, [his] task, [his] responsibility'; he then remains seated without doing anything in 'the non-action, the *Wou-wei*'[48] and wishing to write the novel by being inspired by poetry and even by 'the Haiku and we are going towards something which is more "psychological" and which is closer to a state of mind than to a satori (little mental jolt) and I would argue, so to say, that it is more Persian than Japanese and more Indo-European than Asian, and therefore Western, and already more romantic.'[49]

To create the text is to end up with a 'state of mind' and to fantasize about another romantic writing requiring generosity, love of the world, and the desire to embrace it. In his classes at the Collège de France and in particular his *Préparation du roman*, Barthes tried to do this but it was unsuccessful and this last class had a surprise in store. He increasingly turns to poetry as the only chance to save literature in a world that no longer loves it. The later Barthes is thus 'anti-modern',[50] a poet, and desires to write himself. It is this face that we can examine in the following section.

Rewriting a dream

Barthes's last lectures fulfil a prestigious literary career. He now closely links life and work wishing to prevent, not the *death of the author*, but rather the death of literature. Barthes describes *another* novel-esque space reminiscent of Proust, Tolstoï and Pascal, and redefines a mode of 'interest in everyday reality'.[51] He then gets to a 'writing of oneself' by presenting it in the form of a 'private diary'.[52] However, he defines it as a 'paradoxical genre'[53] still based on notation as in the 'album',[54] also qualified as *Ursuppe*.[55] The autobiographical serves as a model for Barthes who asserts in *Roland Barthes par Roland Barthes*: '*The Book / the life* (take a classic book and compare everything in your life to it for a year)'.[56]

In *Soirées de Paris*, the author himself discusses the need for this genre with É. Marty.[57] His latest texts, such as the *Journal de deuil*, can also be considered as the 'travel diaries of *Vita Nova*'.[58] This work is like the whole fragmentary Barthesian invention, it resumes 'Life'[59] after his own death due to a 'nosocomial infection'.[60] These successive deaths, in particular that one of the mother, lead paradoxically to an artistic renaissance qualified as 'futuro-mania'.[61] Barthes then wants to change furniture and clothes since he wishes to re-make his world. Death is described as a 'logical continuation of existence'[62] and Barthes notes with sadness that of literature.[63]

Barthes is now alone and weakened[64] hopelessly looking for 'salvation' into his text, sometimes he is even deprived of 'food'.[65] He thinks of his own disappearance because he is doomed to leave, just like his mother.[66] He also feels abandoned and compares his condition to the agony of the grandmother in *À la recherche du temps perdu*.[67] Barthes sees himself again in Orpheus[68] and an emotional bond reappears pushing the writer to constitute a code that recreates language as a 'sign of truth'[69] that we must analyze: 'Mother, through whom the child who comes back to life and whom he brings back from the kingdom of Hades by means of the Winter Garden photograph, is indeed an image of Eurydice.'[70]

This new Barthesian literature prefigures, like the abandoned *Contre Sainte-Beuve* by Proust,[71] the presence of an 'absence'.[72] Barthes longs for the future 'new novel',[73] the book of the future, being written about those ones we love. On the path of the novelesque, Barthes is constantly inspired by the death of Proust's mother, which took place in 1905[74] and constitutes the biographical basis of *À la recherche du temps perdu* or the 'path of the life'.[75] These passages are also reminiscent of those in *Time Regained* where we see the photo of Albertine 'dead'.[76]

The *Chambre claire*, a photographic-themed novel, exploits the techniques of the 'seventh art'. Barthes, like Proust, erects a 'stele' to his mother by recalling her memory.[77] *La Préparation du roman* 'attempts a theory' of the novel[78] and Barthes's last two books, *Roland Barthes par Roland Barthes* and *Fragments d'un discours amoureux* can be considered as novels. Just like Sainte-Beuve 'dreaming of writing like Montaigne',[79] Barthes wishes to unify in the text Proust and his narrator, 'that is to say the writer-*in-fieri*'.[80] The link between 'writing and death' actually brings Barthes closer to Proust.[81]

The misfortune of a son who is permanently separated from his family is terrible and his voice has become his mark, his monogram.[82] Any literary project, any *Vita Nova* fails, it now has 'Nothing to do, without any work'.[83] Barthes readily draws on Pascal in describing the '[moral] misery of man'.[84] The disappearance of the mother in Barthes also signifies that of the reader and a new 'prefiguration of the novel'. This is a return of the 'curiosity, . . . of the author'.[85] The *Journal de deuil* constitutes one of the acmes of a 'matrix of sadness' and emotion immortalized in writing.[86] Barthes is here observing an ill patient, reminding him of the past. But the states of mind such as grief and pain described in his *Journal* paradoxically push him to create the masterpiece:

> Each of us is the equal of Proust, Flaubert or Mallarmé. In desire, there is no acceptance of values. There are no better wishes than others. Desire is desire. If I have the desire to write, I am the equal of the greatest writers as to this desire [. . .] it is rather the rhythm of the division of the volume, that is to say its form, a form built upon the opposition continuity / discontinuity. The forms between which I would have to choose (if I were doing the work, the volume) would be [. . .] the

> Story, the Dissertation (the Treatise) and on the other hand discontinuous forms: the Fragments (Aphorisms, pages of Journal, Paragraphs à la Nietzsche), etc.[87]

Barthes expresses himself in the *Journal*[88] just like Ignace de Loyola and Amiel;[89] he is also a reader of more personal works,[90] like Coyaud's and Kafka's diaries.[91] He makes use of this literary genre written '*day by day*'[92] and made of the whole of 'Life + Work'.[93] Besides, he has only one desire: to create *another* literature, because this is the 'only region of Nobility (as mam was)'.[94]

Conclusion

We thus find the 'desire to write' at the beginning as well as at the end of Barthes's work: it redefines the contours of *another* linguistic universe. After an eclectic career, Barthes also dabbled in the novel and restored literature to its nobility. He sketches his book, a *Vita nova* inspired by images from the past, such as the 'winter garden' at the heart of his work. Barthes, like Proust and Gide, goes back in *time* prefiguring a work that may be 'already written' and sketched in the *Journal*, in this imaginary 'matrix of details'. Barthes tells the adventure of a 'novel of the future' in which one has to invest body and soul. He takes his destiny back and reacts to the 'death of literature': an emotional bond is established between this latter and his text. At the end of his career, Barthes found himself on the path of creation, moving from grief and sadness to the 'empty matrix' of the novelesque. Illness and depression paradoxically led him to fantasize about *a book* written in a telegraphic and fragmentary style.

These intimate thoughts guide researchers on the path of the novelesque *learning-to-write*. The *Journal de deuil* foreshadows *another* poetry defined by the absence, the emptiness and the anguish of a man who initiates himself into writing about himself. The fictional autobiography embodied by the diary replaces the figure of Roland Barthes in literary history books by erecting a stele in memory of those who *wished* to write about *nothing* or, just like Flaubert, to create a *novel about nothing*.

Notes

1. Barthes 2002a[q]. The edition of Roland Barthes's complete works used in this article is the five-volume edition of 2002, revised and corrected by Éric Marty, here cited as Barthes 2002a. English translations are my own.
2. Barthes 2002a[h]: 101.
3. Barthes 2002b : 52.
4. Ibid.: 108.
5. Barthes 2002a[c]: 40.
6. Barthes 2002a[h]: 248.
7. See Marty 2006.

8. Barthes 2002a[i]: 433.
9. Barthes 2015: 146.
10. Barthes 2002a[f] : 672.
11. Ibid.: 648.
12. Barthes 2002a[e]: 537.
13. Chevrier 2003: 418.
14. Barthes 2002a[f]: 716.
15. Barthes 2009: 180.
16. Marty 2016: 37.
17. Barthes 2002a[m].
18. Coste 2015: 369.
19. Barthes 2015: 48 (original emphasis).
20. Barthes 2002a[m]: 794.
21. Ibid.: 801.
22. Ibid.: 854.
23. See Gil 2021: 24.
24. Barthes 2002a[m]: 819.
25. See Fallah Nejad 2017.
26. Barthes 2002a[f]: 670.
27. See Fallah Nejad 2016.
28. Barthes 2009: 115.
29. Ibid.: 148.
30. See Gil 2012: 25.
31. Barthes 2002a[c]: 40–1.
32. Barthes 2002a[m]: 850.
33. Barthes 2009: 153.
34. Barthes 2002a[o]: 936.
35. Barthes 2002a[d]: 504.
36. Barthes 2009: 155.
37. Barthes 2015: 54.
38. Forest 2014: 594.
39. Barthes 2015: 55.
40. Ibid.: 57.
41. Ibid.: 423.
42. Barthes 2009: 44.
43. Barthes 2002a[m]: 869.
44. Barthes 2002c: 68.
45. Ibid.: 208.
46. Ibid.: 220.

47. Ibid.: 232.

48. Ibid.: 222.

49. Barthes 2015: 174. See also Fallah Nejad 2015.

50. See Compagnon 2005: 404.

51. Barthes 2002a[g]: 866.

52. Barthes 2002a[c]: 41.

53. Barthes 2002a[a]: 806.

54. Barthes 2015: 347.

55. See Coste 2015: 370.

56. Barthes 2002a[f]: 723. See Coste 2015: 370.

57. Barthes 2002a[p]: 980.

58. Gil 2012: 58.

59. Barthes 2002a[p]: 984.

60. Samoyault 2015: 13.

61. Barthes 2009: 16.

62. Samoyault 2015: 27.

63. Barthes 2015: 55.

64. Barthes 2009: 106.

65. Ibid.: 71.

66. Ibid.: 130.

67. Ibid.: 172.

68. Ibid.: 197.

69. Barthes 2002a[h]: 263.

70. Marty 2010: 70.

71. See Marty 2013: 53.

72. See Gil 2016: 210 and the Introduction to this volume.

73. See Fallah Nejad 2017.

74. Barthes 2015: 222.

75. Barthes 2002a[l]: 467.

76. Proust 2002–3: IV, 21.

77. Compagnon 2002: 210.

78. Ibid.: 231.

79. Lepenies 2002: 470.

80. Coste 2002: 66.

81. Herschberg-Pierrot 2014: 73.

82. Samoyault 2015: 33.

83. Barthes 2009: 249.

84. Barthes 2002a[p]: 984.

85. Barthes 2015: 381.

86. Snauwaert 2016: 111.
87. Barthes 2015: 329.
88. See Kristeva 1997: 158.
89. Barthes 2015: 88.
90. Ibid.: 122.
91. Ibid.: 438.
92. Ibid.: 343.
93. Ibid.: 382.
94. Ibid.: 237.

Works cited

Barthes, R. (2002a), *Oeuvres complètes*, É. Marty (ed.), volumes I–V, Paris: Seuil.

Barthes, R. (2002a[a]), 'Alain Girard: "Le journal intime"', in É. Marty (ed.), *Roland Barthes. Oeuvres complètes* II, 806–10, Paris: Gallimard.

Barthes, R. (2002a[b]), 'La photographie de mode', in É. Marty (ed.), *Roland Barthes. Oeuvres complètes* II, 1201–3, Paris: Gallimard.

Barthes, R. (2002a[c]), 'La Mort de l'auteur', in É. Marty (ed.), *Roland Barthes. Oeuvres complètes* III, 40–5, Paris: Gallimard.

Barthes, R. (2002a[d]), 'Le troisième sens: Notes de recherche sur quelques photogrammes de S.M. Esisenstein', in É. Marty (ed.), *Roland Barthes. Oeuvres complètes* III, 485–506, Paris: Gallimard.

Barthes, R. (2002a[e]), 'De la parole à l'écriture', in É. Marty (ed.), *Roland Barthes. Oeuvres complètes* IV, 537–41, Paris: Gallimard.

Barthes, R. (2002a[f]), *Roland Barthes par Roland Barthes*, in É. Marty (ed.), *Roland Barthes. Oeuvres complètes* IV, 716 ff, Paris: Gallimard.

Barthes, R. (2002a[g]), 'Vingt mots-clés pour Roland Barthes', in É. Marty (ed.), *Roland Barthes. Oeuvres complètes* IV, 855–75, Paris: Gallimard.

Barthes, R. (2002a[h]), *Fragments d'un discours amoureux*, in É. Marty (ed.), *Roland Barthes. Oeuvres complètes* V, 29–296, Paris: Gallimard.

Barthes, R. (2002a[i]), 'Leçon', in É. Marty (ed.), *Roland Barthes. Oeuvres complètes* V, 429–46, Paris: Gallimard.

Barthes, R. (2002a[l]), 'Longtemps, je me suis couché de bonne heure', in É. Marty (ed.), *Roland Barthes. Oeuvres complètes* V, 459–70, Paris: Gallimard.

Barthes, R. (2002a[m]), *La Chambre claire*, in É. Marty (ed.), *Roland Barthes. Oeuvres complètes* V, 785–892, Paris: Gallimard.

Barthes, R. (2002a[n]), 'Du goût à l'extase', in É. Marty (ed.), *Roland Barthes. Oeuvres complètes* V, 929–30, Paris: Gallimard.

Barthes, R. (2002a[o]), 'Sur la photographie', in É. Marty (ed.), *Roland Barthes. Oeuvres complètes* V, 931–7, Paris: Gallimard.

Barthes, R. (2002a[p]), 'Soirées de Paris', in É. Marty (ed.), *Roland Barthes. Oeuvres complètes* V, 977–93, Paris: Gallimard.

Barthes, R. (2002a[q]), 'Transcription de *Vita Nova*', in É. Marty (ed.), *Roland Barthes. Oeuvres complètes* V, 1007–18, Paris: Gallimard.

Barthes, R. (2002b), *Comment vivre ensemble. Cours et séminaires au Collège de France (1976-1977)*, C. Coste (ed.), Paris: Seuil/ IMEC.

Barthes, R. (2002c), *Le Neutre. Cours et séminaires au Collège de France (1977–1978)*, T. Clerc (ed.), Paris: Seuil/ IMEC.

Barthes, R. (2009), *Journal de deuil*, N. Léger (ed.), Paris: Seuil/IMEC.

Barthes, R. (2015), *La Préparation du roman. Cours au Collège de France (1978–1979 et 1979–1980)*, É. Marty (ed.), Paris: Seuil.

Chevrier, J.-F. (2003), 'Proust par Roland Barthes', in A. Compagnon (ed.), *Prétextes: Roland Barthes. Colloque de Cerisy*, 413–27, Paris: Christian Bourgois.

Compagnon, A. (2002), 'Le Roman de Roland Barthes', *Revue des Sciences Humaines* 266/267: 203–31.

Compagnon, A. (2005), *Les antimodernes: de Joseph de Maistre à Roland Barthes*, Paris: Gallimard.

Coste, C. (2002), 'Le Proust radiophonique de Roland Barthes', *Revue des Sciences Humaines* 268: 55–72.

Coste, C. (2015), 'État présent, Roland Barthes', *French Studies* 69: 363–74.

Fallah Nejad, M. R. (2015), 'Le "haïku" et la creation romanesque dans *La Préparation du roman* de Roland Barthes', *Études de langue et littérature française, Revue des Études de la langue Française* 12: 41–54.

Fallah Nejad, M. R. (2016), 'Le Conte de *Combray* et les noms persans: du voyage à l'écriture', *Studii Şi Cercetâri Filologice, Seria Limbi Romanice* 19: 79–93.

Fallah Nejad, M. R. (2017a), 'Le discours politique dans le *Roland Barthes par Roland Barthes*: de la prefiguration fragmentaire au romanesque', *Studii Şi Cercetâri Filologice, Seria Limbi Romanice* 21: 70–83.

Fallah Nejad, M. R. (2017b), 'Biographie et autobiographie dans *La Préparation du roman*', *Revue d'études proustiennes* 6: 471–91.

Forest, P. (2014), 'Dix ans après: *De l'enfant éternel à Tous les enfats sauf un*, Sept propositions pour une poétique du deuil', in B. Hidalgo-Bachs and C. Milkovitch-Rioux (eds), 592–600, Clermont-Ferrand: PU Clermont.

Gil, M. (2012), *ROLAND BARTHES Au lieu de la vie*, Paris: Flammarion.

Gil, M. (2016), '"L'homme affranchi de l'ordre du temps" Pour une ontologie de la *Vita Nova* selon Proust et Barthes', in M. Gil and F. Worms (eds), *La Vita Nova. La vie comme texte, l'écriture comme vie*, Paris: Hermann.

Herschberg-Pierrot, A. (2014), 'Roland Barthes: Marcel Proust, le texte et la vie', *Bulletin d'informations proustiennes* 44: 65–76.

Kristeva, J. (1997), *La révolte intime*, Paris: Fayard.

Lepenies, W. (2002), *Sainte-Beuve au seuil de la modernité*, trans. J. Étoré and B. Lortholary, Paris: Gallimard.

Marty, É. (2006), *Roland Barthes, le métier d'écrire*, Paris: Seuil.

Marty, É. (2010), *Roland Barthes, la littérature et le droit à la mort*, Paris: Seuil.

Marty, É. (2013), 'L'autre Barthes', *Le magazine littéraire, Nouveaux regards*, special issue: L. Nunez (ed.), *Roland Barthes*: 53–8.

Marty, É. (2016), 'Roland Barthes, l'objet photographique', in N. Piégay and L. Zimmermann (eds), *Roland Barthes aujourd'hui*, 33–43, Paris: Hermann.

Proust, M. (2002–3), *À la recherche du temps perdu*, vols I–IV, Paris: Gallimard, Bibliothèque de la Pléiade.

Samoyault, T. (2015), *Roland Barthes, biographie*, Paris: Seuil.

Snauwaert, M. (2016), 'Éthique et poétique du deuil: la nécessité du journal', in N. Piégay and L. Zimmermann (eds), *Roland Barthes aujourd'hui*, 109–21, Paris: Hermann.

PART III
SILENCE AND ENIGMA

CHAPTER 8
EPITOMIZING SILENCE: THE *APOPHTHEGMATA PATRUM* AS AN IMPOSSIBLE ENCYCLOPAEDIA OF UNKNOWING

Jesús Hernández Lobato

> He [Abba James] also said: 'There is need not only of sayings, for there are many sayings amongst folk nowadays. But there is need for action; that is what is sought, not sayings – which bear no fruit.'
>
> Apophthegmata patrum *alph James 4*[1]

> A monk said to Chao-chou, 'I have just arrived in this monastery; may the master please teach me something.'
>
> Chou asked, 'Have you eaten your rice gruel yet?'
>
> The monk said, 'I have eaten my rice gruel.'
>
> Chou said, 'Go wash your bowl.'
>
> The monk comprehended.
>
> Gateless Barrier (Wu-men kuan), *case 7*[2]

The late third and early fourth centuries witnessed the birth of a clearly countercultural movement forged in the bosom of the growing (though at the same time threatened) Christian community of Egypt: the hermit life of the so-called Desert Fathers and Mothers, who in disenchantment with the prevailing life model decided to withdraw from civilization to seek God in solitude, *ascesis*, quietude and silence.[3] The wisdom, sayings, stories and experiences attributed to these pioneering Christian hermits were gathered together in various collections, generally known as *Apophthegmata patrum*.[4] Most of these apophthegms are in the form of a conversation between a younger monk and his spiritual father. Beginning as an oral tradition in the Coptic language and freely transmitted by word of mouth by generations of masters and disciples, it was only subsequently, from the fifth century onwards, that this living legacy, which was suddenly endangered by the continuous raids of Bedouin tribes, was compiled and written down as a Greek text so that it could be safely preserved beyond its original context. From a strictly literary point of view, these extremely unconventional pieces pose many questions and defy categorization. As Peter Brown has pointed out,[5] the *Apophthegmata* 'provided a remarkable new literary genre, close to the world of parable and folk wisdom'. This chapter attempts to approach the peculiarities of this microscopic, multi-authored, and intrinsically fragmentary form of literature though the conceptual lens of epitome, paradox and self-deconstruction, thus integrating it into the bigger picture of the generalized questioning of language and representation, which characterized late antique culture in its entirety – a phenomenon I propose calling 'poetics of silence' when considered in its strictly literary dimension[6] and 'logoclasm' when considered to its full extent, i.e. as a cross-cutting manifestation of a new epochal *episteme*.[7]

What is an apophthegm? Definition and typology

Jean-Claude Guy,[8] the modern editor of the Systematic Collection of the *Apophthegmata Patrum* at *Sources Chrétiennes*, establishes four distinctive characteristics of the apophthegmatic genre that clearly differentiate it from any other known form of literature:

1. C'est d'abord une 'littérature' (mais on hésitera toujours à leur propos à employer un tel mot) fragmentaire. On y recueille un ensemble de conversations, de récits ou de paroles qui sont sans lien les uns avec les autres. Accumulation de fragments qui peuvent donner l'impression extérieure de la disparate.
2. Il s'agit d'un ensemble regroupant des 'doctrines' et des 'pratiques' qui n'ont rien entre elles d'homogène, quand elles ne sont pas incompatibles. Des courants multiples et divergents s'y côtoient de façon tellement imprévisible que cela distingue ce recueil de tous les autres écrits contemporains.
3. Nous sommes en présence d'un recueil dont on serait tenté de dire que, paradoxalement, il n'a été composé par personne et à aucun moment particulier. [. . .] Chaque scribe recopiant un modèle s'autorise à le modifier. Le 'premier' compilateur aujourd'hui repérable n'a pas signé son œuvre; et il définit sa tâche comme celle d'un simple collectionneur. Plus d'une centaine de moines 'auteurs' de paroles ou de récits s'y côtoient sans qu'aucun d'eux n'ait jamais eu l'idée qu'il deviendrait un 'écrivain'. En outre, plusieurs des attributions d'une sentence à tel moine particulier son sujettes à caution. La même peut, d'un manuscrit a l'autre, être attribuée à deux moines différents ou rapportée ailleurs de façon anonyme. [. . .]
4. [. . .] Les premiers qui quittèrent leur ville [. . .] pour aller 'habiter au désert' [. . .] ne disposaient de l'expérience d'aucun prédécesseur qui aurait pu leur enseigner comment y vivre. Ils n'avaient aucun modèle à imiter. [. . .] C'est donc a travers des expériences particulières, parfois heureuses, mais parfois aboutissant à des échecs, qu'ils élaborèrent peu à peu les grandes lois de la vie spirituelle au désert. De ses expériences, les collections d'apophtegmes sont le reportage brut, non encore systématisé. [. . .] On peut les lire comme le guide pratique de l'expérience de Dieu au désert.

As for the structure and typology of apophthegms, three basic patterns can be distinguished:

1. A master–disciple dialogue. Its structure takes the following form: a) a young disciple asks a question; b) the elder gives an answer, which is 'souvent énigmatique';[9] c) the disciple requests further clarification; d) he receives a new answer from the master. Sections a, c, and d are facultative.
2. A collective address aimed at several monks.
3. An inspirational biographical story/anecdote.

Number 1) in this tentative classification is by far the most common type and consequently that which tends to be associated almost automatically with the notion of apophthegm *tout court*. The question is how does this peculiar literary format actually operate? How can we approach this literature from a critical and theoretical point of view? What aesthetic and conceptual parameters does it set in motion? In short, what is its ultimate raison d'être?

The epitomic nature of apophthegms: The absolute epitome?

Approaching such an unconventional literary genre from the conceptual frame of epitome may shed some light on its internal workings and its aesthetic nature. In fact, apophthegms operate in accordance with a principle of reduction, which is not entirely dissimilar to the one regulating epitomes (from ἐπι-τέμνειν 'to cut short'). It is not for nothing that apophthegms have the power to *condense* a whole theological treatise into a single mysterious sentence;[10] the life of a saint into a revealing anecdote;[11] a thought-provoking homily into a pregnant gesture or an apparently trivial or nonsensical action;[12] a whole exercise of Biblical exegesis into an enigmatic passing reference;[13] a monastic rule into a simple word of advice on how to cope with some of the day-to-day difficulties of desert life, regardless of how unimportant they might seem to an average reader or to a highbrow seeker of transcendental truths.[14] Apophthegms should thus be considered a kind of condensation or quintessentialization of religious literature rather than an ordinary summary or reduction of any pre-existing work. They are able to capture in a mere few words the ineffable and ungraspable essence that would take any fully-fletched theologian thousands and thousands of pages to conceptualize (and generally to no avail). Such peculiar ability turns this *sui generis* form of speech into the perfect vehicle for conveying the unspeakable truth of spiritual experience.

However, the strange thing about the literary genre of *apophthegmata* is that, despite its epitomic and compendious appearance, it does not imply in any way the pre-existence of a larger work to be distilled, abridged or summarized. Apophthegms are born as such from scratch – they are but pure fragments, a kind of epitome of themselves with no external references whatsoever. They might thus be regarded as the epitome of nothingness – that is to say, the absolute epitome, the epitome that has been happily freed from the troublesome burden of being a by-product of any preceding work. Apophthegms go even further than epitomes in their peculiar literary workings (in clear contrast to the time-honoured paradigm of Graeco-Roman classicism): whereas both can be considered miniature, unpretentious, compendious, and encapsulated pieces of literature, only apophthegms are also disruptive, fragmentary, multi-authored, microscopic (often one or two sentences long), disperse, asyntactic, and absolutely alien to the taxonomic and hierarchical mechanism that regulates and structures not only literature but also everyday discourse. In the following pages I will explore the paradoxes and potentialities inherent in some of these characteristics.

The ineffable and intangible experience of the hermits' inner and outer life is condensed (or rather *densified*) until it becomes language. The very notion of a verbal embodiment (almost 'solidification' into language) of the unspeakable truth underlying spiritual experience seems to be somehow reminiscent of Christian Incarnation, the cornerstone of theological speculation at that time.[15] If the epitome is deprived of its literary connotations to be more generally defined as an instance representing any wider reality (not necessarily a pre-existing literary work), apophthegms might be considered in their own right to be the epitome – the quintessence – of desert spirituality.

The paradoxical, self-deconstructive and 'logoclastic' nature of apophthegmatic literature: Apophthegms as a form of anti-literature and anti-language

Apophthegms defy almost every single feature, rule and convention that we tend to associate with the idea of literature. They were never set down in writing by any of their many authors, most of whom were illiterate low-class Egyptians who had never contemplated the idea of creating anything even remotely reminiscent of a literary work. Their style is plain and entirely free from any aesthetic pretension. Each apophthegm was basically conceived as an ephemeral, concrete and extremely personalized verbal response to the doubts, fears or difficulties that plagued a specific neophyte in his/her attempt at leading a hermit life. Therefore, no systematicity, consistency or even internal coherence is to be sought in them. The same question may indeed elicit different and even contradictory answers, depending on the external circumstances and the spiritual needs of the specific person formulating it.[16] Apophthegms were not thought to be important in their own right but rather as a mere disposable instrument aiming at achieving a certain spiritual effect – an effect that has nothing to do with language (let alone literature!). Unlike ordinary literature, which according to Jakobson's classical theory tends to focus on 'the message for its own sake', thus being dominated by the so-called 'poetic function',[17] apophthegms are intrinsically centrifugal: they are conceived as mere pointers to an extralinguistic and intangible reality and thus destined to dissolve into silence and objectless prayer (also known as contemplation). They actually work as a more or less explicit invitation to break the chains of language and social life by passing from action to contemplation, from company to loneliness, from the city to the desert, from the word to silence:

> Ἀδελφὸς συνοικῶν ἀδελφοῖς ἠρώτησε τὸν ἀββᾶν Βισαρίωνα· Τί ποιήσω; Λέγει αὐτῷ ὁ γέρων· Σιώπα, καὶ μὴ μετρήσῃς ἑαυτόν.
>
> A brother who shared a lodging with other brothers asked Abba Bessarion, 'What should I do?' The old man replied, 'Keep silence and do not compare yourself with others'.[18]

> Ἔλεγον περὶ τοῦ ἀββᾶ Ἀγάθωνος ὅτι ἐπὶ τρία ἔτη ἔβαλε λίθον εἰς τὸ στόμα αὐτοῦ ἕως οὗ κατώρθωσε τὴν σιωπήν.
>
> It was said about Abba Agathon that for three years he lived with a stone in his mouth, until he had learned to keep silence.[19]

This second apophthegm probably entails an ironic reversal of a famous anecdote of Demosthenes, the father of Western oratory, who is said to have rehearsed his speeches with pebbles in his mouth in order to overcome his stammer and improve his hesitant pronunciation.[20] In the case of Agathon this curious exercise does not lead to a mastery of eloquence but to the silence of contemplation and eternal truths, which unmasks the fallacies and hollowness of language and conceptual thinking.

In this sense apophthegms can be considered to be a kind of self-deconstructive (or even self-destructive) anti-literature, the aim of which is to disappear once the recipient has been led to the realm of silence and speechlessness – the sacred dwellings of God. On this road towards one's inner self, words are nothing more than a provisional and extremely imperfect auxiliary element to be thrown away – as Wittgenstein would put it[21] – once we begin to approach our ultimate spiritual goal. Not even the Bible, the word of God, is to be retained longer than necessary:

> Εἶπεν γέρων· Ὅτι ἐκέκτητό τις τῶν ἀδελφῶν εὐαγγέλιον μόνον, καὶ τοῦτο πωλήσας ἔδωκεν εἰς τροφὴν τοῖς πένησιν, ἄξιον μνήμης ἐπιφθεγξάμενος ῥῆμα· αὐτὸν γάρ φησι, τὸν λόγον πεπώληκα τὸν λέγοντα· *Πώλησόν σου τὰ ὑπάρχοντα καὶ δὸς πτωχοῖς.*
>
> An elder said that one of the brothers possessed only a Gospel. This he sold and gave the proceeds to feed the poor, making this memorable statement: 'I have sold the verse itself which says: 'Sell what you have and give it to the poor' [Mt 19:21].[22]

The comic paradox contained in this apophthegm eloquently reveals these hermits' ultimate distrust of language (especially in written form).[23] The raison d'être of this microscopic form of literature does not lie in its literary qualities or its syllogistic strength but in the transformational effects it has on those who internalize it and dematerialize it by putting its underlying message into practice. The ultimate goal of apophthegms is to disappear. They are a mere verbal instrument deliberately designed to help hesychasts gain access to what is extralinguistic, aniconic and non-dimensional (both timeless and spaceless)[24] – something early Christian tradition used to call the Kingdom of Heaven. This function is explicitly vindicated in the prologue to the collection of *Apophthegmata*:

> Ἐν τῇδε τῇ βίβλῳ ἀναγέγραπται ἐνάρετος ἄσκησις καὶ θαυμαστὴ βίου διαγωγή, καὶ ῥήσεις ἁγίων καὶ μακαρίων Πατέρων, πρὸς ζῆλον καὶ παιδείαν καὶ μίμησιν τῶν τὴν οὐράνιον πολιτείαν ἐθελόντων κατορθῶσαι, καὶ τὴν εἰς βασιλείαν οὐρανῶν ἄγουσαν βουλομένων ὁδεύειν ὁδόν.
>
> This book is an account of the virtuous ascetism and admirable way of life and also of the words of the holy and blessed fathers. They are meant to inspire and instruct those who want to imitate their heavenly lives, so that they may make progress on the way that leads to the kingdom of heaven.[25]

But what does the hackneyed evangelical expression 'kingdom of heaven' really mean? What does this avowed goal of all apophthegmatic literature actually involve? One of the rare Greek-speaking and intellectually trained desert fathers, namely Evagrius Ponticus,[26] provides the clearest (and probably the most surprising) answer to this riddle (*Praktikos* 2): βασιλεία οὐρανῶν ἐστιν ἀπάθεια ψυχῆς μετὰ γνώσεως τῶν ὄντων ἀληθοῦς ('The kingdom of heaven is impassibility of the soul accompanied by true knowledge of beings').[27] According to this definition, it is only the *apatheia* ('impassibility'), a state of internal stillness and receptiveness characteristic of hesychastic spirituality, which grants access to the kingdom of heaven: 'O *hēsychia*! The way to the kingdom of heaven' is written in the *Apophthegmata patrum*.[28]

In order to attain this state of *apatheia* or *hēsychia* one must silence the internal hurly-burly of thoughts (*logismoi*) and concepts (*noēmata*) and push aside all mental images and discursive reasoning by focusing on pure objectless contemplation (*theoria*). This is the very essence of the spiritual practice followed by the desert fathers and mothers, rather than physical isolation or severe ascetic privations, which may even prove to be a waste of time, if they do not lead the practitioner to this state of inner silencing:

> Εἶπεν ἀμμᾶ Συγκλητική· Πολλοὶ ἐν ὄρει ὄντες τὰ τῶν δημοτῶν πράττοντες ἀπώλοντο, καὶ πολλοὶ ἐν πόλεσιν ὄντες τὰ τῆς ἐρήμου ἔργα ποιοῦντες σῴζονται. Δυνατὸν γὰρ μετὰ πολλῶν ὄντα μονάζειν τῇ γνώμῃ, καὶ μόνον ὄντα μετὰ ὄχλων τῇ διανοίᾳ διάγειν.
>
> Amma Synclētikē said: 'There are many in mountains acting like city dwellers who are perishing and many in cities doing the deeds of the desert who are being saved. For it is possible to be alone with one's spirit while in the company of many and also to have one's thoughts with crowds even when one is alone.'[29]

It is not for nothing that one of the values of classical civilization that the desert fathers and mothers most vehemently rejected was its rampant logocentrism. The greatest enemies of a hesychast monk were indeed thoughts, revealingly termed *logismoi* after *logos* itself. *Logos* not only failed to be a means of attaining full knowledge of reality (*gnosis*) but was even the greatest obstacle to achieving this goal. 'Prayer' – as Evagrius Ponticus states – 'is the laying aside of mental representations' (προσευχὴ γάρ ἐστιν ἀπόθεσις νοημάτων).[30] Only a state of *logos*-less *apatheia* ('impassibility, the quietening of mental activity') affords access to real knowledge. Concentration and emptying of the mind of any possible distraction (thoughts, visual representations, memories) are thus the key elements of this practice, which is strikingly similar to certain totally unrelated far-Eastern meditation methods, most particularly Zen. As Abba Poemen used to say, 'the beginning of evils is distraction'.[31] The desert fathers and mothers would certainly subscribe to the view of the twentieth-century philosopher and mystic Simone Weil, who famously described prayer as 'absolutely unmixed attention'.[32]

Εἶπεν ἀββᾶ Ὑπερέχιος· Ἡ ἐνθύμησίς σου ἔστω διαπαντὸς ἐν τῇ βασιλείᾳ τῶν οὐρανῶν, καὶ ταχέως κληρονομήσεις αὐτήν.

Abba Hyperechios said, 'Let your consciousness always dwell on the kingdom of heaven, and soon you shall inherit it'.[33]

Διηγήσατό τις ὅτι τρεῖς φιλόπονοι ἀγαπητοὶ ἐγένοντο μοναχοί. Καὶ ὁ μὲν εἷς ᾑρήσατο τοὺς μαχομένους εἰρηνεύειν κατὰ τὸ εἰρημένον· «Μακάριοι οἱ εἰρηνοποιοί», ὁ δὲ δεύτερος ἐπισκέπτεσθαι τοὺς ἀσθενοῦντας, ὁ δὲ τρίτος ἀπῆλθεν ἡσυχάζειν εἰς τὴν ἔρημον. Ὁ οὖν πρῶτος κοπιάσας διὰ τὰς μάχας τῶν ἀνθρώπων οὐκ ἠδύνατο θεραπεῦσαι πάντας, καὶ ἀκηδιάσας ἦλθεν πρὸς τὸν ὑπηρετοῦντα τοὺς ἀσθενεῖς καὶ εὗρεν αὐτὸν ὀλιγωροῦντα καὶ μὴ φθάνοντα τελειῶσαι τὴν ἐντολήν. Καὶ συμφωνήσαντες οἱ δύο ἀπῆλθον ἰδεῖν τὸν ἐρημίτην καὶ διηγήσαντο αὐτῷ τὴν θλῖψιν αὐτῶν, καὶ παρεκάλεσαν αὐτὸν εἰπεῖν αὐτοῖς τί κατόρθωσεν. Καὶ σιωπήσας μικρὸν βάλλει εἰς λεκάνην ὕδωρ καὶ λέγει αὐτοῖς· Προσέχετε εἰς τὸ ὕδωρ. Ἦν δὲ τεταραγμένον. Καὶ μετὰ μικρὸν πάλιν λέγει αὐτοῖς· Προσέχετε καὶ ἄρτι ὡς κατέστη τὸ ὕδωρ. Καὶ ὡς προσέσχον τῷ ὕδατι, θεωροῦσιν ὡς ἐν ἐσόπτρῳ τὰ πρόσωπα αὐτῶν. Καὶ λοιπὸν λέγει αὐτοῖς· Οὕτως ἐστὶ καὶ ὁ ἐν μέσῳ ἀνθρώπων, ἀπὸ τῆς ταραχῆς οὐ βλέπει τὰς ἁμαρτίας ἑαυτοῦ· ὅταν δὲ ἡσυχάσῃ, καὶ μάλιστα ἐν ἐρήμῳ, τότε βλέπει τὰ ἐλαττώματα ἑαυτοῦ.

Somebody told about three friends, members of a religious philanthropic society, who became monks. The first one chose to pacify those who were in conflict, in accordance with the saying, 'Blessed are the peacemakers' [Mt 5:9]; the second one [elected] to visit the sick, but the third went off to practice *hēsychia* in the desert. Much as the first labored to allay the contentions of people, he was unable to heal them all. Afflicted with *accidie*, he came to the one who was serving the sick and found him despairing of fulfilling the commandment [cf. Mt 25:26]. The two of them came to an agreement and went to visit the hermit. They told him of their affliction, begging him to tell them what *he* had successfully accomplished. After a brief silence, he poured water into a bowl and said to them. 'Look carefully at the water,' for it was disturbed. Then, after a little while, he said to them again, 'Now look carefully [and see] how the water is stilled,' and as they looked at the water, they saw their faces as in a mirror. Then he said to them, 'It is like that too for somebody amidst the people; he cannot see his own sins for the tumult; but when he practices *hēsychia*, especially in the desert, then he sees his own shortcomings.'[34]

Only through *apatheia* and *hēsychia* can one gain access to the kingdom of heaven, i.e. true knowledge of the things around us as they really are. The nature of this mystical knowledge – which Evagrius Ponticus calls 'the knowledge that arises within us by the grace of God' (ἡ ἐκ Θεοῦ χάριτος ἐγγινομένη [γνῶσις]) – differs radically from what we tend to consider actual 'knowledge', i.e. discursive and logical knowledge – in Evagrius' words 'the knowledge that comes to us from outside' (ἡ ἔξωθεν ἡμῖν συμβαίνουσα γνῶσις). The latter demands the mediation of *logos* (both language and reasoning) and merely conveys apparent knowledge, since it is utterly unable to fathom the deepest raison d'être of the things it vainly strives to scrutinize; the former is a direct (αὐτοψεὶ) unmediated apprehension of what things really are. Evagrius expresses this key distinction in words in *Gnostikos* 4:

> Ἡ μὲν ἔξωθεν ἡμῖν συμβαίνουσα γνῶσις, διὰ τῶν λόγων ὑποδεικνύειν πειρᾶται τὰς ὕλας· ἡ δὲ ἐκ Θεοῦ χάριτος ἐγγινομένη, αὐτοψεὶ τῇ διανοίᾳ παρίστησι τὰ πράγματα, πρὸς ἃ βλέπων ὁ νοῦς, τοὺς αὐτῶν λόγους προσίεται·
>
> The knowledge that comes to us from outside attempts to make known material things by means of *reasoning* (διὰ τῶν λόγων); but the knowledge that arises within us by the grace of God presents objects directly to the intellect, and when the mind looks upon them it approaches their reasons (τοὺς αὐτῶν λόγους).[35]

This eloquent passage plays deliberately with two contrasting meanings of the Greek term *logos*. In the first sentence it means 'reasoning, language, conceptualization' and refers to the inescapable and misleading mediation of language in our daily apprehension of reality; in the second sentence it has the technical sense given to this term by the stoics, meaning the ultimate raison d'être of all beings. The first *logos* is an attribute of the knower's mind and is close to the meaning of *logismoi* – the bombarding thoughts which prevent the monk from achieving the long-awaited state of *apatheia*; the second *logos* is an attribute of the things to be known – their deepest essence. Even if this term has been generally translated into Syriac by its literal equivalent ܡܶܠܬ݂ܳܐ *melṯā* ('word'), the revised version opts interestingly for the more insightful ܣܘܟܳܠܳܐ *sukālā* ('intelligence, understanding, meaning, sense').[36] In any case, it is apparent that Evagrius' kingdom of heaven has nothing to do with angelic apparitions or fabulous visions: rather it is all about seeing things as they really are without the distorting filter of language and conceptual thinking. For Evagrius the natural state of man is blindness – looking without seeing. The gnostic (in the Evagrian sense of the term) is the one who comes to see what things truly are by means of an exercise or pure unmediated contemplation, thus gaining access to the so-called kingdom of heaven.[37] The kingdom of heaven therefore seems to equate quite well with the experience that Zen practitioners call *kenshō*. This Japanese term literally means 'seeing (*ken*) the-essence-of-things (shō),' i.e. seeing reality as it really *is* and not as it merely *seems* to be. It can be thus defined as an initial, sudden, and generally ephemeral insight or awakening, which opens up the path to more permanent *satori* (comprehension or enlightenment).[38] It is no wonder that the pioneer of desert spirituality, Antony, publicly proclaimed the immediacy (non-mediatedness) and immanence of the kingdom of heaven in the following terms once he first reached illumination after an extended period of seclusion:

> Ἕλληνες μὲν οὖν ἀποδημοῦσι καὶ θάλασσαν περῶσιν, ἵνα γράμματα μάθωσιν, ἡμεῖς δὲ οὐ χρείαν ἔχομεν οὔτε ἀποδημίας διὰ τὴν βασιλείαν τῶν οὐρανῶν οὔτε περᾶσαι θάλατταν διὰ τὴν ἀρετήν. Φθάσας γὰρ εἶπεν ὁ Κύριος· «Ἡ βασιλεία τῶν οὐρανῶν ἐντὸς ὑμῶν ἐστιν.»
>
> Οὐκοῦν ἡ ἀρετὴ τοῦ θέλειν ἡμῶν μόνου χρείαν ἔχει, ἐπειδήπερ ἐν ἡμῖν ἐστι καὶ ἐξ ἡμῶν συνίσταται. Τῆς γὰρ ψυχῆς τὸ νοερὸν κατὰ φύσιν ἐχούσης ἡ ἀρετὴ συνίσταται. Κατὰ φύσιν δὲ ἔχει, ὅταν ὡς γέγονε μένῃ· γέγονε δὲ καλὴ καὶ εὐθὴς λίαν.
>
> The Greeks leave home and cross the sea in order to be educated, but we have no need to leave home for the kingdom of heaven or to cross the sea for virtue. The Lord has already said, 'The kingdom of God is within you' [Lk 17:21].
>
> All virtue needs, then, is for us to will it, because it is within us and has its origins from us. Virtue comes into being because the soul naturally possesses the rational faculty of understanding. Virtue maintains its nature when it remains as it came into being, and it came into being good and perfectly upright.[39]

The kingdom of heaven was already there right in front of Antony from the very beginning, but he was unable to see it until he suddenly realized its unmediated nature. As Augustine would put it (*conf.* 3.6.11), it was something 'closer to me than I am to myself' (*interior intimo meo*), something that does not demand going far but rather returning to oneself and opening the soul's eyes once and for all.[40] In order to be able to perceive it, you only needed to look at the things around you without the distorting filter of conceptual thinking, i.e. to make internal silence:

> Εἶπε γέρων·Ὥσπερ εἰς πεζευομένην στράταν οὐκ ἀνέρχεται χλωρόν τί ποτε, οὐδὲ κἂν βάλλῃς σπέρμα, διὰ τὸ πατεῖσθαι τὸν τόπον, οὕτως καὶ ἐφ' ἡμῶν ἐστίν.Ἡσύχασον δὲ ἀπὸ παντὸς πράγματος, καὶ βλέπεις φυόμενα ἃ οὐκ ᾔδεις ὅτι ἔνδοθέν σου ἦσαν ἐπειδὴ εἰς αὐτὰ περιεπάτεις.
>
> An elder said: 'In the same way that no plant whatsoever grows up on a well-trodden highway, not even if you sow seed, because the surface is trodden down, so it is with us. Withdraw from all business into *hēsychia* and you will see things growing that you did not know were in you, for you were walking on them.'[41]

Hēsychia thus entails a conquest of something one already possessed without being aware of it – Evagrius' and Antony's kingdom of heaven. The main obstacle to attaining this state of an enhanced apprehension of reality is that of thoughts (*logismoi*) regardless of their content and nature. Antony himself attests to this in the very first apophthegm of the alphabetical collection:[42]

Ὁ ἅγιος ἀββᾶς Ἀντώνιος, καθεζόμενός ποτε ἐν τῇ ἐρήμῳ, ἐν ἀκηδίᾳ γέγονε καὶ πολλῇ σκοτώσει λογισμῶν· καὶ ἔλεγε πρὸς τὸν Θεόν· Κύριε, θέλω σωθῆναι, καὶ οὐκ ἐῶσί με οἱ λογισμοί· τί ποιήσω ἐν τῇ θλίψει μου; πῶς σωθῶ;

Once when the holy Abba Antony was residing in the desert, overcome by *accidie* and a great darkening of *logismoi*, he was saying to God: 'Lord, I want to be saved and my *logismoi* do not leave me alone. What am I to do in my affliction? How I am to be saved?'

Salvation, as is apparent from this text, does not belong to the hereafter but to the here and now. And there is no salvation in conceptual thinking. Fourth-century Graeco-Roman civilization was besotted with *logos*, inebriated with concepts. A way out was urgently required. According to the continuation of this telling anecdote, the answer to the puzzle that vexed Antony was much simpler and easier to implement than he had ever expected: he merely had to stop and concentrate on whatever he was doing at that moment; in order to *see* you just have to *look*:

Καὶ μικρὸν διαναστὰς ἐπὶ τὰ ἔξω, θεωρεῖ τινα ὁ Ἀντώνιος ὡς ἑαυτὸν, καθεζόμενον καὶ ἐργαζόμενον, εἶτα ἀνιστάμενον ἀπὸ τοῦ ἔργου καὶ προσευχόμενον, καὶ πάλιν καθεζόμενον καὶ τὴν σειρὰν πλέκοντα, εἶτα πάλιν εἰς προσευχὴν ἀνιστάμενον· ἦν δὲ ἄγγελος Κυρίου, ἀποσταλεὶς πρὸς διόρθωσιν καὶ ἀσφάλειαν Ἀντωνίου. Καὶ ἤκουσε τοῦ ἀγγέλου λέγοντος· Οὕτως ποίει, καὶ σώζῃ. Ὁ δὲ τοῦτο ἀκούσας, πολλὴν χαρὰν ἔσχε καὶ θάρσος, καὶ οὕτως ποιῶν ἐσώζετο.

Going outside [his cell] a little way, Antony saw somebody like himself, sitting working – then standing up from his work and praying; sitting down again, working at rope-braiding, then standing to pray once more. It was an angel of the Lord sent to correct Antony and to assure him. And he heard the angel saying: 'Act like this and you shall be saved.' He experienced much joy and courage on hearing this and, acting in that way, he went on being saved.

In this inner fight against distracting thoughts the simplicity of an illiterate peasant might prove more useful than any high-flown theological dissertation:

Ἐρωτῶντός ποτε τοῦ ἀββᾶ Ἀρσενίου τινὰ γέροντα Αἰγύπτιον περὶ ἰδίων λογισμῶν, ἕτερος ἰδὼν αὐτὸν εἶπεν· Ἀββᾶ Ἀρσένιε, πῶς τοσαύτην παίδευσιν Ῥωμαϊκὴν καὶ Ἑλληνικὴν ἐπιστάμενος, τοῦτον τὸν ἀγροῖκον περὶ τῶν σῶν λογισμῶν ἐρωτᾷς; Ὁ δὲ εἶπε πρὸς αὐτόν· Τὴν μὲν Ῥωμαϊκὴν καὶ Ἑλληνικὴν ἐπίσταμαι παίδευσιν· τὸν δὲ ἀλφάβητον τοῦ ἀγροίκου τούτου οὔπω μεμάθηκα.

Abba Arsenius was once asking an Egyptian elder about his own *logismoi*. Another person, when he saw him, said: 'Abba Arsenius, how is it that you, who have such a command of Greek and Roman learning, are asking this rustic about your *logismoi*?' But he said to him: 'A command of Greek and Roman learning I have, but I have not yet learned the alphabet of this rustic.'[43]

The silent alphabet of the rustic illiterate has to replace the useless verbosity of discursive thinking (those pounding *logismoi*). The image of the alphabet is generally taken to symbolize the basic rudiments of a discipline, in this case hesychastic contemplation. According to this apophthegm, not even these rudiments were naturally accessible to those who had been academically trained to deal with reality through the distorting filter of *logos* (both reasoning and language). Those would-be mystics with a sound philosophical and rhetorical background (such as Evagrius Ponticus or Arsenius) had to *unlearn* what they had been taught. Only then would they be on the right track to restart their inner search from the beginning.[44] Apophthegms, a kind of ephemeral, ever-changing and originally unwritten anti-literature, which uses language against itself by challenging its monopolistic position in our perception of reality, were actually meant to help initiands to complete this inner transition from the word to silence:

> Ἠρωτήθη πάλιν [γέρων]· Τί δεῖ ποιοῦντα σωθῆναι; Ἦν δὲ σειρὰν πλέκων καὶ μὴ ἀνανεύων ἐκ τοῦ ἔργου, καὶ ἀπεκρίθη· Ἰδοὺ ὡς βλέπεις.
>
> An elder was asked, 'What should one do to be saved?' He was braiding rope and not looking up from his work, and he replied, 'What you see here'.[45]

An openly 'logoclastic' attitude emerges from many apophthegms. Words and explanations prove pointless when it comes to finding your inner silence in the solitude of the desert. At best they can show the fastest way to their own annihilation:

> Ἀδελφὸς παρέβαλεν εἰς Σκῆτιν πρὸς τὸν ἀββᾶ Μωϋσῆν αἰτούμενος παρ' αὐτοῦ λόγον. Λέγει αὐτῷ ὁ γέρων· Ὕπαγε, κάθου εἰς τὸ κελλίον σου καὶ τὸ κελλίον σου διδάσκει σε πάντα.
>
> A brother came to Scetis to visit Abba Moses and asked him for a word. The old man said to him, 'Go, sit in your cell, and your cell will teach you everything.'[46]
>
> Ἀδελφὸς ἠρώτησε τὸν ἀββᾶ Ἡσαίαν λέγων· Πῶς χρὴ ἡσυχάζειν ἐν τῷ κελλίῳ; Καὶ ἀπεκρίθη ὁ γέρων· Τὸ ἡσυχάζειν ἐν τῷ κελλίῳ <ἐστὶ> τὸ παραρρίπτειν ἑαυτὸν ἐνώπιον τοῦ Θεοῦ καὶ τὸ ποιῆσαι τὴν δύναμιν ἑαυτοῦ ἀντιστῆναι παντὶ σπειρομένῳ λογισμῷ ὑπὸ τοῦ ἐχθροῦ· τοῦτο γάρ ἐστι τὸ φεύγειν ἀπὸ κόσμου. Καὶ εἶπεν ὁ ἀδελφός· Τί ἐστιν ὁ κόσμος; Καὶ ἀπεκρίθη ὁ γέρων· Ὁ κόσμος ἐστὶν ὁ περισπασμὸς [. . .]
>
> A brother asked Abba Isaiah, 'How does one maintain *hēsychia* in the cell?' The elder answered, 'To maintain *hēsychia* in the cell is to thrust oneself into the presence of God and, to the best of one's ability, to withstand every *logismos* sowed

> by the enemy, for that is to flee from the world.' The brother said, 'What is the world?' and the elder replied, 'The world is distraction.' [. . .][47]

God can only be experienced in the inmost recesses of the soul where there is no place for human language and reasoning. Hence the elders' complete disinterest in the theological controversies and intellectual speculations on the nature of God that were shaking the world scenario at the time. Convinced as they were of the ineffability of God and the futility of language in the grasping of reality, they would undoubtedly have subscribed to Wittgenstein's famous adage: 'Whereof one cannot speak, thereof one must be silent' ('Wovon man nicht sprechen kann, darüber muss man schweigen').[48] Adhering to orthodoxy without stridency, they did not take the slightest interest in theology – fundamentalism and fanaticism were totally alien to them. They would rather focus on specific everyday aspects of desert life, showing a surprisingly high degree of empathy and a non-judgemental attitude towards their neighbours' flaws and weaknesses.[49] As the twentieth-century American mystic Thomas Merton has rightly pointed out:

> Not the least of the qualities of the 'words of salvation' [i.e. the *Apophthegmata patrum*] is their common sense. This is important. The Desert Fathers later acquired a reputation for fanaticism because of the stories that were told about their ascetic feats by indiscreet admirers. They were indeed ascetics: but when we read their own words and see what they themselves thought about life, we find that they were anything but fanatics. They were humble, quiet, sensible people, with a deep knowledge of human nature and enough understanding of the things of God to realize that they knew very little about Him. Hence they were not much disposed to make long speeches about the divine essence, or even to declaim on the mystical meaning of Scripture. If these men say little about God, it is because they know that when one has been somewhere close to His dwelling, silence makes more sense than a lot of words. The fact that Egypt, in their time, was seething with religious and intellectual controversies was all the more reason for them to keep their mouths shut.

Eloquence and syllogistic argumentation were thus absolutely excluded in the context of desert spirituality. One may even detect a certain irrationalist drift in the content and underlying doctrine of the *Apophtheghmata patrum*, which is of course not unknown to other mystical trends of late antiquity starting with Neoplatonism itself:[50]

> Εἶπεν ὁ αὐτός· Ὃς ἐὰν γένηται μωρὸς διὰ τὸν Κύριον συνετιεῖ αὐτὸν ὁ Κύριος.

> The same [elder] said, 'Whoever has become a fool for the Lord's sake [see 1 Cor 3:18], the Lord will make him wise.'[51]

In the desert language loses its function. It does not communicate anything. It does not inform. It does not mean. Language becomes prayer. Prayer acts indeed as an annihilation of language, a deactivation of its workings and its purpose. After all, prayer may be arguably considered to be a form of anti-language, a condition which is shared to some extent by those words deliberately conceived and uttered (never written down) to lead the neophyte to the silent realm of contemplation: apophthegms. This paradoxical nature of prayer was clearly perceived – and exploited – in late antique philosophical speculation. One of the major concerns of Augustine of Hippo was precisely the highly problematic linguistic statute of prayer, as is apparent from the founding paradox that pervades the whole text of his *Confessions*: how can words address Him who is beyond all language and who moreover has no need to be informed of anything? The following passage from his *De magistro* (1.2) addresses this issue with rare lucidity:

> AUGUSTINUS: Videtur ergo tibi nisi aut docendi aut commemorandi causa non esse institutam locutionem?
>
> ADEODATUS: Videretur, nisi me moueret, quod dum oramus utique loquimur, nec tamen Deum aut doceri aliquid a nobis aut commemorari fas est credere.
>
> AUGUSTINUS: Nescire te arbitror non ob aliud nobis praeceptum esse, ut in clausis cubiculis oremus, quo nomine significantur mentis penetralia, nisi quod Deus, ut nobis quod cupimus praestet, commemorari aut doceri nostra locutione non quaerit. Qui enim loquitur, suae uoluntatis signum foras dat per articulatum sonum, Deus autem in ipsis rationalis animae secretis, qui homo interior uocatur, et quaerendus et deprecandus est; haec enim sua templa esse uoluit. An apud apostolum non legisti: 'Nescitis quia templum Dei estis et spiritus Dei habitat in uobis' et 'in interiore homine habitare Christum'? Nec in propheta animaduertisti: 'Dicite in cordibus uestris et in cubilibus uestris conpungimini. Sacrificate sacrificium iustitiae et sperate in Domino'? Vbi putas sacrificium iustitiae sacrificari nisi in templo mentis et in cubilibus cordis? Vbi autem sacrificandum est, ibi et orandum. Quare non opus est locutione, cum oramus, id est sonantibus uerbis, nisi forte, sicut sacerdotes faciunt, significandae mentis suae causa, non ut Deus, sed ut homines audiant et consensione quadam per commemorationem suspendantur in Deum.

> AUGUSTINE: Then doesn't it seem to you that speaking is undertaken only for the sake of teaching or reminding?
>
> ADEODATUS: It would seem so were I not troubled by the fact that we certainly speak while we're praying, and yet it isn't right to believe that we teach God or remind Him of anything.
>
> AUGUSTINE: I dare say you don't know that we are instructed to pray 'in closed chambers' [Mt 6:6] – a phrase that signifies the inner recesses of the mind – precisely because God does not seek to be taught or reminded by our speaking in order to provide us what we want. Anyone who speaks gives an external sign of his will by means of an articulated sound. Yet God is to be sought and entreated in the hidden parts of the rational soul, which is called the 'inner man'; for He wanted

> those parts to be His temples. Have you not read in the Apostle: 'Do you not know that you are the temple of God and that the Spirit of God dwells within you?' [1 Cor 3:16] and: 'Christ dwells in the inner man' [Eph 3:16–17]. Didn't you notice in the Prophet: 'Speak in your hearts and be stricken in your bedchambers; offer up the sacrifice of justice, and hope in the Lord' [Ps 4:4–5]. Where do you think the 'sacrifice of justice' is offered up but in the temple of the mind and in the bedchambers of the heart? What is more, one should pray where one should sacrifice. There is accordingly no need for speaking when we pray. That is, there is no need for spoken words – except perhaps to speak as priests do, for the sake of signifying what is in their minds: not that God might hear, but that men might do so and by remembering might, with one accord, be raised to God.[52]

In a sense prayer overcomes the limitations of language by transcending the very ideas of meaning and communication: 'We cannot speak' – declares Augustine (*in psalm.* 102.8) – 'and we are not allowed to be silent. [. . .] Therefore, what can we do without speaking and without being silent? We can rejoice', or which amounts to much the same thing, *pray*.[53] The peculiar linguistic, pragmatic and even philosophical dimension of prayer as a *sui generis* act of language has been frequently dealt with in its full deconstructive potential by the post-structuralist thinker Jacques Derrida in the wake of Augustine's pioneering reflections:

> Between the theological movement that speaks [. . .] and the apophatic path [. . .] there is necessarily a passage, a transfer, a translation. [. . .] This experience is that of prayer. [. . .] In every prayer there must be an address to the other as other; [. . .] This first trait thus characterizes a discourse (an act of language even if prayer is silent) which, as such, is not predicative, theoretical (theo*logical*), or constative. [. . .] Neither the prayer nor the encomium is, of course, an act of constative predication. Both have a performative dimension [. . .]. I will hold to one distinction: prayer in itself [. . .] implies nothing other than the supplicating address to the other, perhaps beyond all supplication and giving, to give the promise of His presence as other, and finally the transcendence of His otherness itself, even without any other determination; the encomium, although it is not a simple attributive speech, nevertheless preserves an irreducible relationship with attribution. [. . .] How can one deny that the encomium qualifies God and *determines* prayer, *determines* the other [. . .]? [. . .] [Prayer] does not speak *of*, but *to*.[54]

All these considerations are even truer of objectless prayer, the kind practised and favoured by most hesychasts. In order to attain the mystical state known as the kingdom of heaven, language must cease and only pure, empty, objectless prayer may prevail. But how do apophthegms help to make this happen? Apart from the more explicit methods that we have explored so far (invitations to prayer, meaningful anecdotes, shared experiences, words of advice), apophthegms occasionally choose to make deliberate use of absurdity and paradox in order to de-automatizate and ultimately neutralize the ordinary workings of discursive reasoning. The initiand, who is puzzled by the apparent *non sequitur* of the words that he has just heard, is implicitly invited to make sense of them by resorting to a non-discursive kind of (anti-)logic that can only be achieved through silent contemplation:

> Εἶπεν ὁ ἀββᾶς Ἰωσὴφ τῷ ἀββᾷ Λώτ· Οὐ δύνασαι γενέσθαι μοναχὸς, ἐὰν μὴ γένῃ ὡς πῦρ φλογιζόμενος ὅλος.
>
> Abba Joseph said to Abba Lot: 'You cannot become a monk unless you become altogether like flaming fire' [cf. Heb 1:7, Ps 103:4].[55]

> Ἠρωτήθη πάλιν· Διατί συνεχῶς ῥᾳθυμῶ; Καὶ ἀπεκρίθη· Ἐπειδὴ οὐδέποτε τὸν ἥλιον εἶδες.
>
> He [an elder] was also asked: 'Why am I continually negligent?' 'Because you have never seen the sun', he replied.[56]

> Εἶπε γέρων· Ἐὰν μοναχὸς ὅτε ἵσταται εἰς προσευχὴν τότε μόνον εὔχεται, ὁ τοιοῦτος ὅλως οὐκ εὔχεται.
>
> An elder said: 'If it is only when a monk is standing in prayer that he prays, such a one does not pray at all'.[57]

> Εἶπε γέρων· Ἡ γενεὰ αὕτη οὐ ζητεῖ τὸ σήμερον ἀλλὰ τὸ αὔριον.
>
> An elder said, 'This generation is not looking out for today, but for tomorrow'.[58]

> Ἔλεγον οἱ γέροντες ὅτι· Τὸ ἔργον ἡμῶν καίειν ἐστὶ ξύλα.
>
> The elders used to say, 'Our task is to burn wood'.[59]

This particular type of apophthegm bears a strong resemblance to the brief sayings, anecdotes, and snippets of conversations of the most venerable Zen masters known as kōans.[60] The apparently nonsensical and paradoxical nature of most kōans, which are to be obsessively ruminated on by students during meditation, aims at triggering a sudden non-discursive illumination, which enhances the student's apprehension of reality. Only the student who has been able to internalize the kōan to the point of becoming one with its content suddenly attains a non-conceptual 'solution' to the riddle it poses. Such a solution can only be reached within an extra-logical level of signification in which all paradoxes and dualities dissolve into an all-embracing experience. A single example of kōan will be sufficient to illustrate the nature of these oriental apophthegms: 'A monk asked Dongshan Shouchu, "What is Buddha?" Dongshan said, "Three pounds of flax"'.[61] Interestingly, the emergence of kōans, their original use (which differs substantially from that of today)[62] and even their further compilation in different collections parallels the tradition of Western apophthegms to a greater extent than their role in contemporary Zen practices.[63] It is curious that both oral traditions, as similar as they are genetically unrelated, originate in a relatively limited period of time (the fourth century in the case of Western *Apophthegmata* and the sixth or seventh century onwards in the case of Zen)[64] in parts of the world as far away as China and Egypt. Unfortunately this is not the place to go any deeper into a systematic comparison between apophthegms and kōans, a subject that probably deserves an entire doctoral dissertation.[65]

In the case of both Eastern and Western contemplative practices, overcoming thoughts (*logismoi*) and reaching the kingdom of heaven (illumination) ultimately entails being able to perceive the deep unity of every existing creature, the *coincidetia oppositorum* or non-duality underlying reality, thus superseding the fallacies inherent in all binary thinking. Apophthegms clearly point in this direction:

> Εἶπε γέρων· Εἴκοσι ἔτη ἔμεινα πρὸς ἕνα λογισμὸν πολεμῶν ἵνα πάντας τοὺς ἀνθρώπους ὡς ἕνα βλέπω.
>
> An elder said, 'I have been twenty years fighting against one *logismos* in order to see all men as one.'[66]

The collections of apophthegms: An impossible encyclopaedia of unknowing?

Owing to their isolation and lack of defensive fortifications, the great settlements of Egyptian monasticism (Scetis, Kellia, Nitria) were soon exposed to continuous raids by Bedouin tribes. Scetis, one of the main centres of desert monasticism, was devastated by Mazics initially in 407 and subsequently in 434 or 444, and many of its monks were driven away or simply killed. Those who survived found themselves forced to seek refuge in Palestine. It was there during the fifth century that they first decided to commit to writing the oral tradition of the teachings of the desert fathers and mothers, which was then endangered by the disruption of the original monastic communities.

The task was far from simple. Given the fragmentary, disperse, multi-authored (sometimes even multi-lingual), logoclastic, thematically heterogenous, and asyntactic nature of apophthegms, it was extremely difficult to find a taxonomical principle to gather and organize them all together in a coherent user-friendly collection. Being so unclassifiable and multifarious, they discouragingly defied any attempt at systematization. Different taxonomical criteria were explored and two in particular: alphabetical (based on the initial of the name of the master involved) and thematic (based on the subject treated in the apophthegm). But what of anonymous apophthegmata? Which topics were to be chosen as the most meaningful and which excluded? What of thematically ambiguous apophthegms? What of those not unusual cases in which different and even mutually contradictory answers are given to the same question?[67] The ultimate arbitrariness of both criteria further proves the impossibility of carrying out such a task satisfactorily. In addition, as we have seen, most apophthegms were conceived to question the very workings of language and literature in an invitation to silent prayer and non-discursive concentration. Some of them even flirt with absurdity. All of them ultimately demand their own disappearance. How can the irrational be rationalized? Does it make any sense trying to systematize a kind of apophatic encyclopaedia of silence and unknowing? Does this not entail a contradiction in terms? The prologues to the two main collections (the alphabetical and the thematic, known as systematic) bear witness to the difficulty of the task. Part of the prologue to Alphabetic Collection reads as follows:

> Ἐπειδὴ δὲ συγκεχυμένη καὶ ἀσύντακτος οὖσα τῶν πολλῶν ἡ διήγησις δυσκολίαν τινὰ ἐμποιεῖ τῇ διανοίᾳ τοῦ ἀναγινώσκοντος, μὴ ἐξαρκούσῃ περιλαβεῖν τῇ μνήμῃ τὸν πολυσχιδῶς κατεσπαρμένον τῷ βιβλίῳ νοῦν, τούτου χάριν ἐπὶ τήνδε τὴν ἔκθεσιν κεκινήμεθα τῶν στοιχείων, δυναμένην διὰ τὴν τάξιν [καὶ] περίληψιν ἐναργεστάτην τε καὶ ἑτοίμην τοῖς βουλομένοις τὴν ὠφέλειαν παρέχειν. Ἐπειδὴ τὰ περὶ τοῦ ἀββᾶ Ἀντωνίου, Ἀρσενίου τε καὶ Ἀγάθωνος, καὶ τῶν ἀπὸ τοῦ ἄλφα [ἀρχομένων] .... [Βασιλείου, Βισα]ρίωνος καὶ Βενιαμὶν εἰς τὸ βῆτα στοιχεῖον, καὶ οὕτως καθεξῆς ἕως τοῦ ω.
>
> Ἐπειδὴ δέ εἰσι καὶ ἕτεροι λόγοι γερόντων ἁγίων καὶ πράξεις, μὴ ἐμφαίνοντες τὰ ὀνόματα τῶν τε εἰρηκότων αὐτοὺς καὶ πραξάντων, τούτους μετὰ τὴν συμπλήρωσιν τῶν κατὰ στοιχεῖον ἐν κεφαλαίοις ἐξεθέμεθα.
>
> Πολλὰ δὲ ἐρευνήσαντες βιβλία καὶ ζητήσαντες, ὅσα εὑρεῖν ἠδυνήθημεν, ἐνετάξαμεν εἰς τὰ τέλη τῶν κεφαλαίων, ἵνα ἐκ πάντων ἐρανιζόμενοι τὴν τῆς ψυχῆς ὠφέλειαν, [...] τύχωμεν τῆς αὐτοῦ βασιλείας. Ἀμήν.

> Now, a narrative which is the work of many hands is confused and disorderly, and it distracts the attention of the readers, for their minds are drawn in different directions and cannot retain sayings that are scattered about in the book. Therefore we have tried to gather them together in chapters, so that they will be in order and clear and easy to look up, for those who want to benefit by reading them. Thus, all that is attributed to Anthony, Arsenius, Agathon, and all those whose name begin with 'A' are listed under Alpha; Basil, Bessarion, Benjamin, under Beta, and so on to the end of the alphabet.
>
> But since there are some sayings and deeds of the holy fathers in which the name of him who said or did them does not appear, we have arranged them in chapters after the alphabetical sections.
>
> We have investigated and gone through as many books as we could find, and we have placed the results at the end of the book, so that we may gather spiritual fruit from each one, and [...] gain His kingdom. Amen.[68]

This provisional arrangement did not seem to convince the compilers of the Systematic Collection, who tried to explore another equally unfitting method of organizing and rationalizing such disconcerting and slippery material. It should be noted that the Greek wording of the first lines of the following passage is identical to that of the Alphabetical Collection[69] – although their conclusions diverge dramatically:

> Ἐπειδὴ δὲ συγκεχυμένη καὶ ἀσύντακτος οὖσα τῶν πολλῶν ἡ διήγησις δυσκολίαν τινὰ ἐνεποίει τῇ διανοίᾳ τοῦ ἀναγινώσκοντος, μὴ ἐξαρκούσῃ περιλαβεῖν τῇ μνήμῃ τὸν πολυσχιδῶς κατεσπαρμένον τῷ βιβλίῳ νοῦν, τούτου χάριν ἐπὶ τήνδε τῶν κεφαλαίων τὴν ἔκθεσιν κεκινήμεθα, δυναμένην διά τε τὴν τάξιν καὶ τὴν τῶν ἰσοδυναμούντων λόγων περίληψιν ἐναργεστάτην τε καὶ ἑτοίμην τοῖς βουλομένοις τὴν ὠφέλειαν παρέχειν. Οὐ μικρὸν γὰρ εἰς ἀρετῆς προτροπὴν λόγος ἐκ πολλῶν ἐναρέτων προσώπων ὁμοδόξως προσφερόμενος.
>
> Ὅταν γὰρ ἀββᾶ μὲν Ἀντώνιος λέγει ὅτι ἡ ταπεινοφροσύνη πάσας τοῦ διαβόλου τὰς παγίδας παρέρχεται, ἄλλος δὲ πάλιν ὅτι δένδρον ζωῆς εἰς ὕψος ἐγειρόμενόν ἐστιν ἡ ταπεινοφροσύνη, ἕτερος δὲ ὅτι ἡ ταπείνωσις οὐκ ὀργίζεται οὐδὲ αροργίζει τινά, καὶ πάλιν ἄλλος φησὶν ὅτι ἐάν τις εἴπῃ τινὶ συγχώρησον μετὰ ταπεινοφροσύνης καίει τοὺς δαίμονας, ἐκ πάντων τούτων πληροφορίαν λαμβάνει ἡ τοῦ ἀναγινώσκοντος διάνοια πάσῃ σπουδῇ μεταδιώκειν τὴν ταπεινοφροσύνην. Καὶ ἐν τοῖς ἄλλοις δὲ κεφαλαίοις τὸ αὐτὸ εὑρήσεις. Ἡ γὰρ τάξις ὅλων ὁμοῦ τῶν κεφαλαίων καὶ καθὲν αὐτῶν ἑνὸς ἑκάστου τὰ μέγιστα λυσιτελεῖ τῷ μεταχειριζομένῳ τὴν τοῦ βιβλίου ἀνάγνωσιν.
>
> [. . .] ἕκαστον κεφάλαιον περιέχει πατέρων διαφόρους λόγους ὡρισμένων τε καὶ ἀορίστων [. . .]. Ἀλλὰ καὶ ὁ σύμπας τῶν κεφαλαίων εἱρμὸς οὐκ εἰκῇ οὐδὲ ὡς ἔτυχε κείμενος, ὁμοίως χρησιμώτατος τυγχάνει τῷ βουλομένῳ προσέχειν τὸν νοῦν.
>
> But since the relating of many of the things was confused and disordered – their meaning haphazardly spread throughout the book, which did not help the memory to keep track of it – it caused some difficulty in the readers' mind. That is why we have moved to this arrangement by chapters, for it is able to provide very clear comprehension and ready benefit for those who wish it because a statement unanimously sustained by many virtuous persons make no small contribution to the advance of virtue.
>
> For when Abba Antony says that 'humility evades all the snares of the devil' [see 15.3, Antony 7], another [elder] that 'humility is a tree of life, raised up on high' [see 15.67, Hyperechios, N 699], another that 'humiliation neither angers anyone nor gets angry' [see 21.34; N 115], while yet another says that 'if one says to another in humility, 'Forgive me', he burns the demons' [see 15.98], from all these the mind of the reader receives confidence to make every effort in pursuit of humility. And you will find the same in the other chapters; for the arrangement of the chapters all together and each one of them separately is beneficial in the highest degree to him who undertakes the reading of the book.
>
> [. . .] Each chapter contains the various saying of fathers, named and unnamed [. . .]. The general sequence of the chapters is not arranged without plan or haphazardly; it too is very convenient for him who is willing to apply his mind.[70]

Needless to say, this thematic arrangement proves its unavoidable arbitrariness in many an item. Despite all these editorial efforts, the *Apophthegmata patrum* continued to resist definition and classification as the most curious encyclopaedia of silence and unknowing ever conceived – a *unicum* in ancient (anti-)literature.

The various collections of apophthegms that gradually appeared in different languages and contexts enjoyed enormous popularity and diffusion. It is therefore no wonder that they exerted such a huge influence not only on the development of Christian monasticism but also on the appearance, format, style, and conception of a number of traditionally produced (i.e. single-authored) religious works, such as the theological treatises by Evagrius Ponticus, a hesychast monk himself.[71] One may even speak of a clear apophthegmization of the traditional genre of the theological treatise, with an unprecedented use of extremely short periods, single-sentence chapters, cut-and-paste quotations, enigmatic formulae, apophatic hints, etc. In this manner the *Apophthegmata patrum*, the most accomplished form of anti-literature of the ancient world, not only became a literary genre in its own right, but – paradoxically enough – also succeeded in implementing a new aesthetic model for future creations. But that is another story.

Notes

1. Translation taken from Wortley 2014: 153. This saying also figures in AP syst 10.111.
2. Quoted from Foulk 2000: 39.
3. A good introduction to early monasticism and desert spirituality can be found in Harmless 2004 (with an extensive bibliography).
4. See Harmless 2004: 169–70: 'The *Apophthegmata* has come down to us in two basic forms: the Alphabetical Collection and the Systematic Collection. The Alphabetical gathers some 1,000 sayings and brief narratives under the names of 130 prominent monks and arranges these according to the Greek alphabet. Thus, *Alpha* begins with thirty-eight sayings from Antony and follows with [. . .] Arsenius, Agathon, Ammonas, and so on [. . .]. Attached to certain manuscripts of the Alphabetical Collection is an additional set of sayings and stories that had come down to the ancient editors without names. This series, referred to as the Anonymous Collection, had as its original core some 240 sayings, but eventually 400 more came to be attached to this core. The Systematic Collection contains many of the same sayings and stories but gathers them under twenty-one different headings or themes, such as "discernment", "unceasing prayer", "hospitality", and "humility". The Greek version contains some 1200 sayings. In the mid-sixth century, an early version of this Systematic Collection was translated from Greek into Latin by two Roman clerics, the deacon Pelagius and the subdeacon John (who perhaps became the later Popes Pelagius and John). This version, called the *Verba Seniorum* [. . .] was apparently known to Saint Benedict and powerfully influenced the spirituality of medieval monasticism. In time, vast collections of *Apophthegmata* appeared not only in Greek and Latin, but also in Syriac, Coptic, Armenian, Georgian, Arabic, Ethiopic, and Old Slavonic'. The Alphabetic collection (quoted as AP alph followed by the corresponding name) has no modern critical edition – the standard Greek text is still that of Jean Baptiste Cotelier (1677: 338–712), reproduced in PG 65: 71–440. It has been translated into English by Ward 1984 and Wortley 2014. The Anonymous Collection (quoted as AP N) has been recently edited and translated by Wortley 2013. The Systematic Collection (abbreviated AP

syst) has an excellent bilingual edition in three volumes by Jean-Claude Guy (1993–2003–2005) and an English translation (Wortley 2012).

5. Brown 1971: 100.
6. See Hernández Lobato 2017a.
7. I have coined the term 'logoclasm' in imitation of Byzantine iconoclasm. It implies the idea of a structural crisis in the traditional 'logocentrism' of Graeco-Roman antiquity – i.e. the unchallenged hegemony of *logos* in the understanding, interpretation, and representation of reality. This neologism aims to provide a new critical tool by which to explain the ultimate raison d'être of the epochal shift of late antiquity – and in particular the profound transformations that its new epistemological paradigm (opposed to that of classical logocentrism) brought with it in so many cultural fields (a long list of examples can be found in Hernández Lobato 2018: 53–4): philosophy, semiotics (which originate as such precisely in this period for a reason), religion, literary aesthetics, hermeneutics, artistic creation and how it was decoded by spectators, the perception of the landscape and the surrounding reality, the experience of one's inner being, the conception of the social pyramid, the manner of experiencing the notions of temporality and infinity, the planning of the iconographical and decorative programmes, the town planning of Constantinople, and even textile fashion. The crisis of the third century, the irrationalist drift of neo-Platonic philosophy, the flood of mystical and soteriological currents imported from the East and the countercultural discourse of early Christianity, the heir to a Jewish world view, finally perforated the epistemological certainties of the Roman citizen, gradually instilling a generalized doubt as to the mediating entities in our comprehension of reality, including of course the most important of all: language, the ultimate basis of our understanding of the world and an essential requirement for participation in public life. For the first time late antique man was forced to face the surrounding world without the support of the intermediation of *logos*, which had gone from being the beacon that lights up reality, giving it purpose and sense, to being considered a deceptive mask, a distorting veil, in short a hindrance to full comprehension of what is. This change of epistemological paradigm, brought about by an unprecedented *mise en crise* of the very notions of language and representation (a kind of 'linguistic turn' *avant la lettre*, as suggested in Hernández Lobato 2017a: 279), will be explored in depth in a future monograph currently under preparation. On the notion of *episteme* see Foucault 1966.
8. Guy 1993: 18–21.
9. Guy 1993: 21.
10. See e.g. AP alph Sisoes 40 [tr. Ward 1984: 220]: 'Abba Sisoes said, "Seek God, and do not seek where he dwells".' See also AP alph Poemen 85 [tr. Ward 1984: 179]: 'He [Abba Poemen] also said concerning Abba Pior that every day he made a new beginning.'
11. See AP alph Evagrius 7; syst 16.3 [tr. Wortley 2004: 104]: 'Once there was a meeting at The Cells about some matter and Abba Evagrius spoke. The priest said to him: "Abba Evagrius, we know that if you were in your homeland you would probably have been a bishop and the head of many [clergy]; but now you are living here as an alien." He was pricked in his conscience but not disturbed. Nodding his head, he said to him: "It is true, father; nevertheless, «I have spoken once; I will add nothing the second time» [Job 40:5]".' See also AP alph Arsenius 7; syst 2.6 [tr. Ward 1984: 10]: 'Blessed Archbishop Theophilus, accompanied by a magistrate, came one day to find Abba Arsenius. He questioned the old man, to hear a word from him. After a short silence the old man answered him, "Will you put into practice what I say to you?" They promised him this. "If you hear Arsenius in anywhere, do not go there".'
12. See e.g. AP alph Macarius 23 [tr. Ward 1984: 132]; cf. syst 10.47: 'A brother came to see Abba Macarius the Egyptian, and said to him, "Abba, give me a word, that I may be saved." So the

old man said, "Go to the cemetery and abuse the dead." The brother went there, abused them and threw stones at them; then he returned and told the old man about it. The latter said to him, "Didn't they say anything to you?" He replied, "No." The old man said, "Go back tomorrow and praise them." So the brother went away and praised them, calling them, "Apostles, saints and righteous men." He returned to the old man and said to him, "I have complimented them." And the old man said to him, "Did they answer you?" The brother said no. The old man said to him, "You know how you insulted them and they did not reply, and how you praised them and they did not speak; so you too if you wish to be saved must do the same and become a dead man. Like the dead, take no account of either the scorn of men or their praises, and you can be saved"'. See also AP alph Sisoes 24; syst 20.6 [tr. Ward 1984: 217]: 'It was said of Abba Sisoes that when he was sitting in the cell he would always close the door.'

13. See e.g. AP alph Poemen S 8 [tr. Wortley 2014: 259]: He also said: If Moses had not led the sheep to a fold, he would not have seen what he saw at the bush [Ex 3:1–2].

14. See e.g. AP alph Antony 6; syst 1.2 [tr. Wortley 2004: 32]: 'Abba Pambo asked Abba Antony: "What am I to do?" The elder said to him: "Have no confidence in your righteousness; have no regret about a past action; get control of your tongue and your belly"'. See also AP alph Poemen 112; syst 9.21 [tr. Wortley 2014: 246]: 'Some fathers asked Abba Poemen: "If we see a brother sinning, do you want us to reprove him?" The elder said to them: "For my part, even if I am obliged to go that way and I see him sinning, I pass him by and do not reprove him"'.

15. See e.g. Iren. 3.16.6 [the Latin text is taken from Rousseau and Doutreleau 1974: 312–14; tr. Roberts, Donaldson and Coxe 1885: 442–3]: 'There is [. . .] one God the Father, and one Christ Jesus, who [. . .] gathered together all things in Himself. But in every respect, too, He is man, the formation of God; and thus He took up man into Himself, the invisible becoming visible, the incomprehensible being made comprehensible, the impassable becoming capable of suffering, and the Word being made man, thus summing up all things in Himself' (*Unus igitur Deus Pater* [. . .] *et unus Christus Iesus Dominus noster,* [. . .] *omnia in semetipsum recapitulans. In omnibus autem est et homo, plasmatio Dei; et hominem ergo in semetipsum recapitulatus est, invisibilis visibilis factus, et incomprehensibilis factus comprehensibilis, et impassibilis passibilis, et Verbum homo, universa in semetipsum recapitulans*). On the aesthetic implications of this theology for late antique literature and art see Hernández Lobato 2017: 480–6.

16. For instance, a question such as 'How can I be saved?' (formulated either explicitly or implicitly) has many different answers throughout the apophthegmatic corpus [all translations in this note are taken from Ward 1984]: 'Do this [alternate work and prayer] and you will be saved' (AP alph Antony 1); 'Whoever you may be, always have God before your eyes; whatever you do, do it according to the testimony of the holy Scriptures; in whatever place you live, do not easily leave it. Keep these three precepts and you will be saved' (AP alph Antony 3); 'Without temptations no-one can be saved' (AP alph Antony 5); 'The Gospel says, "if anyone strikes you on one cheek, turn to him the other also." [Mt. 5:39] [. . .] If you cannot offer the other cheek, at least allow one cheek to be struck. [. . .] If you are not able to do that, do not return evil for evil' (AP alph Antony 19); 'Flee from men and you will be saved' (AP alph Arsenius 1); 'Go, make your thoughts like those of the evildoers who are in prison. For they are always asking when the magistrate will come, awaiting him in anxiety. [..] If you give yourself continually to this, you may be saved.' (AP alph Ammonas 1), etc. The answer always varied according to the specific spiritual needs of the initiand as is apparent from the following text (AP alph Ares 1): 'Abba Abraham went to see Abba Ares. They were sitting together when a brother came to the old man and said to him, "Tell me what I must do to be saved." He replied, [. . .]. When the brother had gone, Abba Abraham said to Abba Ares, "Why do you prescribe an easy yoke to all the brethren, while you impose such a heavy burden on

this brother?" The old man replied, "How I send them away depends upon what the brethren came to seek. Now it is for the sake of God that this one comes to hear a word, for he is a hard worker and what I tell him he carries out eagerly. It is because of this that I speak the word of God to him".'

17. Jakobson 1960: 356.

18. AP alph Bessarion 10 [tr. Ward 1984: 42].

19. AP alph Agathon 15; syst 4.7 [tr. Ward 1984: 22].

20. The story is transmitted by Plutarch (*Demosthenes* 11.1).

21. *Tractatus logico-philosophicus* 6.54: 'My propositions are elucidatory in this way: he who understands me finally recognizes them as senseless, when he has climbed out through them, on them, over them. (He must so to speak throw away the ladder, after he has climbed up on it.)' Translations from this work are taken from Wittgenstein 1922.

22. AP N 392; syst 6.6 [tr. Wortley 2013: 251]. The unnamed elder who originally told this story about one of his fellow brothers was probably Evagrius Ponticus, since it first appears in chapter 97 of his *Praktikos* (see Gillaumont 1971: 704–5 n. for further details). It was not unusual for the name of Evagrius to be intentionally omitted from the manuscripts after his posthumous condemnation for Origenism. For a complete account of all the sources transmitting this popular anecdote and its different attributions (with no mention of Evagrius' *Praktikos*) see Butler 1898: 98–9.

23. Cf. e.g. AP alph Theodore of Pherme 1; syst 6.7 [tr. Ward 1984: 73]: 'Abba Theodore of Pherme had acquired three good books. He came to Abba Macarius and said to him, "I have three excellent books from which I derive profit; the brethren also make use of them and derive profit from them. Tell me what I ought to do: keep them for my use and that of the brethren, or sell them and give the money to the poor?" The old man answered him in this way, "Your actions are good; but it is best of all to possess nothing." Hearing that, he went and sold his books and gave the money for them to the poor.' See also AP alph Serapion 2; syst 6.16 [tr. Ward 1984: 227]: 'A brother said to Abba Serapion, "Give me a word." The old man said to him, "What shall I say to you? You have taken the living of the widows and orphans and put it on your shelves." For he saw them full of books.'

24. The fourth-century theologian Gregory of Nyssa famously described God as 'adiastemic', i.e. not extended in space and time (non-dimensional) – and as something that therefore contrasted with the created world, which is unable to escape its dimensional ('diastemic') condition: see e.g. *Eun*. 2.69–70. Since language is but a human invention (see *Eun*. 2.163, 166 and 181) and as such inescapably 'diastemic', it is utterly unable to convey the ultimate reality of things (*Eun* 2.195), which is by definition divine and 'adiastemic' (*Eun* 2, 214; tr. Hall 2007: 105): ὅπου δὲ διάστασις οὐκ ἐπινοεῖται, τὸ συνημμένον πάντως ὁμολογεῖται, τὸ δὲ διὰ πάντων συνημμένον φωνῇ καὶ λόγῳ οὐ μεσιτεύεται ('But where no separation is conceived, close conjunction is surely acknowledged; and what is totally conjoined is not mediated by voice and speech'). See on this subject Hernández Lobato 2016. On the pivotal notion of 'diastema', see Douglass 2005, and Mateo-Seco and Maspero 2010 s.v.

25. AP alph *prol.* [tr. Ward 1984: xxxv].

26. On Evagrius Ponticus see Casiday 2006 and 2013, Corrigan 2009 and Konstantinosky 2009.

27. Greek text taken from Guillaumont 1971: 498. Translation taken from Sinkewicz 2006: 97.

28. AP syst 2.35 [tr. Wortley 2012: 23].

29. AP syst 2.27; PG 28: 1438A [tr. Wortley 2012: 21]

30. Evagrius Ponticus *de oratione* 70 (PG 79 1181) [tr. Sinkewicz 2006: 200]. Due to the posthumous condemnation of Evagrius, this work was transmitted under the name of Nilus

of Ancyra (also known as Nilus of Sinai) by the Greek branch of the manuscript tradition. However, the Syriac and Arabic translations preserved the original attribution, which is further confirmed by a cross-reference in Evagrius' *Peri logismōn* 22.

31. AP syst 2.24; alph Poemen 43 [tr. Wortley 2012: 20].

32. Weil 2002: 117: 'Attention, taken to its highest degree, is the same thing as prayer. [. . .] Absolute unmixed attention is prayer. [. . .] Extreme attention is what constitutes the creative faculty in man and the only extreme attention is religious. The amount of creative genius in any period is strictly in proportion to the amount of extreme attention and thus of authentic religion at that period.'

33. AP syst 11.76; alph Hyperechios 7 [tr. Wortley 2012: 205].

34. AP syst 2.29; N 134 [tr. Wortley 2012: 21–2]. The wording of the final scene is strongly reminiscent of 1 Cor 13:12: 'For now (ἄρτι) we see (βλέπομεν) in a mirror (δι᾽ἐσόπτρου) dimly, but then face to face (πρόσωπον πρὸς πρόσωπον). Now (ἄρτι) I know in part; then I shall know fully, even as I have been fully known' (βλέπομεν γὰρ ἄρτι δι᾽ἐσόπτρου ἐν αἰνίγματι, τότε δὲ πρόσωπον πρὸς πρόσωπον· ἄρτι γινώσκω ἐκ μέρους, τότε δὲ ἐπιγνώσομαι καθὼς καὶ ἐπεγνώσθην). This deliberate intertextual dialogue enhances the generally unnoticed mystical dimension of the whole passage, thus providing an interesting key for its interpretation.

35. Greek text taken from Guillaumont and Guillaumont 1989: 92. Translation slightly modified from Sinkewicz 2006: 280 n. 46.

36. On these two Syriac renditions of Greek *logos* in its technical sense, directly borrowed from stoicism, see Guillaumont and Guillaumont 1989: 29–30.

37. On the notion of the kingdom of heaven in other Church Fathers see Herrick 1903 and Lampe 1948.

38. This amplified perception of reality was indeed a typically late antique experience: from Plotinus' 'philosophical' ecstasies (Hadot 1993) via Ausonius' unmediated encounter with the river Moselle (Hernández Lobato 2016a) to Augustine's sudden epiphanies (see e.g. *conf.* 7.10.16–17.17.23). Proof of the transversality and pervasiveness of such experiences in late antique culture is the fact that they are not restricted to the realm of religion or to a single social milieu. They have even left clear traces in late antique art and visual culture, thus giving birth to what I refer to as 'aesthetics of detail(s)' (Hernández Lobato 2012: 318–401).

39. *Life of Antony* 20.4–6 [tr. Vivian and Athanassakis 2003: 105–7].

40. Cf. August. *uera rel.* 39.72: *Noli foras ire, in te ipsum redi. In interiore homine habitat ueritas* ('Do not go outside, return into yourself, for it is in the inner self that truth dwells').

41. AP syst 2.33; N 463 [tr. Wortley 2012: 22].

42. AP alph Antony 1; syst 7.1 [tr. Wortley 2014: 31].

43. AP alph Arsenius 6; syst 15.7 [tr. Wortley 2014: 41].

44. Anti-intellectual controversies, dominated by the idea of the failure of classical *logos*, arose in several sectors of Christianity. A paradigmatic case is that of Saint Antony, the father of Christian hermit life and a precursor of hesychast mysticism, and the pagan philosophers who came to tempt him with their traps of logic and syllogisms, mocking him because of his lack of academic training (*Vita Antonii* 72–80). Antony expresses his sorrow at the ignorance shown by these intellectuals on the ultimate reality of things, which is always beyond any attempt at logical or linguistic formulation (*Vita Antonii* 74.2). 'Faith', Antony argues (*Vita Antonii* 77.4–78.1: tr. Vivian and Athanassakis 2003: 221–3), 'comes from the disposition of the soul whereas dialectic is a skill that belongs to those who practice it. Therefore, those in

whom faith is actively working have no need of argumentation with words; in fact, it is probably superfluous. Indeed, what *we* [Christians] know through faith, *you* [philosophers] attempt to construct with words; and often *you* are unable to perceive what *we* know. As a result, the working of faith is better and more secure than all your sophistries and syllogizings. We Christians, therefore, do not possess the mystery though the wisdom of Greek words but through the power of faith, [. . .] although we do not know how to write'. The tools of *logos* may be useful for practical matters, but they are utterly unable to provide true wisdom, which is by definition ineffable. This kind of logoclastic controversies is often inspired by the Pauline epistles (e.g. 1 Cor 1:20–25). Another telling example can be found in John Cassian's *Conferences* 15.3, which describes Saint Macarius defeating the 'dialectic arts' and 'Aristotelian subtleties' of an eunomian heretic.

45. AP syst 21.6; N 91 [tr. Wortley 2012: 377].

46. AP alph Moses 6; syst 2.19 [tr. Ward 1984: 139].

47. AP syst 2.15; alph Isaiah 21.3 [tr. Wortley 2012: 18].

48. *Tractatus logico-philosophicus* 7.

49. Section 9 of the *Systematic Collection* is entirely devoted to the requirement of not judging anyone. See e.g. N 11; syst 9.15; alph Theodotus S.1 [tr. Wortley 2013: 13, slightly modified]: 'Do not judge the one who indulges in *porneia* [fornication] if you are chaste, for in that way you transgress the law just as much – because he who says: "Do not indulge in *porneia*" [Mt 5:27] also says: "Do not judge" [Mt 7:1].' As Harmless (2004: 236) acutely observes following Gould (1993: 112), 'modern readers often imagine that for monks, sexuality posed *the* great struggle. But ancient sources indicate otherwise. Anger, not sex, figured more prominently. The challenge was human relations.' Anger was indeed, together with thoughts and mental dispersion, the great enemy of hesychast monks, as is apparent from AP alph Agathon 19; syst 10.16 [tr. Ward 1984: 23]: 'The same abba [Agathon] said, "A man who is angry, even if he were to raise the dead, is not acceptable to God".'

50. Cf. e.g. Rappe 2000.

51. AP syst 21.39; N 120 [tr. Wortley 2012: 380].

52. Translation taken from King 1995: 95–6.

53. *Ecce non possumus dicere, et non permittimur tacere . . . Quid ergo faciamus, non loquentes et non tacentes? Iubilemus.* My translation.

54. Derrida 1992: 110–11.

55. AP alph Joseph of Panepho 6; syst 11.45 [tr. Wortley 2014: 152]. Cf. AP Joseph of Panepho 7; syst 12.9 [tr. Wortley 2014: 152]: 'Abba Lot visited Abba Joseph and said to him: "Abba, to the best of my ability I do my little *synaxis*, my little fasting; praying, meditating, and maintaining *hēsychia*; and I purge my *logismoi* to the best of my ability. What else then can I do?" The elder stood up and stretched out his hands to heaven; his fingers became like ten lamps of fire. He said: "If you are willing, become altogether like fire".'

56. AP syst 21.8; N 92 [tr. Wortley 2012: 378].

57. AP syst 21.23; N 104 [tr. Wortley 2012: 379]

58. AP syst 21.31; N 112 [tr. Wortley 2012: 379].

59. AP syst 21.32; N 113 [tr. Wortley 2012: 379]. Cf. AP syst 21.63 [tr. Wortley 2012: 382]: 'The elders used to say, "In the same way that fire burns wood, so the work of the monk ought to burn the passions".'

60. According to Heine and Wright 2000: 3, 'the term kōan (C. *kung-an*) refers to enigmatic and often shocking spiritual expressions based on dialogical encounters between masters and

disciples that were used as pedagogical tools for religious training in the Zen (C. Ch'an) Buddhist tradition. This innovative practice is one of the best known and most distinctive elements of Zen Buddhism.' On kōans see Herine 1994 and Heine and Wright 2000.

61. *Gateless Barrier* (*Wu-men kuan*) case 18; *Blue Cliff Collection* (*Pi-yen chi*) case 12.

62. Foulk 2000: 15–23: 'Even the aforementioned type of koan practice, which is known in the [. . .] Zen schools as the 'Zen of contemplating phrases' [. . .], has its roots in an older, essentially literary tradition of collecting and commenting on dialogues attributed to ancient masters. [. . .] The practice of contemplating phrases is something that first became widespread among followers of the influential Ch'an master Ta-hui Tsung-kao (1089–1163). Ta-hui was a disciple of Yüan-wu, the compiler of the *Blue Cliff Collection*, but he decried the style of commentary embodied in that text as overly discursive. [. . .] Any attempt to grasp the meaning of the old cases conceptually, Tai-hui argued, was a species of gradualism, whereas the superior 'sudden enlightenment' approach entitled the frustration and final abandonment or transcendence of such merely intellectual approaches.'

63. Cf. Foulk 2000.

64. The Bodhidharma, who is traditionally credited as having introduced Ch'an Buddhism (the seed of Japanese Zen) into China to become the first Chinese patriarch, probably lived in the fifth or sixth century. According to Heine and Wright 2000: 3, Schlütter 2008: 109–11 and McRae 2000, the oral use of kung-ans (later called kōans in Japan) originated in China during the T'ang dynasty (AD 618–907). The first collections to be compiled date from the eleventh century (see Foulk 2000) and contain sayings and stories attributed to past Ch'an masters. These early records were later commented on and expanded, thus giving birth to canonical works such as the *Blue Cliff Collection* or *Pi-yen chi* (twelfth century) and the *Gateless Barrier or Wu-men kuan* (early thirteenth century). Western apophthegmatic tradition, as already explained, had developed centuries earlier.

65. The striking similarities between both textual corpora impressed the Japanese artist Yushi Numura to the point of putting together a curious anthology of translated apophthegms (Numura 1983), each of them calligraphically handwritten and delicately illustrated in the style of traditional Zen pen and ink drawings. On the relationship between Zen and the well-established apophatic tradition of Patristic theology, see Williams 2000.

66. AP syst 21.24; N 105 [tr. Wortley 2012: 379].

67. For examples see above note 16.

68. AP alph *prol.* [tr. Ward 1984: xxxvi].

69. Unfortunately the corresponding English renderings mask this word-for-word repetition.

70. AP syst *prol.* 4–7 [tr. Wortley 2012: 3–4].

71. A good example is Evagrius' *Praktikos Logos*, which consists of a succession of ninety extremely short chapters (most of them one or two sentences long), followed by a short collection of ten apophthegms proper. Something similar can be found in his treatise *Ho Gnostikos*.

Works cited

Brown, P. (1971), *The World of Late Antiquity: AD 150–750*, New York: W. W. Norton.

Butler, C. (1898), *The Lausiac History of Palladius: A Critical Discussion Together with Notes on Early Egyptian Monachism, Volume I*, Cambridge: Cambridge University Press.

Casiday, A. M. (2006), *Evagrius Ponticus*, London: Routledge.

Casiday, A. M. (2013), *Reconstructing the Theology of Evagrius Ponticus: Beyond Heresy*, Cambridge: Cambridge University Press.

Corrigan, K. (2009), *Evagrius and Gregory: Mind, Soul and Body in the 4th Century*, Farnham: Ashgate.

Cotelier, J.-B., ed. (1677), *Ecclesiae Graecae monumenta*, vol. 1, Paris: F. Muguet.

Douglass, S. (2005), *Theology of the Gap: Cappadocian Language Theory and the Trinitarian Controversy*, New York: Peter Lang.

Gould, G. (1993), *The Desert Fathers on Monastic Community*, Oxford: Clarendon Press.

Guillaumont, A., ed. (1971), *Évagre le Pontique. Traité pratique ou Le moine, Volume II* (SC 171), Paris: Éditions du Cerf.

Guillaumont, A. and C. Guillaumont, eds (1989), *Évagre le Pontique. Le Gnostique ou À celui qui est devenu digne de la science* (SC 356), Paris: Éditions du Cerf.

Guy, J.-C. (1993), *Les apopthegmes des pères, Collection systématique. Chapitres I-IX*, Paris: Les Éditions du Cerf (SC 387).

Guy, J.-C. (2003), *Les apopthegmes des pères, Collection systématique. Chapitres X-XVI*, Paris: Les Éditions du Cerf (SC 474).

Guy, J.-C. (2005), *Les apopthegmes des pères, Collection systématique. Chapitres XVII-XXI*, Paris: Les Éditions du Cerf (SC 498).

Derrida, J. (1992), 'How to Avoid Speaking: Denials (tr. K. Frieden)', in H. G. Coward and T. Forshay (eds), *Derrida and Negative Theology*, 73–142, Albany NY: Suny Press.

Foucault, M. (1966), *Les mots et les choses: Une archéologie des sciences humaines*, Paris: Gallimard.

Foulk, T. G. (2000), 'The Form and Function of Koan Literature: A Historical Overview', in S. Heine and D. S. Wright (eds), *The Kōan: Texts and Contexts in Zen Buddhism*, 15–45, Oxford: Oxford University Press.

Hadot, P. (1993), *Plotinus or the Simplicity of Vision* (trans. Michael Chase), Chicago: The University of Chicago Press.

Hall, S. G. (2007), 'Gregory Bishop of Nyssa. The Second Book against Eunomius', in L. Karfíková, S. Douglass and J. Zachhuber (eds), *Gregory of Nyssa: Contra Eunomium II. An English Version with Supporting Studies*, 59–201, Leiden-Boston: Brill.

Harmless, W. (2004), *Desert Christians: An Introduction to the Literature of Early Monasticism*, Oxford: Oxford University Press.

Heine, S. (1994), *Dōgen and the Kōan Tradition: A Tale of Two Shōbōgenzō Texts*, Albany: State University of New York Press.

Heine, S. and D. S. Wright, eds (2000), *The Kōan. Texts and Contexts in Zen Buddhism*, Oxford: Oxford University Press.

Hernández Lobato, J. (2012), Vel Apolline muto: *Estética y poética de la Antigüedad tardía*, Bern: Peter Lang.

Hernández Lobato, J. (2016), 'Más allá del pensamiento. El escepticismo epistemológico de Gregorio de Nisa', in A. I. Bouton-Touboulic and C. Lévy (eds), *Scepticisme et Religion. Constantes et évolutions, de la philosophie hellénistique à la philosophie médiévale* (MON 21), 157–69, Turnhout: Brepols.

Hernández Lobato, J. (2016a), 'Mystic River: Ausonius' *Mosella* as an Epistemological Revelation', *Ramus*, 45 (2): 231–66.

Hernández Lobato, J. (2017), 'Conceptual Poetry: Rethinking Optatian from Contemporary Art', in M. Squire and J. Wienand (eds), *Morphogrammata / The Lettered Art of Optatian: Figuring Cultural Transformations in the Age of Constantine*, 461–93, Paderborn: W. Fink.

Hernández Lobato, J. (2017a), 'To Speak or Not to Speak: The Birth of a 'Poetics of Silence' in Late Antique Literature', in J. Elsner and J. Hernández Lobato (eds), *The Poetics of Late Latin Literature*, 278–310, Oxford: Oxford University Press.

Hernández Lobato, J. (2018), 'Late Antique Foundations of Postmodern Theory: A Critical Overview', in S. Schottenius Cullhed and M. Malm (eds), *Reading Late Antiquity*, 51–70, Heidelberg: Universitätsverlag Winter.
Herrick, H. M. (1903), *The Kingdom of God in the Writings of the Fathers*, Chicago: University of Chicago Press.
Jakobson, R. (1960), 'Linguistics and Poetics', in T. A. Sebeok (ed.), *Style in Language*, 350–77, Cambridge, MA: MIT Press.
King, P. (1995), *Augustine. Against the Academicians and The Teacher*, Indianapolis, IN: Hackett.
Konstantinovsky, J. (2009) *Evagrius Ponticus: The Making of a Gnostic*, Farnham: Ashgate.
Lampe, G. W. H. (1948), 'Some Notes on the Significance of βασιλεία τοῦ θεοῦ, βασιλεία Χριστοῦ, in the Greek Fathers', *JTS*, 49 (193/194): 58–73.
Mateo-Seco, L. F. and G. Maspero, eds (2010), *The Brill Dictionary of Gregory of Nyssa*, Boston: Brill.
Nomura, Y. (1983), *Desert Wisdom: Sayings from the Desert Fathers*, London: Eyre & Spottiswoode.
McRae, J. R. (2000), 'The Antecedents of Encounter Dialogue in Chinese Ch'an Buddhism', in S. Heine and D. S. Wright (eds), *The Kōan: Texts and Contexts in Zen Buddhism*, 46–74, Oxford: Oxford University Press.
Rappe, S. (2000), *Reading Neoplatonism: Non-Discursive Thinking in the Texts of Plotinus, Proclus, and Damascius*, Cambridge: Cambridge University Press.
Roberts, A., J. Donaldson and A. C. Coxe, eds (1885), *The Ante-Nicene Fathers. Volume I: The Apostolic Fathers with Justin Martyr and Irenaeus*, Buffalo, NY: The Christian Literature Publishing Company.
Rousseau, A. and L. Doutreleau, eds (1974), *Irénée de Lyon, Contre les héresies: Livre III, Volume 2* (SC 211), Paris: Éditions du Cerf.
Sinkewicz, R. E. (2006), *Evagrius of Pontus. The Greek Ascetic Corpus*, Oxford: Oxford University Press.
Schlütter, M. (2008), *How Zen became Zen: The Dispute over Enlightenment and the Formation of Chan Buddhism in Song-Dynasty China*, Honolulu: University of Hawai'i Press.
Vivian, T. and A. N. Athanassakis (2003), *Athanasius of Alexandria. The Life of Antony. The Coptic Life and the Greek Life*, Kalamazoo, MI: Cistercian Publications.
Ward, B. (1984), *The Sayings of the Desert Fathers: The Alphabetical Collection*, London: Cistercian Publications.
Weil, S. (2002), *Gravity and Grace* (trans. E. Crawford and M. von der Ruhr), London: Routledge.
Williams, J. P. (2000), *Denying Divinity: Apophasis in the Patristic Christian and Soto Zen Buddhist Traditions*, Oxford: Oxford University Press.
Wittgenstein, L. (1922), *Tractatus logico-philosophicus* (trans. C. Kay Ogden), London: Kegan Paul.
Wortley, J. (2012), *The Book of the Elders: Sayings of the Desert Fathers. The Systematic Collection*, Collegeville, MN: Cistercian Publications.
Wortley, J. (2013), *The Anonymous Sayings of the Desert Fathers: A Select Edition and Complete English Translation*, Cambridge: Cambridge University Press.
Wortley, J. (2014), *Give Me a Word: The Alphabetical Sayings of the Desert Fathers*, New York: St Vladimir's Seminary Press.

CHAPTER 9
DIONYSIUS' IMAGINARY LIBRARY

Virginia Burrus

God creates from *nothing* – an absolute *poiesis*. The humble epitomizer, in contrast, starts with *something*, making less of more. Epitomizing is an apophatic art, then – a negation or subtraction that pares a text down to its core. And yet, paradoxically, that apophasis becomes a kataphasis, not a saying-away but a saying-towards. Indeed, it produces a lavish surplus, as we shall see – thus making more of less, so to speak.

From the perspective of late ancient Christian literature, every writer is an epitomizer, every text the product of a drastic selectivity. Consider the ending of the Gospel of John: 'This is the disciple who is testifying to these things and has written them, and we know that his testimony is true. But there are also many other things that Jesus did; if every one of them were written down, I suppose that the world itself could not make room for [χωρῆσαι] the books that would be written' (21:24-5). John's Gospel is already a fragment, an abridgement, before its ink has dried. Later writers of saints' Lives would echo the rhetoric, if never perhaps matching the power of John's image of cosmic overflow. At the opening of his *Life of Saint Martin*, Sulpicius Severus writes, more pragmatically, 'I cannot hope to set forth all that he was or did. Those excellences of which he alone was conscious are completely unknown. . . . And even of those which had become known to us, we have omitted a great number, because we have judged it enough if only the more striking and eminent should be recorded' (1). The anonymous author of the *Life of Constantina* announces that 'we are compressing with as much brevity as we can material that even a long speech can barely set forth', adding: 'in that way, many things may be known from a few and, through the few things that, once recalled, do become known, those matters that have been omitted may not be denied understanding' (1.1).[1] Torturous prose, but the claim is intriguing: compression and omission somehow allow the text to transcend its own self-imposed limits. For his part, Augustine waxes theatrical when faced with the impossible challenge of giving a full account of the miracles that the saints have worked: 'Now what am I to do? . . . I cannot relate all the stories of miracles that I know' (*City of God* 22.8). And what of those stories he does not know? Such examples could of course be multiplied almost endlessly, but this abridged version will have to suffice for now. Well, maybe one more! 'What shall I say? What shall I leave unsaid?' Basil of Caesarea wonders when confronted with the challenge of putting the marvels of creation into words (Homily 5.4). 'What discourse can touch all?' he queries (5.8).

Jorge Luis Borges seems to be asking a version of this question when he memorably describes a library as boundless as the one the Gospel of John imagines, one that fills, and indeed overfills, the very universe, leaving room for nothing else, cosmic infinitude notwithstanding. 'In order for a book to exist, it is sufficient that it be *possible*', he writes, in the voice of his fictional librarian. Borges's imaginary library is '"total" – perfect, complete, and whole', containing 'all that is able to be expressed, in every language'.[2] Sean Braune comments: 'The possible books that are assembled in this library are supplements to the canon, but also supplements to only partially finished, lost, or burned texts.'[3] Braune's interest, like mine, is in the mutual enfolding of literary fragment and supplement. Lost or imaginary works are particularly revealing of the interdependent relation of the fragmentary remainder – which may be a citation, a summary, or merely a title – to its supplement, 'the imaginary product of the fragment', 'the excess – either imaginary or symbolic – that is constructed in relation to the fragment's potentiality'.[4] Braune notes that in the case of fragments of lost or imaginary works 'a new agentic force is adoptable by both the reader and literary critic in that both reading and literary criticism become a conceptual writing that creates a metatext by extending beyond the physical object of the book/text'.[5] The reader or critic is active in the generation of 'virtual texts' (theoretically infinite, perhaps) that are 'operative – literally a present-absence – within and around any fragment'.[6]

This volume invites us to consider the epitome as 'a *textual embodiment of absence*', giving rise to 'a state of inexhaustible and dynamic tension, of *perpetual self-projection toward perpetually absent objects*'[7] – namely, the 'primary texts' that have been cut and pasted, fragmented and caught up in new compositions that remain haunted with the memory of lost presence or wholeness. It invites us to explore how the 'epitomizing dimension' of a text – that is, its constitutive operations of fragmentation and recomposition – generates a metatextual supplement that might be conceived as a kind of virtual library, in Braune's (and Borges's) terms. My topic is this virtual or imaginary library – the library that emerges as the supplement of fragmentary texts.

Specifically, I want to explore the imaginary library generated by the body of late ancient Christian works attributed to one Dionysius. The Dionysian corpus, which Istvan Perczel dubs 'a late ancient literary fiction', was probably produced in fifth-century Syria.[8] However, the author writes in the name of a first-century Athenian mentioned briefly in the biblical book of Acts: 'Some of them joined [the apostle Paul] and became believers, including Dionysius the Areopagite and a woman named Damaris, and others with them' (17:34). Consisting of four treatises that borrow heavily from both Paul and the philosopher Proclus, as well as ten letters evoking fictional contexts, the Dionysian corpus contains allusions to a number of carefully cross-referenced but otherwise unknown works, including seven that the author claims to have written himself and two that he attributes to his teacher Hierotheus. Scholars are divided as to whether these are lost works, works circulating under a different pseudonym, works planned but never written, or 'entirely fictitious'.[9] I am inclined toward the latter opinion, though in a sense it does not matter. As Perczel notes, 'The entire setting is there to suggest that the most part of the Corpus is missing and that, consequently, what we have in our hands is just a fragment of what had been sometime Christianity's first and most fundamental theological exposition.'[10] My own proposal is that the artful and elaborate construction of the Dionysian corpus as a fragment serves not only to authorize the corpus itself, as Perczel suggests, but also to evoke and sustain desire for a textual integrity, completeness, or unity that will remain elusive. In this way, the corpus performs what it also describes, for the stimulation of desire for an elusive whole, at once cosmic and divine, is at the heart of Dionysian soteriology.

Theological Representations and Symbolic Theology

The Dionysian corpus might itself be read as a supplement to the biblical text. After all, it emerges as an imaginative expansion of one concise verse from the book of Acts. Moreover, Dionysius explicitly identifies the bible as the source of all theological discourse, a principle that our author refers to as the 'scriptural rule' in the treatise *Divine Names*, the longest text in the corpus. 'We must not dare to resort to words or conceptions concerning that hidden divinity which transcends being, apart from what the sacred scriptures have divinely revealed' (*Divine Names* 1.1).[11] Yet the bible is less a fragment requiring supplementation than an overflowing font – self-supplementing, so to speak. In this way, it partakes of the imaginary, being construed as the repository of all possible names for a god who bears the names of all possible creatures.

Celebrating the power of performative naming enabled by the holy scriptures, Dionysius affirms the *via positiva* or kataphatic approach to theology: 'and from all beings whatsoever [divine *pronoia* or providence] is harmoniously hymned and named' (1.7). The divine is not only called by the name of all things; she '*is* all things': 'sun, star, and fire, water, wind, and dew, cloud, archetypal stone, and rock' (1.6). But if the kataphatic naming responds to and re-enacts the god's creative overflow, as manifest in both cosmos and scripture, a corresponding apophatic unsaying responds to and re-enacts the ultimate elusiveness of both god and creation. The divine is not only named by every name; she is also nameless. The divine not only 'is all things' but is also 'none of the things' (1.6). That is to say, the name of god is all names; yet even the totality of all names falls short. God both is and is not identical with the sum total of the created things that sing god's praises by calling her by all their own names – names that are found in the bible.[12]

If the Dionysian corpus emerges as a supplement of the bible, there are other ways in which the corpus in general, and *Divine Names* in particular, is also positioned as a fragment of a larger whole, marked by its partiality and lack. Indeed, *Divine Names* begins in medias res, presenting itself as a continuation of an otherwise unknown work: 'And so, my friend, after *Theological Representations* [ὑποτυπώσεις], I come now to an explication of the divine names, as far as possible' (1.1). *Theological Representations* is mentioned five other times in *Divine Names* and once in another Dionysian work, *Mystical Theology*, where its contents are briefly summarized. *Divine Names* also seems to offer a summary after the opening reference to the text, from which we may infer that *Theological Representations* deals with the divine invoked by the scriptures as monad, trinity, creator, and incarnation, respectively (*Divine Names* 1.1; cf. *Mystical Theology* 3). As Paul Rorem puts it, 'Perhaps *The Divine Names* here begins by "summarizing" a treatise that was never written at all.'[13] One effect of this way of beginning, I suggest, is to perform the apophasis that *Divine Names* attributes to *Theological Representations*. 'I said in my *Theological Representations* that one can neither discuss nor understand the one, the hyperunknown [ὑπεράγνωστον], the hyperbeing [ὑπερούσιον].... It is at a total remove from every condition, movement, life, imagination, conjecture, name, discourse, thought, conception, being, rest, dwelling, unity, limit, infinity, the totality of existence' (*Divine Names* 1.5). Here we see how what might seem like affirmative statements – the divine is being, for example – are rendered apophatic by an attribution of excess. More complex still is the negation of negation: the divine is neither unknown nor known but beyond knowing or not knowing.[14] As our author says elsewhere, the highest forms of theological 'affirmations [τὰ καταφασκόμενα] . . . have the force of a hyperochic negation [ὑπεροχικῆς ἀποφάσεως]' (Letter 4) – that is, an intensifying negation that indicates a 'hyper-having' consisting in both 'having something in excessive measure' and 'exceeding beyond the having of something', as Timothy Knepper puts it.[15] If the divine exceeds knowability and being, the writing of the superabundant divine also exceeds the text on divine naming. The truest or most apt representations (ὑποτυπώσεις) of the divine exist only as an imaginary supplement to the names that can actually be written and read; even that supplement provides no more than outlines or sketches (also ὑποτυπώσεις). *Theological Representations* is a book that can only exist in full in an imaginary library; it is necessarily present only in and as fragments.

This is also the case with another book mentioned in *Divine Names*. Whereas *Divine Names* focuses on noetic designations or concepts found in the scriptures, such as goodness, light, beauty, love, being, life, wisdom, and truth, the scriptures also abound with earthier images. 'I will do my best to speak [of these] in *The Symbolic Theology*', the author promises (*Divine Names* 1.8). These names, or symbols, appear far from suitable when applied to god, yet this second supplementary book is much longer than the first. As Dionysius explains, the further one descends into the realm of materiality, thus of differentiation rather than simplicity, the more the names multiply (*Mystical Theology* 3). Most of them are far easier to unsay than to say, such as body parts – 'eyes, ears, hair, face, and hands, back, wings, and arms, a posterior, and feet' (*Divine Names* 1.8); animals – 'a panther, a leopard, or a charging bear' and even 'what seems the lowliest and most incongruous of all, . . . a worm' (*Celestial Hierarchy* 2.5); or inanimate objects – 'crowns, chairs, cups, and mixing bowls' (*Divine Names* 1.8), 'ointment' or 'stone' (*Celestial Hierarchy* 2.5). Worse still: 'anger, grief, and rage'; 'drunk and hungover'; 'oaths and curses' (*Mystical Theology* 3). *Divine Names* includes three more references to *Symbolic Theology*, which is also mentioned in *Mystical Theology* and two other Dionysian works, *Celestial Hierarchy* and *Letter* 9, where the book is referred to as already written.

Thus *Divine Names* itself is strongly marked by its own limitations and lacks, limitations and lacks that prove distinctly generative, allowing the text to partake (if imperfectly) in the self-exceeding quality of the scriptures. Its main focus is the positive and abstract names for god, names that most easily open up a positive or kataphatic approach to the divine. Yet the power of the work arguably arises not primarily from the relatively fluid discussions of relatively appropriate names but from the ways in which the text reveals itself to be gapped and fragmentary, in need of supplementation, opening onto realms of discourse that are expansive and excessive precisely to the degree that they are apophatic. The god is not 'being' (for example) but *hyper*being, beyond either being or non-being: this appears to be the argument of the imaginary book of *The Theological Representations*, a slim volume, austere and challenging, we might imagine. The god is no more 'goodness' (for example) than the god is a worm or a drunkard or a panther or a stone: this appears to be the argument of the imaginary book of *The Symbolic Theology*, a text as expansive and complex as the cosmos itself, and also as shockingly sensual, it seems.

Erotic Hymns

'One must hymn [ὑμνητέον] the beneficient providence of the thearchy from all created things [ἐκ πάντων τῶν αιτιατῶν]', writes Dionysius in *Divine Names* (1.5). Here *pronoia* or providence names the divine as the overflow of ecstatic *eros* that creates the cosmos, in and as a process of divine incarnation and self-revelation.[16] *Pronoia*'s creative beneficence calls forth a song. The song is a cosmic song, in two senses: it takes its start from the contemplation of the things created, and it arises from among created things. This singing is also a naming of the god, as we have seen, a naming that responds to and mimics the god's own creative outpouring. For the divine is hymned not only 'from all creatures' but also 'from every name' (1.6); that is, the god is praised with the name of every creature, through the voices of all creatures.

That praise is carried on the waves of longing. 'For all things both surround [providence] and are directed toward her, and she is before all things, and all things cohere in her. . . . All things long for [ἐφίεται] her.' Different kinds of things – human, animal, plant, mineral – long for the divine differently, Dionysius goes on to explain. However, each desires for the way appropriate to it: 'Intellectual and rational things, cognitively; things lower than these, sensually; and the rest, according to their vital movement or the fitness of their being and habit' (1.5). Complex beings like humans may long in *all* these ways: as Eric Perl notes, there is 'a continuum of modes of communion with God' and 'the higher types of participation do not exclude the lower'.[17] To long, in whatever way, is to participate in divine love. As John Rist sums it up, for Dionysius, 'God is Eros and the cause of Eros in all other things.'[18] At once lover, beloved, and love itself, the god is, in Dionysius's own words, 'erotic motion . . . pouring out from the good onto all that is and returning once again to the good . . ., always proceeding, always remaining, always being restored' (*Divine Names* 4.14). Thus creaturely desire not only responds to but is continuous with divine eros, completing its circuit, so to speak; it is the overflow of cosmic eros turning back toward its own elusive source.

Dionysius grounds his teaching of divine eros in an otherwise unknown work that he claims his teacher Hierotheus wrote, entitled *Erotic Hymns*. Hierotheus may well be a fiction, along with the work, from which Dionysius cites as follows: 'When we talk of eros . . . we should think of a unifying and co-mingling power that moves those higher to the care [πρόνοια] of those more needy, those of equal rank to mutual support, and finally those subordinate to a return to the stronger and the superior' (*Divine Names* 4.15). It is fitting that Dionysius's musings on eros emerge as glosses on a fragment of an absent text. Like the cosmic hymning of divine providence, the *Erotic Hymns* exist only as an imaginary supplement to Dionysius's own text, a sonorous plenitude as evocative and alluring and ultimately as elusive as the god itself. That this imaginary work is said to be authored by a teacher grants it special authority, an authority that Dionysius can appropriate as he articulates a doctrine that seems to have been controversial in some circles. 'Let no one imagine that in giving status to the term *eros* I am running counter to scripture' (4.11), he asserts defensively', adding, 'In my opinion, the sacred writers regard *eros* and *agape* as having one and the same meaning' (4.12).

Divine Hymns

Dionysius' cosmic hymnody stands in both close and ambiguous relation to his sacramental theology, a topic that is the focus of his treatise *Ecclesiastical Hierarchy*. The sacraments include baptism, eucharist, and ointment, as duly administered by the three hierarchical orders of the clergy; their aim is to ensure 'the salvation and divinization of all reasonable and intelligent beings' (*Ecclesiastical Hierarchy* 1.4). The eucharist, which Dionysius refers to as communion or gathering, is 'the sacrament of sacraments', a prime site of theurgy, or the work of god; 'it draws our fragmented lives together'; 'it forges a divine unity out of the divisions within us' (3.I). Dionysius is attentive to the choreography as well as the soundtrack of this sacrament. He describes how the hierarch, or bishop, begins the ritual with a prayer at the altar and then moves out from the altar, circling the sanctuary with a censer and returning thereafter to the altar; in this 'double movement' he performs the divine dance of erotic procession and return, differentiation and unification, evoking a wider cosmic flow (3.III.3). Back at the altar, Dionysius explains, the bishop sings the psalms 'and the entire assembly joins him in this'; the reading of scripture follows. As Dionysius comments, 'the sacred psalmody is a part of the hierarchic mysteries and should certainly accompany the most hierarchic of them all', while the readings impart edifying lessons. In particular, the psalms offer 'a universal song and narrative of all divine things and they enable everyone who participates in a godly spirit always to receive and to pass on the sacrament of the hierarchy' (3.III.4) – to participate in the 'erotic movement' of the cosmos, that is. In Dionysius' view, the psalms do crucial work not only in preparing human spirits to receive the elements of bread and wine, but also (and more immediately) in preparing them to receive the 'images and proclamations' of other parts of scripture. With respect to the former, psalmody attunes its singers to 'the divine harmony' and brings them into positive relation 'not only with divine realities but with our individual selves and with others in such a way that we make up one homogenous choir of sacred humans'. With respect to the latter, psalmody offers a 'summary and opaque outline' on which the rest of scripture expands with more accessible images (3.III.5).

Following the readings, the deacons and priests lay out the sacred elements of bread and cup and the music continues, as the congregation now sings 'the hymn of universal faith' – a possible allusion to the chanting of the creed (3.II). Dionysius adds: 'This hymn is sometimes called a confession of praise, sometimes a symbol of adoration, sometimes . . . a hierarchic thanksgiving. . .. To me it seems that this song is a celebration of all the work of God on our behalf' (3.III.7). That divine work or theurgy – itself another echo of the erotic procession and return mobilized by human ritual – is concentrated in the sacred act 'when [the hierarch] uncovers the veiled gifts, when he makes a multiplicity of what had originally been one, when the distributed sacrament and those receiving it are made perfectly one, when a perfect communion of all the participants is achieved' (3. III.13). At the close of the rite of communion, bishop and congregation 'end the ceremony with a sacred thanksgiving' (3.III.15).

Hymnody thus suffuses and carries the eucharistic liturgy; sound is the medium of sacrament, though not of course the only one. It is perhaps not irrelevant that Dionysius seems to have lived in a time – the late fifth or early sixth century – and a place – Syria, most likely – in which hymn writing was on the rise. An anonymous *Life of Severus of Antioch* (465–538) reports that 'the Antiochenes rejoiced in song', so much so that Severus 'appointed chanters and composed hymns'; his hymns were 'full of sighs and calling those who hear them unto the tears loved by God' (60).[19] In his treatise *On the Celestial Hierarchy*, Dionysius lets us hear an angelic choir echoing through the human song. 'Theology has transmitted to the people of earth those hymns sung by the first ranks of the angels' (*Celestial Hierarchy* 7.4). 'Theology' here as elsewhere in the corpus means the bible. Dionysius alludes to two biblical hymns in particular, emphasizing their resounding loudness: 'Blessed be the glory of the Lord of many waters' (Ez 3:12, LXX) and 'Holy, holy, holy is the lord of hosts; the whole earth is full of his glory' (Is 6:3). The former as well as the latter is associated with the Sanctus, i.e., the eucharistic prayer, from the early fourth century,[20] and such passages citing angelic song appear in other hymns of the period as well. As with the book of *Erotic Hymns* that he attributes to his teacher, Dionysius makes it clear that these two fragments merely gesture toward a larger hymnic whole: 'In my book *Divine Hymns* I have already explicated, to the best of my ability, the supreme praises sung by those holy intelligences which dwell beyond in heaven' (*Celestial Hierarchy* 7.4). Surely an angelic hymnal could exist only in an imaginary library.

Dionysius the Aereopagite is named in a single verse in the biblical book of Acts. In an audacious act of readerly imagination, our fifth-century author has created a library of works that this first-century Athenian convert to Christianity might be thought have authored. Precisely due to its carefully constructed pseudonymity and fictive character, the Dionysian corpus gives the impression of a high degree of coherence as body of literature, while offering a remarkably totalizing and holistic view of the divine, the cosmos, and the scriptures, encompassing heavenly and earthly domains at once. By focusing on several of the lost or fictitious works included in the internal cross-referencing of the corpus, I have tried to explore how that body is constructed not as a whole but as a fragment of an even larger and more complete body of writing – an imaginary library perhaps as vast as the one fantasied by Borges, coextensive with the cosmos itself. The Dionysian corpus is an epitome of that imaginary library and also a gateway to it. As such, it is crucially incomplete. Like the god who is at once hidden and revealed in the cosmos, the supplemental texts of which we can only ever read fragments incite the reader's desire and lure her imagination, thereby drawing her into the movement of divine eros itself.

The texts that we have before us can only say what can be said. The texts that are absent can say what has also been unsaid. They are apophatic texts, in Dionysian terms, written and unwritten at once, simultaneously negated and excessive, nearly silent and also resounding with the clamour of creation itself. They are the potential inhering in every fragment, the possibility that seduces all writing.

Notes

1. Conti, Burrus, and Trout 2020: 51.
2. Borges 1998: 117 n. 3, 115.
3. Braune 2013: 253.
4. Braune 2013: 253.
5. Braune 2013: 241.
6. Braune 2013: 253.
7. See the Introduction to this volume pp. 11–12.
8. Perczel 2015: 212.
9. Perczel 2015: 213.
10. Perczel 2015: 213.
11. For Dionysius' works, I have used the editions in Suchla, Heil, and Ritter 1990–1. Translations generally follow Luibheid 1987; see also Parker 1897–9.
12. While this chapter focuses on the relationship of the fragment to the supplement, we should also note that the technique of generating lists of names constructs the text as a *totality of fragments*; in this, it mirrors both cosmos and divinity, as Dionysius understands them. Here we can compare the Dionysian corpus to other late ancient literary compendia, such as Symphosius' *Aenigmata*, as discussed by Philip Hardie in this volume. Hardie argues that 'the *Aenigmata* performs dismemberment and recomposition at the level of both the individual epigram, and the collection as a whole', adding that individual riddles fragment the unity of objects both by breaking them into their constitutive parts and by 'decomposing [them] conceptually into oppositions' (p. 179). The latter technique is fundamental to the Dionysian corpus, which relies heavily on opposition and paradox.
13. Luibheid 1987: 52 n. 10.
14. Compare Jesús Hernández Lobato's exploration in this volume of the Christian *Apophthegmata* as 'an impossible encyclopaedia of unknowing'. Lobato prefers his own neologism 'logoclasm' to the more traditional 'apophasis'. There may be good reason to hang on to the latter as well. Collections of sayings do not merely stage a battle between silence and words, with their penchant for extreme condensation; they also hold the linguistic restraint of the individual saying together with the linguistic excessiveness of the compendium itself. The collection is not and can never be complete. The number of possible sayings is infinite, and no order (alphabetical, thematic) can limit or contain the work.
15. Knepper 2008: 627–8.

16. This identification of *pronoia*, *eros*, and the one god is apparently original with Dionysius. See Rist 1966: 239–40; de Vogel 1981: 70–3; and Smith 2012: 212–14.

17. Perl 1994: 324.

18. Rist 1966: 243.

19. Brock and Fitzgerald 2013: 126–7.

20. Spinks 1991: 117.

Works cited

Borges, J. L. (1998), 'The Library of Babel', in *Collected Fictions*, trans. Andrew Hurley, 112–18, New York: Penguin.

Braune, S. (2013), 'How to Analyze Texts That Were Burned, Lost, Fragmented, or Never Written', *Symplokē* 21 (1–2): 239–55.

Brock, S. and B. Fitzgerald, trans. (2013), *Two Early Lives of Severos, Patriarch of Antioch*, Liverpool: Liverpool University Press.

Conti, M., V. Burrus and D. Trout, eds (2020), *The Lives of Constantina*, Oxford: Oxford University Press.

de Vogel, C. J. (1981), 'Greek Cosmic Love and the Christian Love of God: Boethius, Dionysius the Areopagite and the Author of the Fourth Gospel', *Vigiliae Christianae* 35: 57–81.

Knepper, T. D. (2008), 'Not Not: The Method and Logic of Dionysian Negation', *American Catholic Phlosophical Quarterly* 82 (4): 619–37.

Luibheid, C. (1987), *Pseudo-Dionysius: The Complete Works*, trans. Luibheid, C., with P. Rorem, New York: Paulist Press.

Parker, J. H., trans. (1897–9), *The Complete Works of Dionysius the Aereopagite*, London: James Parker.

Perczel, I. (2015), 'Dionysius the Areopagite', in Ken Parry (ed.), *Wiley Blackwell Companion to Patristics*, 211–25, Malden, MA: John Wiley & Sons.

Perl, E. J. D. (1994), 'Symbol, Sacrament, and Hierarchy in Saint Dionysios the Areopagite', *The Greek Orthodoxy Theological Review* 39 (3/4): 311–56.

Rist, J. M. (1966), 'A Note on Eros and Agape in Pseudo-Dionysius', *Vigiliae Christianae* 20: 235–43.

Smith, J. W. (2012), 'Divine Ecstasy and Divine Simplicity: The Eros Motif in Pseudo-Dionysius's Soteriology', *Pro Ecclesia* 21 (2): 211–27.

Spinks, B. D. (1991), *The Sanctus in the Eucharistic Prayer*, Cambridge: Cambridge University Press.

Suchla, B. R., G. Heil and A. M. Ritter, eds (1990–1), *Corpus Dionysiacum* I and II, Berlin: De Gruyter.

CHAPTER 10
THE KALEIDOSCOPIC WORLD OF SYMPHOSIUS' *AENIGMATA*

Philip Hardie

Symphosius' *Aenigmata* is not technically an epitome, in the sense of an abbreviated version of a longer pre-existing text or group of texts (this 'epitomic quality', divorced from the abbreviation of a larger work, they share with the *Apophthegmata Patrum*, discussed by Jesús Hernández Lobato in Chapter 8).[1] Rather, the *Aenigmata* is a single-authored poetry book of one hundred three-line riddling epigrams, of uncertain date, but most probably of the late fourth or early fifth century. With regard to the formal features and aesthetics of the epitome, I shall argue that the *Aenigmata* presents itself as a totality of fragments, an encyclopaedia of distorted and fractured perspectives on a world whose coherence and instant intelligibility we normally take for granted. With reference to the editors' conceptualization of the 'epitomic dimension',[2] I shall suggest that the *Aenigmata* performs dismemberment and recomposition at the level of both the individual epigram, and the collection as a whole.

At the level of the individual epigram, a riddle may fragment the unity of an object in two ways:

1. By decomposing a composite whole **physically**, into its constituent parts, so that, in order to solve the riddle, we have mentally to put the pieces back together again to arrive at the solution. One of Timothy Leary's 'thematic links', the categories by which he traces thematic continuities across a number of separate epigrams, is 'Composite wholes', of which an example is 77 *rotae*, where the four separate wheels of a cart have to be put together to realize the gestalt of the four-wheeled cart:

> quattuor aequales currunt ex arte sorores
> sic quasi certantes, cum sit labor omnibus unus;
> et prope sunt pariter nec se contingere possunt.
>
> Four equal sisters run skilfully as if in this way striving, although the task for all is one and the same, and they are equally close and yet cannot touch one another.
>
> *Trans. T. J. Leary 2014*

2. By decomposing a single object **conceptually** into oppositions, turning everyday things into surprising paradoxes. The defamiliarization of the quotidian to the point where it is temporarily unrecognizable, is followed by recognition of that with which we were, in fact, already familiar, recomposing what was fragmented, although a trace of the unfamiliar remains once we have returned to our everyday world. An object that has

been subjected to the process of riddling may never look quite the same again. The trick in many of the epigrams is to identify an opposition or antithesis between different aspects of an object, often expressed through a balanced contrast between the two halves of the hexameter. A good example is number 5:

5 *catena*
nexa ligor ferro, multos habitura ligatos.
uincior ipsa prius, sed uincio uincta uicissim;
et solui multos, nec sum tamen ipsa soluta.

A chain. I am bound, fastened with iron, and will hold many bound. I am restrained myself first but, having been restrained, I restrain in turn; and I have loosed many and am nonetheless set loose myself.

In each line the opposition hinges at the third-foot caesura, and the antitheses are worked through verbal polyptoton, with a contrast between active and passive uses of the same verb in lines two and three. The chain, something whose essence it is to be connected (*nexa*), is prised apart into linguistic and metrical disconnections. Here a word should be said on the way in which the riddles are presented in the *Aenigmata*: the solution, in the form of the lemma, is given before the riddle itself. We start from the familiar object, and are then invited to contemplate the strangeness of the familiar. Once we have matched the playful cleverness of the three-line epigram to the lemma (in most cases of a single word), the lemma remains, as it were, inhabited by the strangeness of the riddling perspective.

Elsewhere paradox is engineered through puns and wordplay, for example 16:

16 *tinea*
littera me pauit, nec quid sit littera noui.
in libris uixi, nec sum studiosior inde.
exedi Musas, nec adhuc tamen ipsa profeci.

A bookworm. Literature has nourished me, but I do not know what literature might be. I have lived in books, but I am not more learned in consequence. I have devoured the Muses, but I myself have not yet made progress.

Here paradox is generated through the figurative senses available for the verbs in the first half of each of the three lines, *pauit*, *uixi*, *exedi*, of the reader's 'feeding on', 'living in or with' and 'devouring' books. Here the linguistic division is semantic rather than morphological (as in the case of the contrasting actives and passives of *catena*), but the semantic division is again mirrored in the metrical division, whereby the first part of each line, up to the third-foot caesura, invites the reader to take the verbs in the figurative sense, applicable to what he or she is doing in the act of reading this riddle, while the remaining part of each line requires that the reader refocus on the literal sense of the verbs in order to arrive at the solution of the riddle.

Turning to the status of a collection of riddles: each individual riddle demands a separate act of attention. The mental energy employed on a riddle reaches a point of closure or stasis once we have arrived at a solution, or have seen the point of any particular riddle. This tends to seal off a riddle as a self-contained monad. Recent work on the *Aenigmata* has, however, produced strong readings for the unity of the one hundred epigrams, working against the tendency of a collection of riddles to be no greater than the sum of its parts. Timothy Leary provides a detailed 'Overview of Symphosius' book structure',[3] listing 'Thematic links and links embracing several riddles', and 'Links between successive riddles'. Once the reader has been encouraged to look for these connections, yet others will readily spring to the eye. There is thus an extensive network – one might say 'con-catenation' – of verbal and conceptual links between poems adjacent or near to each other in the sequence, as well as parallels and repetitions that reach over longer sections of the collection. The game of spotting these connections is another aspect of the mental gymnastics that are called for by the individual riddles, in an extension into a more free kind of play of the matching up of the single riddles to their solutions.

When it comes to the suggestion that, in the case of a literal epitome, the epitome 'undermines the *primary meaning* (that is, the apparent meaning of the *primary object*)',[4] i.e. a text, one might look for an analogy in the way that a riddle displaces our attention from our unexamined, everday, perception of a (non-textual) object, to see it in that unfamiliar light. And, related to this, if we think of epitome as the 'textual embodiment of absence', the riddle has the effect of altering or displacing the way an object makes itself present in the world. That absence of the quotidian is also registered in other ways, both of which might be thought of rather as the presence of something that is normally absent. First, the most common form of riddle gives a voice to the usually inanimate object by making it the speaker in the first person (cf. the modern 'What am I?' riddles). Second, the *praefatio* to the *Aenigmata* presents the riddles as the product of the Saturnalia (or of a post-Saturnalian moment). The world of the riddling objects of the text emerges as the product of Saturnalian *ludus*. The recurrent paradox of the riddle reflects the inversions of the Saturnalian world-upside-down, an alternative world to the world we normally inhabit. The everyday world is made anew in the mirror of the Saturnalia. Erin Sebo speaks of Symphosius' creation of 'a Saturnalian view of the world which stresses cyclical change, reversal and above all else, plurality in all things.'[5]

* * *

I turn now to ask what kind of a world is constructed by the one hundred brief poems of the *Aenigmata*, and how this small world, this 'microcosm' – to use a word applied to riddle collections by Zoja Pavlovskis[6] – relates to larger worlds. First, I consider the world of the book of *Aenigmata* as an intratextual object.

The book as a whole is framed by riddling epigrams that refer to the activity and products of the riddle poet himself. The first two describe writing implements, a stylus and a reed pen. The first, *graphium*, is programmatic in two ways: first, the object, that with which this book of epigrams is being written, draws renewed attention to the statement in the *praefatio* that, in contrast to the orally improvised riddles of his companions at the Saturnalia, and in order to avoid the shame of having remained silent himself (*praef.* 13 *ne solus foede tacuisse uiderer*), Symphosius has subsequently gone away and written some riddles (15 *hos uersus feci subito*). Second, the form of this epigram is a classic example of the 'divided self' kind of riddle, combining linguistic and metrical oppositions:[7]

1 *graphium*
de summo planus sed non ego planus in imo
uersor utrimque manu. diuerso munere fungor:
altera pars reuocat quicquid pars altera fecit.

A stylus. Flat as to the top, but not flat at the bottom, I'm turned either way in the hand. I discharge a conflicting duty: one end undoes whatever the other has done.

The last line contains an allusion to a Horatian tag that points up by contrast the difference between spoken and written (and as yet unpublished) production of language, *Ars poetica* 390 *nescit uox missa reuerti* 'a word once sent abroad cannot return'. The contrast between oral and written also structures the following epigram, 2:

2 *harundo*
dulcis amica dei, semper uicina profundis,
suaue canens Musis, nigro perfusa colore,
nuntia sum linguae digitis signata magistris.

A reed. Sweet girlfriend of a god, always neighbour to deep waters, singing sweetly for the Muses, steeped in the colour black, I am the tongue's Messenger, having been distinguished by a master's fingers.

The object, *harundo*, turns out to be a reed pen, but the lemma undergoes semantic metamorphosis as we read the epigram: a reed growing on a river-bank, an object in the natural world produced by the metamorphosis of the body of Syrinx, turns into an object in the world of arts and crafts, the pan-pipes that Pan constructed from the reeds, and then changes once more, into the pen of the writer, not the musical instrument of the singer. The intertexts in this epigram are Ovidian, rather than Horatian.[8] Epigram 2 is thus programmatic for a recurrent metamorphic strain in the *Aenigmata*, which constructs a world of metamorphosis, as well as a world of paradox.

Ovidian and Horatian converge in the last epigram, which seals Symphosius' aspiration to literary fame, 100 *monumentum*. This comes after a sequence of four poems, 96–99, on 'Shadowy or insubstantial phenomena' (as Timothy Leary labels them), which can all be also read as containing poetic or metapoetic meanings (*uerba*, *umbra*, *Echo*, *somnus*):

100 *monumentum*
nomen habens hominis post ultima fata relinquor.

nomen inane manet, sed dulcis uita profugit.
uita tamen superest morti post tempora uitae.

A monument. Bearing the name of a man, I am left after his final destiny. The empty name remains, but sweet life has fled. Yet life survives death after the time of his life.

This is the riddle poet's variation on Horace's *Odes* 3.30 *Exegi monumentum*, with Ovidian overlays: *uitae* is Symphosius' last word, as *uiuam* is the last word of Ovid's *Metamorphoses*. Opening and closing epigrams draw Symphosius into his own world of riddling paradox and metamorphosis, beginning with the point of origin of the text, the stylus, and ending with the survival of its author's name through the survival of the text.

If the fragments of the *Aenigmata* compose themselves as a coherent literary whole, can one also see this little Saturnalian world as reflecting a larger world outside the text? One might point to an encyclopaedic quality, admittedly of a very non-systematic kind, in the selection of a hundred objects. I am reminded of the BBC Radio 4 series *A history of the world in 100 objects*, presented by Neil MacGregor, Director of the British Museum, based on objects in the British Museum's collections.[9] Symphosius' hundred objects are drawn from both the natural and human worlds. In this respect, too, number 2 *harundo* might be taken as programmatic, charting as it does the transition from natural to technological objects (and one might go further and see in the person of the nymph Syrinx, the ultimate origin of both plant and plant product, a licence for the persistent anthropomorphization of objects through the first-person-singular form of the riddle. The riddle is an inherently personifying form, changing dumb objects into speaking persons). The range of things in the natural world that is covered is quite wide: weather, animals and birds small and large, flowers and crops. In general terms, the epitomic universalizing pretensions of the *Aenigmata* have something in common with the epitomic qualities of Dionysius the Areopagite's 'imaginary library', as discussed by Virginia Burrus in Chapter 9.

There is also a recurrent framing of small, discrete objects or creatures within a synoptic view of the four elements or world-divisions, in some cases pointing up a paradoxical confusion of elements:

6 *tegula*
terra mihi corpus, uires mihi praestitit ignis.
de terra nascor; sedes est semper in alto,
et me perfundit qui me cito deserit umor.

A tile. The earth provided my body, fire my strength. I am born of the earth; my seat is always in the sky, and a wave of water washes over me which quickly leaves me.

61 *anchora*
mucro mihi geminus ferro coniungitur uno.

cum uento luctor, cum gurgite pugno profundo.
scrutor aquas medias, ipsas quoque mordeo terras.

An anchor. My twin point is joined in a single piece of iron. I strive with the wind, I fight with the ocean deep. I search through the midst of the waters, and I also bite the very earth.

62 *pons*
stat nemus in lymphis, stat in alto gurgite silua,
et manet in mediis undis immobile robur.
terra tamen mittit quod terrae munera praestat.

A bridge. A grove stands in the waters, in the deep stream stands a wood, and the oak remains unmoving in the midst of the waves. However, the earth puts forth that which performs the duties of the earth.

74 *lapis*
Deucalion ego sum crudeli sospes ab unda,
adfinis terrae sed longe durior illa.
littera decedat, uolucris quoque nomen habebo.

Stone. I am a Deucalion,[10] safe from the cruel sea, a relation of the earth but much harder than it. Let a letter be subtracted, I shall also have the name of a winged creature.

One of Leary's 'Thematic links' is 'The four elements, technology and building', in epigrams 70-76: 70 *clepsydra* ('waterclock'): water; 71 *puteus* ('well'): earth and water; 72 *tubus* ('a pipe'): earth and water; 73 *uter* ('bellows'): fire, air (and water); 74 *lapis* (air), earth and water; 75 *calx* ('lime'): fire and water; 76 *silex* ('flint'): fire and water. By setting usually small, and sometimes very small, objects in a cosmic frame, riddles of this kind engineer striking contrasts between large and small, the grand and the lowly. Through a pun on *mundus* ('clean'/'universe') the humble broom is humorously elevated to the position of cosmic creator, guiding all things in the universe (if *mundi magna parens* is the correct reading):

79 *scopa*
mundi magna parens, laqueo conexa tenaci,
iuncta solo plano, manibus compressa duabus,
ducor ubique sequens et me quoque cuncta sequuntur.

A besom. Great mother of the world, held together by a firm noose, conjoined with a level surface, pressed to it by two hands, I am drawn everywhere in following and everything also follows me.

The flask, or wine-jar, has the grandest of parents in the first line of epigram 81, followed by the diminutive *auriculae* in line 2.

81 *lagena*
mater erat Tellus, genitor est ipse Prometheus,
auriculaeque rigent redimitae uentre cauato.
dum cecidi subito laniauit me mea mater.

A flask. My mother was Earth, my father is Prometheus himself, and my little ears stick up, crowned with – a hollowed belly. When I fell unexpectedly, my own mother mangled me.

The contrast of large and small is a structuring principle for example in 25 *mus* 'mouse', which lives in a *parua domus* 'small house', feeds itself *exiguo sumptu* 'at small expense', but shares its name with a great Roman consul (P. Decius Mus); 34 *uulpes* 'fox', which has *exiguum corpus, sed cor mihi corpore maius* 'a small body, but my heart is greater than my body' (where paradoxically the monosyllabic *cor* is 'greater' than the trisyllabic *corpore* that contains it); 40 *papauer* 'poppy', 1–2 *grande mihi caput est, intus sunt membra minuta; | pes unus solus, sed pes longissimus unus* 'My head is large, my organs inside are tiny; I have just one foot, but one foot that is very long'; 46 *uiola* 'violet', *magna quidem non sum, sed inest mihi maxima uirtus. | spiritus est magnus, quamuis sim corpore paruo* 'To be sure I am not big, but there is in me the greatest potency. Although I might be of small stature, my perfume is large'; 49 *ebur* 'ivory', *dens ego sum magnus populis prognatus Eois. | nunc ego per partes in corpora multa recessi* 'A great tusk I was born to the peoples of the East. Now I have declined bit by bit into many bodies.' One might see a programmatic signalling of the contrast between large and small in the reference in the *praefatio* to the great effort expended in composing trifling riddles at the Saturnalia, *praef.* 8–10 *tum uerbosa cohors . . . nescio quas passim magno tentamine*[11] *nugas | est meditata diu* 'then the wordy company pondered on all sides, for a long time, with great effort, some trifles or other'.

The *Aenigmata* has a distinct interest in the miniature, although by no means all of the hundred objects are small in scale. One might also speak of an interest in miniaturization, for example in 67 *lanterna*:

cornibus apta cauis, tereti perlucida gyro,
lumen habens intus diuini sideris instar,
noctibus in mediis faciem non perdo dierum.

A lantern. Fitted with curved horn, translucent with my smooth surround, containing light within, like the divine star, in the middle of the night I create the appearance of day.

Leary suggests that *gyro* 'has cosmic associations, being applied to the orbit of heavenly bodies'. The 'divine star' is the sun; Leary comments 'That the sun should be contained by a lantern is . . . ridiculously humorous.' But it is also symptomatic of what has been seen as a late antique vogue for the miniature and the miniaturist. Jaś Elsner speaks of 'exquisite miniatures' as typical of a late antique aesthetic,[12] and Jesús Hernández Lobato points to 'late-antique aesthetic miniaturization'.[13] Claudian is an artful practitioner of cosmic miniaturization, for example in a short poem (*carm. min.* 51) on the subject of the sphere of Archimedes, a famous miniature working model of the universe, which begins (1–2) 'when Jupiter saw the heavens in a little sphere of glass, he laughed' (*Iuppiter in paruo cum cerneret aethera uitro | risit*): laughter on the part of the god, but admiration on the part of human beholders. The animation of the small sphere of Archimedes and the magnet uses the language that Virgil applies in *Aeneid* 6 to the breath that nurtures and sets in motion the whole universe: with *carm. min.* 51.7–8 (Archimedes' sphere) *inclusus uariis famulatur spiritus astris | et uiuum certis motibus urget opus* 'a spirit enclosed within serves the various courses of the stars and activates the living work with defined motions' compare *Aeneid* 6.726–27 *spiritus intus alit, totamque infusa per artus | mens agitat molem et magno se corpore miscet* 'a spirit within sustains [the universe], and mind, spread through the limbs, moves the whole mass and mingles with the mighty body'.

Miniaturization could also be thought of as an essential part of the aesthetics of the epitome, and hence of the *Aenigmata* as a whole, to the extent that it is legitimate to see the collection as having an 'epitomic dimension'. The mise en abyme is a device that Lucien Dällenbach associates with miniaturization.[14] It is not difficult to find in the *Aenigmata* individual epigrams that can be read as mises en abyme, miniaturizations, of the book as a whole. For example:

3 *anulus cum gemma*
corporis extremi non magnum pondus adhaesi
(ingenitum dicas, ita pondere nemo grauatur),
una tamen facies plures habitura figuras.

A ring with a gem. I have clung fast, no great weight at the body's end (so unburdened is anyone by this weight, you would declare it inborn), a single countenance but one nonetheless which will have many impressions.

The contrast between one and many recurs in a number of the epigrams, pointing up an inner division in the nature of an object; but, beyond that, it can be taken of the unity in plurality that characterizes a book of poems homogeneous in their metrical form and size (each of three lines), but multifarious in their subject-matter. Fragmentation of an original whole that preserves a unitary appearance is the subject of 49 *ebur*:

dens ego sum magnus populis prognatus Eois.
nunc ego per partes in corpora multa recessi;
nec remanent uires, sed formae gratia mansit.

Ivory. As a great tusk I was born to the peoples of the East. Now I have declined bit by bit into many bodies. My strength does not remain, but the charm of my beauty has remained.

The hundred epigrams are like the steps of a ladder, each separate, but all contained in a single order:

> 78 *scalae*
> nos sumus ad caelum quae scandimus, alta petentes,
> concordi fabrica quas unus continet ordo,
> ut simul haerentes per nos comitemur ad auras.
>
> Ladder.[15] We are what climbs to the sky, seeking the heavens, we whom a single series holds in a unified structure so that clinging together we are accompanied to the heights by means of ourselves.

The steps of the ladder work harmoniously together (*concordi fabrica*, *simul*). Might one also detect the aspiration of the poet to a heaven-reaching fame, anticipating the *monumentum* (100) that closes the book? *Exegi monumentum ... regali ... situ pyramidum altius* (Horace, *Odes* 3.30.1–2).

The parts of the 'composite whole' (to use Leary's label) in the previous epigram, 77, also work together, but as if in competition with each other:

> 77 *rotae*
> quattuor aequales currunt ex arte sorores
> sic quasi certantes, cum sit labor omnibus unus;[16]
> et prope sunt pariter nec se contingere possunt.
>
> Wheels. Four equal sisters run skilfully as if in this way striving, although the task for all is one and the same, and they are equally close and yet cannot touch one another.

This is the image of a *concordia discors*. The four wheels look as if they are trying to get away from each other, engaged in a competition that would lead to a disastrous fragmentation of the wagon, but in fact their 'com-position' is not broken, although they are unable to '*con-tingere*' each other.

* * *

How typical of a late antique aesthetics is the *Aenigmata*? I have tried to show that, although not an epitome *stricto sensu*, it has features that conform to the 'epitomic dimension'. One late antique text with which the *Aenigmata* has often been compared, and which may have influenced the *Aenigmata*, is Ausonius' *Griphus ternarii numeri*.[17]

This poem in 90 lines is not actually a riddle, despite its title, but it has a riddling quality in its elaborate enumeration of things connected through the number three. Like the *Aenigmata*, the *Griphus* purports to be the jesting and trifling product of drinking games. But, again like the *Aenigmata*, it has an encyclopaedic – and epitomic – quality, ranging the natural and human worlds in search of things that come in threes (perhaps not coincidentally, three is the number of lines of each of the epigrams that make up the

Aenigmata).[18] This nugatory poem begins with the *mystica lex* of the symposium, *Ter bibe*, but this frivolity is soon followed by the statement that (4) *iuris idem tribus est, quod ter tribus: omnia in istis* 'three has the same power as thrice three: all things are contained by them.' The universality of the numbers three and nine begins with the laws that govern the life of human beings, the nine months of gestation, and the nine times nine (81) limit of the number of a man's years. Universalizing trios later in the *Griphus* include the three elements of an Orphic cosmography of the *orbis*, 74 *Orpheos hinc tripodes, quia sunt tria: terra, aqua, flamma*, and the demographic structure of the *urbs*, Rome, 78 *Martia Roma triplex, equitatu, plebe, senatu*. The last three lines of the poem begin with a return to the opening *ter bibe*, but now in a striking juxtaposition of the ludic and the sublime, 88 *ter bibe. tris numerus super omnia, tris deus unus*. The Triune Christian God is greater even than the *omnia* of line 4. The concluding two lines then take a self-reflexive turn, 89–90 *hic quoque ne ludus numero transcurrat inerti, | ter decies ternos habeat deciesque nouenos* 'And that this game may not run its course without a significant number, let it have verses thrice ten times three, or nine times ten' – a self-reflexivity that is also shared with the *Aenigmata*.

* * *

But if we were to conclude that the *Aenigmata* bears the unmistakable hallmark of a late antique aesthetic, we should stop to reflect on the fact that many of the features that I have been considering find precedents in texts that predate late antiquity. It is well recognized that the most important models for the *Aenigmata* are Martial's two books of epigrams that consist of gift-tags for objects given as presents during the Saturnalia, the *Xenia* (book 13) and the *Apophoreta* (14). Recent criticism has shown how these collections of apparently random and disunited fragments from the world of the Roman consumer are given unity by complex and sophisticated associations and juxtapositions.[19] A tension between fragmentation and cohesion is of course to be found in any artfully composed poetry book, going back to Catullus and Hellenistic books of epigram and the *libellus* (or *libelli*) of Catullus. Horatian books of odes are one of the progenitors of Symphosius' book of *Aenigmata*: Michèle Lowrie states at the outset of her study of Horace's *Odes*, 'A concern that runs throughout this book is the relation of unity to disunity.'[20]

I have identified *concordia discors* as a principle of aesthetics and organization in the *Aenigmata*, both at the level of the individual riddles and of the book as a whole. Michael Roberts concludes his anatomy of the poetics of late antiquity, in his influential book *The Jeweled Style*,[21] by elevating *concordia discors* to an overarching aesthetic principle:[22] 'The jeweled style itself is the literary embodiment of *concordia discors*.'[23] It is certainly true that late antiquity has a particular fascination with *concordia* and *discordia*, and with the tension between them, both in the spheres of politics, ideology and theology, and in the fields of aesthetics and poetics;[24] but this is a development, and heightening, of phenomena that can be traced much earlier in antiquity. *Concordia discors* is already central to the poetics of Horace and Ovid.

When it comes to the *Aenigmata*'s foregrounding of contrasts of large and small, and its interest in miniaturization, Martial again emerges as an important predecessor, notably in Victoria Rimell's reading of Martial's epigrams: 'Martial captures a Rome in miniature, an oxymoronic microcosm of monumental spaces made tight and constraining. At the same time he visualises the most minute and humble of poetic forms expanding to fill and become the greatest city on earth.'[25] Rimell sees an analogy with that other construction of the Flavian period, the Colosseum, an image of the world at the centre of Rome: 'that ultimate epigrammatic microcosm, the Colosseum'.[26] The Colosseum is an epitome of the world ruled by Rome, the city which is itself the ἐπιτομὴ τῆς οἰκουμένης (Athenaeus, *Deipnos.* 1.36).

But epigrammatic *multum in paruo* goes further back, to the Hellenistic period, and spills over into other genres and other media, for example the statuette type of Herakles Epitrapezios, the mighty Herakles small enough to be placed 'on the table, perhaps originally the work of Lysippus, and the subject of poems by Statius (*Silv.* 4.6: 36–38 *seseque tuendum | indulsit, Lysippe, tibi, paruusque uideri | sentirique ingens* 'He granted you, Lysippus, to behold him, small to the eye but huge to the sense'; 43 *tam magna breui mendacia formae* 'so great is the deception in that tiny form') and Martial (9.43–44: 43.2 *exiguo magnus in aere deus* 'a mighty god in a small bronze').[27] The *Tabulae Iliacae*, tiny relief carvings with inscribed texts (probably mostly to be dated between the late first century BC and early first century AD), miniaturize the *Iliad* in both text and image: one of the *Tabulae* is a sculptural realization of the Homeric Shield of Achilles, small enough to be held in the hand, a miniaturization of the 130-line long Homeric description of the Shield, a passage that is long for a poetic ecphrasis, but small-scale as a textual miniaturization of the cosmos, of which it is an image, εἰκόνα κόσμου as Claudian labels a crystal with its drop of water (*AP* 9.753.2).[28]

The *Aenigmata*, the first surviving structured book of riddling epigrams, may be grouped together with other examples of extreme kinds of wordplay and formal patterning in late antique poetry – pattern poems, the cento, and the figured poems of Optatian. But if the *Aenigmata* is typically late antique, it is not through a revolution in form and content, but through the evolution of features whose history may be traced much earlier in Classical Antiquity.

Notes

1. For commentaries, see Bergamin 2005; Leary 2014. On Symphosius' reworking of the riddle form see Sebo 2013. The present paper goes over some of the ground covered in my discussion of Symphosius in Hardie 2019: 183–7, but here viewed through an epitomatory lens.
2. I refer to the editors' formulations in the Introduction.
3. Leary 2014: 15–26.
4. As formulated in the editors' Introduction, see p.4.
5. Sebo 2013: 187.
6. Pavlovskis 1988.
7. Pavlovskis 1988: 222 'In a charming combination of two standard ways of constructing a riddle (mentioning what a thing is *or* what it is not), the stylus is described as being *and* not being flat; accomplishing *and* revoking.'

8. With *nuntia sum linguae digitis signata magistris* cf. Ovid, *Tr.* 5.13.29–30 *sic ferat et referat tacitas nunc littera uoces, | et peragant linguae charta manusque uices*; *Tr.* 3.7.2 *littera, sermonis fida ministra mei.*
9. https://www.bbc.co.uk/programmes/b00nrtd2 (accessed 20 December 2021)
10. If the text is correct, apparently a metonym for 'stone' from the survivor of the Flood, Deucalion, who threw stones that turned into men.
11. The text is very uncertain: *tentamine* Harrison; *conamine* Buenemann; *molimine* Baehrens.
12. Elsner 2004: 283–4 on the shift from large-scale sculpture to 'exquisite miniatures' in ivory, silver, glass, precious stones, painted manuscripts.
13. Hernández Lobato 2012: 320–50 'La obra como "detalle": la miniaturización estética tardoantigua'.
14. Dällenbach 1989.
15. The Latin for 'ladder' is *scalae* in the plural (cf. English 'steps' = step ladder); the epigram exploits that plural for the play on one and many.
16. Cf. *Verg. Georg.* 4.184 *omnibus una quies operum, labor omnibus unus*, of the concordant society of the bees.
17. See Leary 2014: 5–6. On Ausonius' *Griphus* see Lowe 2013.
18. *Aenigm.* 82 *conditum* and 92 *mulier quae geminos pariebat* are riddles on the number three.
19. E.g. Fitzgerald 2007.
20. See Lowrie 1997: 1; see also her index s.v. 'unity', 'fragmented'.
21. Roberts 1989. At 28–30 Roberts comments on the 'dismembering' of sentences into cola and commata, and on the display of 'antithesis and parallelism, variation and concinnity'.
22. Roberts 1989: 144–77. Roberts returns to the topic of *concordia discors* in his later book on Venantius Fortunatus, where aesthetic harmony matches the harmonious coexistence of barbarians and Latin-speakers: Roberts 2009: 53–60 'In praise of kings and dukes': cf. e.g. Venant. Fort. *Poems* 6.2.7–8 *hinc cui barbaries, illinc Romania plaudit: | diuersis linguis laus sonat una uiri*; 7.8.61–70 in praise of Duke Lupus, pointing to the harmony of diverse subjects and voices; 69–70 *nos tibi uersiculos, dent barbara carmina leudos: | sic uariante tropo laus sonet una uiro.*
23. Roberts 1989: 145.
24. See Hardie 2019: 103–34.
25. Rimell 2008: 182; 64 Martial's epigram as like the Colosseum, wanting 'to swallow and package up the Roman world'.
26. Rimell 2008: 205.
27. See Squire 2011: 267–9.
28. For a game-changing study of the *Tabulae Iliacae* see Squire 2011, a very big book on some very small objects.

Works cited

Bergamin, M. (2005), *Aenigmata Symposii: La fondazione dell'enigmistica come genere poetico*, Florence: SISMEL edizioni del Galluzzo.

Dällenbach, L. (1989), *The Mirror in the Text*, trans. J. Whiteley and E. Hughes, Chicago: Chicago University Press.

Elsner, J. (2004), 'Late Antique Art: The Problem of the Concept and the Cumulative Aesthetic', in S. Swain and M. Edwards (eds), *Approaching Late Antiquity: The Transformation from Early to Late Empire*, 271–309, Oxford: Oxford University Press.

Fitzgerald, W. (2007), *Martial: The World of the Epigram*, Chicago: Chicago University Press.

Hardie, P. (2019), *Classicism and Christianity in Late Antique Latin Poetry*, Oakland: University of California Press.

Hernández Lobato, J. (2012), Vel Apolline muto: *Estética y poética de la Antigüedad tardía*, Bern: Peter Lang.

Kwapisz, J., D. Petrain, M. Szymanski, eds (2013), *The Muse at Play: Riddles and Wordplay in Greek and Latin poetry*, Berlin: De Gruyter.

Leary, T. J. (2014), *Symphosius. The Aenigmata: An Introduction, Text and Commentary*, London: Bloomsbury.

Lowe, D. (2013), 'Triple Tipple: Ausonius' *Griphus ternarii numeri*', in J. Kwapisz, D. Petrain and M. Szymanski (eds), *The Muse at Play: Riddles and Wordplay in Greek and Latin Poetry*, 335–52, Berlin and Boston: De Gruyter.

Lowrie, M. (1997), *Horace's Narrative Odes*, Oxford: Oxford University Press.

Pavlovskis, Z. (1988), 'The Riddler's Microcosm: from Symphosius to St Boniface', *C&M*, 39: 219–51.

Rimell, V. (2008), *Martial's Rome: Empire and the Ideology of Epigram*, Cambridge: Cambridge University Press.

Roberts, M. (1989), *The Jeweled Style: Poetry and Poetics in Late Antiquity*, Ithaca, NY: Cornell University Press.

Roberts, M. (2009), *The Humblest Sparrow: The Poetry of Venantius Fortunatus*, Ann Arbor: University of Michigan Press.

Sebo, E. (2013), '*In scirpo nodum*: Symphosius' Reworking of the Riddle Form', in J. Kwapisz, D. Petrain and M. Szymanski (eds), *The Muse at Play: Riddles and Wordplay in Greek and Latin poetry*, 184–95, Berlin: De Gruyter.

Squire, M. (2011), *The Iliad in a Nutshell: Visualizing Epic on the* Tabulae Iliacae, Oxford: Oxford University Press.

PART IV
MATERIALITY

CHAPTER 11
'DISFIGURED' WRITING? THE CASE OF ANTONIN ARTAUD'S 503 NOTEBOOKS

Ana Kiffer

This article sets out to investigate the two largest editions to date of the work of Antonin Artaud (1896–1948). A great part of Artaud's work was written in conditions of extreme precariousness, in French psychiatric asylums during the second world war. Artaud's work invites constant rereading and reappraisal. This does not mean to underestimate what has already been done, but then nor should a single direction be pursued by Artaud's scholars. In fact, it should be emphasized, as I shall try to do here, that critics have approached Artaud from three key perspectives, which are also not at all exclusive of one another. One of these perspectives concerns itself with how, within a certain historical context, meaning (which includes also sensory, visual and tactile qualities) of Artaud's work has been produced. In this direction it is necessary to question how we have focused too much on certain layers of meaning that we judge to be significant when we are faced with the author's manuscripts, which then can be emphasized by given editions. I should highlight that these questions are not aimed to undermine the efforts of editors, but rather to explore in a broader way a certain horizon of meaning that brings together, guide and safeguard particular readings within a given period.

In a different way, I think it extremely important – especially in the case of writings which, in their material and conceptual aspects, pose questions about the limits of the textual form (as Artaud's notebooks do) – that we probe how editions of these works have been materially constructed, and the difficulties and the challenges encountered in creating such editions. Every researcher who works with manuscripts is obliged to reflect on notions of text, of the book and of representation. The resulting criticism can be both imaginative and archaeological as it engages with the discourses the researcher has uncovered. But particularly with Artaud's works, it is vital, at least in my opinion, to design modes of editorial constructions that can circulate between the critical and the curatorial, between the book and the *mis en scène*, as the editor represents to their readers Artaud's excavation of the linear and Western notion of 'text'.

These concepts will be explored over the course of the five sections of this article. In all of them, I will seek to highlight the tensions testing the stability of the ideas and preconceptions about texts in Western culture, since these tensions are laid bare by other kinds of writings, such as notebooks. Moreover, this discussion within a modern setting can hardly avoid being political, for it mirrors other conversations about the contradictions of the contemporary world and the rigid separations and borders through which it is instantiated.

Historical background

Antonin Artaud (1896–1948) was a writer, an actor both on the stage and on film, theorist of the theatre, and even a member of a surrealist research group, the *Bureau de recherches surréalistes*, until he was expelled from it. He was a crucial figure in the European *avant-garde*, but even by his fellow pioneers he was considered controversial. He advocated many ideas that proved divisive, such as the *theatre of cruelty* or his writings about his experiences of the peyote rites with the Taraumara Indians in Mexico in 1936, contentious not only in the intellectual spheres of his era but also in the contemporary political climate.

To retain the title of his *Theatre of Cruelty* (1936), he wrote many letters to his publisher, Gallimard, justifying the pregnancy of the term. A year later, during his visit to Mexico as an envoy of the French Ministry of Foreign Affairs, in a lecture he gave in his official capacity at the University of Mexico, Artaud strongly objected to the constant drive towards political revolution among the European left (and a drive shared by many in Mexico), which, he felt, exerted an overbearing influence on their aesthetic ambitions.

To his Mexican audience, Artaud argued for the superiority of the indigenous culture of Mexico, a culture that had propelled him to reconsider the whole white European notion of culture. This put him starkly at odds with the ageing revolutionaries who had made up the Mexican elite since 1920. In his view, these admirers of European culture had foolishly disdained the ancestral culture of indigenous peoples: 'Government policy is not Indianist, I mean it does not have an Indian spirit. It is not pro-Indian, regardless of what the newspapers say. Mexico does not seek either to become Indian or to return to being Indian. Simply the Mexican government protects the Indians *as men*, it does not defend them as Indians.' (Artaud 2017).

Such sentiments from Artaud, which run so counter to the prevailing spirit of his time (whose legacy of Eurocentrism is still so dominant in our own), would only increase in strength upon his return from Mexico and his encounter with a Europe darkened by the evils of Fascism.

Artaud was arrested in Ireland in 1937. The story of his arrest would only become public knowledge in the 1980s. He was accused of disturbing the peace in Dublin and sentenced to deportation. During his deportation, believing he was being attacked, Artaud was violent towards the crew. He was subsequently sent to a psychiatric asylum in France. He went forgotten until 1939, when, after a great collective effort, he was found in a miserable state: disfigured, starving, and sick. The experience of the asylums had not only distorted his physical appearance, but also affected the way he thought and wrote.

For sure, even before his incarceration, Artaud already struggled to give full expression to his words and ideas, possessing as they did a certain radicality that distinguished him from the groups and ideologies of that milieu. However, this disjoint became all the greater with his experiences during the Second World War. Until 1943, Artaud was in the Parisian asylum of Ville-Évrard, in the German-occupied zone. Rescued by Robert Desnos from Ville-Évrard, Artaud was transferred to an asylum in Rodez and into the hands of Gaston Ferdière, the chief doctor there. Ferdière was an advocate of electric shock treatment, an experimental procedure at the time, and it formed part of the treatment he prescribed for Artaud. Artaud's doctors struggled both to diagnose and to treat him. But unlike other artists or thinkers, his time in these asylums did not paralyse or impede the continuance of his work. He remained lucid despite the suffering inflicted by the electric shocks and by the judgement of society. His most fiery and potent texts were written in this period of 1943–1948, while he was interned in Rodez and afterwards in Ivry sur Seine in Paris, when he wrote, for example, *Van Gogh le suicidé de la sociéte* (Goncourt Prize in 1947) and *Pour en finir avec le jugement de Dieu* (1948). Moreover, in these last five years of his life he worked in a newly intricate and intense manner. It became difficult to read and received a complicated reception subsequently. His work in this period, which touches on aesthetics, poetics, and philosophy, is comprised of manuscripts and notebooks. But much of this body of work is still unpublished, although what has been published makes up 18 of the 26 volumes of his *Complete Works*. Even today editors and critics are stilled puzzled by how best to proceed in the task of approaching this open, unstable, and heterogenous body of work.

It does not seem coincidental that Artaud's thought and his writings only found a proper reception in the 1960s, when the prevailing aesthetic and political paradigms started to fall apart under the pressure of the counterculture, and especially the reading of post-structuralist philosophers: Foucault, Derrida, and Deleuze-Guattari.

The notebooks

A total of 503 notebooks were first published thanks to Paule Thévenin, the fruit of a long effort from the 1960s to the 1980s, although even this did not exhaust all of Artaud's written material.[1]

In this edition, published within the *Collection Blanche Gallimard*, 10 volumes, each around 300–600 pages, are texts from the notebooks, written over a period of only five years. Moreover, in this short five-year period, Artaud also wrote numerous other texts which constitute eight volumes of the *Collected Works*. If we consider there are also eight volumes covering a period from the early 1920s to 1937, we can note a creative intensity seldom rivalled, which leads us to pose questions about his writing processes in this context.

It is also worth considering Artaud's conception of writing during this intense period of creativity. His writing, as I will try to show here, disfigures some of the stable characteristics of the text. But it also seems to me that the composition of his notebooks can be analysed in a singular manner through this writing. In other words, we should pay careful attention to how exactly Artaud wrote this material, from examining the manuscript evidence, so that we can understand what has been included and what has been lost in the published form of the *Gallimard* edition.

In short, I will explore how this writing, which is as varied in form to include not just fragments of text but also sketches, was incorporated in publication by its subsequent editors, what on the page was represented and what was not. For instance, frequently the drawings which are tightly intertwined with the text displace that text from the central position on the page. Often the text demands to be interpreted in light of the drawing or sketch with which it is juxtaposed. Such a juxtaposition invites a reading that combines the physical, tactile, visual, and auditory. The pages can possess directionality that is not necessarily the usual left-to-right that has near total dominance in Western culture. It demands from its readers a new kind of reading that forces us to question our underlying preconceptions about writing, text, and creative works.

Intensive writing and the first edition of the notebooks

I start with of one of Artaud's letters to Jacques Rivière in 1924. These letters are collected in the first volume of his *Collected Works*. Nothing is radically altered in these letters, as regards their composition and visual arrangement, from their manuscript form to their edited and published form.

Let us move on to the writings of Artaud made while he was in the psychiatric hospitals at Rodez and Ivry-sur-Seine, in copybooks given to him by the head doctor Gaston Ferdière, in which he practised calligraphy. These writings form the entirety of his work from 1943 to 1948, the year of his death.

It must be noted how the drawings and the text are interwoven in their visual and material aspects. Furthermore, it can be observed that his actual handwriting, compared to his earlier script as seen in the 1924 letter, has gained volume and thickness, and it does not occupy, at least not exclusively, a position of centrality on the page. In addition, we can note the appearance of 'words of sound', which make no sense in any language and inhabit a central position in many of his texts and notebooks.

We can now start to seek to understand the phenomenon of this writing put into practice by Artaud. Judgements of these texts, which depend only on notions of insanity, are insufficient to analyse and appreciate what Artaud has achieved. Of course, his history in the asylums cannot be completely ignored, but we should take care to avoid mythologizing or romanticizing insanity or reducing Artaud's vision to his psychiatric history.

This reading requires from us a twofold perspective: we can take some stock of the ways in which Artaud's life might have shaped his work,[2] which perhaps comes to the fore in the views of his friends and acquaintances, as well as some influential later critics, and yet at the same time begin to glance in a different direction from the path that most criticism of Artaud has taken. The former perspective emerges when we consider a few individuals whose responses to Artaud perhaps deserve privileging: the editor-in-chief of Gallimard, Gaston Gallimard, who, while Artaud was still alive, invited him to publish his complete works; artists contemporary to Artaud who supported him, including André Breton, André Gide, Arthur Adamov, Roger Blin, and Pierre Loeb, who owned an art gallery; Artaud's friend and the editor of his *Collected Works*, Paule Thévenin; Gaston Ferdière, the chief psychiatric doctor at Rodez; and certain critics who at the beginning of the 1960s stated the importance of Artaud's work, including Maurice Blanchot, Michel

Foucault, Jacques Derrida, Gilles Deleuze, and Felix Guattari. It would be naive at the very least to view the challenges of Artaud's work as coming exclusively from his psychotic state and neglecting the interest that this work provoked and still provokes.

Nevertheless, I would like to argue that the contemporary setting demands from us a different perspective, that above all crystallizes in discourses appearing from the end of the 1960s, a certain belief that something essential was passing between the artistic regime and the regime of insanity. My question is not at all an attempt to 'normalize' the figure of Artaud. Rather, the purpose is to question up to what point this romanticizing of madness and art meant that the disruptive impact of his final work, above all his notebooks, came to be based on its transgressive content, its blasphemous strength, and its strange mix of mystical and quasi-religious conceptions of art and culture, which shook almost all the contemporary sources of authority: the state, the Church, and the family.

It was in this context that the publication of his notebooks was embarked upon by Paule Thévenin. No mention whatsoever was made of Artaud's drawings, sketches, figures, and outlines by the publisher. No mention of the strength of the pen stroke in Artaud's writing. Nor the justification of the decision for the prevalence of a chronological order when the actual notebook disobeys this order. This is a fundamental point of difference between the notebooks and the diaries.

Finally, no mention was made of the choice for the total linearization of the texts, as there was also no mention of how much of what was written in the margins was either brought into the body of the text or removed entirely, nor the total erasure of the superimposition and interweaving of the writing with the pictorial drawing. Nor was any attention paid to the glossolalia as a scanned and exclusively sound-based language, repeatedly deployed by Artaud. Instead, there was an attempt to make the glossolalia into words with conventional meaning.

This was the predominant reception of the notebooks until well into the 1990s. At the end of that decade, at the time when I arrived in Paris to study and meet other researchers, including my supervisor, Evelyne Grossman, who would later publish a new version of the Artaud's works,[3] the prevailing notion was that the fragment was a micro-text that mirrored a macro-text. The fragment's own uniqueness was not appreciated. Instead, a text was conceived as being made exclusively from the fabric of language, neglecting such dimensions as the texture of the pen strokes, the importance of sound and any pictorial aspects. However, any publication of Artaud's notebooks cannot avoid the singularity of the notebook and isolate a body of text while neglecting the other elements of this fragmented text, whether that be the poems, prose, drawings, or glossolalia.

Obviously, there is no wish here to belittle the Herculean efforts of Paule Thévenin, much less the readings made of Artaud as an anomalous example of deviant subjectivities or as a precursor of the counterculture, as has been claimed from May 1968 onwards. What is required is a consideration of how this scriptural event of the notebooks demands a reformulation of our Western conception of the text – more specifically of an over-determination of the text as a logocentric regime, and of what effects this reformulation may provoke in the fields of literature and art.

A first observation should be concerned with noting that Artaud's practice in his notebooks radically differs from his earlier practice in his diaries. The diaries were easily comprehensible within the existing literary practices and conventions of Western culture. But unfortunately, in publication the notebooks were subjected to the same oppressive chronological regime as the diaries, to a linearization of events – even though the notebooks indicate, in their own singular chaos of a space that evades linearity, an intensive stroke (of its own marking of time?) on the page from the weight of a hand, which situates the writing in a relationship of co-dependence upon corporeal rhythms, as if they sprouted from a verbal soil far anterior to the text.

These elements by themselves alone disturb the conventional textures of text, if we understand text as a link, a synthetic concatenation, a regularity, or an alignment. The intensity of these elements ends up indicating a rhythm of disconnection, disjunction, and dislocation. However, it is also this disjunctive movement that urges the simultaneous presence of heterogeneous regimes such as those that move from the letter to the stroke, from the word of meaning to the word of sound, from the sketch to the drawing.

In the modern tradition we have the impression that disjunctive movements exclude, or at least blur, interiority, and what this psychological notion places as the sustenance of the text, its own subject of enunciation. I understand that the first edition of Artaud's notebooks sought to textualize these disjunctive movements as far as possible, including the filling in of the blanks suggested by incomprehensible or missing words. This attempt means that not only is the evidence of these disjunctive regimes removed, but also that many of the contradictions inherent in the process of self-abnegation, which Artaud went through after 1937, are suppressed. Many of the religious contradictions of this period, which are often regarded as a religious delirium suffered by Artaud, appeared in blasphemous marginal notes that were not included in the published volumes. Literature's difficulty to handle the presentation of the notebooks without domesticating it in a diary format also points to this fact of Artaud's writing, that it is writing which defies any possibility of unification.

The second edition of the notebooks

The second edition of Artaud's works, undertaken by Evelyne Grossman in 2014, lacked from the very beginning any commitment to the idea of compiling a *Complete Works* – alerting readers to the numerous unpublished texts and notes in the notebooks.

It also opted initially:

> To respect (as far as possible) the disposition on the page made by Artaud, as well as the rhythm which he impressed on the lines traced out on the pages. When a word is obscure, it is chosen to leave a blank space between brackets, preferring not to invent hypothetical words. Nor at any moment is it attempted to construct texts based on sparse fragments of notebooks. In addition, whenever there is a particular graphic interest a copy of the manuscript is placed alongside the printed text.[4]

This decision, which was heavily criticized by Derrida, and more recently by Bridet,[5] is, however, the only way in which the heterogenous regimes of Artaud's notebooks could be respected, as well as, and I would like to emphasize this, calls for a reader capable of living with imperfection – to cope with this aborted work, as Artaud himself referred to it. For him this was the *sine qua non* condition for reflection on our conceptions and expectations of artistic works (as well as peoples' lives). Coexisting with this broken line seems to require new forms of publication, but also of production of meaning. Up to a certain point this is not so dissimilar of the perspectives of our own day and age, of the necessity to move between inconstant and uncertain languages and references.

In the case of Artaud, I can affirm that this disjunction, whether it is grammatical, textual, or even in speech, becomes instead an invitation towards aesthetic and affective contact with materials. He calls it 'relating words with the physical movements from which they are born' (1933, Letter to Paulhan). It was in this way that for him 'literature was recomposed'.

We can then say that disjunction and imperfection are not related to a vacuum, or to a type of *nonsense* as a rule, but rather, affectively offer us radically different universes, which we could call enigmatic, uncivilized, and containing symbolic precariousness, with other types of cosmologies and passages between what is sensed and the sign, which we so often disregard. These are universes with which the white man still lacks any real empathy or contact. This is what Artaud saw in the indigenous culture of the Tarahumaras mountains. They can also be found in the indigenous or Afro-centred cultures that are still disregarded when Western Eurocentric interpretative systems are imposed upon the world.

Becoming a book?

In relation to this aspect there is a third kind of recomposition, which has still not been achieved in terms of publishing, but which I propose here as a critical exercise and an inflection that characterizes in a different way the relationship between literature and the other arts (visuals, sound, scenic) in the contemporary world. An inflection that, in my point of view, still needs to be deepened. Artaud's medium (*milieu*)[6] of writing in the notebooks (in other words, the notebooks seen as a medium, and not just as passive support) would seem to demand this thickening.

This recomposition of literature is related to a demonstration of their processes of composition and decomposition. As an art, literature, fixed in the book form (whether digital, serial, or in paper), creates an intrinsic contradiction between the process and the final product. We can read one thousand interviews with authors who declare that their works are not finished but are abandoned; we can see the constructs and experiments of 'open works', or inter-textual, interrupted, suspended, or anti-narrative works; yet the reader will still find there a 'book tomb',[7] a set of fixed and printed letters, frozen on the page, finished.

Without the marks of the missteps of that 'finished' construction, literature sets out to participate in the contemporary world, but at the same time resists it. Aesthetics has progressively decomposed its predictable forms: breaking out of the frame, escaping from the perspective of the look, and consequently demanding the participation of the spectator.

In one way or another the challenge of this decomposition through which art passed between the second half of the twentieth century and the present was already germinating in Artaud's notebooks. For me, this seed is related to the need to share processes more than conclusions. Artistic processes should be viewed as something halfway between the proposer and the work of art. They are up to a certain point subjective strokes, but not intimate or confessional. They are like dregs, remnants, pieces of bodies – bodies of thought, affection, ideas – which live within our processes of creation. Impasses. Absences. Unthinkable. It seems to me fundamental in this way that the sharing of this vulnerable and imprecise aspect of the process appears today in the recomposition of artistic texts, and in the long-ago torn social and symbolic fabrics of our contemporary world.

In the case of Artaud's notebooks, one of the possible paths for this recomposition is to see them within, or in relation to, the texts or drawings that he to a greater or lesser extent 'finalized'. The notebook represents the imperfect part of this great aborted work.

At some moments this requires understanding that the centrality of that notebook does not go through written text, for we must abandon the regime of literature and move to the pictorial regime, to understand the book as belonging to the artist or the museum. As if it were be possible for a moment to understand that Artaud's demand for an aesthetic-poetic language was achieved in the form of drawings-writings.

Nevertheless, more than an investigation of the instability of genres, this demonstration of the processes of composition and decomposition of writing appears to me to be fundamental for the recomposition of intermediate or border zones, between different artistic or subjective regimes. These border zones can be explored through more open publications willing to question what came before them historically and to question the hegemony of what, for numerous reasons yet to be fully evoked and considered, still occupies the centre of the page, or of an epoch, or a genre, or a place, or a corpus. In relation to this aspect, the emphasis on highlighting such works which might explore these border zones, works which contemplate and show such processes, also becomes an emphasis on questioning everything which at one moment or another we want to erect and stabilize as a centre. Processes always cross borders. Imperceptible or subtle, they help us question the rigid and unified centralities. The theme of disconnection appears to me to be fundamental today for us not to think of the text merely as a texture that links, brings together, closes, and unifies.

Notes

1. See Artaud 1980.
2. See Thévenin 1993; Virmaux 1996; Rosolato 1976.
3. Grossman 2014.

4. Grossman 2014: 15.
5. See Derrida 2004a, 2004b, and Bridet 2016.
6. I treat the notebooks as a *milieu* (a concept proposed by Deleuze-Guattari through the reading of the biologist Jakob Von Uexkull) because I understand that the support does not provoke the comprehension I seek to use with the notebooks, in other words: that of something that is actively passed between the corpus – from who writes, the writing, and the 'paper' or 'screens' or 'skins' of the notebooks, which singularize the event of writing, obliging us to see them under other intricacies and paths.
7. See Artaud 1980: 1934.

Works cited

Artaud, A. (1980), *Oeuvres Complètes*. Cahiers de Rodez – février-avril 1945. Volume VX, ed. Paule Thévenin, Paris: Gallimard.

Artaud, A. (2004), *Oeuvres*, ed. Evelyne Grossman, Paris: Gallimard.

Bridet, G. (2016), 'Artaud, de l'appropriation symbolique à la neutralisation patrimoniale?', *Les Temps Modernes* 687–8: 117–45.

Derrida, J. (2004a), 'Une nouvelle "Affaire Artaud"?', *La Quinzaine Littéraire* 885: 31.

Derrida, J. (2004b), 'N'oublions pas Paule Thévenin. . .', *La Quinzaine Littéraire* 886: 31.

Grossman, E., ed. (2014), *Antonin Artaud: Œuvres*, Paris: Gallimard, Quarto, 2014.

Rosolato, G. (1976), 'L'Expulsion', *Revue Oblique* 10–11: 41–9.

Thévenin, P. (1993), *Antonin Artaud, ce désespéré qui vous parle*. Paris: Seuil.

Virmaux, Alain and Odette (1996), *Antonin Artaud. Collection Qui est-vous?* Lyon: Éditions La Manufacture.

CHAPTER 12
VISUAL EPITOME IN LATE ANTIQUE ART

Jaś Elsner[*]

Epitome, brevity, exemplarity

One picture is worth a thousand words.[1]

My epigraph, an English proverb surprisingly first attested only in the 1920s, conveys the power of visual epitome in the popular imagination. The *Oxford English Dictionary* offers two basic meanings for the word *epitome* in English usage, both dating back to the early Renaissance.[2] The first represents the way we usually use the idea in classical philology – namely as an abridgement, summary or condensed account. The second takes that condensation to represent the essence in miniature of the thing referred to – in other words, to be a kind of ideal or perfect embodiment of its quality or type. It is in this sense that a picture as a visual epitome can be worth a thousand words and that it may function as a special form of exemplarity, a topic that has had some recent exposure in Classical studies.[3] I take it to be the case that the two meanings are not necessarily mutually exclusive and that both may be in play if we are to extend our understanding of the workings of epitome in late antiquity beyond the strict abbreviation of texts to a wider cultural spectrum that might include images.

Let me summarize my argument here. I will assume that epitome in the sense of the abbreviation of narratives, when it functions in the visual sphere, is actually ubiquitous in Roman art since all images from narratives effectively cut down a long diachronic process of reading or telling a story into a synoptic frame (or sometimes several) that effectively summarizes its key features and spurs the imagination or memory to fill in the rest.[4] In Roman art this goes with a particular quality of replication in which certain stock forms and figures are repeated with variations across different narratives (whether mythological, historical or biographical) and are made identifiable through their attributes.[5] The story of Narcissus, for example, as told at some length by Ovid, becomes a pictorial snapshot of a youth by a pool with his reflected head inside it.[6] A particular interest of this feature – one I will not discuss here – is that the forms of epitome in this model are actually independent of the specific narratives that they represent, and hence constitute a visual discourse and semiotics that is in conversation with itself as well as with the stories they epitomize. That independence also allows a distancing from the narratives they exemplify and a more generalized, even allegorical, range of reference – something I will claim is implicit in the ancient theoretical literature on abbreviation and something that becomes available to radical appropriation for new rhetorical models of meaning and signification in Christian late antiquity, with the rise of typology (the use of images that are, in part, specifically evocative of a canonical series of Scriptures) and with the transformation of book culture from roll to codex. I will concentrate for the longest section on the implications of visual epitome and exemplarity for how images aided and enabled the codex, as a new kind of book, to function through a kind of pictorial epitomic paratextuality.

There has recently been a rich and thoughtful strand of work on the theme of epitome in Greek and Roman writing, of which of course this collection is a part.[7] That literature places the epitome within the large ancient rhetorical and scholarly culture generated in the Hellenistic world which throve during the period known as the Second Sophistic in Roman imperial times and carried on into late antiquity and the middle ages, significantly transgressing the barriers imposed on many aspects of earlier Classical culture by Christianity. Epitomes enabled collections, anthologies, commentaries, glossaries, lexicographies, grammaticographies, doxographies, and other scholarly genres (what have been called auxiliary texts)[8], themselves immensely conducive to the new book technology of the codex, which came to replace the roll roughly during the fourth century AD.[9] Likewise, epitomes were essential to education (and remain so!) – both in the provision of shortened texts and summaries (from biographies of exemplary characters to the *hypotheses* of plays) for school use, and of commentaries,[10] as well as in the management of large-scale histories.[11] The deep-play of epitome within the genesis of Greek and Roman writing can be seen in the extent of what has been called 'self-epitomization' in the use of narrative recapitulations (*kephalaia*) and other models of abbreviation by ancient writers of all periods.[12]

Although the term epitome does not appear among the technical figures of ancient rhetorical theory or training (unlike elaboration, *exergasia*, which broadly implies its opposite),[13] the concept of keeping things short and crisp (*brachylogia* in Greek or *brevitas* in Latin) has traction in both Greek and Latin rhetorical primers. On the Greek side, the *Rhetorica ad Alexandrum*, transmitted with the manuscripts of Aristotle but nowadays attributed to Anaximenes of Lampsachus (perhaps compiled from a fourth-century BC source in its current form),[14] refers to *brachylogia*,[15] and is followed in the first century BC by the *de tropis* attributed to Tryphon of Alexandria (*c.* 60 BC–AD 10) which has sections on *brachytes* (brevity) and *syntomia* (concision),[16] and in the imperial period by the *ars rhetorica* 1.136–37, traditionally attributed incorrectly to Aelius Aristides but perhaps finally assembled from earlier models towards the end of the fifth century AD,[17] which has a section on *brachytes* and *syntomia*.[18] Notably, on the Latin side, the concept of *brevitas* appears in passing as a figure in the major rhetorical textbooks that survive from the Roman Republic – the *ad Herennium* (4.54.68), and several of Cicero's works on oratory (*orator* 40.139, *de partitione oratoria* 6.19 and 9.32, *de oratore* 3.202). Publius Rutilius Lupus, who was a Latin rhetorical theorist in the early first century AD, includes *brachylogia* as a figure in his *de figuris sententiarum et elocutionis* II.8;[19] he is followed by Quintilian (*Institutio Oratoria* 9.3.99) who cites him explicitly, the late Roman *carmen de figuris et schematibus* 46–48,[20] and by two fourth-century treatise writers, Julius Victor and Marius Victorinus.[21] This Latin tradition persists at least until Alcuin in the eighth century,[22] and includes an intriguing late antique fragment from an eighth-century manuscript in Paris on *brevitas* as a virtue in the writing of history.[23] What this theoretical and text-book literature implies is that the skills of abbreviation and précis were a normal part of the educational armature of Hellenistic and later *paideia*, both in Greek- and in Latin-speaking contexts, which means that the arts, practices and instincts of epitomization were inculcated from an early age.

The range of scholarly approaches to epitome has largely remained in the area of texts and textuality, despite the clear potential of miniatures, that attempt to embody the quintessence of a subject, to be visual and pictorial as well as textual. If we take the concept of epitome to be entirely formal – about abbreviating particular texts – then it is a narrowly applicable term, useful in specific contexts. But it is reductive, in missing the clear cultural resonance of the art of epitome and the range of possibilities that abbreviation enables. And if we insist on textual abbreviation as the defining paradigm, we disable exploration of parallel processes in visual media. In the same way, we may insist that any of the epitomized versions of a classic work of fiction, such as *Pride and Prejudice*, from shortenings and parodies via graphic novels to audio adaptations, television series and films are simply irrelevant to modern culture's grasp of the original novel. But it is manifestly the case that in the current era many more people will have had various intermedial forms of vicarious contact with Jane Austen's literary world as conceived in that book through such media, than from actually reading the original. I will take an extended and cultural understanding of the concept of epitome as a theoretical assumption underpinning this paper, and attempt to explore some aspects of its resonance and uses in Roman and late antique visual culture.

It may be objected that concision and brevity are not the same thing as epitome. But consider the following passage from the *Rhetorica ad Alexandrum* (22):

> Βραχυλογεῖν δὲ βουλόμενον ὅλον τὸ πρᾶγμα ἑνὶ ὀνόματι περιλαμβάνειν, καὶ τούτωι ὅ ἄν ὑπάρχηι βραχύτατον τῶι πράγματι . . . καὶ παλιλλογίαν τὴν σύντομον ἐκ τῶν μερῶν ἀφαιρεῖν, ἐν δὲ ταῖς τελευταῖς μόνον παλιλλογεῖν.
>
> If you wish to speak briefly, you should include your whole subject in a single word and that word the shortest which is applicable to your subject. . . . you must do away with brief iterations in the separate divisions of the speech and only employ iteration in your final conclusion.

The art of finding the summarizing word is the skill of epitome in its sense of searching for the quintessential; that of cutting iteration is the skill of précis and abbreviation by which epitome must have been taught. It is striking that this whole section of the text lays out strategies for speeches that are prolonged, brief and of moderate length – with the implication that success lies in the art of 'as far as possible adapting the character of your speech to that of your audience'. Its training must constitute the acquisition of flexibility in both expansion and abbreviation. That flexibility – like the art of memory – effectively becomes a cultural trope in dealing with creativity that extends beyond the purely literary world to visual and material culture.[24]

Visual epitome and the figural

τῆι δὲ λέξει εἰς δύο χρῆσθαι …

'You must make your language serve a double purpose'

Rhetorica ad Alexandrum 22

In the same passage from the *Rhetoric to Alexander*, quoted above, which refers to brevity, the quotation that serves as epigraph to this section appears as well. Beyond the avoidance of repetition, rhetorical concision has the power of using language for a double purpose. It is epitome that points elsewhere or that essentializes in ways that take the listener or reader to a different place. The quintessential, which epitomizes a topic, has the potential for figural power – tending towards allegorical or metaphorical meanings.[25] In the visual arts of late antiquity, this double purpose – associated with simplification and abbreviation – is particularly marked, and has been described by the German literature as *Entmythologisierung*, the demythologization of narratives to render essential or symbolic themes, whether exemplary virtues or exemplifications of mortality.[26] The quality is particularly marked in both the main corpora of images from the later Roman world, namely mosaics and sarcophagi.[27] Exemplary simplifications are in fact completely normal across Roman art – one thinks of personifications, such as all those female figures for provinces,[28] or narrative epitomes where a single episode inevitably stands for an entire mythological story or cycle.[29]

One of the most powerful aspects of Roman art in general is the ability of figures through their formal appearance and allusion to earlier (semi-canonical) forms to hold meaning in what has been described as 'semantic system'.[30] This effectively means that the same type of a nude reclining youth becomes – in Pompeian painting for instance – an epitome for a variety of mythical narratives, such as that of Endymion, Narcissus, Cyparissus or Ganymede, with only a given set of attributes (Selene's presence for Endymion, the reflected head in a pool for Narcissus, a stag for Cyparissus, the eagle-lover for Ganymede) defining which story a viewer should bring to mind (Figure 1).[31] What is new with demythologization is the increased potential for figural meaning (already of course present in the figure of a female as a personification for a given province, for example, or that of a male for a river). In early Christian art, this feature of visual production achieves increased emphasis. The typological method, whereby the juxtaposition of Old Testament themes from the Hebrew Bible (like Jonah and the Whale or Daniel in the Lions' Den) are set side-by-side with scenes from the New Testament or with figures like the Good Shepherd that intimate Christian meanings, effectively creates a new Scriptural language for the visual arts.[32]

To cash out these general reflections in terms of material examples, let us take the interesting mid to late third-century Endymion lenos (tub-shaped sarcophagus) from Naples, once in the Cook collection and now in the British Museum (Figure 2). This shows the hero, carved with the portrait of the deceased, in a recumbent posture but with open eyes, surrounded by putti – some holding torches, one with a garland, two playing musical instruments and a number with baskets of grapes or apples.[33] Here there is no figure of Selene to mark the full mythological narrative, which normally shows her approaching the sleeping figure of her beloved, and the piece was certainly recut in antiquity from a reclining Ariadne sarcophagus (with the removal of the breasts, the insertion of a penis and the change of portrait features to a male with close-cropped hair that may be as late as the Tetrarchy, potentially dating the recarving to the 280s).[34] When the image represented Ariadne, she too had no accompanying Dionysus, and one might argue that the iconography in the abbreviated form of the deceased as sleeper in a paradisal setting is not incompatible with interpretation as Jonah (who sleeps beneath the gourd vine at the close of the visual account of the Biblical Jonah narrative). Whichever narrative we choose, the figure is an epitome whose meanings serve a 'double purpose' in signalling – away from the narrative action of the myth – the various intimations of a happy sleep in death among erotes that such imagery might evoke.[35] What is striking is the ability of the same figure – with a little sculptural adaptation – to shift epitomic status from one narrative to another. In this case the simplification of content that goes along with abbreviation (the removal of Dionysus and all his retinue from Ariadne, the absence of Selene from Endymion) aids a generalization of meaning that extends beyond any one narrative frame.

If we move to a Christian example also from the late third century – the famous lenos from the church of Santa Maria Antiqua in Rome (Figure 3),[36] these kinds of isolated figure (either with some narrative referents or with none) juxtaposed against each other, create extraordinary potential for rich interpretative resonance. Here, on the far left side, Neptune is seated with his trident and beside him a ship. This segues into the sea monster (*ketos*) who swallowed Jonah, although the juxtaposition of monster and ship does not mean that this ship must necessarily be the one on which Jonah sailed. Beside the monster on the front of the sarcophagus lies Jonah sleeping beneath the vine, above which three sheep are grazing. Again the actual narrative of Jonah being swallowed and spewed by the beast is avoided. In the centre of the front are a female orant, a seated philosopher reading from a scroll (both of which have blank heads) and the Good Shepherd (or at any rate, a shepherd carrying a sheep). To the right of this is the Baptism of Christ and over the curve on the right-hand side are two figures who may be fishermen mending their nets. These certainly have a potential Christian meaning, but also pick up the marine imagery on the left end. Only two of the scenes here are narrative-related (Jonah and the Baptism), but the others all acquire potential symbolic resonance in relation to these and to each other. The imagery certainly does not abandon non-Christian Graeco-Roman thematics (notably the figure of Neptune, the ship, the philosopher and the fishermen) but it is also susceptible to strong Christian interpretation. Each image is exemplary and at least those with a narrative reference are epitomic. But it is the rhetorical potential for generating meaning through these symbols that marks the typological genius of early Christian culture, in this case with the Old Testament as represented by the recumbent Jonah (himself a figure for the Resurrected Christ) in juxtaposition with the Incarnation as defined by the fundamental act of Christian initiation in the Baptism.

Visual epitome and the codex

I will concentrate for the rest of this discussion on manuscripts. I have just indicated that the possibilities for visual epitome and its liberation of figures from the constraints of narrative structure to all kinds of rhetorical purposes (exemplary, metaphorical and so forth) was fundamental – although in rhetorically different ways – for all the visual arts both in the Roman world and in Christian late antiquity. I should say at the outset here that epitome was by no means the only purpose of illumination and that other ways in which pictures are worth a thousand words are well illustrated by the extraordinary naturalistic drawings of plants and herbs in the sixth-century Vienna Dioscorides,[37] or the fine drawings of buildings in the Agrimensores manuscripts.[38] We need not assume that all uses of images are epitomic or exemplary, but rather that their functions are rhetorically flexible and attuned to the contexts in which they were employed.[39]

The particular issue of visual epitome in the new medium of the codex and at a heightened level of intermedial juxtaposition with the painted picture set against or alongside the written text, makes the creative options developed by manuscript illumination of particular interest for the late antique moment. If we take visual decoration in books to have qualities of epitome and exemplarity that are exceptionally close to textual models, late antique examples nonetheless play in numerous ways. I will focus here on the variety of such issues inside illustrated manuscripts, rather than on the epitomic arguments made – for instance – by the decorated bindings of early books, which could represent complex themes and could be executed in valuable materials, for the consumption of a much wider public than the interiors of the same codices.[40] My focus will be on the complex visual strategies of epitome first in non-Christian books, although ones very likely produced in Christian contexts, and then in Bibles and Gospel books.

Let us begin with the surviving illuminations of a remarkable manuscript probably made towards the end of the fifth century in Rome. The so-called Roman Vergil (Ms. Vat. Lat. 3867 in the Vatican Library) was an enormous book of 410 fine sheepskin parchment folios, each measuring about 350 x 335 mm in size, containing the *Eclogues*, *Georgics* and *Aeneid*.[41] The book was richly illustrated. A small header illumination was supplied at the beginning of each of the *Eclogues* (the first seven of which survive), a double-page spread at the opening of each of the four *Georgics* (of which only two images survive from before the third Georgic) and a double-page spread with two illustrations at the opening of each book of the *Aeneid* (of which ten pictures survive out of the original twenty-four).[42] The text was written in highly legible large rustic capitals in brown ink with rubric for emphasis. I want to claim that the illuminations do effective epitomic work, of different kinds, in relation to the text they illustrate, and that as a sequence or collection of epitomes they make a major contribution to the formal effect and handling of the codex as well as offering interpretative or exegetic emphases (in the choice of what to illustrate) and creating a visual paratext through which – for instance – a non-literate peruser of the volume might nonetheless gain some sense of its contents.[43] We need to understand the illuminations as an essential part of the book technology of an expensive luxury manuscript like the Roman Vergil,[44] so as to avoid modernizing errors in misunderstanding why some do not show what might to us seem like obvious narrative subjects.[45]

The illuminations of the *Eclogues*, at the first part of the book, are the only non-full-page pictures. In each case they illustrate the speaking voice of the given poem – giving the reader a visual cue as to whether she is being addressed by the poet directly or by a dialogue between speakers within the text. This works in an alternating fashion: *Eclogues* 1, 3, 5, 7 and 9 (this last now lost from the manuscript) are poetic conversations, with the speakers marked in rubric annotations to the left of the margin where the voice changes in the surviving poems, while *Eclogues* 2, 4, 6, 8 and 10 (the last two of these now lost) are works in a single voice. This vocal difference between alternating poems is performed by the miniatures. Vergil himself appears as a framed author portrait for the even-numbered poems in a single voice (even where that is largely the voice of a persona). Hence in Eclogue 2, a lament by the herdsman Corydon which carries the rubric heading 'POETA CORYDON' below the image, the marginal annotation 'POE' to the left of the first line, clearly indicating that the poet speaks and in the voice of Corydon, whose actual speech opening at line 6 is marked in the margin of fol. 4r. (Figure 4). The picture has a seated frontal author in tunic with clavi and a cloak, his feet on a footstool, holding a scroll with a lectern to his left and a capsa for containing rolls to his right (fol. 3v.).

This pattern is repeated for poems 4 and 6, though with the capsa and lectern reversed, the poet looking to the left and his feet (with no footstool) crossing the band that constitutes the picture's frame as though he were about to step into the space of the poem itself. The image for Eclogue 4 appears at the bottom of fol 9r. (at the end of poem 3), while the text only begins as you turn the page, where again the marginal annotation for the speaking voice reads 'POE' (fol. 9v.). The opening of the sixth Eclogue appears after the last line of poem 5 almost at the top of fol 14r (Figure 5). There is a long rubricated title line below the author portrait summarizing the poem's contents ('FAUNORUM SATYRORUM ET SILENORUM DELECTATIO') whose last letters taper away into the right margin, and again the cue for the speaking voice ('POE') in the left margin before the poem's first verse. In each of these cases, the illumination is an epitome of the poem (in the sense of choosing, and focalizing on, one quintessential aspect) that emphasizes its speaking voice as its author, and affirms the antiquated writerly context of a papyrus roll as opposed to the contemporary modernism of a parchment codex.

The pictures for the even-numbered *Eclogues* must be seen in dialogue with the very different visual strategy chosen for the odd poems, which are all conversations. In these cases, the header-picture always illustrates the speakers within the poem: two in the first Eclogue, three in the third, two in the fifth and three again in the seventh poem – although there a fourth herdsman, Daphnis, is mentioned as being present in the conversation (vv. 1–8) but omitted in the picture, one may surmise because he does not speak. We may assume that the ninth poem, now lost, would have reverted to two figures for its speakers Lycidas and Moeris. The range of images for the odd-numbered *Eclogues* provide collectively a chiasmic pictorial pattern of 2 figures, 3, 2, 3, 2. The somewhat abraided opening page of Eclogue 1 (fol. 1r.) has an image unlike any other in the book (Figure 6).

The illumination has no frame, extending across the upper half of the page (and has been cut down at the top when the folio was trimmed at some later point). The poem has no titular enumeration of its speakers in red ink (as in all the subsequent *Eclogues*) though their names are inscribed against their figures in the image; its first line is rubricated. As in the texts of later poems, the speaker is indicated at the right margin of the text, usually in red. The image appears specifically to illustrate the poem's opening verses, with Meliboeus standing and making a gesture of speech to the seated Tityrus, who is relaxing beneath a beech tree playing his pipe (as in vv. 1–2). Tityrus' pipe, virtually the first visual gesture of the entire codex, is the manuscript's only pictorial nod to the theme of pastoral music in the *Eclogues* (pipes are mentioned at the openings of Eclogue 1, v. 2; Eclogue 5, v. 2; Eclogue 6, v. 8 and at poem 10, v. 34), but the topic is visually revived in the left frontispiece to Georgic III (fol. 44v.).

The remaining Eclogue pictures are all within frames, the figures wreathed in bay crowns (perhaps reflecting Silenus' wreath in Eclogue 6, vv. 16–19) and carrying staffs, like the herdsmen in the prefatory images of Georgic III, fols. 44v. and 45r. In each case what has been identified as a herdsman's rustic shelter, a kind of tent perhaps made of reeds, with a flask suspended at the opening, appears within the illustration. The images do not represent the subjects or narrative content of their poems (for instance any love interest) but rather their setting, both rural and dramatic. The header for Eclogue 3 (fol. 6r.), at the top of the page, has the three speakers (Menalcas, Damoetas and Palaemon who will be the judge of their contest) seated, each making a gesture of speech. The rubric title, immediately below, names the three speakers in that order from left to right, but in fact the image depicts Palaemon on the left facing right, as the judge of the other two, who face him at the centre and to the right of the picture. No part of the picture extends beyond its frame. The image for poem 5 appears at the bottom of the page where the fourth Eclogue finishes (fol. 11r.), so that the text (including the rubric title with the speakers' names, Menalcas and Mopsus) is over the page on the other side of the folio (fol. 11v.). Here there is a rustic hut beside each figure – the one on the left greatly extending beyond the painting's left margin. The page with the image for Eclogue 7 (fol. 16v.) – again at the bottom of the folio, where the sixth poem ends – is the last in the run of the *Eclogues* to survive (Figure 7). This means the titulus and the text of the poem (which would have opened at the recto of the next page, facing this image) have been lost. This time the judge, Meliboeus, reclines on a rock in the centre of the visual field, listening to the two speakers, Corydon and Thyrsis, to his left and right. Again, the rustic hut and the feet of the dog beside it jut out beyond the frame to the right.

In the odd *Eclogues*, the frontispiece as pictorial epitome, while still insisting on the visual embodiment of the poem's speaking voices, gestures to the poems' dramatic content and context. The even *Eclogues* – as interiors with the poet in his imagined space of composition – visualize not the poem but the extra-textual figure of its creator; the odd *Eclogues* – as bucolic landscapes, with trees, grass, sheep, goats or cattle as well the herdsmen who are the speakers – picture a world and characters internal to the text they prefigure. In moving from the *Eclogues*, with their part-page prefatory single images for each poem, to the *Georgics* and the *Aeneid*, the *Roman Vergil* keeps the model of frontispiece illuminations but shifts gear. From the *Georgics*, each book (admittedly much longer than any Eclogue) is given a double page pictorial spread before the start of the text, on what is frequently an inserted bifolium where the pages on the reverse of each illustration are left blank (Figure 8a and 8b). The images are not drawn in the centre of the page but with a wider margin to the outside, so that they sit relatively close to the central binding, but within the generous space afforded by the book's size.

The epitomic model – as two full-page pictures with no adjacent text, preceded by textual summary – is very different from the *Eclogues*, but remains prefatory. Moreover, as with the full prefatory scheme for the books of the *Aeneid* (only surviving complete for Books II and X), this is a complex mix of epitomic text and image. The double-page spread of images are preceded by a closing colophon for the preceding book and an *incipit*, in a border above and below made of red and brown ink, on one page (which may also include the last lines of the preceding book); this is followed on a separate page by a prose summary – itself a textual epitome – of the content of the next book in alternating red and brown ink lines (four lines for Georgic 3, eleven lines including title for the books of the *Aeneid*) again within a red brown ornamental border at top and bottom of the page; then there are blank pages before and after the pictures and finally the opening of the new book on a new page, signalled by three lines of rubric (see the Appendix).[46]

In the Georgics, only the two images from Book III have been preserved (Figure 8a and 8b). These are bucolic idylls with animals, herdsmen (one playing a flute) and rustic tents, which pick up the imagery and even the colour scheme of the odd *Eclogues* pictures but greatly expand the pictorial surface and ambition. They appear not to make any specific narrative reference to the text of the poem itself. However, there seems a potential exegetic inflection in the way they borrow much of their imagery (herdsmen, pipes, rustic hut) from the odd *Eclogues* yet their yellow colour scheme from the interiors of the even *Eclogues*, as if bringing the earlier set of poems together in a crowning synthesis.[47]

By contrast the ten full-page miniatures in a richer and more varied palette that survive (out of twenty-four) in the *Aeneid* are largely definitive selections from the narrative of the given book, almost as if they were quotations, excerpted from the main thrust and set aside at the front as a kind of summarizing pictorial epitome. In Book I only one image survives, the right half (i.e. the second picture) of the original pair, depicting Aeneas' response to the storm at sea (*Aen.*1.93–96, fol. 77r.). Book II preserves the original double illustration pattern as its frontispiece opening (Figure 9a and 9b). The first illustration shows Dido's banquet with Aeneas (fol. 100v.), Dido in the centre and Ascanius (who is in fact Cupid in disguise) reclining at table. Dido's hand is raised indicating her request to her guest to tell his tale (the closing lines of *Aen.*1.753–56) and Aeneas' hand is raised as he recounts his story (*Aen.* 2.1–2). The second picture shows the story of Sinon bringing the Wooden Horse to Troy (*Aen.* 2.57–194, fol. 101r.), which is both the first major episode of Book II and part of the content of Aeneas' speech as depicted in the preceding picture. This image may thus stand for itself as an epitome of the narrative and may also be a kind of speech bubble, summarizing what Aeneas is saying in the previous painting. No picture survives from Book III and only the second of the two from Book IV. This is a sober and fully-clothed depiction of the love-making of Dido and Aeneas in the cave (*Aen.* 4.160–68), with the bulk of the scene including trees, horses and an ochre pastoral background recalling the imagery of the odd *Eclogues* and the *Georgics*. The one surviving miniature from Book V, mis-bound at fol. 76v., shows a very loose version of the sacrifice in honour of Anchises (*Aen.* 5.42–103); it is less clearly tied to the text of the *Aeneid* than any of the other miniatures.[48] No image survives from Book VI and from Book VII only that on the right hand side of the original pair, which shows a crucial episode, Ascanius shooting Silvia's pet stag (*Aen.* 7.496–99, fol. 163r.). No picture remains from Book VIII but from Book IX the left half of the original pair shows Iris appearing to Turnus (from the very opening of the Book, 9.1–5, mis-bound at fol. 74v.). The double page spread from Book 10 shows two frontal images of the Council of the Gods (10.1–95, fol. 234v. and 235r.) both beneath a dome-like rainbow flanked by sun and moon.[49]

The final surviving miniature from the *Aeneid* (mis-bound at fol. 188v.) is the left side of the two frontispiece images (Figure 10). It clearly indicates a battle scene, perhaps from the last book of the epic. It has been suggested this is the single combat of Aeneas and Turnus on which the epic climaxes (*Aen.* 12.704–24) before Turnus turns to flight (from verse 731), but in that episode no one has a bow and arrow (as does the leading warrior in the Phrygian cap on the left with his quiver emphasized on the ground between the two heroes in the painting)[50] and their duel is explicitly by sword (*Aen.* 12.695 and 709 (*ferro*), 729 (*ensem*), 731 (*ensis*)).[51] If we stress the pictorial emphasis on an archer as the main protagonist to the left, then other options arise. At 12.266, Tolumnius the Rutulian augur breaks the truce by hurling his dart (*telum contorsit*): could this have been understood by the draughtsman as shooting an arrow rather than throwing a spear? At 12.311–23, in response to the rise of battle, Aeneas attempts to hold back the Trojans from responding, and is struck explicitly by an arrow (*sagitta*) shot from an unknown hand. But in this passage Aeneas is described as bare-headed with right hand unarmed (which is to say, certainly without the helmet and shield of the lead-warrior to the right of the miniature): *dextram tendebat inermem/nudato capite*, 12.311–12. And the miniature makes a major protagonist of the archer by contrast with the poem's insistence on uncertainty (*incertum qua pulsa manu, quo turbine adacta*, 12.320). Also, in principle, the artist has distinguished Trojans from Rutulians by their helmets (Phrygian caps for the Trojans on the left and plumed helmets on the right): both the last two options I have suggested from the text have the archer as an Italian, rather than a Trojan, whereas in the painting the archer is clearly leading the Trojans. At the same time, since the image has been displaced and misbound, it is not impossible it refers to a contest in a different book. A strong candidate whose textual detail fits most of the pictorial intimations is Aeneas's son Ascanius' victory with bow and arrows over Turnus' brother-in-law Numanus Remulus (9.590–637). Unfortunately, the miniature is a left-hand opening, just like the one surviving picture from Book 9 (fol. 74v.), which appears to make this identification impossible or at any not possible for the opening of Book 9.[52] Perhaps the search for illustrative precision is misguided, and the point of this visual epitome is a generalized evocation that can stand for each of these episodes or all together, in effect an epitomic summary of all the battles that characterize the second half of the *Aeneid*. Indeed, if the scene evokes (or also evokes) the killing of Achilles by Paris's arrow, foretold at his death by Hector at *Iliad* 22.358–60 and recapitulated in Aeneas' prayer as he enters the underworld at *Aeneid* 6.56–58, then the miniature is an epitome of the entire *aristeia* tradition of individual battles in epic. Certainly, this is a case where no one passage in the text fully coheres with the visual details, and so 'illustration' (if that were ever the intent) is not precise.

By contrast with the miniatures of the *Eclogues* and *Georgics*, where the epitomic strategy avoids narrative quotation from within the text, those of the *Aeneid* are largely drawn from the narrative as illustrations, with the interesting exception of fol. 188v., just discussed, but by virtue of their being pulled out to the front and emphasized they function also as an exegetic emphasis that potentially directs the reader's interpretation of what is important. An illiterate peruser of the manuscript would gain some version of its narrative content through looking only at the selection of 24 pictures. At the same time, the visual strategy is one that abbreviates the text radically in choosing what to illustrate. If we take all the illustrations together, then clearly each is an epitomic frontispiece, but the strategies of summary and abbreviation are radically different. The varied strategies include emphasizing the speaking voice within a given poem (in the *Eclogues*); evoking a poem's general character (in the case of Georgic III); and selecting from a long and complex epic narrative (in the case of the *Aeneid*), which also implies imposing a potential interpretive scheme upon it. The twenty-four pictures that made up the epitome of the *Aeneid* were themselves of course effectively a mini-narrative in pictorial form, a medial transformation of the textual narrative into discrete visual segments constructing a kind of chronology. Finally, the images all define the beginnings of independent poems or books within a longer cycle, which means they also aid the reader in knowing where an earlier poem has ended. There is no surviving overall image for the entire collection of the three canonical works of Vergil, although there might well have been one (for example a portrait) to accompany an overall title. Visual epitome here has a pragmatic function in aiding a reader's navigation through the monolithic blocks of text that constitute a codex of over 400 folios, but it also has a series of exegetical functions in stressing particular aspects of the text that it introduces. Here the difference in palette between the illuminations of the *Eclogues* and *Georgics*, on the one hand, and the *Aeneid*, on the other, may have some significance, as might the repeated visual motifs – such as rustic huts and suspended flasks in the bucolic books and military gear like shields and quivers in the epic. It is worth noting that the images of the *Roman Vergil*, even as they visualize Vergil's poetic works, make no reference to the rich textual visualizations within his poems in the form of ekphrasis.[53] The illuminations of the *Roman Vergil*, quite apart from their art-historical significance and their place in the history of the illustrated codex, are a contribution to and out of the rich late antique culture of the reception of Vergil.[54] This is a world steeped in epitome – from the passages picked out for commentary by Servius,[55] to the making of new poems out of selected spolia from Vergil's verses in the art of the cento.[56]

The richness of functions – effectively arising from the 'double purpose' of brevity as defined by the *Rhetorica ad Alexandrum* – is typical of late antique illumination. In the now lost manuscript of the plays of Terence, made in Rome about 400 AD, which was copied along with its illuminations in a series of major Carolingian and later versions,[57] there was an initial frontispiece to the entire collection showing the author, Terence, in an imago clipeata within a square frame on a pedestal, held by two figures in theatrical masks (Figure 11).[58] Each play was then given a separate frontispiece – a fine aedicule flanked by coloured columns containing shelves, on which were placed theatrical masks in the same number as the given play's speaking parts (Figure 12).[59] These are highly formalized epitomic strategies with significant functions in the book's ancient handling – to indicate the single authorship of the collection and to define the opening of each play as well as its voices. But then within each play a very rich range of miniatures offer illustration of particular chosen episodes, with several figures, usually labelled, as well as a speaking figure for each prologue (Figure 13). Here a complex strategy of emphasis of particular scenes within the dramatic action is enacted through representation, a literal visualization of the given play alongside and interspersed within its written text.[60] It has generally been accepted that these illustrations of the dramatic action coincide with scene divisions.[61] Here we have different kinds of epitomic strategies again – on the one hand, prefatory and formal, on the other, forms of condensing a written text into brief visual vignettes.

That mixture appears beyond ancient pagan texts in the miniatures of the Christian visual tradition. For example, in the sixth- or early seventh-century Syriac Bible in Paris, known as Syr. 341, each book in both the Old and the New Testaments is prefaced by an illumination.[62] The book is unfortunately incomplete but it offers three kinds of epitomes: author portraits for several of the prophets and for St James the apostle (fol. 174r., 175r., 178r., 178v., 179v., 180r., 180v., 181r., 181v., 182r., 212r., 218v., 248r., e.g. Figure 14), narrative vignettes for books such Exodus, Numbers, Job and Ezekiel (fol. 8r., 25r., 46r., 162r., e.g. Figure 15), and a fascinating typological image as the frontispiece for the Book of Proverbs (fol. 118r., Figure 16). This shows the Virgin standing between Solomon who holds a book (presumably the text of Proverbs itself, of which he is the author) with his right hand raised in blessing and a female personification who carries a cross and a Bible – conceivably Ecclesia (the Church) or Sophia, Wisdom, the subject of Proverbs (who is personified female within it, e.g. Proverbs 3:13–18). The Virgin holds a blue mandorla containing the Child, who stands inside (as if in her womb) and makes a blessing with his right hand in emulation of Solomon. Here the image of Solomon is a portrait of the book's author, but the Christian resonances of the text are signalled by the Virgin and Ecclesia, as well as the way Christ is presented – both incarnate and at the same time inside his mother. In this manuscript, very similar combinations of prefatory and epitomic visual strategies are in use but with the addition of Christian typology in an exegetic frame to show how Solomon's proverbs effectively prefigure the coming of Christ.

The immense complexity and range of possibilities for prefatory epitome in the visual culture of the Christian late antique codex may be glimpsed by looking at the manuscript of the Rossano Gospels,[63] written in Greek in the sixth century and from the Eastern Mediterranean (scholarship currently assumes Syria or Palestine),[64] which is now in the Diocesan Museum of Rossano in Calabria. This book was of about the same grandeur as the Roman Vergil – roughly half of it survives, comprising the Gospels of Matthew and most of Mark, at 188 parchment folios or 366 pages with a size of 300 × 250 mm per page but this after some later trimming.[65] But it was more lavish than the Vergil – all its pages dyed purple and its text written in silver ink, with the opening three lines of each Gospel in gold.[66] The images – of which fourteen remain and many (including the Canon Tables) have been lost – were painted on thicker parchment than the rest of the manuscript and were collected in a spectacular burst at the front,[67] with an additional evangelist portrait probably prefacing each Gospel in the original binding, of which only Mark (fol. 121r.) survives (Figure 17).[68] In particular, the Rossano Gospels, like the sixth-century Syriac Rabbula Gospels and the spectacular eighth-century full Bible known as Codex Amiatinus,[69] makes use of a model of the preliminary gathering of an extended cycle of images to give a rich visual and exegetic introduction to the book.[70]

The splay of prefatory miniatures in its surviving form (which includes some images bound in the wrong places as well as losses) represents an extended Passion cycle, starting with the Entry into Jerusalem (fol 1v.) and in its current condition ending with the Trial of Christ in two miniatures back to back on the same leaf (foll. 8r. and 8v.), intermixed with miracle scenes (the raising of Lazarus, fol. 1r.) and the healing of the blind man (fol. 7r.) and parables (the Wise and Foolish Virgins, fol. 2v. and the Good Samaritan, fol. 7v.). It has been suggested that in addition to the now lost Eusebian Canon tables, and their prefatory folio depicting the four evangelists in a ring surrounding the title to the Canons that reads 'Structure of the Canon of the harmony of the Gospels' (fol. 5r.), there may have been four leaves of initial miniatures (perhaps with Nativity narratives) and two further leaves with concluding miniatures.[71] In the eight pages that remain bound in their original order (foll. 1r.–4v.), a relatively detailed Passion narrative is outlined – the Entry to Jerusalem (fol. 1v.), the Expulsion of the Money Changers from the Temple (fol. 2r.), the Last Supper and Washing of the Feet (fol. 3r.), two versions of the Communion to the Apostles on facing pages (foll. 3v. and 4r.), and the Agony in the Garden (fol. 4v.) – but headed by the Raising of Lazarus (fol. 1r.) and with the insertion of the Parable of the Virgins (fol. 2v.). This mixture is enforced by the deliberate use of episodes from all four Gospels to create the images as a unified diatessaron.[72]

The total effect of the visual cycle at the book's opening is to summarize a series of key narrative events of scripture, through visual epitomes that are displaced from direct relation to the flow of the Gospel text or juxtaposition with the specific texts or titles to which they relate (by contrast to other illuminated sixth-century manuscripts).[73] Moreover the narrative thus created, at any rate in the elements of the cycle that survive, combines events from Christ's Passion with his miracles and his teaching in the form of parables. The visual epitomes of the two parables supply significant interpretative exegesis in that in both cases the male protagonist is represented as Christ himself (the Good Samaritan and the Bridegroom that comes for the Wise Virgins, Figure 18). This is extra-textual in relation to the Gospel narratives illustrated, but deeply embedded in traditions of Patristic commentary.[74] Since the visual epitomes allude to texts from all four Evangelists, they together enact a harmonization in visual form of the four Gospels.[75] This unification of Scripture as a prefatory pictorial sequence itself appears to have framed the Canon tables, which enact the model of harmonization in textual form and through visual tabulation. In other words, the pictorial preface of the Rossano Gospels uses the juxtaposition of Scriptural imagery to construct a visual summary of the book for which it is frontispiece and to frame the written Scripture that follows in a highly interpretative, although entirely orthodox, fashion.

If we move to the level of the individual page, then the subtlety of the typological use of pictorial epitomes becomes still more clear. Ten of the illuminated pages employ the following format. A title or *kephalaion* is written in silver letters at the top of the page and the image related to this titulus is painted in the top third of the page, with a ground line that runs across the entire width. Below that there are four bust-length portraits of Old Testament prophets, themselves identified by written inscriptions, pointing upwards; either they hold open scrolls on which their texts are written (although with some seepage across the scroll into the background)[76] or they appear atop white-framed transparent columns over which extracts from their books in the Septuagint version are placed.[77] These excerpts and their placement reflect considerable scholarly and exegetic care in their selection, and several appear – alongside a liturgical focus in the images chosen for epitome (for instance a double-page opening of the Eucharist to the Apostles (foll. 3v. and 4r.) – to be quotations used in early liturgy.[78] Let us take an example. The page with the Good Samaritan (fol. 7v, illustrating Luke 10.30–36) has the title 'Concerning one who fell among thieves' (see Figure 18).[79] The miniature shows a walled city to the left, presumably Jerusalem from which the robbed man makes his journey (Luke 10. 30), then a scene of him lying naked while Jesus himself, as the Good Samaritan, in blue tunic and gold cloak with a gold cruciform halo tends to him, accompanied by a white-robed angel holding a golden bowl with veiled hands. To the right Jesus as the Samaritan leads the naked man, whom he has seated on his donkey, to the innkeeper into whose hands he puts the two pennies (Luke 10.34–35). It is worth noting that – as in a number of the other Scriptural miniatures – more than one episode is rendered, with Christ shown twice.[80]

Beneath the ground line are the names of the four Prophets or authors of the four texts that are written out as columns below the portraits of the Prophets. They are (left to right) David, Micah, David (repeated) and Sirach (Ecclesiasticus). The bust portraits of the figures below the inscribed names all have haloes and point upwards with their right hands directly signalling the Scriptural image above. These images effectively move the epitomic discourse from the visual abbreviation of narratives with exemplary pictures illustrating its content to the defining of a book (or excerpt) through its author, something also effectively done through the ring page with Evangelist portraits that prefaced the Canons (fol. 5r.). As we saw, both strategies are used in the Roman Vergil and the Vatican Terence, but not together on the same page as part of the same total synthesis of images and texts (including the epitomic *kephalaion*). David wears a golden crown and is dressed like Christ in blue and gold (probably the most expensive pigments – lapis lazuli and gold),[81] announcing the royal heritage of the Messiah. He is by a long way the figure who appears most frequently across the surviving Rossano illuminations in this context,[82] probably reflecting the liturgical significance of the selected texts since he is invariably present as author of the Psalms. The texts beneath are from Psalm 93.17: 'Unless the Lord came to my aid, my soul would have soon dwelt in Hades'; from Micah 7.19: 'He will turn and will have compassion upon us because he is the one who desires mercy'; from Psalm 117.7: 'The Lord is my helper and I will gaze upon my enemies'; from Sirach 18.13: 'The mercy of a man is on his neighbour, but the mercy of God is on all flesh.'[83] The texts are themselves excerpted epitomes that stand figurally or typologically for the New Testament episode to which their portrayed speakers point. But the choice of four creates a dynamic of foretelling voices that emphasize respectively the perspective of the robbed traveller (to whose aid the Lord has come in the first Psalmic quotation), the action of the Samaritan as Jesus (in the second quotation about compassion), the sense of being saved by the help of the Lord (in the third passage, and the image of the naked man on the donkey) and a general commentarial reflection on the entire episode in the reflection on the mercy of man and the mercy of God in the last excerpt.[84] This immense richness of meaning is itself underpinned by the Patristic tradition that aligned the Samaritan with Christ, but which is not cited explicitly in the page. The fact that the four texts appear as if they were columns on which their authors sit gives the sense, visually, that they not only foretell but uphold the Incarnational dispensation of the upper image, which not only shows Jesus but actually illustrates his spoken words from the Gospel – the epitomic work being visually parallel to that of the odd *Eclogues* in the Roman Vergil (illustrating the frame and action depicted in the text) but in this case conflating speaker with actor, by contrast with the author portraits, which only illustrate their respective speaking voices.

Conclusion

I have argued that visual epitome was essentially a rhetorical trope in Roman culture – parallel and related to the literary model of concision for a double purpose and its relation to exemplarity. In Roman art it was one of the key features of the freedom that motivated replication (figural and non-figural), which underpins what I would describe as the discursive (rather than semantic) nature of Roman visual culture,[85] in which the decorative and the ornamental are quite as powerful as figures,[86] the frame quite as substantial as the content, from the rhetorical point of view.[87] But in keeping with the late antique focus of this collection, I have concentrated particularly on the remarkable richness of strategies whereby an epitomic image used to encapsulate text, often a frontispiece, performs radically different functions in the new medium of the illuminated codex. The multiplicity of options – including the juxtaposition of verbal epitomes with visual ones – comes to a climax in the brilliant word-and-image conflations of the greatest early Christian codices, with their use of this rhetorical structure to perform significant exegetical and interpretative work.

It is worth noting the vast quantity of issues I have not mentioned – such as the richness of visual epitome as portraiture as well as abbreviated mythology in the Roman art of the mid-to-late empire (for instance in the use of portrait heads on figures or in medallions on sarcophagi, including ones whose features are left blank, as are the heads of the philosopher and the orant in the Santa Maria Antiqua sarcophagus).[88] And, of course in turning to manuscripts, I have neglected the range of epitomic uses of Christian narratives not only on all kinds of small-scale objects from liturgical implements to reliquaries, from household cutlery and crockery to textiles and gems, but also on the large-scale painted and mosaic cycles that came to decorate church space as well as funerary contexts. That is, in addition to the relatively small-scale and specific but immensely intricate process of inventing the Christian book as a material artefact, there is a vast world of Christian visual epitome – drawing on that of pre-Christian Roman art, and developing from it in a wide range of creative ways – that would need a full account. late antiquity is of particular interest as being a crucial hinge point where rhetorical models of visual culture both remained close to and indeed drew on the long and vibrant tradition of Roman imperial art, on the one hand, but at the same time developed radically new models that would come to define the arts of the Middle Ages, on the other.

Appendix

The prefatory structure of the Books of the *Georgics* and the *Aeneid* in the Roman Vergil

The three places where the full run of these pages survives are:

Fol. 43r. end of G II/incipit G III, in a double red/brown border above and below, beneath the last 3 lines of G II on same page
Fol 43v. summary of G III in 4 lines (alternating in red and brown ink) within a red/brown ornamental border at top and bottom of page
Fol 44r. blank
Foll 44v. and 45r. picture pages
Fol. 45v. blank
Fol 46r. opening of G III (first 3 lines in red)

Fol 99r. end of A I/incipit A II, in a double red/brown border at top and bottom of page
Fol 99v. summary of A 2 in 11 lines (first one a title, alternating in red and brown ink) within a red brown ornamental border at top and bottom of page
Fol 100r. blank
Foll 100v. and 101r. picture pages
Fol. 101v. blank
Fol 102r. opening of A II (first 3 lines in red)

Fol 232v. end of A IX/incipit A X with a single red/brown border above and below, beneath the last 5 lines of A IX on same page
Fol 233r. blank
Fol 233v. summary of A X in 11 lines (first one a title, alternating in red and brown ink) within a red brown ornamental border at top and bottom of page

Fol 234r. blank
Foll 234v./235r. picture pages
Fol 235v. blank
Fol 236r. opening of A X (first 3 lines in red)

Notes

* This paper was commissioned by the editors for this volume. I gave versions in person before the Covid-19 crisis at the Ethical Reading Seminar run by Constanze Güthenke and Hindy Najman in Oxford and during the crisis at the Late Antique and Byzantine Art seminar organized by Robert Nelson and Vasileios Marinis at Yale via Zoom. I am grateful to all who participated, commented and sent me notes by email – they helped me sharpen both my argument and my observations.

1. Proverb, first attested in 1927, according to the *Oxford Dictionary of Quotations and Proverbs* (proverb 726).
2. See OED online under 'epitome'. For epitome in early modern English literature, see Wheatley 2011: esp. 1–38 and Osorio Whewell 2019 with interesting reflections on issues of paratextuality.
3. E.g. Lowrie and Lüdemann 2015; Goldhill 2017; Roller 2018; Langlands 2018; Rood, Atack and Philips 2020: 145–68. Oddly, this literature does not address issues of abbreviation or epitome that always accompany the choice and use of examples.
4. On synopsis, see e.g. Stansbury O'Donnell 1999: 5–7, 89–91; Squire 2011: 252–9. Recently on the visual figuration of Ovidian narratives, see Salvo 2015.
5. E.g. Pearson 2015: 158–62, or Elsner 2020a: 19–22.
6. Narcissus: Ovid, *Metamorphoses* 3. 339–510; Hodske 2007: 166–71 for a repertoire of images.
7. Notable earlier accounts include Opelt 1962. More recently, see Risch 2003; Gärtner and Eigler 2004; Nosarti 2009: 30–42; Horster and Reitz 2010; Gasti 2015: 345–67; Schwedler, Schwitter and Dusil 2017; Borgna 2018: 47–105; Grethlein 2019; Manafis 2020.
8. See Dubischar 2010: 40–8.
9. For the revolution from roll to codex, see Turner 1977; Roberts and Skeat 1983; Blanck 1992: 75–101; Cavallo 1997 and 2010; Mazal 1999: 125–51; Szirmai 1999: 7–94; Schipke 2013: 143–52; Boudelis 2018. For the Christian book in particular, see e.g. Halbertal 1997; Gamble 2000; Stanton 2004; Hurtado 2006: 43–94; Grafton and Williams 2006; Klingshirn and Safran 2009; Wallraff 2013; Stroumsa 2014.
10. E.g. Luhtala 2010.
11. For instance, in Latin Livy, with e.g. Chaplin 2010 and Horster 2017; in Greek Dio Cassius with e.g. Mallan 2013.
12. See for instance Dubischar 2010: 48–50 (on Galen and self-synopsis); Müller 2010; Whitmarsh 2010: 316–19; Dyck 2010; Ingelbert 2010.
13. See e.g. the *progymnasmata* of Aelius Theon 16, ed. Patillon and Bolognesi 1997: 110–12.
14. See Patillon 1997; Chiron 2007: 101–4.
15. Anaximenes of Lampsachus, *ars rhetorica* 6, in Spengel 1853: 209; Fuhrmann 2000: 30; Chiron 2002: 38.

16. Tryphon, *de tropis* in Spengel 1856: 202.

17. See Patillon 2002, vol. 1: viii–x.

18. Spengel 1853: 500; also Patillon 2002, vol. 1: 151–2.

19. See Halm 1863: 17; Barabino 1967: 192; Brooks 1970: 33.

20. Halm 1863: 65; d'Angelo 2001: 56 and 93–4 for discussion.

21. Julius Victor, *ars rhetorica* 419, 423–24, in Giomini and Celentano 1980: 65, 71–2; Marius Victorinus, *commenta in Ciceronis rhetorica* 1.20 and 22, in Halm 1863: 204–5, 210 and Ippolito 2006: 90–1, 99; see also Riesenweber 2015, vol. 1: 13–17 for authorship.

22. Alcuin (Albinus Magister), *disputatio de rhetorica et de virtutibus* 23–25: Halm, 1863: 536–7; translation in Howell 1965: 102–5. Note section 23: 'reduce the speech to main points which are brief in statement, comprehensive in scope and few in number . . .'

23. Anonymous, *excerpta rhetorica ex codice Parisino 7530*: Halm, 1863: 588; http://digiliblt.lett.unipmn.it/upload/pdf/DLT000178.pdf at p. 3 'de historia'.

24. See e.g. Elsner and Squire 2016. The uses of images (*Imagines*) placed in particular spaces (*loci*) in the instructions for the art of memory in Roman textbooks is a clear example of visual epitome being instrumentalized: see e.g. the anonymous *ad Herennium* 3.29.

25. For allegorical signification of myths on sarcophagi, see e.g. Newby 2016: 273–319.

26. See e.g. Raeck 1992: 71–8; Borg 2013: 162–3, 164–78, 209–11; Borg 2014; Allen 2022.

27. Mosaics: Dunbabin 1978: 38–45 (although unfortunately focused around 'decline'); Muth 1998: 282–9. Sarcophagi: Sichtermann 1966: 82–7; Brandenburg 1967: 210 and 240–3; Blome 1978; Wrede 1981: 171–5; Koch and Sichtermann 1982: 615–17; Koortbojian 1995: 138–41; Muth 2004; Borg 2013: 161–211; Borg 2014: 328–51; Allen 2022 *passim*.

28. For instance: Smith 1988; Hughes 2009.

29. This is archetypally true of the so-called Iliac tablets of the first century BC, where a single minuscule picture represents a whole book of the Iliad. See the recent accounts of Squire 2011, and Petrain 2014.

30. See esp. Hölscher 2004: 2–3, 86–101, 113–16, 125–7. For some discussion, see Elsner 2006: 270–6, 293–4.

31. See Pearson 2015: 151–8 on ephebic figures and 159–60 on 'accoutrements, background scenery and subordinate figures to build up layers of meaning' and to 'make a precise mythological character identifiable'; Elsner and Squire 2016: 191–203. A handy collection of illustrated examples from Pompeii are available in Hodske, 2007.

32. On Christian typology in art, see Thümmel 1985; Schrenk 1995; Elsner 1995: 271–87; Mohnhaupt 2000; Tkacz 2002: 51–62; Elsner 2014b: 338–47.

33. See Sichtermann 1992: 54–5 (under 'Robert nr. 92') and https://www.britishmuseum.org/research/collection_online/collection_object_details.aspx?assetId=376347001&objectId=459806&partId=1. There is a rich discussion including Gerke 1940, 17–19 and 331 (no. II, 27); Sichtermann 1966: 68–75; Fittschen 1969; Engemann 1973: 29–30; Walker 1990, no. 36; Koortbojian 1995: 91–2, 137–41; Birks 2013: no. 576 and pp. 146–7.

34. See esp. Sichtermann 1966: 68–75. Other isolated Endymion sarcophagi include that in the Palazzo Braschi (with Sichtermann 1992, no. 102), while other isolated Ariadne sarcophagi include one in Naples (with Matz 1969, no. 229 and Birks 2013, no. 559) and one in Copenhagen (with Wrede 1981, no. 54 and Birks 2013, no. 21).

35. See Zanker and Ewald 2012: 100–2.

36. See Bovini. and Brandenburg 1967, no. 747; Engemann, 1973: 70–6; Huskinson 2008: 290–2; Zanker and Ewald 2012: 262–3.

37. Codex Medicus Graecus 1, Austrian National Library: with Mazal 1998–9.

38. See e.g. Carder 1978.

39. For mss. illustration within the larger pattern of relations between image and text in Roman culture, see Squire and Elsner forthcoming.

40. See Lowden 2007; Boudelis 2018: 97–145.

41. See Effenberger 1977; Bertelli 1985; Wright 1992: 15–34 and 131–40 for codicological reconstruction; Wright 2001 and the fine digitized version at https://digi.vatlib.it/view/MSS_Vat.lat.3867.

42. See Wright 1992: 17–23.

43. For these reasons and because my topic is visual epitome, I will not engage in the discussion about the extent to which the images of the *Roman Vergil* come from stock themes or are copies of some lost earlier exemplar. See Wright 1992: 58–9, 70–3, 75–6, 80–1, 84, 89–90, 93, 96–7, 101–2, 106, 108–9, 114, 118–19, 122–4.

44. This is one reason why I am hesitant about the 'illustration' model for studying the images in manuscripts (on which e.g. Penny Small 2003: 118–54). For more on prefatory images within the structure, apparatus and reception of the early codex, see Elsner 2020b.

45. Wright systematically falls into such errors: e.g. Wright 2001: 19 'the illustration . . . does not correspond to any specific moment in the narrative and so must be thought of as an improvisation out of stock elements . . . rendered with less than complete understanding', or 20 'taking the easy path by avoiding mythological content'. This kind of thing is nonsense, fundamentally (and anachronistically) misconstruing what the illuminations are doing.

46. This pattern appears, in cases where there have not been losses or mis-bindings, for Georgic III, fol. 43r. to 46r.; *Aeneid* 2, fol. 99r. to 102r.; *Aeneid* 10, fol. 233r. to 236r. See the Appendix.

47. My thanks to Tobias Reinhardt for this suggestion.

48. Wright 2001: 33.

49. The rainbow picks up that raised by Iris in fol. 74v. from Book 9.

50. The quiver on the ground with arrows inside between figures is an odd repeated fixture of a number of the surviving *Aeneid* miniatures, rather like the rustic hut of the *Eclogues*. It recurs in the surviving images from Books 7 (fol 163r.), relatively comprehensible in the shooting of the stag, and very oddly between Iris and Turnus in the image from Book 9 (fol 74r.)

51. Wright 2001: 43. Wright places Aeneas as the figure on the left with the Phrygian cap and the bow, although he admits there is no bow in the text. Thanks to Christina Shuttleworth Kraus for discussion of the episode and miniature.

52. The problem here is that fol. 188v. is certainly a left-side opening, as is fol. 74 r. which is most likely from Book 9. Only one of these could have occupied that position, which is the strong argument for pushing 188 v. to Book 12. Of course, it is not impossible that, exceptionally, Book 9 might have had two images painted for the left-hand side and then bound together either consecutively or to face each other, but this strays into realms of speculation that cannot be tested or proven.

53. See e.g. Kainia 2016: 82–8 on the 'notional ekphrasis' in Georgic III.1–48, which has no place in the manuscript's visual programme . . .

54. See e.g. Rees 2004; Ziolkowski and Putnam 2008; for bibliography see: http://virgil.org/bibliography/

55. For a bibliography of Servius, see http://virgil.org/bibliography/.

56. On the cento see e.g. Polara 1990; McGill 2005; Bažil 2009; Formisano and Sogno 2010; Pelttari 2014: 96–112; Hinds 2014, 171–98; Elsner 2017.

57. See Webber Jones and Rufus Morey 1931; Wright 2006; with https://digi.vatlib.it/view/MSS_Vat.lat.3868 and http://gallica.bnf.fr/ark:/12148/btv1b84525513/f1.image.

58. Jones and Morey 1931, plates 1–4; Wright 2006: 6–7.

59. Jones and Morey 1931, plates 7–8 (Andria), 323–4 (Heauton timoumenos), 448–9 (Adelphoe), 582–3 (Hecyra), 678–9 (Phormio); Wright 2006: 8–9 (Andria), 66–7 (Heauton timoumenos), 94–5 (Adelphoe), 126–7 (Hecyra), 148–9 (Phormio). The aedicule for Eunuchus appears to have been lost from the original late antique exemplar before it could be copied: see Wright 2006: 35.

60. See Dodwell 2000: 1–100, for some discussion.

61. E.g. Grant 1973: 90.

62. See Sörries 1991 and Sörries 1993: 89–93 with plates 47–50.

63. The fundamental literature includes: Gebhardt and von Harnack 1880; Haseloff 1898; Muñoz 1907; Ainalov, 1961: 108–24 (originally published in Russian, 1900); Cavallo, Gribomont and Loerke 1987 (with long review by Sevrugian 1989); Sevrugian 1990; Sörries 1993: 70–7, plates 38–40. See also http://www.codexrossanensis.it/en/.

64. But see the doubts about such assumptions (doubts with which I agree) in Lowden 1999: 21.

65. Details in Cavallo 1987: 24.

66. Cavallo 1987: 27.

67. The most comprehensive discussion of the prefatory sequence with codicological reconstruction is by Loerke 1987: 111–14. Thickness of parchment: Cavallo 1987: 24 and Loerke 1987: 109.

68. The portrait of St Mark, inspired by an unnamed female personification (who may be Sophia), is the only image without silver ink – both the title and the scroll on which he writes are inscribed in a red-orange ink, apparently cinnabar: see Bicchieri 2014: 14151, https://arxiv.org/ftp/arxiv/papers/1404/1404.6414.pdf. On the basis of the different ink and of the page's palaeography, some have argued that this image is not original to the book but a later pastiche (by no means unimpressively produced and of high quality): see Kresten and Prato 1985; Cutler 1989: 407; Lowden 1999: 20–1; Krueger 2004: 220, n. 67 (*contra* e.g. Sörries 1993: 76 and Loerke 1995). Recent scientific analysis has argued that the page is authentic and was not afflicted by the invasive and irreversible restoration to which the prefatory group of miniatures were subjected in 1917–19: see Bicchieri 2014: 14156.

69. On the Rabbula Gospels (Florence, Biblioteca Medicea Laurenziana, MS syr. Plut. 1.56), see Cecchelli, Furlani, and Salmi 1959; Bernabò 2008 and 2014. On Codex Amiatinus (Florence, Biblioteca Medicea Laurenziana, MS Amiatino 1), see Gameson 2018 and Chazelle 2019.

70. The placement and function of the Eusebian canon tables in Gospel Books is key to this model of a parade of frontispiece miniatures, which then appears to have acquired extra images beyond the arcades of the tables themselves. On the canon tables, see now Bausi, Reudenbach and Wimmer 2020. For rich discussion in relation to the eclectic selection of images in the preliminary gathering of Amiatinus, see Chazelle 2019: 311–449.

71. Loerke 1987: 111–14.

72. Loerke 1987: 110–11 for details and discussion.

73. For instance, the forty-three remaining folios from the Gospel of Matthew of the once huge Sinope Gospels, now in Paris, written entirely in gold on purple parchment, where on the five

illuminated pages the images appear at the bottom margin and in direct relation both to the Biblical episode illustrated and to the *kephalaion* or chapter title at the head of the page (which were supplied as organizing paratexts to Scripture in the fourth century). See e.g. Omont 1900; Muñoz 1907; Grabar 1948; Sörries 1993: 78–80; Lowden 1999: 21–4. One might also cite the two great sixth-century Genesis mss that are known to us, the Cotton Genesis (all but destroyed by fire in 1731) and the Vienna Genesis, both with half page illustrations interspersed in the text: see (with their bibliographies) Mazal 1980; Weitzmann and Kessler 1986; Sörries 1993,: 45–66; Lowden 1999: 13–18.

74. See Loerke 1987: 130 and 144 for some examples, although there are many more.

75. Loerke, 1987: 110.

76. For the view that they are scrolls, see Weitzmann 1977: 89; Loerke 1987: 122; Lowden 1999: 20. In the Sinope fragment, similar Old Testament figures as busts appear above similar framed texts alongside the miniatures. There the case for the frames representing scrolls rather than columns is stronger because the Prophets appear to be holding onto the thick bar at the top. But in the Rossano Codex their hands appear to be resting on the top as if on a parapet.

77. See Loerke 1987 for fullest discussion of the imagery; on the texts see now Hixson 2016.

78. See esp. Hixson 2016: 541; also Loerke 1975: 69, 72–3; Loerke 1987: 126–45.

79. περὶ *τοῦ ἐμπεσόντος εἰς τοὺς λῃστάς* (the italics here being a direct quotation from Luke 10.36); for transcription see Hixson 2016: 512, also 537. On the page's imagery, see e.g. Wetizmann 1977: 93–4; Loerke 1987: 143–5; Sevrugian 1990: 41–3

80. Other examples are fol 3r. (the Last Supper and Washing of the Feet, again with Jesus shown twice), fol. 4v. (the Agony in the Garden, with Jesus shown twice) and fol. 7r. on the reverse of the Samaritan page (the Healing of the Blind and the Washing at the Pool of Siloam).

81. See the table at Bicchieri 2014: 14150.

82. Twice at fol. 1r., fol. 1v., fol. 2r., fol. 3v., fol. 4r., fol. 4v., fol. 7r. fol. 7v.; three times at fol. 2v., fol. 3r. For more on David and pairing, see Loerke 1975: 69; Hixson 2016: 539–40. On the consistency of the David portrait across 22 instances, see Loerke 1987: 122.

83. Loerke 1987: 130; Hixson 2016: 512 (whose version I quote).

84. For some discussion, see Loerke 1987: 145; Hixson 2016: 533–4.

85. On art as rhetoric in Roman culture see especially Elsner 2014a.

86. On issues of Ornament, see Dietrich and Squire 2018.

87. On the question of framing, see Platt and Squire 2017.

88. For instance, on sarcophagi and portraiture, recently and in a long literature: Newby 2011; Studer-Karlen 2012; Birk 2013. On blank heads: Huskinson 1998; Russell 2013: 301–7; Elsner 2018.

Works cited

Ainalov, D. (1961), *The Hellenistic Origins of Byzantine Art*, New Brunswick: Rutgers University Press.

Allen, M. (2022), *The Death of Myth on Roman Sarcophagi: Allegory and Visual Narrative in Late Antiquity*, Cambridge: Cambridge University Press.

d'Angelo, R., ed. (2001), *Carmen de figuris et schematibus*, Hildesheim: Olms.

Barabino, G., ed. (1967), *P. Rutilii Lupi, Schemata dianoeas et lexeos*, Genoa: Istituto di filologia classica e medioevale.

Bausi, A., B. Reudenbach and H. Wimmer, eds (2020), *Canones: The Art of Harmony: The Canon Tables of the Four Gospels*, Berlin: De Gruyter.

Bažil, M. (2009), *'Centones Christiani': Métamorphoses d'une forme intertextuelle dans la poésie latine chrétienne de l'antiquité tardive*, Paris: Institut d'études augustiniennes.

Bernabò, M., ed. (2008), *Il Tetravangelo di Rabbula: Firenze, Biblioteca medicea laurenziana, Plut. 1.56; l'illustrazione del Nuovo Testamento nella Siria del VI secolo*, Rome: Edizioni di storia e letteratura.

Bernabò, M. (2014), 'The Miniatures in the Rabbula Gospels: Postscripta to a Recent Book', *Dumbarton Oaks Papers*, 68: 343–58.

Bertelli, C. (1985), *Vergilius Romanus*, Zurich: Belser.

Bicchieri, M. (2014), 'The Purple Codex Rossanensis: Spectroscopic Characterization and First Evidence of the Use of the Elderberry Lake in a 6th Century Manuscript', *Environmental Science and Pollution Research* 21: 14146–157.

Birks, S. (2013), *Depicting the Dead: Self-Representation and Commemoration on Roman Sarcophagi with Portraits*, Aarhus: Aarhus University Press.

Blanck, H. (1992), *Das Buch in der Antike*, Munich: Beck.

Blome, P. (1978), 'Zur Umgestaltung griechischer Mythen in der römischen Sepulkralkunst. Alkestis-, Protesilaos- und Proserpinasarkophage', *Mitteilungen des Deutschen Archäologischen Instituts, Abteilung Rom* 85: 435–57.

Borg, B (2013), *Crisis and Ambition: Tombs and Burial Customs in Third-Century* CE *Rome*, Oxford: Oxford University Press.

Borg, B (2014), 'Rhetoric and Art in Third Century AD Rome', in J. Elsner and M. Meyer (eds), *Art and Rhetoric in Roman Culture*, 235–55, Cambridge: Cambridge University Press.

Borgna, A. (2018), *Ripensare la storia universale: Giustino e l'*Epitome *delle* Storie Filippiche *di Pompeo Trogo*, Hildesheim: Olms.

Boudelis, G. (2018), *The Codex and Crafts in Late Antiquity*, New York: Bard Graduate Center.

Bovini, G. and H. Brandenburg (1967), *Repertorium der christlich-antiken Sarkophage I. Rom und Ostia*, Wiesbaden: Steiner.

Brandenburg, H. (1967), 'Meerwesensarkophage und Clipeus-Motiv', *Jahrbuch des Deutschen Archäologischen Instituts* 82: 195–245.

Brooks, E., ed. (1970), *P. Rutilii Lupi, De figuris sententiarum et elocutionis,* Leiden: Brill.

Carder, J. (1978), *Art Historical Problems of a Roman Land-Surveying Manuscript*, New York: Garland.

Cavallo, G. (1987), 'The Purple Codex of Rossano: Book, Object, Symbol', in G. Cavallo, J. Gibromont and W. Loerke, *Codex purpureus Rossanensis, Museo dell'Arcivescovado, Rossano calabro: commentarium*, 23–41, Rome: Salerno.

Cavallo, G. (1997), 'Du volumen au codex: la lecture dans le monde romain', in G. Cavallo and R. Chartier (eds), *Histoire de la lecture dans le monde occidental*, 85–114, Paris: Seuil.

Cavallo, G. (2010), 'Libri, lettura e biblioteche nella tarda antichitá: un panorama e qualche riflessione', *Antiquité Tardive* 18: 9–19.

Cavallo, G., J. Gribomont and W. Loerke (1987), *Codex purpureus Rossanensis, Museo dell'Arcivescovado, Rossano calabro: commentarium*, Rome: Salerno.

Cecchelli, C., G. Furlani, and M. Salmi (1959), *The Rabbula Gospels: Facsimile Edition of the Miniatures of the Syriac ms. Plut. 1, 56 in the Medicaean-Laurentian Library*, Olton: Urs Graf.

Chaplin, J. (2010), 'The Livian Periochae and the Last Republican Writer', in M. Horster and C. Reitz (eds), *Condensing Texts – Condensed Texts*, 451–67, Stuttgart: Franz Steiner Verlag.

Chazelle, C. (2019), *The Codex Amiatinus and Its 'Sister' Bibles*, Leiden: Brill.

Chiron, P., ed. (2002), *Pseudo-Aristote, Rhétorique à Alexandre,* Paris: Belles Lettres.

Chiron, P. (2007), 'The Rhetoric to Alexander', in I. Worthington (ed.), *A Companion to Greek Rhetoric*, Oxford: Oxford University Press, 90–105.

Cutler, A. (1989), 'The End of Antiquity in Two Illuminated Manuscripts', *Journal of Roman Archaeology* 2: 401–12.

Dietrich, N. and M. Squire, eds (2018), *Ornament and Figure in Greek and Roman Art*, Berlin: De Gruyter.

Dodwell, C. (2000), *Anglo-Saxon Gestures and the Roman Stage*, Cambridge: Cambridge University Press.

Dubischar, M. (2010), 'Survival of the Most Condensed? Auxiliary Texts, Communications Theory and Condensation of Knowledge', in M. Horster and C. Reitz (eds), *Condensing Texts – Condensed Texts*, 39–67, Stuttgart: Franz Steiner Verlag.

Dunbabin, K. (1978), *The Mosaics of Roman North Africa: Studies in Iconography and Patronage*, Oxford: Oxford University Press.

Dyck, A. (2010), 'Cicero's Abridgement of His Speeches for Publication', in M. Horster and C. Reitz (eds), *Condensing Texts – Condensed Texts*, 369–74, Stuttgart: Franz Steiner Verlag.

Effenberger, C. (1977), 'Die Miniaturen des Vergilius Romanus, Codex Vat. Lat. 3867', *Byzantinische Zeitschrift* 70: 58–90.

Elsner J. (1995), *Art and the Roman Viewer*, Cambridge: Cambridge University Press.

Elsner, J. (2006), 'Classicism in Roman Art', in J. Porter (ed.), *Classical Pasts: The Classical Traditions of Greece and Rome*, 270–97, Princeton: Princeton University Press.

Elsner, J. (2014a), 'Art and Rhetoric in Roman Culture: Introduction', in J. Elsner and M. Meyer, *Art and Rhetoric in Roman Culture*, 1–34, Cambridge: Cambridge University Press.

Elsner, J. (2014b), 'Rational, Passionate and Appetitive: The Psychology of Rhetoric and the Transformation of Visual Culture from non-Christian to Christian Sarcophagi in the Roman World', in J. Elsner and M. Meyer, *Art and Rhetoric in Roman Culture*, 316–34, Cambridge: Cambridge University Press.

Elsner, J. (2017), 'Late Narcissus: Classicism and Culture in a Late Roman *Cento*', in J. Hernandez Lobato and J. Elsner (eds), *The Poetics of Late Latin Literature*, 176–205, Oxford: Oxford University Press.

Elsner, J. (2018), 'The Embodied Object Recensions of the Dead on Roman Sarcophagi', *Art History* 41: 546–65.

Elsner, J. (2020a), 'Mutable, Flexible, Fluid: Papyrus Drawings for Textiles and Replication in Roman Art', *The Art Bulletin* 102.3: 7–27.

Elsner, J. (2020b), 'Beyond Eusebius: Prefatory Images and the Early Book', in A. Bausi, B. Reudenbach and H. Wimmer (eds), *Canones: The Art of Harmony: The Canon Tables of the Four Gospels*, 99–128, Berlin: De Gruyter.

Elsner, J. and M. Meyer, eds (2014), *Art and Rhetoric in Roman Culture*, Cambridge: Cambridge University Press.

Elsner, J. and M. Squire (2006), 'Vision and Memory', in M. Squire (ed.), *Sight and the Ancient Senses*, 188–212, London: Routledge.

Engemann, J. (1973), *Untersuchungen zur Sepulkralsymbolik der späteren römischen Kaiserzeit*, Münster: Aschendorff.

Fittschen, K. (1969), 'Review of Sichtermann (1966)', *Göttingische Gelehrte Anzeigen* 221: 41–9.

Formisano, M. and C. Sogno (2010), 'Petite poésie portable: The Latin Cento in Its Late Antique Context', in M. Horster and C. Reitz (eds), *Condensing Texts – Condensed Texts*, 375–94, Stuttgart: Franz Steiner Verlag.

Fuhrmann, M. ed. (2000), *Anaximenes, Ars rhetorica*, Leipzig: Teubner.

Gamble, H. (2000), *Books and Readers in the Early Church: A History of Early Christian Texts*. New Haven, CT: Yale University Press.

Gameson, R. (2018), 'Codex Amiatinus: Making and Meaning', *Jarrow Lecture 2017*, Jarrow: The Parish Church Council of St. Paul's Church.

Gärtner, H. and U. Eigler (2004), 'Epitome', *Brill's New Pauly* 4: 1154–6.
Gasti, F. (2015), *'La forma breve della prosa nella storiografia latina d'età imperiale tarda'*, *Koinonia* 39: 345–67.
Gebhardt, O. and A von Harnack (1880), *Evangeliorum codex Graecus purpureus Rossanensis S, seine Entdeckung, sein wissenschaftlicher und künstlicher Wert*, Leipzig: Giesecke and Devrient.
Gerke, F. (1940), *Die christlichen Sarkophage der vorkonstantinischen Zeit*, Berlin: De Gruyter.
Giomini, R. and M. Celentano, eds (1980), *Julius Victor, ars rhetorica*, Leipzig: Teubner.
Goldhill, S. (2017), 'The Limits of the Case Study: Exemplarity and the Reception of Classical Literature', *New Literary History* 48: 415–36.
Grabar, A. (1948), *Les peintures de l'évangéliaire de Sinope*, Paris: Bibliothèque nationale.
Grafton, A. and M. Williams (2006), *Christianity and the Transformation of the Book: Origen, Eusebius, and the Library of Caesarea*, Cambridge, MA: Harvard University Press.
Grant, J. (1973), 'T and the Miniatures of Terence', *Classical Quarterly* 23: 88–103.
Grethlein, J. (2019), 'Epitome und Erzählung. Die Rekapitulationen am Ende der Odyssee', *Poetica* 50: 169–92.
Halbertal, M. (1997), *People of the Book: Canon, Meaning, and Authority*, Cambridge, MA: Harvard University Press.
Halm, C., ed. (1863), *Rhetores Latini Minores*, Leipzig: Teubner.
Haseloff, A. (1898), *Codex purpureus Rossanensis, die Miniaturen der griechischen Evangelien-Handschrift in Rossano*, Berlin: Giesecke and Devrient.
Hinds, S. (2014), 'The Self-Conscious Cento', in M. Formisano and T. Fuhrer (eds), *Décadence: 'Decline and Fall' or 'Other Antiquity'*, 171–98, Heidelberg: Winter.
Hixson, E. (2016), 'Forty Excerpts from the Greek Old Testament in Codex Rossanensis (Rossano, Museo Diocesano, S.N.), a Sixth-Century Gospels Manuscript', *Journal of Theological Studies* 67: 507–41.
Hodske, J. (2007), *Mythologische Bildthemen in den Häusern Pompejis: die Bedeutung der zentralen Mythenbilder für die Bewohner Pompejis*, Ruhpolding: Rutzen.
Hölscher, T. (2004), *The Language of Images in Roman Art*, Cambridge: Cambridge Unversity Press.
Horster, M. and C. Reitz, eds (2010), *Condensing Texts – Condensed Texts*, Suttgart: Steiner.
Horster, M. (2017), 'Livius-Epitome: Ein spätantiker Blick auf die (kurzgefasse) römische Republik', in G. Schwedler, R. Schwitter and S. Dusil (2017) *Exzerpieren – Kompilieren – Tradieren: Trasfortmationen des Wissens zwischen Spätantike und Fühmittelalter*, 25–48, Berlin: De Gruyter.
Howell, W. (1965), *The Rhetoric of Alcuin and Charlemagne*, New York: Russell and Russell.
Hughes, J. (2009), 'Personifications and the Ancient Viewer: The Case of the Hadrianeum "Nations"', *Art History* 32: 1–20.
Hurtado, L. (2006), *The Earliest Christian Artifacts: Manuscripts and Christian Origins*, Grand Rapids: Eerdmans.
Huskinson, J. (1998), '"Unfinished Portrait Heads" on Later Roman Sarcophagi: Some New Perspectives', *Papers of the British School at Rome* 46: 129–58.
Huskinson, J. (2008), 'Degrees of Differentiation: Role Models on Early Christian Sarcophagi', *Memoirs of the American Academy in Rome. Supplementary Volumes* 7, *Role Models in the Roman World. Identity and Assimilation*, Ann Arbor: University of Michigan Press, 287–99.
Ingelbert, H. (2010), 'Lactance abbréviateur de lui-même', in M. Horster and C. Reitz (eds), *Condensing Texts – Condensed Texts*, 491–515, Stuttgart: Franz Steiner Verlag.
Ippolito, A, ed. (2006), *Marii Victorini, Explanationes in Ciceronis rhetoricam*, Turnhout: Brepols.
Kainia, R. (2016), '"Unbounded Views": Incomplete Ekphrasis and the Visual Imagination in Virgil' *Ramus* 45: 74–101.
Klingshirn, W. and L. Safran, eds (2007), *The Early Christian Book*, Washington, DC: Catholic University of America Press.
Koch, G. and H. Sichtermann (1982), *Römische Sarkophage*, Munich: Beck.

Koortbojian, M. (1995), *Myth, Meaning and Memory on Roman Sarcophagi*, Berkeley: University of California Press.

Kresten, O. and G. Prato (1985), 'Die Miniatur des Evangelisten Markus im Codex Purpureus Rossanensis: Eine spätere Einfügung', *Römische Historische Mitteilungen* 27: 381–403.

Krueger, D. (2004), *Writing and Holiness: The Practice of Authorship in the Early Christian East*, Philadelphia: University of Pennsylvania Press.

Langlands, R. (2018), *Exemplary Ethics in Ancient Rome*, Cambridge: Cambridge University Press.

Loerke, W. (1975), 'The Monumental Miniature', in K. Weitzmann, W. Loerke, E. Kitzinger and H. Buchtal (eds), *The Place of Book Illumination in Byzantine Art*, 61–97, Princeton, NJ: Princeton University Press.

Loerke, W. (1987), 'The Rossano Gospels: The Miniatures', in G. Cavallo, J. Gribomont and W. Loerke (eds), *Codex purpureus Rossanensis, Museo dell'Arcivescovado, Rossano calabro: commentarium*, 109–73, Rome: Salerno.

Loerke, W. (1995), 'Incipits and Author Portraits in Greek Gospel Books: Some Observations', in D. Mouriki et al. (eds), *Byzantine East, Latin West*, 377–81, Princeton, NJ: Princeton University Press.

Lowden, J. (1999), 'The Beginnings of Biblical Illustration', in J. Williams (ed.), *Imaging the Early Medieval Bible*, 9–60, University Park: Pennsylvania State University Press.

Lowden, J. (2007), 'The Word Made Visible: The Exterior of the Early Christian Book as Visual Argument', in Klingshirn, W. and L. Safran (eds), *The Early Christian Book*, 13–47, Washington, DC: Catholic University of America Press.

Lowrie, M. and S. Lüdemann eds (2015), *Exemplarity and Singularity: Thinking Through Particulars in Philosophy, Literature, and Law*, London: Routledge.

Luhtala, A. (2010), 'Late Schulgrammatik and the Emergence of Grammatical Commentaries', in M. Horster and C. Reitz (eds), *Condensing Texts – Condensed Texts*, 209–43, Stuttgart: Franz Steiner Verlag.

McGill, S. (2005), *Virgil Recomposed: The Mythological and Secular Centos in Antiquity*, Oxford: Oxford University Press.

Mallan, C. (2013), 'The Style, Method and Programme of Xiphilinus' *Epitome* of Cassius Dio's *Roman History*' *Greek, Roman and Byzantine Studies* 53: 610–44.

Manafis, R. (2020), *(Re)writing History in Byzantium: A Critical Study of Collections of Historical Excerpts*, Abingdon: Routledge.

Matz, F. (1969), *Die Dionysischen Sarkophage 3, ASR 4.3* Berlin: Mann.

Mazal, O. (1980), *Kommentar zur Wiener Genesis: Faksimile-Ausgabe der Codex theol. gr. 31 der Österreichischen Nationalbibliothek in Wien*, Frankfurt am Main: Insel-Verlag.

Mazal, O. (1998–9), *Der Wiener Dioskurides*, 2 vols., Graz: Akademische Druck- und Verlagsanstalt.

Mazal, O. (1999), *Geschichte der Buchkultur. Band I: Griechisch-römische Antike*, Graz: Akademische Druck- und Verlagsanstalt.

Mohnhaupt, B. (2000), *Beziehungsgeflechte: typologische Kunst des Mittelalters*, Bern: Lang.

Müller, M. (2010), 'Die Epitome: Das Bessere Original?', in M. Horster and C. Reitz (eds), *Condensing Texts – Condensed Texts*, 69–89, Stuttgart: Franz Steiner Verlag.

Muñoz, A. (1907), *Il codice purpureo di Rossano e il frammento sinopense*, Rome: Danesi.

Muth, S. (1998), *Erleben von Raum – Leben im Raum: Zur Funktion mythologischer Mosaikbilder in der römisch-kaiserzeitlichen Wohnarchitektur*, Heidelberg: Verlag Archäologie und Geschichte.

Muth, S. (2004), 'Drei statt vier. Zur Deutung der Feldherrsarkophage', *Archäologischer Anzeiger*: 263–73.

Newby, Z. (2011), 'In the Guise of Gods and Heroes: Portrait Heads on Roman Mythological Sarcophagi', in J. Elsner and J. Huskinson (eds), *Life, Death and Representation: Some New Work on Roman Sarcophagi*, 189–227, Berlin: De Gruyter.

Newby, Z. (2016), *Greek Myths in Roman Art and Culture: Imagery, Values and Identity in Italy, 50 BC-AD 250*, Cambridge: Cambridge University Press.

Nosarti, L. (2009), *Forme brevi della letteratura latina*, Bologna: Pàtron.

Omont, H. (1900), *Notice sur un très ancient manuscript grec de l'évangile de Saint Matthieu*, Paris: Imprimerie Nationale.

Opelt, I. (1962), 'Epitome' *Reallexicon für Antike und Christentum* 5: 944–73, Stuttgart: Hiersemann.

Osorio Whewell, E. (2019), 'For the Sake of Arguments: Reading the Headnotes to the *Fairie Queene*', *The Review of English Studies* 71: 460–85.

Patillon, M. (1997), 'Aristote, Corax, Anaximène et les autres dans la *Rhétorique à Alexandre*', *Revue des études grecques* 110: 104–25.

Patillon, M. and G. Bolognesi, eds (1997), *Aelius Théon, Progymnasmata,* Paris: Belles Lettres.

Patillon, M., ed. (2002), *Pseudo-Aelius Aristide, Ars rhetorica*, 2 vols., Paris: Belles Lettres.

Pearson, S. (2015), 'Bodies of Meaning: Figural Repetition in Pompeian Painting', in S. Lepinski and S. McFadden (eds), *Beyond Iconography: Materials, Methods, and Meaning in Ancient Surface Decoration,* 149–66, Boston: Archaeological Institute of America.

Pelttari, A. (2014), *The Space that Remains: Reading Latin Poetry in Late Antiquity*, Ithaca, NY: Cornell University Press.

Penny Small, J. (2003), *The Parallel Worlds of Classical Art and Text*, Cambridge: Cambridge University Press.

Petrain, D. (2014), *Homer in Stone: The* Tabulae Iliacae *in Their Roman Context*, Cambridge: Cambridge University Press.

Platt, V. and M. Squire, eds (2017), *Framing Antiquity*, Cambridge: Cambridge University Press.

Polara, G. (1990), 'I centoni', in G. Cavallo, P. Fedeli and A. Giardina (eds), *Lo spazio letterario di Roma antica: v.3. La ricezione del testo*, 245–75, Rome: Salerno.

Raeck, W. (1992), *Modernisierte Mythen: Zum Umgang der Spätantike mit klassischen Bildthemen*, Stuttgart: Steiner.

Rees, R., ed. (2004), *Romane memento: Vergil in the Fourth Century*, London: Duckworth.

Riesenweber, T., ed. (2015), *C. Marius Victorinus, Commenta in Ciceronis Rhetorica*, 2 vols., Berlin: De Gruyter.

Risch, F. (2003), 'Was tut ein Epitomator? Zur Methode des Epitomierens am Beispiel der pseudoclementinischen "epitome prior"', *Das Altertum* 48: 241–55.

Roberts, C. and T. Skeat (1983), *The Birth of the Codex*, London: The British Academy.

Roller, M. (2018), *Models from the Past in Roman Culture: A World of Exempla*, Cambridge: Cambridge University Press.

Rood, T., C. Atack and T. Philips (2020), *Anachronism and Antiquity*, London: Bloomsbury.

Russell, B. (2013), *The Economics of the Roman Stone Trade*, Oxford: Oxford University Press.

Salvo, G. (2015), *Miti scolpiti, miti narrati: riflessioni sulla produzione di sarcofagi romani tra arte e letteratura*, Padua: Padua University Press.

Schipke, R. (2013), *Das Buch in der Spätantik. Herstellung, Form, Ausstattung und Verbreitung in der westlichen Reichshälfte des Imperium Romanum*, Wiesbaden: Reichert.

Schrenk, S. (1985), *Typos und Antitypos in der frühchristlichen Kunst*, Munster: Aschendorff.

Schwedler, G., R. Schwitter and S. Dusil, eds (2017), *Exzerpieren – Kompilieren – Tradieren: Transformationen es Wissens zwischen Spätantike und Fühmittelalter*, Berlin: De Gruyter

Sevrugian, P. (1989), Review of G. Cavallo, J. Gribomont and W. Loerke (1987) *Codex purpureus Rossanensis*, *Jahrbuch für Antike und Christentum* 32: 233–40.

Sevrugian, P. (1990), *Der Rossano-Codex und die Sinope-Fragmente: Miniaturen und Theologie*, Worms: Wernersche Verlagsgesellschaft.

Sichtermann, H. (1966), *Späte Endymion-Sarkophage: Methodisches zur Interpretation*, Baden-Baden: Grimm.

Sichtermann, H. (1992), *Die mythologischen Sarkophage 2. Apollon biz Grazien, ASR 12.2*, Berlin: Mann,

Smith, R. R. R. (1988), '*Simulacra Gentium*:The Ethne from the Sebasteion at Aphrodisias', *Journal of Roman Studies* 78: 50–77.

Sörries, R. (1991), *Die syrische Bibel von Paris: Paris, Bibliothèque Nationale, syr. 341; eine frühchristliche Bilderhandschrift aus dem 6. Jahrhundert*, Wiesbaden: Reichert.

Sörries, R. (1993), *Christlich-Antike Buchmalerei im Überblick*, Wiesbaden: Reichert.

Spengel, L., ed. (1853), *Rhetores Graeci* II, Leipzig: Teubner.

Spengel, L., ed. (1856), *Rhetores Graeci* III, Leipzig: Teubner.

Squire, M. (2011), *The Iliad in a Nutshell: Visualizing Epic in the* Tabulae Iliacae, Oxford: Oxford University Press.

Squire, M. and J. Elsner (forthcoming), 'Latin Literature and Material Culture', in R. Gibson and C. Whitton (eds), *Cambridge Critical Guide to Latin Literature*, Cambridge: Cambridge University Press.

Stansbury O'Donnell, M. (1999), *Pictorial Narratives in Ancient Greek Art*, Cambridge: Cambridge University Press.

Stanton, G. (2004), 'The early Christian preference for the codex', in C. Horton (ed.), *The Earliest Gospels: The Origins and Transmission of the Earliest Christian Gospels. The Contribution of the Chester Beatty Gospel Codex P45*, 40–9, London: T&T Clark.

Stroumsa, G. (2014), 'On the Status of Books in Early Christianity', in C. Harrison, C. Humfress and I. Sandwell (eds), *Being Christian in Late Antiquity*, 57–72, Oxford: Oxford University Press.

Studer-Karlen, M. (2012), *Verstorbenendarstellungen auf frühchristlichen Sarkophagen*, Turnhout: Brepols.

Szirmai, J. (1999), *The Archaeology of Medieval Bookbinding*, Aldershot: Ashgate.

Thümmel, H. (1985), 'Typologische und analogische Argumentation in der christlichen Kunst', in J. Rogge and G. Schille (eds), *Theologische Versuche*, IV, 195–214, Berlin: Evangelische Verlags-Anstalt.

Tkacz, C. (2002), *The Key to the Brescia Casket*, Notre Dame, Indiana: University of Notre Dame Press.

Turner, E. (1977), *The Typology of the Early Codex*, Philadelphia: University of Pennsylvania Press.

Walker, S. (1990), *Catalogue of the Roman Sarcophagi in the British Museum*, London: British Museum Press.

Wallraff, N. (2013), *Kodex und Kanon: Das Buch im frühen Christentum*, Berlin: De Gruyter.

Webber Jones, L. and C. Rufus Morey (1931), *The Miniatures of the Manuscripts of Terence*, Princeton, NJ: Princeton University Press.

Weitzmann, K. (1977), *Late Antique and Early Christian Book Illumination*, New York: George Bazilier.

Weitzmann, K. and H. Kessler (1986), *The Cotton Genesis: British Library, Codex Cotton Otho B VI*, Princeton: Princeton University Library.

Wheatley, C. (2011), *Epic, Epitome, and the Early Modern Historical Imagination*, Farnham: Ashgate.

Whitmarsh, T. (2010), 'Epitomes of Greek Novels', in M. Horster and C. Reitz (eds), *Condensing Texts – Condensed Texts*, 307–20, Stuttgart: Franz Steiner Verlag.

Wrede, H. (1981), *Consecratio in formam deorum. Vergöttlichte Privatpersonen in d. röm. Kaiserzeit*, Mainz: Von Zabern.

Wright, D. (1992), *Codicological Notes on the Vergilius Romanus*, Vatican City: Biblioteca Apostolica Vaticana.

Wright, D. (2001), *The Roman Vergil and the Origins of Medieval Book Design*, London: British Library.

Wright, D. (2006), *The Lost Late Antique Illustrated Terence*, Vatican: Biblioteca apostolica Vaticana.

Zanker, P. and B. Ewald (2012), *Living with Myths: The Imagery of Roman Sarcophagi*, Oxford: Oxford University Press.

Ziolkowski, J. and M. Putnam, eds (2008), *The Virgilian Tradition: The First Fifteen Hundred Years*. New Haven, CT: Yale University Press.

PART V

FROM THE FRAGMENTS TO THE WHOLE?

CHAPTER 13
THE *AENEID* MORE OR LESS: THE VERSE *ARGUMENTA* OF THE SO-CALLED 'TWELVE WISE MEN'

Scott McGill

It is possible to read the *Aeneid* in less than five minutes – just not Virgil's *Aeneid*. One must instead turn to hexameter *argumenta*, or summaries of the *Aeneid*, that shrink the epic down to epigrammatic size. Several *argumenta* are gathered in editions of the *Anthologia Latina*. Unique among them are five-line summaries of each book of the *Aeneid*, which very likely date to late antiquity and are attributed to twelve named authors known collectively as the *duodecim sapientes*, or Twelve Wise Men (*Anthologia Latina* [*AL*] 591–602 Riese [R^2] = 97–108 Friedrich [F]).[1] The summaries form the ninth cycle of poems in a collection of twelve cycles, with each of the Twelve Men contributing one piece to each cycle – hence each author summarizes one book of Virgil's epic. In addition, there is a single poem within the twelfth cycle that gives a précis of the entire *Aeneid* in twelve lines (*AL* 634 R^2 = 141 F). These are the only *argumenta* from antiquity that belong to a larger group of poems and that are attributed to different authors. The summarizers, however, are probably not what they appear to be: critics have plausibly argued that the Twelve Wise Men are in fact one author writing under twelve assumed names.[2] Anne Friedrich proposes that the author in question was Lactantius, and that the collection was a work of his youth, when he was a teacher at a grammatical or rhetorical school.[3] But her claim has encountered cogent resistance, and the author must remain unidentified in the shadowland of pseudonymity.[4]

Like any epitomizing text, the Twelve Wise Men's *argumenta* cut a huge amount of their source work. The demands of space are the obvious reason for this: they cause the author to omit many story and plot elements in the *Aeneid* and to compress dramatically the content that he does summarize. What is more, as thumbnail sketches of the subject matter of Virgil's epic, the *argumenta* offer almost entirely present-tense, third-person accounts of what the summarizer considers the essential action in each book.[5] Clearly, this is to reproduce the bones of the *Aeneid* but not its marrow. Still, the reduction of Virgil's epic demands to be viewed not just as an exercise in subtraction and loss. The *argumenta* are ludic textual performances that fit a reduced *Aeneid* to a new literary context and to new purposes. What is more, they not only distil what happens in the epic, but also recast its language and pass its content through different interpretive filters. The summarizer's handling of the *Aeneid* thus involves more than simply making it less, more than condensing it and flattening it out. The *argumenta* are by definition derivative and lesser texts. But they are also reception poems that in different ways remake the *Aeneid*.

A game of numbers

The summaries of the *Aeneid* belong to a collection of poems mainly on learned topics. Along with Virgil, subjects include Cicero, the zodiac, mythology, the seasons, the mirror effect of frozen water, and the letter Y. For Friedrich, the topics place the collection in the tradition of learned banquets: they largely correspond to *quaestiones convivales*, or topics – e.g., natural phenomena, ethical issues, and literary and grammatical matters – for such banquets.[6] The cycle constitutes not a parody of such a party, but a fictional version of one: the *duodecim* are made-up deipnosophists who follow each other in treating subject areas befitting a banquet, and who produce sympotic poetry out of that matter.[7] This reading is very attractive, although it cannot be proven outright, because no frame situates the poems in such a setting.

At the very least, the Twelve Wise Men are clearly presented as men of learning and culture. It is tempting to identify them more precisely as grammarians, as well as to suppose that the author was the same, writing about and – at least in the first ring of the poems' circulation – for his fellow teachers.[8] The attention given to Virgil in the collection is consistent with that authorial identity. Virgil is the most prevalent subject in the collection: along with the *argumenta*, there are two-line and four-line variations on his epitaph (*AL* 507–18 R^2 = 13–24 F, *AL* 555–66 R^2 = 61–72 F). Grammarians were intimately familiar with Virgil because he was a central author in Western schools of grammar into late antiquity wherever the traditional curriculum survived, with the *Aeneid* the central grammatical text.[9] Given the place of Virgil in the schools, a grammarian is a prime candidate to be the author of a collection that features him so prominently.[10] Gabriella Senis has proposed, moreover, that grammarians would summarize books of the *Aeneid* as a first step in teaching them.[11] This raises the possibility that the author was drawing on and reflecting his own experience as a teacher when composing his verse *argumenta*.

The summaries that the author produces under the guise of the Twelve Wise Men, however, are no instructional texts. While they sketch the content of the *Aeneid*, their essential purpose is not to serve as a practical conduit to the poem and to enable readers to know in a short compass what happened in it. The *argumenta* are meant instead to entertain. This they do first as part of a fictional performance of literary fellowship, with each of the Twelve Wise Men taking turns contributing a piece on a theme.[12] The collection depicts a cultured group of men enjoying the social practice of poetry, and it implies an intended readership that will appreciate and enjoy the show.[13]

But the *argumenta* also entertain in themselves as compact versions of the *Aeneid*. Like all verse summaries, the texts are exercises in defamiliarization, i.e., of making the familiar look different and strange. The author performs that task based on ad hoc rules governing length that create a closed textual field in which he must operate.[14] The poems are about technique, i.e., about the ways that the author negotiates the (self-)imposed formal restrictions that define his endeavour. They are a form of literary play in which the what of the poem directs the reader to focus on the how of the poem – i.e., how the author shrinks the *Aeneid* to small bits of text.[15] The summarizer wants audiences to read the *argumenta* for the story, but only insofar as this leads them to register, and to appreciate, his ability to play the game of miniaturizing skill and to make a little out of a lot.[16] The ability to shrink down the *Aeneid* is most powerfully emphasized in a radically condensed summary like the twelve-line version of the entire *Aeneid* that appears in the twelfth cycle of Wise Men poems (*AL* 634 R² = 141 F).[17] Yet in all the *argumenta*, it is form, defined in this case by length, that gives the texts their essential identity and meaning.

We might wonder if the author considered Virgil to be a kind of summarizer himself, reducing the 24-book *Iliad* and 24-book *Odyssey* by three quarters, to a 12-book epic. But even if he did, his point was not to place his *argumenta* on a continuum with Virgil's reduction of Homer. It is the summaries' difference in size from the *Aeneid* that matters, and the author's procedures for creating that difference. The game is not one of authorial identification or impersonation, but of putting a new, defamiliarizing spin on Virgil's material.

The canonicity of the *Aeneid* is crucial to all of this. The central place of the poem in Roman imperial literary culture, which was immune to shifts in taste and the wear of time through some combination of artistic merit, institutional forces (notably the school curriculum), and the power of tradition, creates the familiarity with the poem that is necessary to writing the summaries. But the cultural standing of the epic is also fundamental to the impact of the texts. Their effect lies in the difference between large and small. This is simultaneously a difference between major and minor, i.e., between the familiar canonical standing of the *Aeneid* and the minor work into which the summarizer transforms it – with minor defined especially by textual form and function, but also by the text's place in the tradition.[18] Virgil's standing is a foil to the poems; it is the thing from which the pieces depart and the thing that casts them into relief. As examples of active, writerly reception,[19] the summaries are an extension of the original, but they are also distant from it and its canonicity. They move their source poetry into different textual territory and come to occupy a Virgilian hinterland, one connected to the centre of the canon, but existing on the non-canonical periphery.[20] The game of compression not only turns a long text into something short but also turns a hugely authoritative text in a high genre into its opposite.[21]

The Twelve Wise Men author plays at shortening Virgil's epic within another game, one that extends through his entire cycle of poems. Across the twelve sets of poems, he rotates his writers, so that the first one in one cycle is the last author in the next, while the second moves to the first position, the third to the second, and so on.[22] As the collection proceeds, moreover, the poems increase in length. An opening cycle has one-line inscriptions for boards used in the dice-game *alea*; each line consists of words of six letters, a number that matches the number of sides of a die.[23] The second, third and fourth cycles, meanwhile, contain two-line poems; the fifth, three-line; the sixth, seventh and eighth, four-line; the ninth (our *argumenta*), five-line; the tenth and eleventh, six-line; and the twelfth, pieces of differing length. A pattern of the number of cycles devoted to a particular length of poem is thus in place – one/three/one/three/one, with the end of the collection then breaking the pattern. Each cycle is devoted to a single topic except the final one, where the poems are on miscellaneous subjects. The last cycle also deviates from a metrical pattern found in the rest of the collection: the author alternates between dactylic hexameters (in the first cycle and subsequent odd-numbered cycles) and elegiac couplets (in the even-numbered cycles) until the twelfth cycle, which contains poems in hexameters but is a polymetric set.

The entire Twelve Wise Men collection is thus a broad-scale game comprising different formal and numerical patterns, governed by their own ad hoc rules. The place of the summaries within that larger game reveals another way that the *Aeneid* could be turned into literary play – with play again understood as the negotiation of formal restrictions that in this case include but also extend beyond the conventional ones of metre, and as an entertaining display of technique in working within those strictures to produce poetry with the appropriate structure. Both the inset *ludus* of the *argumenta* and the collection's overarching ludic pattern show the author adapting the *Aeneid* to his own creative needs and treating it as a mobile text, able to be fitted to new forms, contexts, and purposes.[24] The epic's canonicity is a partial foil to the collection's macro-game, because the *argumenta* belong to that game. The place of the poem in the canon invests it with the cultural standing and weight against which the ninth cycle, not only as a miniaturization of the *Aeneid* but also as an entry in the large-scale game, stands in pointed contrast.

A game of words

When summarizing the *Aeneid* in a short compass, authors obviously must choose what details to include and what to leave out, because they cannot reproduce what happens in Virgil in its entirety. This is to present a reading of the source text, inasmuch as the summarizer offers his audience a partial version of the *Aeneid*, which grows out of his choice of attention and decisions over what to preserve and what to omit.[25] Thus while the Twelve Wise Men author hits on most of Virgil's major plot points, he overlooks some significant details – for instance, the encounter with Dido in *Aen.* 6; Hercules and Cacus, the tour of archaic Rome, and the ecphrastic account of the Battle of Actium in *Aen.* 8; and the reconciliation of Juno to the fate of the Trojans in *Aen.* 12.

In the twelve-line *argumentum* of the entire *Aeneid*, meanwhile, the summarizer has to choose what he considers to be the most defining action from each book. In *Aen.* 10, he decides that the death of Pallas does not rise to that level, while in *Aen.* 11 he focuses on the Italian defeat in battle after Camilla's death rather than on the funeral of Pallas earlier in the book. While it is hard to question his choices in the other books, it remains the case that the *argumentum* is by definition a radically limited version of the *Aeneid*, which is filtered through the summarizer's interpretation of what constitutes the crucial content of the *Aeneid* when the poem is boiled down to its essence.

But it is not just the choice of Virgilian plot points in the *argumenta* that reflects and reveals readings of the *Aeneid*; it is also the language the summaries contain. That language is itself pervasively Virgilian.[26] The many echoes show that the engagement with the *Aeneid* in both the five-line and twelve-line summaries involved more than pruning content to arrive at very lean narration, and that it extended to culling individual words and phrases that the summarizer remembered from his reading. This links the Twelve Wise Men author to other summarizers of the *Aeneid* in the *Anthologia Latina*, who recurrently recycle Virgil's language.[27] While it is natural for the summarizers to reuse *verba* from the relevant books or passages, none of them is under compulsion to do so, and each generally goes about it in his own way.[28] On top of that, the parallels are very rarely exact, which means that there is at least some measure of creative adaptation of a kind that resembles conventional imitation. The authors also take language from places in the *Aeneid* other than the passages they are summarizing; these can be other sections in the relevant book or other books in the epic.[29] Such adaptation of Virgil's language and assimilation of it to a new place and purpose is again akin to *imitatio*.[30] It shows that the summarizers took a bird's eye view of the entire *Aeneid* when condensing individual books and felt free to move language between them.

The twelve-line summary of the entire *Aeneid* provides several examples where the Twelve Wise Men author recasts Virgil's language. Most are straightforward cases where the author adapts snippets from the relevant book.[31] Yet one example demonstrates a more creative hand. It comes in the summary of *Aen.* 4: *quartus item miserae duo vulnera narrat Elissa*e (the fourth then narrates the two wounds of wretched Elissa). *Miserae* and *Elissae* echo an adjective and epithet that are repeatedly used of Dido in *Aen.* 4.[32] With *duo vulnera*, meanwhile, the summarizer combines Virgilian imagery and action: *vulnera* refers both to Dido's love for Aeneas, described as a wound at *Aen.* 4.2 (*vulnus alit venis* [she feeds the wound with her life-blood]) and 4.67 (*tacitum vivit sub pectore vulnus* [the silent wound lives beneath her breast]), and to her suicide by stabbing, described as a wound at 4.689 (*infixum stridit sub pectore vulnus* [the deep wound hissed beneath her chest]).[33] The constraints of the form allow for a flash of wit via the combination of the metaphorical and the literal, which develops from a reading of the wound-theme in Virgil's book.

The first of the five-line summaries, meanwhile, exemplifies how extensively the author recasts the language of the *Aeneid* in that set of *argumenta*:

> Aeolus inmittit ventum Iunone precante
> Troianis, Libycasque vagos expellit in oras.
> solatur Venerem dictis pater ipse dolentem.
> Aenean recipit pulchra Carthagine Dido,
> cui Venus Ascanii sub imagine mittit Amorem.

> With Juno praying for it, Aeolus sends the wind against the Trojans, and he drives them, scattered, onto Libyan shores. The father consoles the grieving Dido with words. Dido receives Aeneas in lovely Carthage; Venus sends Cupid to her in the image of Ascanius.

Libycasque . . . expellit in oras derives from *Aen.* 1.377, *Libycis tempestas appulit oris* (the storm drove [us Trojans] to Libyan shores). *Solatur* in the next line then comes partly from *Aen.* 1.239, *hoc equidem occasum Troiae tristisque ruinas / solabar* (with this I found solace for the fall of Troy and its sad ruin, 1.238–39). The summarizer takes a verb used by Venus to say that she comforted herself for the destruction of Troy by thinking of the great fate that Jupiter had in store for the Trojans (the *hoc* of 1.238) and has it describe how Jupiter comforted the goddess by affirming that fate. But a second Virgilian source for that verb and the entire line is *Aen.* 4.393–94, on Aeneas' wish to soothe the sorrowing Dido: *quamquam lenire dolentem / solando cupit et dictis avertere curas* (although he wishes to calm her in her grief by comforting her and to get rid of her distress with words). The summarizer fits the Virgilian line to a new context that, he presumably saw, contrasts with the original: whereas Aeneas does not proceed to comfort Dido – a victim of Venus' and Juno's scheming – and prepares instead to depart for his fated Italy, Jupiter comforts Venus with the promise that the Trojans' fate remains inviolate, despite Juno.

Aen. 4 is also a source in the next two lines of the summary; the evidence makes it clear that books one and four of Virgil's epic were closely connected in the author's mind. Line four adapts *Aen.* 4.214, *dominum Aenean in regna recepit* ([Dido] welcomed Aeneas into her kingdom as lord), and varies 4.192, *cui se pulchra viro dignetur iungere Dido* (to which man/husband fair Dido deigns to join herself); the summarizer shifts *pulchra* from Dido to *Carthagine.*[34] Line five then recasts language from *Aen.* 4.84, *Ascanium, genitoris imagine capta* (*detinet*) ([Dido], enraptured by the likeness of his father, holds Ascanius). The author reuses a line showing Dido in love with Aeneas and, consequently, holding Ascanius because he resembled his father to describe how Venus implanted that love by disguising Cupid as that boy. The connection is one of narrative cause and effect, though it also lies in the theme of physical likeness.

On the one hand, the adaptation of Virgil's language in this and other *argumenta* reinforces the derivative, ancillary status of the texts; within summaries of the *Aeneid* are words and phrases that themselves originate in the epic. On the other hand, the changes to Virgil distinguish the summaries from their source. The result is simultaneous likeness and difference, indebtedness and independence: while the echoes cause the *argumenta* to read like the *Aeneid*, they are also instances of original expression – and of course the stronger and more creative the changes, the greater the degree of originality. Both Virgil and the summarizer contribute to the language of the *argumenta*; the latter is not a passive recipient of the model text who mechanically reproduces its words, but rather an active inheritor who reshapes what he takes from the *Aeneid.*[35]

The extensive reuse of Virgil's language adds an element to the game that the summarizer was playing. While showing that he could work within extreme constraints to relate what happened in each book of the *Aeneid*, he also demonstrates his detailed command of that poetry by echoing and adapting specific verses. This implies that he was writing for an audience who would identify the debts and appreciate his mastery of that feature of his summaries – further proof, if any was necessary, that the *argumenta* were not intended to introduce tyros to the *Aeneid*. The game relies on expertise: the author shows that in his reception of Virgil's poem he has acquired both wide and precise knowledge of it, down to the details of its language, while the audience is informed enough to recognize the extent of what he knows.

At moments beyond those already noted in the *argumentum* of *Aeneid* 1, the summarizer shows himself via his echoes of Virgil to be a reader capable of drawing connections between the books of the epic, and of putting their content into dialogue. An example appears in lines four and five of the summary of *Aen.* 5, *Venus anxia placat / Neptunum* (anxious Venus conciliates Neptune). This takes its cue from 5.779, where Venus, *exercita curis* (distressed with cares, i.e., concern for her Trojans), implores Neptune to preserve the Trojans as they sail and to allow them to get to Italy. With *placat*, the author includes a form of the verb found only once in the *Aeneid*, at 1.142, where Neptune calms the sea storm that had lashed the Trojans (*tumida aequora placat* [he calms the swollen seas]). By all appearances, this is an instance where the summarizer deliberately echoes a word describing Neptune as he saves the Trojans from a sea storm when describing how Venus prayed for Neptune's aid to protect the Trojans on the water.[36] Venus' allusion to the storm in her speech to the god (5.789–91) could easily have put the author on the track of *Aen.* 1.142. But he still had to take that cue and look across books, and still had to draw the connection between the preserving Neptune in both *Aeneid* 1 and 5.[37]

Further examples come in the final two lines of the summary of *Aen.* 6:

> congressusque patri discit genus omne suorum,
> quove modo casus valeat superare futuros.

> Having met his father, he learns the entire race of his own men and how he might be able to overcome future perils.

Discit in the first of these lines probably owes something to *Aen.* 6.755, where Anchises, along with Aeneas, climbs a mound from which to 'note the faces' (*discere vultus*) of the Roman souls as they file past. The line-end *omne suorum*, meanwhile, echoes *omnemque suorum* at *Aen.* 6.681, which occurs in the same position: once more, the subject in Virgil is Anchises, who is in the process of surveying and and reviewing the souls of future Romans. Yet the summarizer also takes *discit genus omne suorum* from *genus omne tuum . . . disces* at *Aen.* 5.737. There the ghost of Anchises visits Aeneas and tells him that he must visit the Underworld, where he will learn all his race. In addition, *genus omne* appears in the same verse position at *Aen.* 8.628, which describes how Mulciber fashioned on Aeneas' shield the *genus omne futurae* [*stirpis ab Ascanio*], 'the entire race of the stock to come from Ascanius'. The parallel and the summarizer's use of *futuros* in his following verse indicate that he also had that Virgilian line in mind. He therefore echoes a passage in *Aen.* 8 on the Roman descendants of Aeneas to describe those descendants at a different moment of historical prolepsis in the poem. What we find in the fourth line of the *argumentum* of *Aen.* 6, then, is the simultaneous recollection of several Virgilian lines that are all thematically related: the author not only compresses the *Aeneid*, but also coherently fuses multiple models in that very tight compass.

The final verse of the *argumentum* of *Aen.* 6 then responds primarily to *Aen.* 6.892, *et quo quemque modo fugiatque feratque laborem* (and how [Aeneas] is to flee and to face each toil), where Anchises tells Aeneas how to deal with the Italian War that he is soon to face. But there is a second debt to *Aen.* 11.244, *casus superavimus omnis* (we overcame all perils). The echo of that line creates a more optimistic note than that at *Aen.* 6.892: rather than just learning to escape and bear his struggles, the summarizer's Aeneas learns how to overcome them.[38] The speaker at *Aen.* 11.244 is Venulus, who reports to the Council in King Latinus' city about an unsuccessful mission to recruit Diomedes to fight as an ally; at 11.244, he tells the Latin Council how the embassy prevailed over all dangers to get to Diomedes. The summarizer thus adapts a verse from deep inside the story of the war in Italy while also adapting a verse in *Aen.* 6 in which Anchises instructs Aeneas on how to deal with that war. Diomedes' refusal to fight the Trojans as a Latin ally, moreover, significantly paves the way for Aeneas to overcome the perils of the Italian war. It seems possible that the summarizer recognized this, and that it led him to reuse *Aen.* 11.244.

These examples are sufficient to confirm that the summarizer read across Virgilian books and reused and combined lines from them not simply out of convenience, but because he identified substantive links between them. Yet other details in the *argumenta* reveal even more about him as a reader of the *Aeneid.* One such detail appears in the last line of the summary of *Aeneid* 8: [*in clipeoque*] *res fingit Latias et fortia facta nepotum* ([Mulciber] fashions [on the shield] the Latin story and the descendants' brave deeds). In the second half of the verse,[39] the summarizer takes *nepotum* from the last line of *Aen.* 8 (8.731), *attollens umero famamque et fata nepotum* (lifting on his shoulder the fame and fortunes of his descendants).[40] At the same time, he adapts *fortia facta* from *Aen.* 1.641, *fortia facta patrum*; these are the deeds of Dido's ancestors, embossed in gold upon silver plates at a banquet in Carthage.[41] The summarizer turns to Virgil's micro-ecphrasis in his first book when summarizing the grand ecphrasis of *Aen.* 8 and changes the deeds of Dido's forbears to the deeds of Aeneas' descendants; images of the great Sidonian past of Dido's Carthage become images of the great future of Rome. The suggestion is that the author sees a contrast between the 'great deeds' of each of the two great historical enemies, and that he pointedly rewrites the one as the other. In the process, he gives *facta* an adjective that it did not have in *Aen.* 8.731, and one that invests the deeds with heroic shading. This is in keeping with the tenor of Virgil's own ecphrasis, especially its description of Actium. The incorporation of the adjective reveals a summarizer who wished to underline that aspect of Virgil's account, and thus to imply that it is a gilded passage of praise.[42]

Of course, the *Aeneid* is not simply a celebration of empire and Augustus, but is also a poem of loss and pathos. Another adjective, this time in the summary of *Aen.* 2, responds to that feature of the poem. In the third line of the *argumentum*, the author states that the inset narrator Aeneas of *Aen.* 2 describes the 'most awful fate of Priam' (*Priamique miserrima fata*). This adapts *Aen.* 2.506, *forsitan et Priami fuerint quae fata, requiras* (and perhaps you might ask what was Priam's fate). The summarizer adds *miserrima* perhaps with a glance to another *argumentum* (*AL* 1 SB), which has *Priami fatum miserabile* (*AL* 1.II.7 SB) – although it is impossible to establish priority between works of uncertain date. Yet the superlative is thematic in *Aen.* 2 (see 2.5, 411, 519, and 655), and it is safe to suppose that the summarizer looked back to Virgil for it, even if he was influenced too by the other *argumentum*. By including it, the author shows that he was sensitive to the extreme and exquisite pathos of Priam's death. As with *fortia facta* in the summary of *Aen.* 8, there is nothing deep or surprising about this response. What we have is a form of minimal interpretation, located in a single word within a sharply constrained poetic form, and responding to a manifest feature of the source text. Even so, the choice of adjective points to what in the *Aeneid* struck the summarizer, and it leaves a trace of an emotional reaction to Virgil's majestic sadness.

Something similar occurs in the last line of the last five-line *argumentum*, on *Aen.* 12: *Pallantea necem misero dant cingula Turno* (Pallas' belt gives death to unfortunate Turnus). The characterization of Turnus recalls the use of *miser* for him three times in the last third of *Aen.* 12 (12.636, 813, and 881). All three lines are spoken by characters sympathetic to Turnus (the hero himself, Juno, and Turnus' sister Juturna); and all are at least partially focalized through Juturna, Turnus' desperate defender on the battlefield.[43] But the sympathy towards him as *Aen.* 12 approaches its climactic close is also authorized in the narrative more broadly: the feelings conveyed by these uses of *miser* are not aberrant, but are part of Virgil's sympathetic (though not uncritical) treatment of Turnus as he moves inexorably towards death.[44] The summarizer registers that aspect of the final book and echoes the thematic adjective to capture it.[45] In this final line of his *argumenta*, he once more introduces a hint of emotion, one suggesting that his own sympathy extended to this culminating casualty of Aeneas' fated mission.[46]

These examples further demonstrate that the *argumenta* are documents of reception. The game of compression is primarily a game of nouns and verbs, which enable the summarizer to describe what he considers to be the defining people, places, things, and actions of the *Aeneid* while meeting the demands of economy. Yet space is occasionally made for adjectives that lend interpretive colour. The summarizer-as-reader comes into view not only through his choice of material but also through his verbal choices: the addition of certain adjectives at certain moments provides snapshots of the author's responses to Virgil, and thus of how (re)writing is the product and expression of reading.

A final example shows the summarizer interpreting Virgil in a more active, transformative way. It comes in the fourth line of the *argumentum* of *Aen.* 9, a summary of the Nisus and Euryalus episode: *Euryalus Nisusque luunt nece proelia noctis* (Euryalus and Nisus expiate with death the nighttime battle).[47] *Luo* implies atonement for an offence, as in the third line of the *argumentum* of *Aen.* 12, *Rutulique luunt periuria victi* (the defeated Rutulians atone for their breach of oath).[48] Hence the verb casts the nighttime raid of Nisus and Euryalus in a negative light and presents it as a wrongful act. This perspective on the scene contrasts with the treatment of it in another verse summary of the *Aeneid*, attributed to Sulpicius Carthaginiensis, which focuses on the pious fidelity of the pair (*Nisus et Euryalus morte et pietate fideles* [Nisus and Euryalus were faithful in death and piety], *AL* 653.58 R^2). The contrast reinforces the obvious truth that the Wise Men author need not have represented Nisus and Euryalus in the fashion that he did. In taking that approach, the summarizer also differs from his source. Virgil's version of the Nisus and Euryalus story contains characteristic moral complexity but is, at bottom, sympathetic to the two; thus he famously concludes their episode by apostrophizing them as a 'fortunate pair' (*fortunati ambo*, *Aen.* 9.446) whom the *Aeneid* will commemorate as long as Rome remains (9.446–49).[49] The summarizer gives such sympathetic honour no room. In this, he remakes the Nisus and Euryalus episode as he abridges it, turning it from a tale that, however complicated, is worthy of undying epic renown to one of crime and atoning punishment, and thus advancing a particular way of thinking about the scene.[50] This departure from Virgil illustrates still more that the *argumenta* are distinct from the *Aeneid*, even as they are second-degree texts entirely dependent on and encompassed by it, and shows another way that the summarizer transformed the *Aeneid* in his reception of the poem while also recording what happened in it.[51]

Conclusion

The verse *argumenta* attributed to the Twelve Wise Men are not symbols of cultural exhaustion, in which an unoriginal poetaster feebly turns to a classic of the past and regurgitates it. Rather, they are expressions of the stability of the ancient Latin poetic canon, but also of how that stability made room for, and indeed produced, new forms of expression. Centuries after Virgil wrote the *Aeneid*, it remained a canonical touchstone in late antiquity, set deep and immovable in literary culture. The poem was both a distant monument and a living presence, with the capacity to generate an extraordinarily wide range of responses to it. This includes para-literary Virgilian texts, of which a good number of examples survive from the period.[52] The verse summaries of the Twelve Wise Men, like the other works comprising this body of satellite material, are curiosities. But literary history is incomplete without the curious footnotes to it. Thus the *argumenta* demonstrate the adaptability of the major *Aeneid* to minor poetry and of lofty, serious verse to a literary game. Close examination of the texts, moreover, leads to a better understanding of how one such game was played, including how its author recast Virgil's language, imitation-like, and how he read his source poetry. To explore the summaries in detail is to get a clearer sense of little moments in Virgil's ancient afterlife – a few tesserae in a great mosaic – and to dig down into his Late-Antique reception on the granular level.

Like other epitomizing works, the verse *argumenta* possess thick textuality: they have two layers of text, their own and that of the *Aeneid*. The summaries are at once familiar and strange as new versions of Virgil's poem; and they emerge from an already existent 'world of words', which establishes a framework for writing and for reading.[53] By definition, the texts do not, and cannot, transcend that world. But they do carve out new space in it, as minor literary games that combine continuity and change by both recapping and remaking the *Aeneid*.

Notes

1. I use the text of Friedrich 2002 for the Twelve Wise Men collection. On it, see also Rosellini 2014 and Martorelli 2018. Critics have typically dated the Twelve Wise Men poetry to the fourth or fifth century CE; see, e.g., Friedrich 2002: 4–6 and 189; Stok 2013: 154; Martorelli 2018: cxlvii–cl.
2. Friedrich 2002: 8–11; Martorelli 2018: cxlv. Contra, see Rosellini 2002: 113.

3. Friedrich 2002: 481–508.
4. Paolucci 2011: 84 and 96–7; Stok 2013: 153; and Martorelli 2018: cliii–cliv.
5. Such narration is a feature of summaries generally; see Genette 1997: 240.
6. Friedrich 2002: 438–48.
7. On poetic performances at symposia by the attendees, see Collins 2004: 63–163.
8. Friedrich 2002: 449–61; Stok 2013: 154; and Martorelli 2018: cl–cli similarly situate the collection in a scholastic milieu. Friedrich 2002: 473–6 suggests that the collection was written by a colleague of a *grammaticus* referred to by the name Asmenius, one of the Twelve Wise Men, and the addressee of the dedicatory final poem (*AL* 602 R^2 = 145 F); another possibility Friedrich entertains is that Asmenius was a pseudonym for the author himself. See also Martorelli 2018: cli. The poems perhaps come from Gaul, although North Africa is not out of the question. A Gallic author of the collection would resemble another Gallic grammarian-poet in late antiquity, Ausonius, in his taste for learned, arcane subject matter and for ludic verse. For possible intertextual connections between the collection and Ausonius, see Martorelli 2018: cxlvii–cxlviii. (It bears mentioning that there are summaries of Homer's *Iliad* and *Odyssey* ascribed to Ausonius; but they do not in fact belong to the poet. See Green 1991: 677–95.) See also Sowers in this volume on Ausonius.
9. Bonner 1977: 213–14, Maurice 2013: 73.
10. The other author who features prominently in the collection is Cicero (*AL* 603–14 R^2 = 102–20 F), a central figure in the schools of rhetoric. It seems entirely plausible that the Twelve Wise Men poet included Virgil and Cicero because of their respective places in the curricula. For another fictional gathering where Virgil is a predominant subject, see Macrobius' *Saturnalia* (esp. books 3–5), set at the Saturnalia of probably 383 CE.
11. Senis 1984: 310–11.
12. This further aligns the collection with a banquet: on the communal aspects of sympotic poetry, see Collins 2004: 66–8; and on turn-taking in such poetry, see Collins 2004: 68, 86–8, and 131. Quite possibly, the Twelve Wise Men are to be understood as competing with each other with their poetic efforts; competition was elsewhere an aspect of sympotic poetry (Collins 2004: 63–163).
13. The names of all the Twelve Wise Men appear to be fictional 'speaking names' (Friedrich 2002: 418–38). We cannot know if the Twelve Wise Men were twelve masks for an intended inner circle of twelve readers. Of course, if 'Asmenius' was a pseudonym for a dedicatee (see n. 8), then he would stand in for at least one intended reader.
14. I echo McGill 2005: 8–9. The term 'closed field' comes from Kenner 1962: 597–613; see esp. pp. 599–601.
15. Cf. Sherzer 2002: 4.
16. Similarly, Gioseffi 2012: 140–1.
17. Friedrich and Martorelli attribute the *argumentum* to Asmenius; *AL* 634R^2 attributes it to Basilius. On the order of the Twelve Wise Men's names throughout the collection in the manuscript tradition (and on the spelling of names), see Martorelli 2018: cxxxiii–cxlv. Cf. *AL* 717R^2, whose anonymous author tallies the number of lines in the *Eclogues*, *Georgics*, and *Aeneid* at 12,847 (*AL* 717 R^2 2–4) before summarizing the *Eclogues* and *Georgics* in a single line and the entire *Aeneid* in five lines (*AL* 717 R^2 7–11). The author gives the length of the Virgilian corpus (which differs from modern editions, where the number of lines is 12,913 lines) to underscore just how great the discrepancy is between its size and his miniscule version of it.

18. Of course, what is minor in one period might not be in another if certain institutional forces or tastes change. Still, it is impossible to imagine a shift in institutional practices/structures or in taste that would elevate the verse *argumenta* above the minor.

19. See Peirano Garrison 2017: 23, citing Barthes 1974: 4–5 on writerly works (texts that invite creative intervention) and readerly works (texts that resist intervention and are considered fixed).

20. On 'deterritorializing' in minor literature, see Hexter 2012: 38; the idea originates with Deleuze and Guattari 1986.

21. Cf. McGill 2018: 264 and 286, on the marginality of Virgilian verse summaries.

22. One author, Pompelianus, is omitted from the final two cycles. This could be because in the fiction, he leaves the banquet, as one guest typically does (or threatens to do) in the history of literary symposia; see Friedrich 2002: 418–20.

23. On the game of *alea*, see Purcell 1995: 3–37. Purcell discusses and cites board-inscriptions, including examples from the Twelve Wise Men, at 19–28 and 35. The name of one particular game was *duodecim scripta* (twelve writings; see Purcell 5). The topic of dicing is possible in a collection on a fictionalized banquet; references to dice and ἀστράγαλοι (knucklebones, and a dice-game) are scattered in Athenaeus' *Deipnosophistae*.

24. I echo Rigney 2012: 12.

25. Cf. Genette 1997: 230, on how cutting a text is 'a practice of *reading*, in the strong sense: i.e., a choice of attention'.

26. This corrects McGill 2018: 279 n. 51.

27. For examples in one *argumentum*, *AL* 1 SB, see McGill 2018: 280–4.

28. There are a few moments when the summaries echo each other, and in ways that suggest either inter-summary imitation or reliance on a common earlier *argumentum*. A couple of the *argumenta* (*AL* 653 R^2, *AL* 2a SB = 654 R^2) also resemble each other in echoing closely the first line of each book of the *Aeneid*, although even then there is some variety, because they reproduce different amounts of those lines.

29. This applies to the longer *argumenta*, although I have found one moment in the twelve-line *argumentum* of the *Aeneid* in our cycle where the author might summarize one book with the language of another: in the first line, *primus habet, Libycam veniant ut Troes in urbem* (the first has how the Trojans came to the Libyan city), *Libycam . . . urbem* might derive from *Aen.* 4.348 (Aeneas to Dido) *Libycaeque aspectus detinet urbis* ([if] the sight of the Libyan city holds [you]). Perhaps, however, the summarizer was responding to *Aen.* 1.338–39, *Agenoris urbem; / sed fines Libyci* (the city of Agenor; but the borders are Libyan). For the *Aeneid*, I use the text of Conte 2009.

30. So McGill 2018: 282, quoting Russell 1979: 16.

31. So line two, *edocet excidium Troiae clademque secundus* (the second imparts the destruction of Troy and disastrous defeat) combines 2.361 *quis cladem illius noctis* (*explicet*) (who could unfold that night's disaster) and 2.643, *vidimus excidia* (we saw the destruction); line five, *manibus Anchisae quinto celebrantur honores* (in the fifth honours are celebrated to the shades of Anchises), echoes *Aen.* 5.58 *celebremus honorem* (let us celebrate the sacrifice); line eight, *dat simul Aeneae socios octavus et arma* (the eighth gives allies and arms together to Aeneas), modifies *Aen.* 8.120, *socia arma rogantis* ([captains of Troy] requesting allied arms), with *arma* changed from the Virgilian metonymy for a Trojan alliance with Evander to Aeneas' divinely crafted arms; and line eleven, *undecimo Rutuli superantur morte Camillae* (in the eleventh the Rutulians are defeated by the death of Camilla), has its line-end from *Aen.* 11.796 and 11.839, *morte Camillam*.

32. For *misera*, see *Aen*. 4.315, 420, and 429; for *Elissa*, see *Aen*. 4.335 and 610, as well as 5.3.

33. This is a good indication that the author wrote for an intended audience that already knew the *Aeneid* well; otherwise, the reference to the two wounds would make little sense.

34. This could be (admittedly faint) evidence that the author was himself Carthaginian, and proud of it (see n. 8).

35. Levene 2015, on the *periochae* of Livy, is an influence here.

36. The summarizer also reaches to another book of the epic for language in the second line of the *argumentum*: *tumuloque patris persolvit honorem* (he renders honour to the tomb of his father). This derives from *Aen*. 8.61–62 *mihi victor honorem / persolves*. There does not seem to be a meaningful connection between the Virgilian material, however: the fact that Anchises appears to Aeneas with prophetic instructions at *Aen*. 5.719–39, while at *Aen*. 8.61–62 the Tiber offers its own prophetic instructions, seems too indirect a link, since the summary is dealing only with the funeral games for Anchises and not his subsequent appearance to his son.

37. Neptune of course keeps all the Trojans safe in the fifth book, with the notable exception of Palinurus; see *Aen*. 5.814–15, with 5.840–60.

38. Perhaps the author understood this idea of overcoming to inhere in Virgil's line, as the Late-Antique commentator Tiberius Claudius Donatus did (*Inst. Verg*. I.618 [Georgii]): *quo firmiorem dimitteret, docuit quomodo unumquemque laborem aut vinceret aut vitaret aut certe ferendo toleraret. ipsam sententiam poeta et in quinto libro* (710) *posuit sic: 'superanda', inquit, 'omnis fortuna ferendo est'; quod enim vinci non potest resistendo vel ferendo superatur* (so that he might send him away more resolute, he taught how he might either best every toil or avoid it or certainly endure it by bearing it. In his fifth book, the poet put this idea thus; he said, 'All fortune is to overcome by bearing it.' For a thing that is not able to be bested is overcome by resisting or bearing it).

39. In the first half, *res . . . Latias*, comes from *Aen*. 8.626, and *fingit*, from *finxerat* at 8.726.

40. Perhaps, too, the summarizer knew the reading *facta nepotum*, as DServius did in his commentary on the line (2.306 [Thilo and Hagen]).

41. The only other appearance of *fortia facta* in Virgil is at *Aen*. 10.369, where Pallas implores his troops *per . . . fortia facta*. Clearly, *fortia facta patrum* is a far more plausible source for *fortia facta nepotum*, with *patrum* reversed to *nepotum*.

42. Cf. Tiberius Claudius Donatus (n. 38), who states that Virgil so composed the ecphrasis *ut Caesaris praesentis gesta laudaret* (so that he might praise the deeds/achievements of the current Caesar) (*Int. Verg*. II.182 [Georgii]).

43. In 12.636, *an fratris miseri letum ut crudele videres* (for you to see the cruel death of your wretched brother), the second-person subject is Juturna, and *miseri* seems partly to reflect how she sees Turnus; and in 12.813, *Iuturnam misero, fateor, sucurrere fratri* [*suasi*] (I admit it, [I led] Juturna to help her wretched brother), *misero* appears to reflect how both Juno and Juturna viewed him. 12.881, *nunc certe et misero fratri comes ire per umbras* (now surely [I could] go to the shades at the side of my wretched brother), spoken by Juturna, then captures how she thinks of him.

44. For an excellent, concise discussion of this issue, see Tarrant 2012: 11–12.

45. This does not occur in other verse *argumenta* in the *AL*. In contrast to his characterization of Turnus here as *miser*, the Twelve Wise Men author calls Turnus a 'proud victor' (*victorque superbus*) in the fourth line of his summary of *Aen*. 10. This adapts *Aen*. 10.514, an apostrophe to Turnus, proud with the recent killing of Pallas (*te, Turne, superbum / caede nova*, 10.514–15). Again, this use of an adjective to depict Turnus is unique among the summaries in the

AL. The summarizer is clearly attuned to Virgil's characterization of Turnus, and his use of adjectives reflects the changes to that characterization.

46. Comparable sympathy is visible in the use of *misera* for Dido in the twelve-line summary of the entire *Aeneid* (see p. 237).

47. The line-end *proelia noctis* perhaps derives from *Aen*. 2.397, *proelia noctem*: if so, the summarizer takes a Virgilian line on how Aeneas and his comrades, disguised as Greeks, surprise and slay many enemies during the night that Troy fell to describe another surprising nighttime attack.

48. This line is adapted from *G*. 1.502 *Laomedonteae luimus periuria Troiae* (we have atoned for the breach of faith of Laomedon's Troy) – the sole example I have located of an echo in these *argumenta* of another Virgilian poem.

49. For a fine overview of the Nisus and Euryalus episode and the issues it raises, see Hardie 1994: 23–34. An anonymous verse summary in the *Anthologia Latina* picks up on Virgil's apostrophe and promise of fame: *Euryali et Nisi caedes et fata canuntur* (the massacre and deaths of Euryalus and Nisus are sung, *AL* 2a.IX.3 SB). *Canuntur* suggests a heroic epic tale sung and, in response to *Aen*. 9.446–49, immortalized by the poet.

50. Cf. Noens's conclusion in this volume, on how epitomizing literature has the power to produce new patterns of thinking about earlier texts.

51. 'Second-degree' comes from the subtitle of Genette 1997.

52. Along with other verse *argumenta*, examples are Virgilian centos and several pieces in the *Anthologia Latina* on Virgilian characters and themes. On the centos, see, e.g., McGill 2005 and Bažil 2009. For Virgilian pieces in the *Anthologia Latina*, see *AL* 33, 36, 47, 65, 71, 214, 237, and 249 SB.

53. I echo Horster and Reitz 2018: 453.

Works cited

Austin, R. G., ed. (1964), *P. Vergili Maronis Aeneidos liber secundus*, Oxford: Clarendon Press.

Barthes, R. (1974), *S/Z: An Essay*, trans. Richard Miller, New York: Hill and Wang.

Bažil, M. (2009), *Centones Christiani: Métamorphoses d'une forme intertextuelle dans la poésie latine chrétienne de l'Antiquité tardive*, Paris: Institute d'études augustiniennes.

Bonner, S. F. (1977), *Education in Ancient Rome: From the Elder Cato to the Younger Pliny*, Berkeley: University of California Press.

Collins, D. (2004), *Master of the Game: Competition and Performance in Greek Poetry*, Cambridge, MA: Harvard University Press.

Conte, G. B., ed. (2009), *P. Vergilius Maro: Aeneis*, Berlin: De Gruyter.

Deleuze, G. and F. Guattari (1986), *Kafka: Toward a Minor Literature*, trans. Dana Polan, Minneapolis, MN: University of Minnesota Press.

Friedrich, A., ed. (2002), *Das Symposium der XII Sapientes: Kommentar und Verfasserfrage*, Berlin: De Gruyter.

Genette, G. (1997), *Palimpsests: Literature in the Second Degree*, trans. C. Newman and C. Doubinsky, Lincoln: University of Nebraska Press.

Gioseffi, M. (2012), '"Introducing Virgil": Forme di presentazione dell'Eneide in età tardoantica', in P. F. Alberto and D. Paniagua (eds), *Ways of Approaching Knowledge in Late Antiquity and the Early Middle Ages*, 120–43, Nordhausen: Verlag Traugott Bautz.

Green, R. P. H., ed. (1991), *The Works of Ausonius*, Oxford: Clarendon Press.

Hardie, P., ed. (1994), *Virgil Aeneid IX*, Cambridge: Cambridge University Press.

Hexter, R. J. (2012), 'Canonicity', in R. J. Hexter and D. Townsend (eds), *The Oxford Handbook of Medieval Latin Literature*, 25–45, Oxford: Oxford University Press.

Horster, M. and C. Reitz (2018), 'Handbooks, Epitomes, and *Florilegia*', in S. McGill and E. J. Watts (eds), *A Companion to Late Antique Literature*, 431–50, Malden, MA: Wiley-Blackwell.

Kenner, H. (1962), 'Art in a Closed Field', *Virginia Quarterly Review* 38.4: 597–613.

Levene, D. S. (2015), 'Three Readings of Character in the Periochae of Livy', in R. Ash, J. Mossman, and F. B. Titchener (eds), *Fame and Infamy: Essays on Characterization in Greek and Roman Biography and Historiography*, 313–25, Oxford: Oxford University Press.

Martorelli, L., ed. (2018), *Versus sapientum de diversis causis: Introduzione, testo critico, traduzione poetica e commento filologico*, Hildesheim: Weidmann.

Maurice, L. (2013), *The Teacher in Ancient Rome: The Magister and His World*, Lanham, MD: Lexington Books.

McGill, S. (2005), *Virgil Recomposed: The Mythological and Secular Centos in Antiquity*, Oxford: Oxford University Press.

McGill, S. (2018), '*Minus opus moveo*: Verse Summaries of Virgil in the *Anthologia Latina*', in M. Formisano and C. S. Kraus (eds), *Marginality, Canonicity, Passion*, 263–86, Oxford: Oxford University Press.

Paolucci, P. (2011), 'Larga è la via (a proposito di *AL* 632 R^2)', in T. Privitera and F. Stok (eds), *Sedula cura docendi: Studi sull' Anthologia Latina per/con Riccardo Scarcia*, 83–112, Pisa: ETS.

Peirano Garrison, I. (2017), 'Between Biography and Commentary: The Ancient Horizon of Expectation of *VSD*', in A. Powell and P. Hardie (eds), *The Ancient Lives of Virgil: Literary and Historical Studies*, 1–28, Swansea: The Classical Press of Wales.

Purcell, N. (1995), 'Literate Games: Roman Urban Society and the Game of *Alea*', *Past & Present* 147: 3–37.

Rigney, A. (2012), *The Afterlives of Walter Scott: Memory on the Move*, Oxford: Oxford University Press.

Rosellini, M. (2002), 'Di nuovo sui Carmina XII sapientum', *Rivista di filologia e istruzione classica* 130: 105–25.

Rosellini, M. (2014), 'Esercizi di stile in forma di ghirlanda (*Anth. Lat.* 519–54 e 615–26 Riese^2)', in G. Piras (ed.), *Labor in studiis: Scritti di filologia classica in onore di Piergiorgio Parroni*, 201–16, Rome: Salerno.

Russell, D. A. (1979), 'De imitatione,' in D. West and T. Woodman (eds), *Creative Imitation and Latin Literature*, 1–16, Cambridge: Cambridge University Press.

Senis, G. (1984), 'Argumenta Vergiliana,' in *Enciclopedia Virgiliana I*, Rome: Istituto della Enciclopedia Italiana.

Sherzer, J. (2002), *Speech Play and Verbal Art*, Austin TX: University of Texas Press.

Stok, F. (2013), 'Epitaphia Vergilii', *AL. Rivista di studi di Anthologia Latina* 4: 153–66.

Tarrant, R., ed. (2012), *Virgil Aeneid Book XII*, Cambridge: Cambridge University Press.

CHAPTER 14

A PERSISTENT 'CHRONOPHOBIA': COMPOSITION, TIME AND MEMORY IN PLINY THE YOUNGER'S *EPISTULAE* AND VLADIMIR NABOKOV'S *SPEAK, MEMORY*

Tim Noens[*]

In 1966, the Russian-American author Vladimir Nabokov published the 'autobiographical memoir' *Speak, Memory*. The book consists of fifteen chapters and covers the author's life from his childhood in Russia around the beginning of the twentieth century until his emigration to the United States in 1940. From the moment it appeared, critics have considered it a masterpiece and one of the 'few truly great autobiographies' in modern literary history.[1]

One of the features that makes the work so exceptional and worth reading is its fascinating structure. Contrary to most autobiographies, *Speak, Memory* does not tell the story of Nabokov's life by chronologically going through its most important events. Nabokov offers a much more episodic picture of himself by constructing the work as a sequence of smaller episodes, which give an account of the big moments in his life as well as narrating rather insignificant anecdotes about himself or members of his family or household. Furthermore, the way in which these episodes are arranged within the work is not bound in strictly chronologically fashion. Although the fifteen chapters over which the episodes are divided roughly follow the progress of his life, Nabokov frequently violates the linear course of time. When, for instance, something that (allegedly) happened to him as a child thematically corresponds to an event that took place during his teenage years *or* twenties, Nabokov does not refrain from postponing this childhood experience and treating it a few chapters later, together with the later incident. He thereby brings distant moments in time into contact with one another and blends diverse periods from his life.

The question that has occupied many of Nabokov's readers, namely why he exactly composes his own life in this manner,[2] may somehow remind us of the challenges with which scholars of pre-modern 'autobiographical' texts have been faced.[3] Comparable to *Speak, Memory*, many works with an 'autobiographical potential' from Antiquity, late antiquity and the Middle Ages do not grant the reader a unified, easily comprehensible narrative about the writer's life but rather display a series of chunks of it that is assembled according to a logic that is often not immediately clear at first sight. Think, for instance, of Augustine's *Confessions*, a (seemingly) autobiographical text that is characterized by its many interruptions of the main narrative, its philosophical-theological digressions and deviations. Another obvious example are letter collections wherein an author gives insight into his life via a sequence of 'fragments', i.e. his private or public correspondence, that disclose details about himself, his addressees and particular historical circumstances. As Pliny the Younger, whose *Epistulae* will be central to this chapter, metaphorically implies in 2.5, this means that readers of letter collections can never see the author's 'entire statue at once'. Instead, they are successively given a 'close-up' of the different 'parts of the statue', close-ups that Pliny believes to be admirable in their own right.[4]

The way in which Pliny divides his 247 letters, the 'chunks of his life', over his nine books of *Epistulae* has some affinities with the structure of Nabokov's autobiography. There is a general consensus in scholarship that the composition of his collection is well-considered,[5] although Pliny himself denies in the second sentence of his first letter that there lies a pre-set design behind it: (*Collegi non servato temporis ordine, neque enim historiam componebam, sed ut quaeque in manus venerat*). Most scholars have agreed that this statement is a rhetorical trope by which Pliny aims to indicate the opposite of what he says, namely that the order of his letters is far from arbitrary.[6] As Bodel illustrates,[7] in the individual books, Pliny adopts a scheme of varied but meaningful order, while the nine books as a collection roughly follow chronology and mimic the order of events in Pliny's adult life: the first books mostly contain letters depicting Pliny's early career; the letters in the middle books portray his years as consul and augur; and the letters of the last books the period after his consul- and augurship.[8] According to Gibson and Morello, this chronological lead causes Pliny's *Epistulae* to be 'relatively hospitable, by the standards of ancient letter collections, to readers attempting to follow the story of the author's life'.[9]

Yet, this chronological mode is not consistently maintained throughout the collection, which, at several points, shows deviations that somehow resemble the 'time-related violations' of Nabokov's autobiography. Pliny repeatedly deflects from the linear course of time by sometimes incorporating in one of the later books a letter that addresses an event that, from a chronological perspective, should have been placed earlier in the collection. Narratives of, and references to Pliny's youth and early manhood appear, thereby, in unpredictable places over the course of the *Epistulae*.[10] In this way, Pliny's readers, we could say, are invited to ask similar questions as Nabokov's: why would a writer, in the literary representation of his life, deliberately cause ruptures in its order of events? For what reason would he bring remote moments from his past together and in this way generate a conflict in chronology?

In what follows, I will argue that the deviations from chronology in the *Epistulae* are part of a larger strategy by which Pliny seeks to protect the artistic representation of his life against the passing of time. By violating linearity, he aims to create a literary form that can safeguard a place for him in the world of immortality. This argument will be developed by reading Pliny's letter collection through Nabokov's *Speak, Memory*. I do not argue for any ties of reception between the two works. Instead, departing from the similarity in narrative structure, Nabokov's autobiographical memoir will serve as a constant point of comparison for the Latin text in question and will be shown to contain some features that may help us think about and reflect upon the *Epistulae*'s composition.

A persistent 'chronophobia'

A good starting point for answering the questions asked above, at least those about *Speak, Memory*, we can find in Will Norman's *Nabokov, History and the Texture of Time* (2015). In the introduction to his chapter on the autobiography, Norman makes clear that it would be useless to try to analyse the structure of the work in its own terms. He believes that a study of the composition should go hand in hand with an exploration of some of the key concepts in *Speak, Memory*, which have, in his view, determined the way in which Nabokov has arranged the story of his existence. This section will, therefore, elaborate upon two central notions in the autobiography, the 'relation between art and life' and 'time'.

In Nabokov's oeuvre, we can see a close connection between art and reality, between life and text. Almost every novel is suggested to have an autobiographical undertone and to be grounded to a certain extent in experiences the author went through in his life. As Apple has remarked, however, we should not let ourselves be misled by this autobiographical posture.[11] Nabokov did not write a 'disguised transcription' of things that happened to him in reality.[12] He uses his art to transform elements from his life, lets them go through a creative metamorphosis and embeds them into an artistic and fictional space. This is not different, Apple says, in *Speak, Memory*. We should not read this work as a somewhat embellished but relatively authentic account of the events that occurred from his childhood to adulthood. We must always remember that life has been modified into art where there are other rules and laws than in reality.

Despite the clear affinities with the novelistic works in his oeuvre, Norman believes that *Speak, Memory* holds a somewhat exceptional position. The work is first of all framed as a truly autobiographical text and thus suggests an even tighter relationship than usual between art on the one hand and the author and his personal experiences on the other. Furthermore, the autobiographical memoir is represented as having been created as an act of rebellion against a phenomenon that has held not only the author but humanity as a whole in its grip for a long time, namely time itself.[13] The 'matter of time' (Nabokov 1989: 24) forms a recurring theme in *Speak, Memory*. References to and comments upon this matter can be found everywhere in the work, from the beginning onwards. The first chapter opens with a long reflection on the topic, which immediately makes clear that Nabokov, at least so he alleges, does not seem to be very happy about the conditions that time has forced upon him. Nabokov states that time always seems 'so boundless at first blush'. Yet, in reality, it functions as 'a prison (…) without exits' that entirely controls, determines and defines human life and our existence (25).

Later in the autobiography, Nabokov hints at diverse reasons why he says that he feels so constrained by time. But they all seem to go back to the same essential problem, a problem that he appears to have with the way time has been conceptualized and experienced since Isaac Newton's treatment of it as an absolute phenomenon. Time has been represented as something mathematical, spatial and measurable that exists independently of the perceiver. It progresses in a linear way, at a consistent pace throughout our universe. This absolute conceptualization of time, Nabokov implies, has become determinant for our view on and experience of different aspects of reality, not least life itself. We have become used to thinking about our life as a strictly linear phenomenon that directly and almost mechanically proceeds from a point of beginning towards an inevitable end. We look at ourselves as growing from childhood over adulthood towards being aged (the last stage before death) and define our daily lives in terms of 'clock- and calendar-time'.[14] One of the consequences of this conception of life is that we are in a constant state of awareness of the temporariness of our existence, realizing that it is 'but a brief crack of light between two eternities of darkness' (24).[15] This understanding, so Nabokov suggests, renders many people, at some point in their lives, to be overtaken by a serious attack of the disease which he calls 'chronophobia' (24), an anxiety caused by the awareness of the linear progression of time, of life (towards death), a 'fear of non-existence'.[16]

Nabokov not coincidentally claims to feel somewhat nostalgic for his childhood. As a child he did not yet think about time in the mathematical terms Newton proposed. He was not as occupied as he would become later with measuring the exact chronological distance between two events in his life or history. He experienced time much more personally, as a relative phenomenon that could not exist independently of the perceiver. He felt himself the centre of this experience during which he could rather subjectively decide how two or more events are situated and related to one another, regardless of the actual, mathematical distance between them. He did not yet conceptualize his own life in terms of mathematical 'clock- and calendar-time', as a linear phenomenon that progresses from birth to death. Being a child, he remarks, felt like sitting in a sort of 'primordial cave (...) before the beginning of history' (31).[17]

In the opening pages of the first chapter, after having complained about the imprisonment to which time has convicted him, Nabokov states that he decided to 'rebel against this state of affairs' and to search for ways to free himself from its constraints ('Short of suicide, I have tried everything': 26). His attempts to find an adequate 'strategy of resistance', so he wants readers to believe, ultimately led him to the domain of art and resulted in the creation of the autobiographical narrative he is going to sketch in the remainder of the work. 'Armed with his writing talents', he has tried to free his life from the chains imposed by the Newton-experience of time, considering a literary creation as his only hope to break through 'the walls of time that separate him from the free world of timelessness' (27).[18] For a literary work, he believed, could not only offer him the opportunity to transfer elements from his existence into an artistic medium in which they could be granted 'a new life', with new ways of experience and with alternative conceptions, rules and laws.[19] It could also function, as he wrote in the form by which he applied for financial support to write *Speak, Memory*, as the 'proof of his existence'.[20] His work could crystallize his life, rendering it to be 'frozen in art, halted in space, timeless'.[21] It could 'protect' his existence against the linear passing of time and undermine the established idea that every life is hurtling towards an end, a point of non-existence. *Speak, Memory* can be seen as Nabokov's 'prison-break', which should prevent him from (further?) falling prey to the persistent chronophobia by which some of the members of his family and household, the characters that will appear later in his work, have been afflicted.[22]

Nabokov's ambition to create a work that should convey 'conclusive evidence' of his existence (12) probably does not sound unfamiliar to readers acquainted with pre-modern autobiographical texts.[23] Of course, the latter lack the strong fictional embedment so typical of *Speak, Memory*, though they also offer far from authentic representations of the author's lives. But Nabokov's aspiration to deliver a proof of his existence via his autobiography has affinities with an idea reverberating in many pre-modern literary (autobiographical) works, namely that a text or art piece has the potential to eternalize itself and its creator. Several indications of this idea, for example, can be found in the Latin work around which this chapter revolves. In the *Epistulae*, Pliny recurrently tells his addressees that writing a literary text is the only manner to successfully immortalize your own or someone else's image (3.10: *immortalem effigiem*).[24] Right away in the third letter of his first book, as an implicit programmatic statement, he even declares to Caninius Rufus that an artistic product is the only thing or possession that remains eternally connected to the name of its creator or the person it celebrates (1.3: *Effinge aliquid et excude, quod sit perpetuo tuum. Nam reliqua rerum tuarum post te alium atque alium dominum sortientur, hoc numquam tuum desinet esse si semel coeperit*). Although Pliny's multiple reflections upon the persistent nature of a literary work have already been recorded several times in scholarship, they have mostly been considered as a literary convention or as a strategy to emphasize the high aspirations of the collection.[25] As will be shown in this section, however, it could also be argued that the statements have a deeper function and meaning in the work and could be seen as a part of Pliny's broader Nabokov-like concerns about and reflections upon the linear progress of time.

Quite recently, scholars have started paying attention to the importance of time (*tempus*) in Pliny's collection.[26] The subject of time is brought up in multiple letters over the course of the nine books. Pliny and his addressees are often suggested to be a bit troubled by it as they know that time is a phenomenon that is difficult to control. Famous in this respect is letter 3.5, in which Pliny tells his addressee Baebius Macer about the warnings he frequently received from his uncle and adoptive father, Pliny Caecilius Secundus,[27] about the slipperiness of time. His uncle, so Pliny recounts, always felt chased by time and kept on stressing how volatile and ephemeral it is. Time, his uncle said, is an extraordinary and precious possession, that could, however, 'easily be lost without someone noticing it' (3.5: *tempus eriperet; 'poteras' inquit 'has horas non perdere'*). Therefore, his uncle tried to handle this possession as 'economically and frugally' as possible (3.5: *tanta erat parsimonia temporis*), and repeatedly advised his nephew to do the same (e.g. 3.5: *qua ex causa Romae quoque sella vehebatur. Repeto me correptum ab eo, cur ambularem (. . .). nam perire omne tempus arbitrabatur, quod studiis non impenderetur*).[28]

Although taking his uncle's advice to heart, Pliny in several letters admits that he nevertheless often feels powerless over the passing of time. He has not only noticed his impotence in daily life, where he suffers a constant lack of time to carry out the plans and projects that he has in mind,[29] but more tragically, he also experiences a strong sense of helplessness when seeing friends and acquaintances passing away more prematurely than they deserved, while he can do nothing for them. When deploring the loss of

Fundanus' daughter in letter 5.16, for example, he indicates that it was not 'death itself but the moment of its coming' that made her fate so cruel (5.16: *O triste plane acerbumque funus! O morte ipsa mortis tempus indignius!*). Tragedies like these, especially when suffered by young children or adolescents, strongly remind him of the unpredictability of the mechanisms behind time and death. Again and again, they make him aware, as he pathetically exclaims in a letter bemoaning the decease of Silius Italicus, of the 'fragility' and 'narrowness' of human existence' (3.7: *fragilitatis humanae*; *angustis terminis tantae multitudinis vivacitas ipsa concluditur*), which sometimes seems nothing more, to express it with a phrase borrowed from Nabokov, than only 'a brief crack of light between two eternities of darkness'.

In multiple letters, however, Pliny seems to be driven by the desire to rebel against this state of affairs, thinking of ways that could make human existence resistant to the impact of time. His search for 'methods of opposition' becomes most noticeable in letters dedicated to his closest friends and older role-models. In Pliny's view, they are not only praiseworthy because of their impeccable morals or political and administrative insights. What makes many of them also inspiring is their continuous fight against the march of time.

Significant in this respect is the opening letter of the third book (a book in which the subject of time forms a recurring theme). Letter 3.1 is addressed to Calvisius Rufus, to whom Pliny writes about his visits to Vetricius Spurinna, a former consul of Rome. Pliny does not try to hide his enormous admiration for Spurinna, particularly marvelling at the little influence that time seems to exert on him. Although his friend has passed his seventy-seventh year (*post septimum et septuagensimum annum*), Pliny tells that he remains 'physically agile and energetic' (*inde agile et vividum corpus*). His 'sight and hearing are unimpaired' (*aurium oculorum vigor integer*) and his old age has brought him 'nothing but wisdom' (*solaque ex senectute prudentia*). According to Pliny, this mental and physical vigour radiates directly from Spurinna. When in his company, nobody seems to be concerned anymore about the passing of time. Everything has become so pleasant and cheerful that no one cares about how long something lasts or about a 'meal prolonged into the night' (*sumit aliquid de nocte et aestate; nemini hoc longum est; tanta comitate convivium trahitur*).

By beginning his third book with a celebration of Spurinna, as a paragon of vitality, longevity and endurance, Pliny counterbalances the more sombre opening and closure of the previous book. Reports on death, pain and loss, which are the topics of 2.1 and 2.20, must make space for the hopeful story of a man on whom the passing of time appears to have no effect. If we can believe Pliny, Spurinna's secret lies in his extraordinary ability to organize his existence in accordance to 'cyclical principles'. The way he leads his life is repeatedly defined by Pliny in a vocabulary that suggests 'circularity' (*velut orbe*; *ut certus siderum cursus*), referring to the strict routine that Spurinna has chosen to follow. By implementing a circularity into his life, Spurinna has, at least at first sight, found an effective strategy to counterbalance the linearity of time and 'fight off ageing'.[30]

This way of organizing a life seems to have inspired Pliny, who admits wishing that his own life would be like Spurinna's (*hanc ego vitam voto*). It would, however, be a mistake to think that he considers Spurinna's circularity as the absolute method of opposition against the transience of time that could help him to avoid, for instance, the tragic fate of those mentioned in letters 2.1 and 2.20. Despite his admiration for Spurinna, Pliny appears to comprehend that Spurinna's strategy of resistance is nothing more than a temporary solution. He suggests this most explicitly near the end of the letter. There, he expresses the desire that, as soon as the 'thought of his years permits him to sound a retreat' (*ratio aetatis receptui canere permiserit*), he may approach his death in the same manner as Spurinna (*eundem mihi cursum, eundem terminum statuo*). In this way, he closes the letter with a reference to his own ageing as well as to Spurinna's mortality. This brief allusion to the moment of his own and Spurinna's death in the end slightly subverts the potential gains of the circular mode of living implied earlier. Both he and Spurinna remain subject to the linear logic of time, chained, one could say, within a Nabokov-like 'prison without exits'.

Throughout the rest of the third book (and the collection), Pliny mentions several other friends and role-models who, despite their best efforts, could not win their fight against time and avoid the arrival of death. For some, time has provided an even more cruel destiny and induced them to fall prey to oblivion.[31] This repeatedly brings Pliny to the conclusion that the only, reliable key to the 'world of immortality', can be found in a literary creation (e.g. 3.7: . . . *certe studiis proferamus, et quatenus nobis denegatur diu vivere, relinquamus aliquid, quo nos vixisse testemur*).[32] Thereby, he appears to ascribe a function to the *Epistulae* which resembles the one Vladimir Nabokov has attributed to *Speak, Memory*. Nabokov frames the autobiography as an attempt to 'rebel' against the mathematical experience of time which has been imposed on humanity. He has turned to a literary medium and transferred his personal experiences into art, which would crystallize his existence and preserve 'conclusive evidence' of it. In a related fashion, Pliny's statements about the eternalizing potentials of a literary text may not merely be considered as a literary convention but must be understood within the context of his broader search for a strategy to guard himself against the impact of time. The way in which Pliny conceptualizes time differs, of course, to Nabokov's Newtonian description. But he too sees it as something one should rebel against. Since a strategy like the one of Spurinna ultimately appears to be insufficient, the letter collection, so Pliny implies, is his only hope of conveying 'a proof of his existence', in Nabokov's words, rendering his life, in a sense, to be 'frozen in art, halted in space, eternal'. It should function as his ticket to immortality and as the medicine that can finally release him from his worries about death and oblivion, from, to say it with a term borrowed from Nabokov, his persistent chronophobia.

A resistant literary form

As Norman points out, it is precisely Nabokov's ambition to rebel against time that has formed the remarkable structure of the work. Autobiographical writings flourished in the twentieth century. Many authors felt the need to write down the story of their lives, often presenting it in a narrative that consistently follows a chronological thread and rigorously respects the order of experienced events. Nabokov, however, rejects this way of representation, seeming to understand the risks and inconsistencies of the act of rebellion he undertakes by writing *Speak, Memory*. If he had given form to the artistic transformation of his life in a rigorously chronological order, in terms of clock- and calendar-time, this would have meant that he would have constructed *Speak, Memory* in accordance with the linear logic of time against which he paradoxically wants to rebel by creating the work. He would have imposed the same constraints as those from which he claims to be suffering in reality on his literary life, which might have put his entire project, his ambition to free himself from the chains of absolute, mathematical time, 'under pressure'.[33]

Therefore, instead of adopting the compositional technique typical of many autobiographical texts, he brings episodes together that, speaking from a strictly chronological point of view, are not adjacent. By frequently violating chronology, Nabokov undermines the traditional, linear way in which he has been taught to think about human life. He attempts to avoid letting the literary proof of his existence become subject to the Newtonian time-laws 'against which he seeks to stand up'.[34] He prefers a mode of representation that does not rigorously respect the periodical terms usually imposed on a human life (childhood, then adolescence, then young-adulthood, and so on) and allows for bringing distant moments from his existence together (as he metaphorically suggests in the following sentence: 'I like to fold my magic carpet, after use, in such a way as to superimpose one part of the pattern upon another': 109). The deviations from chronology thus should be understood in terms of resistance, as Nabokov's attempt to 'structurally arm' the literary proof of his existence against the impact of time.[35]

As Foster remarks, this structural strategy of resistance seems to be related to Nabokov's childhood experience of time.[36] As mentioned in the previous section, Nabokov portrays his childhood as a period in which the time-relation between two or more events was rather subjectively experienced and defined by him as a young boy, not by the mathematical clock- and calendar-time. Although this experience has become lost in 'real life', through the chronological deviations he seems to have found a technique to implement a variation of it in the artistic medium into which he has transferred elements from his personal experience. In *Speak, Memory*, chunks of his life are grouped together because he subjectively thinks they belong together, regardless of the actual chronological distance between them. By suggesting this analogy with his childhood, Nabokov aims to enforce the impression that the autobiographical form he has developed serves as an adequate protection mechanism, which succeeds in dismantling time's usual constraints and making his life no longer susceptible to its passing, thus preventing his existence from disappearing into the 'abyss' of death.[37]

Given the affinities pointed out above with *Speak, Memory*, we may wonder whether a comparable relationship can be observed between Pliny's conceptualization of time and the recurrent deviations from the linear thread within the collection. Are the violations of chronology somehow connected with Pliny's ambition to protect his existence, via a literary medium, from the passing of time?

A good starting point for answering these questions might be the very first letter of the *Epistulae*. In the second sentence, which has already been quoted in the introduction, Pliny himself attracts the readers' attention to the notion of chronology by stating that, while composing his collection, he 'has not preserved the order of time' (*collegi non servato temporis ordine*). This does not only serve to incite the curiosity of the readers, who may start wondering what method of arrangement Pliny has applied instead. Pliny is also implying that the text we are going to read could have been arranged otherwise, i.e. strictly chronologically, but that for some reason he has decided not to do so.[38]

Pliny justifies this structural choice by saying that he 'was not writing a history' (*neque enim historiam componebam*).[39] This statement has received much scholarly attention, as it contains the first reference in Pliny's work to the genre of historiography, to which Pliny will continue to come back over the course of collection. Numerous letters praise practitioners of the genre for their literary efforts. Others discuss the stylistic requirements of historiography or celebrate its potential to preserve great deeds from past and present times for future generations. In other letters, Pliny even seems to have incorporated thematic or formal features conventional in historiography, thereby giving his collection a historiographical flavour.[40] The reference to *historia* in the first letter, as Marchesi and Tzounakis argue, indicates from its very beginning the work's strong engagement with the historiographical genre.[41]

This interpretation, however, fails to ask why Pliny, despite his fondness of the genre of historiography, so explicitly rejects the chronological ordering principles with which he characterizes it. Although the ancient literary tradition brought forth some letter collections that follow a strictly chronological lead,[42] overall, the composition of these kinds of works much more often depended on the (non-chronological) technique of *variatio*. There was thus no need for Pliny to justify that he has not consistently preserved the order of time. Why, then, does he underline that he has not wanted to adopt the historiographical linear manner of representation? What does it imply about the compositional choices he has made in his collection?

A letter in which Pliny extensively reflects upon historiography and the great potentials of the genre is 5.8. This letter is framed as a response to Titinius Capito, who encouraged him a while before to start writing historiography. Pliny feels flattered by Capito's request and admits being tempted by the idea. Unfortunately, he says, he must decline the proposal, as he does not have enough time to engage himself in yet another literary enterprise. At this moment, Pliny writes, he is completely preoccupied with publishing his rhetorical speeches, which is such a great undertaking that it cannot possibly be combined with something else, especially not with writing in a high and demanding genre as historiography (*utrumque tam magnum est, ut abunde sit alterum efficere*).[43] It would be foolish to initiate a new literary project of which he cannot be certain if he will even have the time to complete it. For, as he said earlier in his letter, 'anything left unfinished is no different to something not even begun' (*quidquid non est peractum, pro non incohato est*). An unfinished text, in Pliny's view, is very likely doomed to vanish into oblivion, to 'die with its author' (*mecum pariter intercidat*).

These lines may remind the readers of a similar statement he made three letters before, in 5.5, wherein he lamented the death of Gaius Fannius. The letter especially commemorates Fannius' qualities as a writer. He would have been quite well-known in Rome as the author working on a piece about the times under Nero, particularly about those who were put to death or banished by the emperor (*exitus occisorum aut relegatorum a Nerone*). According to Ash, the vocabulary Pliny uses to describe the work indicates that it concerned a sort of historiography.[44] Unfortunately, at the time of his death Fannius had only completed three books (*tres libros absolverat*). Pliny therefore states that it is very unlikely that Fannius' work, in its unfinished state (*opus imperfectum reliquit*), will ever achieve eternal fame. 'Death', he complains, 'always seems to be untimely when it comes to those who have the plan to create something immortal' (*mihi autem videtur acerba semper et immatura mors eorum, qui immortale aliquid parant*).

It seems to be no coincidence that the letters regarding the death of Gaius Fannius and Titinius Capito's proposal about writing historiography follow almost immediately on one another in the fifth book. Both letters revolve around the art of writing *historia* and reflect upon the dangers of incompletion and oblivion. Pliny nowhere explicitly claims that there is a connection between these matters, that the chance to leave a work unfinished would be significantly higher when writing a history than in another genre. But Pliny hints a couple of times in this direction in 5.5 and 5.8. He seems to suggest two reasons that are both remarkably related to the genre's linear representation of time.

The first implicit explanation for why there would be a correlation between composing *historia* and the *opus imperfectum* concerns the nature of the material around which a historiographical work revolves. A historiographer usually gives an account of a series of events that are well-defined in time, space and subject (for instance, a generation of emperors or the victims under Nero). His work can only be considered finished when it has reported on all the main events that happened in the demarcated period and has reached the chosen chronological end point. In cases where the author might feel that death is near (like Gaius Fannius did: *quod accidit, . . . praesensit*), the defined material makes it difficult for him to bring his text hastily to a close. Furthermore, working with well-demarcated material entails that the author, before he starts writing, must make a well-considered choice that he cannot rethink. Someone with as broad interests as Pliny could therefore be faced with insoluble dilemmas. At the end of the letter to Capito, for example, Pliny declares that, even if he did decide to become a historiographer, he would have no idea on what topic he should focus, whether on the recent or the more remote past (*vetera et scripta aliis? . . . intacta et nova*?). Pliny understands that if he chose to be a historiographer, he would not be allowed to tackle both the recent and the remote pasts and include events from different periods in time within a single work. In this way, his account of the past would almost by definition remain 'incomplete'.[45] The conceptualization of historiography as a temporally bound genre, offering a linear representation of the events within a certain period, seems to exclude the possibility of creating a 'complete history', one in which the entire past is recounted.

The second reason for why there may be a link between historiography and incompleteness concerns the constant state of awareness, into which the historiographer is brought by writing history, of the ephemerality of his existence. In 5.5, Gaius Fannius' death is said to have been forecasted in a dream. While sleeping, Fannius saw an image of himself being ready to continue working out his history of the times under Nero. Suddenly, the ghost of the former emperor turned up and started reading the volumes Fannius had already completed (in his dream). After three volumes, Nero's ghost was tired of reading and departed as abruptly as he showed up. Fannius comprehended this dream as a sign, Pliny recounts, that his 'writing would end at the point where Nero stopped reading, and so this came to pass' (5.5: *tamquam idem futurus esset scribendi finis, qui fuisset ill legendi; et fuit idem*). One way to understand Fannius' dream is by seeing it as an embodiment of the awareness of mortality that will affect every historiographer at some point.[46] By concentrating on figures that already belong to the past, the historiographer, perhaps more than practitioners of other genres, is confronted with the fact that the course of everyone's life is linear and inevitably leads towards an end. The historiographer realizes that he will once fall prey to the passing of time and become part of the past himself (like Fannius, who is overtaken by the history he was describing in his present). On a more metaphorical level, and considered from the viewpoint of the historiographer himself, this turns historiography (once more) into an 'art of incompletion'. As history will continue progressing after he himself belongs to the domain of 'what was gone', he understands that there will always be 'things that will be' that he will not be able to include.

Although Pliny favours the historiographical genre, he suggests that the strictly linear way in which it usually treats and conceptualizes the past is a feature that increases the risk of incompletion, which means the work runs the risk of vanishing into oblivion. His refusal to comply with Titinius Capito's proposal to start writing historiography in 5.8, therefore, may have a deeper 'chronophobic' reason than one might think at first glance, being grounded in the fear that the genre's linear representation of time would potentially not allow its author to finish his creation, the creation that would ensure his name survives on when his own time comes.

This reading of Pliny's view on historiography allows us to formulate a new hypothesis about the composition of the collection and the explicit rejection of the historiographical method of arrangement in the very first letter. More than only being a programmatic allusion to the work's engagement with the genre, this rejection can perhaps also serve as an indication of Pliny's belief that the 'preservation of the order of time' would have produced a literary form of which he could not be entirely certain that it would be 'resistant enough' to protect the literary proof of his existence against the linear logic of time. If Pliny had adopted the linear historiographical mode of representation and arranged his collection in a strictly chronological manner, he suggests, he would have told the story of his life in a way that he himself associates with the dangers of incompletion and oblivion; he would have exposed the artistic representation of his life to the risk of running the same fate as will befall his body (passing away, instead of surviving), which would put his 'entire literary project under pressure'. If we continue this line of thinking, we could hypothesize that the recurring violations of chronology over the course of the collection serve as a strategy to help him avoid the dangers inherent to a strictly historiographical mode of composition.

To test this hypothesis, it might be useful to return once more to 5.8, which appears to offer an implicit reflection upon the function and value of the deviations from chronology. As discussed above, Pliny's main reason to refuse Titinius Capito's proposal is that writing historiography would be too demanding an endeavour, which would prove to be difficult to combine with his other writing plans. Instead of initiating a new literary project, he explains to Capito, it would be better to finish first the undertakings, in particular his oratorical work, that he has already begun. As soon as he has completed these texts and 'executed the last revisions', he would be released from the pressure to publish a completed literary testimony before his death (*egi magnas et graves causas. has, etiamsi mihi tenuis ex iis spes, destino retractare, ne tantus ille labor meus, nisi hoc quod reliquum est studii addidero, mecum pariter intercidat*).

Although the latter statement makes perfect sense within the context of 5.8, we may wonder whether his mentioning of 'revising old work' (*destino retractare*), as the preferred alternative of writing *historia*, might have a wider significance. As Morello cogently argues, the verb *retractare*, like *emandare*, is a loaded term in the *Epistulae*. It is not only used in its everyday sense of clerical work, proofreading and correcting written texts.[47] In several letters, Pliny also uses the verb in a more metaphorical sense to refer to some cyclical gestures that can be observed in the collection. Since Pliny only addresses a quite limited set of subjects throughout the nine books, it frequently occurs that, for example, a later letter treats a topic that was already handled somewhere earlier on and of which will be spoken again later on. This creates repetitive patterns running through the work via which certain matters, as Pliny implies, are 'revised' or 'revisited' (*retractare/emendare*) over and again. The letters responsible for the deviations from chronology form an important part of this tendency. Mostly referring to Pliny's youth and early career, they keep on reminding the readers of periods, themes and issues that were already portrayed and discussed in the first books.

These cyclical tendencies, including those caused by the deviations of the letters from strict chronology, have predominantly been understood as a way to guide his readers through the collection in an interesting and intellectually stimulating manner. By incorporating letters revisiting themes and events that have already been treated earlier in the collection, Pliny invites his readers to think them over once more and approach them from a slightly different angle.[48] But the implicit reference to these tendencies in 5.8 opens up a complementary interpretation that allows us to comprehend them in relation to Pliny's concerns about the linear representation of time. The statement that Pliny prefers to 'revise' his earlier (oratorical) work, instead of writing historiography, does not necessarily suggest that he favours the former genre more than the latter. But, in keeping with the metaphorical meaning of the verb *retractare*, Pliny might want to indicate that the cyclical manner of representing life, causing certain aspects and periods of his existence to be 'revised' over and again, is more suitable than the historiographical mode of arrangement associated with the dangers of incompletion and oblivion.[49] By integrating cyclical movements in his collection, even those that violate strict chronology, he may be suggesting, he can avoid exposing the literary proof of his life to the risks he would run if he ordered the story in his existence in a rigorously linear-historiographical way. He would thereby better prevent the 'conclusive evidence of his existence' which he wants to deliver via the *Epistulae* from being subdued to the laws and 'transience of linear time against which he aims to stand up'.

Why would cyclical movements, in particular those generated by the deviations from chronology, decrease the danger of incompletion related to the historiographical method of arrangement? First, these cyclical patterns help Pliny to make sure that his collection is at any time 'concluded' by suggesting 'multiple endings'. As several scholars have illustrated,[50] the ninth book of the *Epistulae* contains a remarkably large number of letters that somehow refer to themes from the first book. By linking the opening and the ending of his collection, Pliny succeeds at bringing us back to the beginning and in this way offers a satisfying conclusion to his work. Yet, as Whitton has argued, this technique seems not to be restricted to the last book alone. He points, for instance, to the final letter of the seventh book (7.33), addressing a treason trial that happened in Pliny's early career. Whitton has recorded several elements within the letter that create a 'sense of an ending' and which suggest that it would have made a 'superb conclusion' to the collection.[51] Something similar can be observed, in his view, within some letters in the second, third and fifth book.[52] By integrating these 'false endings' in the *Epistulae*, partly caused by the deviations from chronology,[53] it appears that Pliny seeks to guard the literary evidence of his life against the danger of incompleteness. Whenever death might happen to befall him, his letter collection would always have an end and be ready for immortality.[54]

A second reason why the cyclical patterns produced by the violations of chronology would help him to make the literary proof of his existence resistant to the impact of time is that they create affinities between the artistic representation of his life and Vetricius Spurinna's way of living that Pliny so admired. As explained in the previous section, Pliny expresses his strong admiration for Vetricius Spurinna in letter 3.1, who fights off ageing by organizing his life in a circular manner. Although Pliny realizes that this method of opposition will ultimately not be sufficient, he understands the possibilities offered by circularity. The implementation of cyclical movements via the deviations from chronology can be seen as an attempt to simulate in his own text Spurinna's techniques of resistance. What may not sufficiently work in 'real' life can work instead in the literary representation of his existence. The deviations from chronology in the collection both in their mirroring of Spurinna's way of living and in the creation of multiple endings, seem to help Pliny to 'structurally arm' – to echo Norman's judgement on Nabokov's *Speak, Memory* – the literary proof of his existence against the passing of time, a passing that he and many of his addressees seem to fear so much.

To turn to Norman's assessment, Nabokov has rejected linearity, which we can find for example in traditional autobiographies, being aware that it might have put his entire literary project under pressure. By bringing distant moments in his life into contact with one another, Nabokov aims to subvert the mathematical and linear experience of time to which humanity has been condemned since Newton's conceptualization and to provide a literary form that could safeguard his life's spot into the domain of timelessness. In a similar way, we could explain the function of the many references to Pliny's youth and early manhood spread over the course of the collection. The deviations from chronology serve as the core of Pliny's Nabokov-like method to make the literary representation of his life resistant to the impact of time.[55] They help him to avoid the dangers of incompletion and oblivion associated with the historiographical mode of arrangement. Via the violations of chronology, it seems, Pliny hopes to develop a literary form that could prevent his life disappearing into the abyss of death and guaranteeing its place in the world of eternity. He seems to have found, in other words, a resistant literary form, which is the ultimate medicine to release himself from a chronophobia quite as persistent as Nabokov's.

Speak, existence, through the reader's memory

In an article examining some modern and early modern editions of letter collections from Antiquity, Gibson notices that during the last centuries, more and more editors were apparently disturbed by the compositional choices made by ancient authors. Especially when recording violations of chronology, editors often felt the need to 'restore' these deviations and sometimes rearranged the entire collection:

> For eight – i.e. nearly three quarters – of our letter collections have been chronologically re-ordered in modern or early modern editions. Of these eight editorial rearrangements, seven have taken place in editions that were either authoritative or widely used in their day. In several cases, the editions, in fact, remain either authoritative or widely used.[56]

Gibson consequently points out that the chronological violations in ancient letter collections are not 'mistakes' but must be understood in a literary-historical context wherein the reader expectations differed from ours.

Gibson's observation gives rise to the question to what sort of reading process Pliny's *Epistulae*, via its composition, gives form. Pliny several times indicates to understand that his ambition to eternalize the literary proof of his existence can never be fulfilled without readers, whatever the literary form his collection is shaped in. Only when the readers preserve the *Epistulae* deep in their memories will Pliny be granted the state of immortality he has been hoping for.[57] But do Pliny's compositional choices help him to impose the artistic evidence of his life on his reader's memory? As the behaviour of the editors mentioned above shows, some readers since the early modern period have preferred a narrative that rigorously respects the course of time. But have they failed to appreciate the form of Pliny's work?

In his analysis of the task of the reader in Nabokov's autobiography, Rodgers starts with a discussion of the alleged literary genesis of the work. Nabokov on several occasions represented the text as the outcome of an intense mental process, of a profound investigation of his own memory.[58] As he confided to his friend Edmund Wilson, *Speak, Memory* could be seen as 'a new type of autobiography'. It should be considered as 'a scientific attempt' to trace back 'all the tangled threads of his personality'.[59] He declared to have worked through his mind and the snatches of his past with the aim of offering a 'correlated assemblage of personal recollections' (10). This strong reliance on memory during the genesis of his work, so Nabokov implies multiple times in the text, has informed almost every single aspect of the autobiography, not least in the the remarkable structure discussed in the previous sections. For example, a mnemonic principle to which he frequently refers over the course of *Speak, Memory* is 'association', a term that already turns up at the very first page. While making his trip down memory lane, he remarks, he has let himself be led by the associative links and connections that could be observed between different episodes in his life. This mnemonic principle, so it is suggested, has (partly) helped him to set up the resistant structure described above. Via associative thinking, he has been enabled to develop the non-chronological 'experiential patterns' that can be observed in the work and offer an artistic transformation that would be capable of protecting his life against the progress of time.[60]

The framing of his autobiography as the outcome of a mnemonic investigation has various implications. One of them, Rodgers explains, is that Nabokov causes his text to seem to be 'functioning as a memorial object'. Like 'tombstones, statues or photographs', the book as an object 'forever depicts, and commemorates, particular instances of life'. This does not only entail that it seeks to 'memorialize the real and imagined events' depicted inside of it. It also indicates that it wants these depictions never to 'change regardless of the number of times we return to them'.[61] By firmly linking his literary creation to memory and presenting it as a written assemblage of personal recollections, Nabokov seems to reinforce the impression that he hopes his life to become frozen in a piece of art that would serve as a commemorating medium and to memorialize the events that he believed in his mnemonic investigation worth preserving, thereby rendering his existence to be resistant to 'death's caprices'.[62]

According to Rodgers, Nabokov has developed several strategies to 'allow the readers to experience his memory'. He does not want his readers merely to register the real and imagined events depicted in the work indifferently (from this point of view, Rodger's above-mentioned comparison to tombstones might be less suitable). He aims to transform his memories, as he states, 'into something that can be turned over to the reader[s] in printed characters' (127), to ensure that they 'remember' what they have read.[63] One of the methods he applies to bring out the readers' experience of his recollections is 'his coupling of descriptive power and sensory evocation'. Nabokov evokes his personal experiences in a deliberately suggestive way, using many details and creating a 'multisensory tableau'.[64] Another and perhaps even more important strategy is his appeal to the readers to actively explore the many connections between the episodes in *Speak, Memory*. Just like Nabokov himself, who states that he has tried to explore all the tangled threads of his personality, the readers are expected to look for possible connections between Nabokov's memories in *Speak, Memory*. They are encouraged to reflect on why he has juxtaposed a non-chronological series of recollections, to see relations over two or more chapters, to record traces running through the mnemonic constellation of his entire life, and so on. Reading the work, so it is implied, can be compared to solving a 'scrambled picture' (450), where the final image is not immediately clear. The readers should sift through the recollections, trying to discover links between them and discern broader patterns, as if they are shifting different pieces of the scrambled puzzle around in order to make out the picture. Nabokov, as he does in his entire oeuvre, constantly misleads his readers and puts them on the wrong track, yet he promises them that, as soon as they will have figured out how the puzzle works, they 'cannot unsee' anymore what they have seen (450).[65] By requiring such a strong participation, Nabokov compels his readers to really 'experience his memories'. They are obliged to become 'engaged in the activity of remembering', imprinting the memories and recollections of Nabokov's existence in their minds, and contribute thereby to the 'negation of the efficacy of death' he seeks to achieve.[66]

If an editor had proposed to chronologically re-order *Speak, Memory*, as has been done with ancient letter collections, Nabokov would certainly have protested. The editor would not only dismantle the artistic structure that has been developed to liberate Nabokov's existence from the constraints of Newtonian time, but would also have undermined Nabokov's strategy to appeal to his readers, stimulating them to explore the relationships between the recollections over the course of the work and to engage themselves in the activity of remembering 'Nabokov'. The question this section wants to ask is whether Pliny, if he had had the chance to confront the editors Gibson has described, would have made a similar protest. Would he have indicated that the arrangement of his letters, including the deviations from chronology, somehow help him to enforce the memorialization of the literary proof of his existence?

To explore this issue, it might be useful to first take a look at how Pliny frames his collection and its literary genesis. If we know how he has (allegedly) set up the composition, we might get an indication of what he expects with it from us. A possible starting point for this research can be found almost at the end of the collection. In 9.36, Pliny tells his addressee, Fuscus Salinator, about his daily routines when he is spending summer in his villa in Tuscany. Although Pliny is busy with many things, several hours a day are devoted to writing. The letter interestingly comments upon some of the writing habits that Pliny asserts he has developed:

> *Evigilo cum libuit, plerumque circa horam primam, saepe ante, tardius raro. Clausae fenestrae manent; mire enim silentio et tenebris ab iis quae avocant abductus et liber et mihi relictus, non oculos animo sed animum oculis sequor, qui eadem quae mens vident, quotiens non vident alia. Cogito si quid in manibus, cogito ad verbum scribenti emendantique.*

From the moment he wakes up, Pliny claims to be completely occupied by his writing tasks. Lying in the dark and feeling detached from any distraction, he occupies himself with his mind's eye' (*sed animum oculis sequor*). The things 'that are at hand', he says, he works out in his head (*cogito si quid in manibus*) and mentally writes and rewrites (*cogito ad verbum scribenti emendantique*). Consequently, he calls his secretary to dictate the matters to which he has just before given shape (*quae formaveram dicto*).[67] What this passage makes clear is that writing, for Pliny, is first and foremost a mental activity. A literary work is not something that spontaneously flows from an author's pen. Instead, the writing process starts in the writer's head, as the writer lets himself be led along paths set out in his mind and mentally gives form to the text.

Pliny's general reflections upon his writing methods near the end of his collection invite us to return once more to the opening letter of the *Epistulae*, which is thematically connected to 9.36.[68] In that letter, he comments upon the genesis of his letter collection and particularly informs his readers about his composition techniques. Whereas 9.36 represents Pliny as a meticulous writer, 1.1 offers, at least at first sight, a more nonchalant image of him. He declares to Septicius Clarus that he has composed his letters 'with some care' (*paulo curatius*) and consequently arranged them in a collection 'as they came to his hand' (*quaeque in manus venerat*). As already pointed out in the introduction, the latter phrase has mostly been interpreted as a rhetorical trope by which Pliny wants to create the false impression that the *Epistulae* was ordered at random but in essence aims to indicate that the opposite is true.

A complementary interpretation of this phrase may come to the fore when reading 1.1 through 9.36. For, the formulation 'as they came to his hand' may remind us of a very similar expression from the letter in the ninth book (*si quid in manibus*) and variants of this expression which can be found elsewhere in the collection (cf. 5.5: *quae inter manus*; 9.1: *si quid aliud in manibus*). In all these letters, the metaphor revolving around *manus* does not refer to arbitrariness but is used in the context of mental activities and alludes to the matters that 'occupy and revolve within an author's mind'. This opens up a different interpretation of the second sentence of the first letter. Apart from functioning as a rhetorical play that falsely implies the randomness of the composition, *ut quaeque manus* may also suggest that Pliny has arranged his letters in the order 'they came up in his mind', in the sequence he handled them while mentally preparing the *Epistulae* (so in accordance with the process he sets out in 9.36). As in his other writings, his letter collection, in particular through its composition, is implied to be the outcome of a thorough mental process of preparation.

Apart from the letters concerning the literary genesis of his writings, Pliny frequently addresses the subject of the mind in the collection. He mostly does so within the context of discussions of oratory and rhetorical training. Pliny represents himself at several points in the *Epistulae* as an experienced orator who enjoyed a profound rhetorical education. He does not only try to convince his readers of his rhetorical capacities via the implementation of letters boasting about his *moments de gloire* in the senate and in court. He also repeatedly demonstrates his oratorical knowledge by reflecting upon a variety of rhetorical techniques that held a key place in Roman education. He pays especial attention to the best strategies by which an orator can train his mental and mnemonic capacities. Gibson and Morello, for example, have pointed to a cluster of letters in which Pliny comments upon how the orator should mentally master a large body of text. He advises his addressees to divide the text in smaller parts and go over these parts again and again in their minds (9.40: *memoriae frequenti emendatio proficitur*). Only by mentally re-reading the text, in an implicit echo of the precepts of Pliny's teacher Quintilian, will an orator be able to master the textual material.[69] In other letters, Pliny goes a step further to demonstrate his familiarity with rhetorical principles. Instead of theorizing about them, he brings them into practice within the context of a letter. According to McEwen, for instance, Pliny's famous letters containing the descriptions of his Tuscan and Laurentian villas (2.17; 5.6) appear to be inspired by the well-known technique of the memory palace.[70] The remarkably systematic way in which the '*dispositio*' (5.6) of the houses is set out may remind the readers of an orator imagining the mental space (*locus*) in which he will later place the images (*imagines*) that should help him to remember the *res* or *verba* of a speech.

Apart from contributing to Pliny's self-fashioning as a skilled orator, these letters might have an additional function in the collection. Especially when reading them with letters like 1.1 and 9.36 in mind, in which a connection has been suggested between the genesis of the *Epistulae* and the writer's mental activities, they may serve as an invitation to the readers to reflect upon the composition of the text they are reading. By repeatedly drawing attention to how a rhetorically trained mind orders and processes textual material, Pliny may be encouraging his readers to consider whether there might be some sort of interrelation with the structure of his work, which has been set up by a self-declared rhetorically trained mind. When reading the advice about how best to master a large body of textual material, which entails that one should divide the speech in small portions and re-read these over and again, for instance, the readers may notice a parallel with the way in which the 'story' of Pliny's life is presented to them in the *Epistulae*. Pliny has chosen to disclose the 'text of his existence' in small separate portions (a sequence of letters) in which a relatively limited number of themes are revisited again and again (the cyclical mode). The letters violating chronology, containing references to Pliny's youth and early adulthood, cause the story of his life, and its readers, to return, in a sense, to the beginning of his life.[71] The structure of the composition, we could say, corresponds to the rhetorical practices for which Pliny pleads.

Another correlation between the arrangement of the *Epistulae* and the way in which the functioning of the rhetorical mind is portrayed seems to be suggested via a remarkable series of metaphors that Pliny uses throughout the collection. He frequently speaks about his letters, especially of those in which he praises a living or deceased friend, in terms of portraits (*picturae*), statues (*statua*) or images (*imagines*) exhibited in private or public. As Henderson argues, this creates the impression that the *Epistulae* is set up as a gallery in which the readers can admire the achievements of great men, including those of the author.[72] When Pliny is depicted in some letters as looking at the statues or monuments that are standing on the forum or a villa domain, this might be understood as a meta-literary invitation to the readers to similarly 'contemplate the exceptional memorials showed in the text, to turn back to look at them, stand at their foot and finally walk past them' (2.7: *effigiem eius subinde intueri subinde respicere, sub hac consistere praeter hanc commeare*; 8.6: *delectus est celeberrimus locus, in quo legenda praesentibus, legenda futuris proderentur*). This causes the *Epistulae* to function to a certain extent as an *objet de mémoire*. Like a statue or a portrait, it should memorialize the persons and events depicted inside of it as well as immortalize them, making them resistant to the 'caprices of death'.

This perception of the *Epistulae* seems to be enforced by a suggested correlation to the memory palace technique. The framing of the collection as a textual space in which one can move from one *imago, statua* or *pictura* to another may have affinities with the mnemonic principle with which Pliny plays in the depictions of his villas. As Bergmann has shown, several pieces of art in Antiquity present themselves as a sort of artistic adaptations of this mnemonic principle. Bergmann illustrates her point by means of an analysis of a Roman living place in Pompeii, which seems to have been constructed in accordance with 'influential rhetorical and mnemonic models'.[73] The owner of the house ordered his space and installed objects and paintings in it in such a way that it appears as if he wants his visitors to move through the 'text or memory of his life'. Similarly, we could say, Pliny in the *Epistulae* offers a 'walking tour' in the 'monument of his existence' (*locus*) in which he has placed a series of objects (*imagines*) that should represent him as a multifaceted figure within the complex social context of Rome. Just as the owner of the Pompeii house, seemingly following the rhetorical theories, has not ordered the objects telling the story of his life chronologically but rather associatively,[74] Pliny's method of arrangement has predominantly been based on techniques of association and patterning. The letters violating chronology and generating the cyclical movements, for instance, are never arbitrarily positioned but, as in a house of memory,[75] are connected to other letters in their immediate environment, thereby adding an extra layer of meaning to their surroundings and bringing diverse moments in time together in a small (textual) space.

The suggested correspondences between the compositional and mnemonic techniques of the *Epistulae* thus do not only reinforce the impression that the collection has been curated by a rhetorically trained mind, who conceptualizes the story of his existence and the writing of this story in rhetorical terms. It also underlines the work's function as a *objet de mémoire* whose depictions inside of it should be remembered. As mentioned in the beginning of this section, this is one of the reasons why Pliny recurrently stresses the importance of the readers. They should walk through the monument of his life, admire the images, statues and pictures installed in the memorial object and save them in their memory. Pliny, not coincidently, favours those addressees who have allegedly told him that they like his work so much that they have learnt parts of it by heart (4.19: *meos libellos habet lectitat ediscit etiam*; 6.33: *tu facillime iudicabis, qui tam memoriter tenes omnes, ut conferre cum hac dum hanc legis possis*).[76]

Importantly, instead of deeply hoping that his readers will be willing to save the collection in their memory, Pliny, so it seems, really wants to 'impose' his work on them. Via his composition, he seeks encourage readers to 'engage themselves in the activity of remembering'. By setting up the *Epistulae* in accordance with rhetorical-mnemonic principles, he persuades us to process his text in a way that resembles the manner in which an orator tries to imprint his speech in his mind. We are compelled to work through the story of his existence in small portions and, due to the cyclical patterns, re-read and re-visit parts of his life that have already been treated before.[77] We are expected to move ourselves through his textual space, looking for connections between the images, statues and portraits and trying to comprehend all the 'tangled threads of his personality'.

This causes the readers of the *Epistulae*, in a sense, to carry out a similar task as those of Nabokov's autobiography, to shift around the pieces of its author's existence in order to build up an image of him (though Pliny does not mislead his readers, nor does he suggest that there is only one solution). By requiring such a strong participation from readers, leading them through a sort of rhetorical-mnemonic trajectory, Pliny, so it seems, seeks to ensure the ongoing memorialization of his work and his existence. The structure of the letter collection is created, in other words, to let the text of his life endlessly 'speak through and within its readers' memory', obliging them to contribute to the 'negation of the efficacy of death' Pliny aims to achieve.

Conclusion

Contrary to many other texts discussed in this volume, Pliny's and Nabokov's autobiographical works do not contain an epitomary dimension in the strictest sense of the word. It could perhaps be argued that their texts are the product of a process of dismemberment and re-composition, which the volume's editors see as two fundamental movements in the creation of epitomary literature. Both authors, we could say, have split up their existence into small pieces which they have consequently rearranged into an artistic constellation. Yet this does not make the letter collection and the autobiography examples of epitomary literature (which requires the procedures of dismemberment and re-composition to be applied to existent texts). What value, then, may the analysis of the *Epistulae* and *Speak, Memory* add to the debate on epitomary gestures?

First of all, this contribution has concentrated on those features in Pliny's and Nabokov's works that seem to have affinities with epitomary literature, and which, therefore, may help us think about the latter's functioning. An aspect of epitomary literature on which the autobiographical texts may throw a new light, for instance, is the notion of (in)completion. Works with an epitomary dimension have often been considered as derivative forms of literature. They have been said to lack the richness of the texts they are epitomizing. For, much of the original texts is asserted to have gone missing in the epitomizing process. As a result of the procedures of dismemberment, selection, compression, fragmentation and re-composition, epitomary works can only present the original texts in a partial, incomplete and less meaningful way. The above analysis of the *Epistulae* and *Speak, Memory* invites us to question this assumed interconnection between epitomary literature and incompletion. Both Pliny and Nabokov do not choose to tell the stories of their lives in a coherent, continuous narrative form that chronologically recounts all the minor and major events that have happened to them. Instead, they work with a selective set of aspects and episodes from their existence, which they present to the readers as a series of relatively brief fragments. Especially in Pliny's view, this literary form serves as the only way to guarantee the preservation of his life in its integrity. For him, the selective and fragmented nature of his collection constitutes its own kind of completion and presents his life in a more meaningful way than a continuous narrative would have done, as it allows him to suggestively interconnect the different aspects and episodes of his existence. We may wonder whether epitomary literature might be conceptualized in a similar way, i.e. as a textual form in which the procedures of dismemberment, selection and compression are not mutually exclusive with the aspiration for integrity. In epitomary literature, as in Pliny's and Nabokov's works, is less more?[78]

Another feature of epitomary literature about which the *Epistulae* and *Speak, Memory* may help us think concerns the notions of time, space and memory. In their respective works, Pliny and Nabokov frequently try to disrupt time's linearity. They bring distant episodes from their life into contact with one another, seeking to counteract time's effects and to protect their existence against its transience. They want their autobiographical texts to function as *objets de mémoire* that can guarantee the immortalization of their life by structurally imposing it on the reader's memory. As explained near the end of the third section, Pliny emphasizes the mnemonic dimension of his collection by presenting his text not as a temporal constellation but as a spatialized construct. The *Epistulae* serves as a monumental space, a gallery, in which the readers are expected to move from one mnemonic image of his life to another, regardless of the actual temporal distance between the pictured episodes. Like Pliny's and Nabokov's works, texts with an epitomary dimension frequently bring distant moments in time into contact with one another. An epitomary work often juxtaposes and confronts excerpts of texts originating from different literary periods. It has the capacity to compress a large timespan of literature onto a few pages.[79] Keeping the *Epistulae* and *Speak, Memory* in mind, we may ask whether epitomary literature similarly serves as a textual form that also counteracts time's effects. And if so, what paradigms replace temporality, as constitutive factors of narrative? Could we, for instance, observe in texts with an epitomary dimension a similar conversion from time into space as in Pliny's collection? Should we, perhaps, understand them as a spatialized form of literature?

The second reason why this contribution is relevant within the context of this volume is that it has tried to integrate some of the central principles of epitomary aesthetics into its own research practice. In my view, the power of epitomary literature lies in its ability to produce new patterns of thinking. As a result of the movements of dismemberment and re-composition, texts are removed from their original context and integrated into a new whole, into a new network of textual interactions. In this way, an epitomary work – whether this was the intention of its author or not – may provoke alternative perspectives upon the texts it has epitomized and induce different modes of understanding.[80] Adopting this idea into my own research practice, I have set up a rather unusual textual encounter between Pliny and Nabokov. Observing a similarity in the works' narrative structure, I have disrupted the *Epistulae* and *Speak, Memory* from their contexts of origin and cancelled out the temporal distance that exists between them. This unexpected confrontation has generated new ways of interpretation, an alternative viewpoint to think about matters of composition. The study of epitomary literature, therefore, may not only prove to be useful because of its literary-historical importance. It may also invite reflection upon and innovation within our own modes of research.[81]

Notes

* I would like to thank the volume's editors for the stimulating conversations we had about my work. I am also very grateful to Prof. Wim Verbaal (Ghent University), whose feedback tremendously improved this contribution.

1. Epstein 2014.
2. For a general discussion of Nabokov's play with narrative form and literary structure, see Toker 1989.
3. For a discussion of the complex relationship between pre-modern texts depicting someone's life and modern definitions of biography and autobiography, see Most 1989: 122; Gibson and Morello 2012: 9–19 and De Temmerman 2016: 3–25.
4. Whitton 2015: 131–8.
5. E.g. Sherwin-White 1966; Murgia 2016; Gibson and Morello 2012; Marchesi 2015; Gibson and Whitton 2016.
6. See Gibson and Whitton 2016: 29–30 for an overview of the scholarly debate on this sentence.
7. Bodel 2015.
8. By combining chronological order with *variatio*, Gibson and Morello (2012: 16) remark that Pliny's *Epistulae* fuses the 'large-scale linear progression of the letters of Cicero to Atticus (or Seneca to Lucilius)' with the compositional techniques of 'certain books of Cicero's *Ad Familiares*'. As Marchesi 2008 illustrates, Pliny's composition techniques may have been inspired by Horace's *Epistles* or Roman love elegy as well.
9. Gibson and Morello 2012: 13.
10. Gibson and Morello 2012: 14.
11. Apple 1991: xxi.
12. Apple 1991: xxii. See also Diment 2006: 175–80.
13. Norman 2015: 53–61. See also Foster 1993: 178–203.
14. Toker 2002: 139.
15. This is only one interpretation of the opening sentence of the first chapter. For other possible readings of this phrase, see Apple 1991: ix–xx.
16. Toker 2002: 138.
17. Norman 2015: 56–7. Toker 1995; 2002 suggests a link between Nabokov's conceptualization of time and the philosophy of Henri Bergson.
18. Norman 2015: 53.
19. Apple 1991: xxiii.
20. Norman 2015: 54.
21. Apple 1991: xxiii.
22. In scholarship, there has been much discussion whether Nabokov presents himself as suffering from 'chronophobia' or just realizes that he runs the risk, like some his characters, of falling prey to it. See Toker 2002 for an overview of this scholarly debate.
23. In his prologue, Nabokov indicates that he considered giving his autobiography the title of 'Conclusive Evidence'.
24. Cf. Lefèvre 2009: 286: '*Plinius versucht durch seine studia – durch literarische Werke – Nachruhm zu erringen*'.

25. Auhagen 2003: 3–15; Lefèvre 2009: 285–9.

26. See Gibson and Morello 2012: 248–51 and especially the third chapter of Henderson 2002, that extensively explores Pliny's relation to time.

27. On the function of Uncle Pliny in the *Epistulae*, see Lefèvre 2009: 123–6; Henderson 2016 and Eco 2016.

28. For an elaborate discussion of the Elder Pliny's relation with time, see Henderson 2002: 69–102.

29. E.g. 1.9; 1.10; 2.8; 2.14; 3.1; 3.12; 3.21; 8.9; 9.35. For a discussion of Pliny's lack of time in the context of the Roman concept *otium*, see Johnson 2010: 32–62; Gibson and Morello 2012: 169–200; Fitzgerald 2007.

30. Henderson 2002: 79. He adds: 'The 'astrolabe' image removes teleology. . . . At Spurinna's, time is cosmic eternity, the astrolabe's capture of time'.

31. Probably the most deplorable example can be found in 6.10, in which Pliny tells about the tomb of Verginius Rufus, a monument completely neglected and forgotten by his heirs.

32. Similar claims are made in several other letters in the third book, most explicitly in 3.5; 3.21.

33. Norman 2015: 57.

34. Norman 2015: 58.

35. Norman 2015: 64. See also Foster 1993: 186.

36. Foster 1993: 186–95.

37. Norman 2015: 57.

38. Pliny's rejection of historiographic linearity in the first letter has mostly been interpreted as a reference to the internal organization of each individual book, in which the letters are arranged in a varied but meaningful order. Keeping the deviations from the linear progress of time in mind that frequently appear across the work, however, the statement may also programmatically comment upon the order of the nine books as a collection.

39. Woodman 1989: 135 observes that chronological ordering was recognized as 'above all a historiographical technique in Antiquity'.

40. Traub 2016; Newlands 2010; Ash 2003.

41. Marchesi 2008: 144; Tzounakas 2008: 47.

42. Think, for instance, of Cicero's letters to Atticus or Seneca's epistles to Lucilius.

43. Baier 2003 and Woodman 2012 explore the dynamic interrelation that Pliny develops in 5.8 between historiography and oratory. See also Gibson and Whitton 2016: 30 for further references.

44. Ash 2003: 221–5; see also Gibson and Morello 2012: 298.

45. Marchesi 2008: 170 offers a more optimistic reading of the end of the letter: 'In a final twist of his argument, Pliny turns the impossibility of historiography into a commitment to write history. Capito should accept Pliny's challenge and pick a topic anyway. His choice will pave the way for Pliny's historical writing'. I believe we could also understand Pliny's demand the other way around, seeing the choice Capito must make as an unsolvable dilemma (and thus as another indication of the impossibility for Pliny to start writing history).

46. For other possible readings of this letter, see Felton 1999: 74; Ash 2003.

47. Morello 2015. See also Gibson and Morello 2012: 246–50.

48. Morello 2015: 184: 'His persistent invitations to 'look again, read again and think again' spur on a reader's intellectual engagement not only with the world around him/herself, but with Pliny's own collection'.

49. Gibson and Morello 2012: 239: 'As readers, we too should consider returning to, and refining, interpretative work already done. . . . It reflects and supports the literary mission which he has already defined for himself in 5.8, the famous letter in which he resists Titinius Capito's encouragement to turn his hand to historiography. . . . Pliny's modesty makes him revise and review even the work in which he has professional expertise, and his message to his readers to think again about everything they have learned in their earlier experience as readers of his collection reflects his attitude to his own career'.

50. Gibson 2015; Whitton 2013: 54–61.

51. Whitton 2013: 48.

52. Whitton 2013: 46–7.

53. Whitton 2013: 45.

54. Although not explicitly referring to letter 5.8, Ash 2003: 214 draws a similar conclusion, yet from a different angle (the actual editorial practice): 'Pliny, by rejecting a continuous historical narrative, not only dispenses with the problem of chronological order, he also allowed himself to scope letters which he had not yet written, about events which had not yet happened. The advantage was that Pliny could simply keep going on: even if he died before his project was finished, the value and standing of his literary endeavour as a whole would not be undermined as a result'.

55. I thus do not agree with Gibson 2012: 69 who suggests that the 'macro-chronology' in the *Epistulae* is 'perhaps not so immediately evident or important as the existence of thematic connections between adjacent letters'. As I have illustrated, from the first letter on there is a constant tension between chronological and non-chronological progress.

56. Gibson 2012: 62.

57. Lefèvre 2009: 285–9. See also a series of letters in the ninth book on this matter: 9.8; 9.11; 9.20; 9.23; 9.25; 9.28; 9.31.

58. Apple 1991: xix.

59. Boyd 1999.

60. Norman 2015: 66. See also Foster 1993: 189–95.

61. Rodgers 2018: 39.

62. Rodgers 2018: 41.

63. Rodgers 2018: 39.

64. Rodgers 2018: 40.

65. Apple 1991: xi. For the link between the patterning in *Speak, Memory* and Nabokov's departure to the United States at the end, see Greyson 2002: 1–7. For a discussion on the relation between the idea of the text as a scrambled picture and the ethical, philosophical and moral aspects of Nabokov's literary project, see Apple 1991: xx–xxiv.

66. Rodgers 2018: 41.

67. Gibson and Morello 2012: 95 notices in this description a 'slightly Ovidian setting of closed shutters and half-light'.

68. 9.36 and its twin letter 9.40, deliberately placed at the close of the collection, are addressed to Fuscus (Salinator). The choice of this addressee may be seen as a response to the opening letter of the collection, written to a long-standing admirer, named (Septicius) Clarus. Throughout the *Epistulae*, we move, thereby, from 'dawn' to 'dusk'. After having dived into the dark of the final letters, the reader is encouraged to return to the light and re-read the collection. See Barchiesi 2005: 330; Marchesi 2008: 248.

69. Gibson and Morello 2012: 247.
70. McEwen 1995. See also Goalen 2001.
71. The link between Pliny's reflections upon the 'piecemeal approach to texts' and the structure of the *Epistulae* is profoundly explored in Gibson and Morello 2012: 238–48.
72. Henderson 2002: 84.
73. Bergmann 1994: 254.
74. Bergmann 1994: 226.
75. Bergmann 1994: 249: 'Memory collects and reconnects moving fragments from the past'.
76. As Morello 2015: 150 convincingly argues, Pliny, at some points in his collection, represents himself as a teacher, who wants to 'educate' his reader: 'I suggest that he is also setting up a fundamentally didactic programme to educate his readers not only in choosing proper moral positions in tricky social or emotional situations but also in acquiring one of the most important technical skills for reading the whole letter collection: the ability to reconsider one's understanding of whatever one has read or thought, and the willingness to change one's mind'.
77. Gibson and Morello 2012: 236–44 extensively discusses the concept of re-reading.
78. In the previous chapter of this volume, Scott McGill draws a similar conclusion regarding the *argumenta*. In his view, the summarizer's handling of the *Aeneid* involves 'more than simply making it less' (p. 237). The *argumenta* are 'ludic textual performances' that do not only 'fit a reduced *Aeneid* to a new literary context and new purposes' but also 'recast' the epic's language and content (p. 237). Epitomary literature, one could say, forces us to rethink the paradigms that we have used to judge literary works to be 'complete', to be 'meaningful'.
79. McGill illustrates this several times in his section on intertextuality in the *argumenta*. One line in the *argumenta* often refers to multiple episodes in the *Aeneid*, so functioning as a 'simultaneous recollection of several Virgilian lines' (p. 237). The *argumenta* thus cancel out narrative time, bringing distant moments in the epic together in one line.
80. McGill beautifully illustrates this in the previous chapter by his analysis of the *argumenta*. He describes the verse summaries as 'exercises in defamiliarization, i.e., of making the familiar look different and strange' (p. 237) One could describe my methodology in similar terms, as an attempt of defamiliarization, an attempt to 'approach my research subject in terms that are both alien to the subject itself and to the discourse and the expectations through which we have been used to shape our understanding of it' (see Noens 2019a: 273).
81. For a more extensive reflection upon a research practice based on unexpected textual encounters, see Noens 2019a, 2019b.

Works cited

Alexandrov, V., ed. (1995), *The Garland Companion to Vladimir Nabokov*, New York: Routledge.
Apple, A. (1991), 'Introduction', in V. Nabokov, *Lolita. Revised and Updated*, xi–lxxv, New York: Vintage Books.
Ash, R. (2003), '"Aliud est enim epistulam, aliud historiam . . . scriber": Pliny the Historian?', *Arethusa*, 36 (2): 221–5.
Auhagen, U. (2003), '*Lusus* und *Gloria*': Plinius' *Hendecasyllabi*', in L. Castagna and E. Lefèvre (eds), *Plinius der Jüngere und seine Zeit*, 3–15, München-Leipzig: K. G. Saur.
Baier, T. (2003), 'Plinius über historischen und rhetorischen Stil (*Epist.* 5.8)', in L. Castagna and E. Lefèvre (eds), *Plinius der Jüngere und seine Zeit*, 66–88, München-Leipzig: K. G. Saur.

Barchiesi, A. (2005), 'The search for the perfect book', in K. Gutzwiller (ed.), *The New Posidippus: A Hellenistic Poetry Book*, 320–42, Oxford: Oxford University Press.

Bergmann, B. (1994), 'The Roman House as a Memory Theatre: The House of the Tragic Poet in Pompeii', *The Art Bulletin*, 76 (2): 255–6.

Bodel, J. (2015), 'The Publication of Pliny's Letters', in I. Marchesi (ed.), *Pliny the Book-Maker: Betting on Posterity in the* Epistles, 13–108, Oxford: Oxford University Press.

Boyd, B. (1999), 'The butterfly, memory', *The Guardian* (April 17).

Castagna, L. and Lefèvre, E., eds (2003), *Plinius der Jüngere und seine Zeit*, München-Leipzig: K.G. Saur.

Connolly, J., ed. (2005), *The Cambridge Companion to Nabokov*, Cambridge: Cambridge University Press.

De Temmerman, K. (2016), 'Ancient biography and formalities of fiction', in K. De Temmerman and K. Demoen (eds), *Ancient Biography and Formalities of Fiction*, 3–26, Cambridge: Cambridge University Press.

De Temmerman, K. and K. Demoen, eds (2016), *Ancient Biography and Formalities of Fiction*, Cambridge: Cambridge University Press.

Diggle, J., J. Hall and H. Jocelyn, eds (1989), *Studies in Latin Literature and Its Tradition in Honour of C.O. Brink*, Cambridge: Cambridge University Press.

Diment, G. (2005), 'Nabokov's biographical impulse: art of writing lives', in J. Connolly (ed.), *The Cambridge Companion to Nabokov*, 170–85, Cambridge: Cambridge University Press.

Eco, U. (2016), 'A Portrait of the Elder as a Young Pliny', in R. Gibson and C. Whitton (eds), *The Epistles of Pliny*, 185–201, Oxford: Oxford University Press.

Epstein, J. (2014), 'Masterpiece: Nabokov looks back at life before Lolita', *The Wall Street Journal* (June 13).

Felton, D. (1999), *Haunted Greece and Rome: Ghost Stories from Classical Antiquity*, Austin: University of Texas Press.

Fitzgerald, W. (2007), 'The Letter's the Thing (in Pliny Book 7)', in R. Morello and A. Morrison (eds), *Ancient Letters: Classical and Late Antique Epistolography*, 191–210, Oxford: Oxford University Press.

Foster, J. (1993), *Nabokov's Art of Memory and European Modernism*, Princeton: Princeton University Press.

Frischer, B. and I. Brown, eds (2001), *Allan Ramsay and the Search for Horace's Villa*, London: Ashgate.

Gibson, R. (2012), 'On the Nature of Ancient Letter Collections', *The Journal of Roman Studies*, 102: 56–78.

Gibson, R. (2015), 'Not Dark Yet . . .: Reading to the End of Pliny's Nine-Book Collection', in Marchesi (ed.), *Pliny the Book-Maker. Betting on Posterity in the Epistles*, 185–222, Oxford: Oxford University Press.

Gibson, R. and R. Morello (2012), *Reading the* Letters *of Pliny the Younger: An Introduction*, Cambridge: Cambridge University Press.

Gibson, R. and C. Whitton, eds (2016), *The Epistles of Pliny*, Oxford: Oxford University Press.

Goalen, M. (2002), 'Describing the villa: *un rêve virgilien*', in B. Frischer and I. Brown (eds), *Allan Ramsay and the Search for Horace's Villa*, 37–50, London: Ashgate.

Grayson, J. (2002), 'Reading Nabokov', in J. Grayson, A. McMillin and P. Meyer (eds), *Nabokov's World*, 1–7, New York: Palgrave.

Grayson, J., A. McMillin and P. Meyer, eds (2002), *Nabokov's World*, New York: Palgrave.

Grewing, F., B. Acosta-Hughes and A. Kirichenko, eds (2013), *The Door Ajar: False Closure in Greek and Roman Literature and Art*, Heidelberg: Winter Verlag.

Gutzwiller, K., ed. (2005), *The New Posidippus: A Hellenistic Poetry Book*, Oxford: Oxford University Press.

Henderson, J. (2002), *Pliny's Statue: The* Letters, *Self-Portraiture and Classical Art*, Exeter: University of Exeter Press.

Henderson, J. (2016), 'Knowing Someone Through Their Books: Pliny on Uncle Pliny (*Epistles* 3.5)', in R. Gibson and C. Whitton (eds), *The Epistles of Pliny*, 378–419, Oxford: Oxford University Press.

Johnson, W. (2010), *Readers and Reading Culture in the High Roman Empire: A Study of Elite Communities*, Oxford: Oxford University Press.

Lefèvre, E. (2009), *Vom Römertum zum Ästhetizismus. Studien zu den Briefen des jüngeren Plinius*, Berlin: De Gruyter.

Marchesi, I. (2008), *The Art of Pliny's Letters: A Poetics of Allusion in the Private Correspondence*, Cambridge: Cambridge University Press.

Marchesi, I. (2015), 'Uncluttered Spaces, Unlittered Texts: Pliny's Villas as Editorial Places', in I. Marchesi (ed.), *Pliny the Book-Maker: Betting on Posterity in the* Epistles, 225–54, Oxford: Oxford University Press.

Marchesi, I., ed. (2015), *Pliny the Book-Maker: Betting on Posterity in the* Epistles, Oxford: Oxford University Press.

McEwen, I. (1995), 'Housing Fame: In the Tuscan Villa of Pliny the Younger', *Anthropology and Aesthetics,* 27: 11–24.

Miller, J. and A. Woodman, eds (2010), *Latin Historiography and Poetry in the Early Empire Generic Interactions*, Leiden: Brill.

Mommsen, T. (1873), *Étude sur Pline le Jeune*, Paris: A. Franck.

Morello, R. (2007), 'Book 8: Two Viewpoints and the Pedestrian Reader', in I. Marchesi (ed.), *Pliny the Book-Maker: Betting on Posterity in the* Epistles, 144–85, Oxford: Oxford University Press.

Morello, R. and A. Morrison, eds (2007), *Ancient Letters: Classical and Late Antique Epistolography*, Oxford: Oxford University Press.

Most, G. (1989), 'The stranger's stratagem. Self-disclosure and self-sufficiency in Greek culture', *Journal of Hellenistic Studies,* 109: 114–33.

Murgia, C. (2016), 'The Chronology and Arrangement of Pliny's Letters', in R. Gibson and C. Whitton (eds), *The Epistles of Pliny*, 146–59, Oxford: Oxford University Press.

Nabokov, V. (1989), *Speak, Memory. An Autobiography Revisited*, New York: Vintage Books.

Nabokov, V. (1991), *Lolita. Revised and Updated*, New York: Vintage Books.

Newlands, C. (2010), 'The Eruption of Vesuvius In The Epistles Of Statius And Pliny', in J. Miller and A. Woodman (eds), *Latin Historiography and Poetry in the Early Empire Generic Interactions*, 105–22, Leiden: Brill.

Noens, T. (2019a), 'A Reader's Dialogues. Discussing Latin Literature of the First Century through Modernism', PhD diss, Ghent University, Ghent.

Noens T. (2019b), 'Catching the Collapse of Time. Reading Ornytus in Statius' *Thebaid* 12 through Malone in Samuel Beckett's *The Unnamable*', *Quaderni Urbinati di Cultura Classica,* 122: 157–78.

Normann, W. (2012), *Nabokov, History and the Texture of Time*, New York: Routledge.

Plinius, C.S. (1969), *Letters.* ed. and trans. Betty Radice, Cambridge, MA: Harvard University Press.

Proskurina, V. (2002), 'Nabokov's *Exegi Monumentum.* Immortality in Quotation Marks', in J. Grayson, A. McMillin and P. Meyer (eds), *Nabokov's World*, 27–40, New York: Palgrave.

Rodgers, M. (2018), *Nabokov and Nietzsche: Problems and Perspectives*, New York: Bloomsbury.

Sherwin-White, A (1966), *The Letters of Pliny: A Historical and Social Commentary*, Oxford: Oxford University Press.

Toker, L. (1995), 'Nabokov and Bergson', in V. Alexandrov (ed.), *The Garland Companion to Vladimir Nabokov*, 367–73, New York: Routledge.

Toker, L. (1989), *Nabokov. The Mystery of Literary Structures*, New York: Cornell University Press.

Toker, L. (2002), 'Nabokov and Bergson on Duration and Reflexivity', in J. Grayson, A. McMillin and P. Meyer (eds), *Nabokov's World*, 132–41, New York: Palgrave.
Traub, H. (2016), 'Pliny's Treatment of History in Epistolary Form', in R. Gibson and C. Whitton (eds), *The Epistles of Pliny*, 123–45, Oxford: Oxford University Press.
Tzounakas, S. (2007), '"Neque enim historiam componebam": Pliny's First Epistle and His Attitude towards Historiography', *Museum Helveticum*, 64: 42–54.
Whitton C. (2013), 'Trapdoors. False Closure in Pliny', in F. Grewing, B. Acosta-Hughes and A. Kirichenko (eds), *The Door Ajar: False Closure in Greek and Roman Literature and Art*, 43–61, Heidelberg: Winter Verlag.
Whitton, C. (2015), 'Grand Designs: Unrolling *Epistles* 2', in I. Marchesi (ed.), *Pliny the Book-Maker: Betting on Posterity in the* Epistles, 109–144, Oxford: Oxford University Press.
Wolff, E. (2003), *Pline le jeune ou le refus de pessimism*, Rennes: Presses universitaires de Rennes.
Woodman, A. (1989), 'Virgil the Historian', in J. Diggle, J. Hall and H. Jocelyn (eds), *Studies in Latin Literature and Its Tradition in Honour of C.O. Brink*, 132–45, Cambridge: Cambridge University Press.
Woodman, A. (2012), *From Poetry to History. Selected Papers*, Oxford: Oxford Scholarship Online.

INDEX NOMINUM

Abensour, Miguel 25, 31 n.8, 31 n.12, 31 n.13
Accius 98
Adamov, Arthur 196
Adorno, Theodor 24, 31 n.8
Aelian 123 n.7
Aelius Aristides 203
Aelius Theon 218 n.13
Aethiopis 74
Agamben, Giorgio 14 n.3
Agathon (monk) 145, 157, 159 n.4, 162 n.19, 164 n.49
Alcuin (*disputatio de rhetorica et de virtutibus*) 203–4, 219 n.22
Ambrose 23
Amiel, Henri-Frédéric 134
Ammianus 108 n.60
Ammonas (monk) 159 n.4, 161 n.16
Anaximenes of Lampsachus 203, 218 n.15
Anthologia Latina, *see Carmina XII sapientum*
Antony (monk) 149–50, 157, 158, 159 n.4, 161 n.14, 16, 163 n.39, 42, 44
  see also Vita Antonii
Apollodorus of Athens 123 n.2
Apollonius Rhodius 52 n.31
Apophthegmata partum 13, 141–65, 175 n.14, 177
Appian of Alexandria (*Iberica*) 69 n.44
Apuleius 95, 108 n.58
Argumenta of the Twelve Wise Men, *see Carmina XII sapientum*
Aristophanes of Byzantium 115, 123 n.7, 124 n.21
Aristotle 107 n.48, 123 n.7, 164 n.44, 203
  Arist. *Ath. Pol.* 107 n.48
Arsenius (monk) 150–1, 157, 159 n.4, 160 n.11, 161 n.16, 163 n.43
Artaud, Antonin 13, 193–201
Athenaeus 187, 244 n.23
Augustine 15 n.25, 23, 103 n.13, 104 n.29, 108 n.59, 149, 153–4, 163 n.38, 40, 168, 248
  Aug. *Civ.* 108 n.59, 168
  Aug. *Conf.* 149, 153, 163 n.38, 248
  Aug. *Mag.* 153–4
  Aug. *in Ps.* 154, 164 n.53
  Aug. *Vera rel.* 163 n.40
Ausonius 13, 34–51, 51 n.3, 51 n.5, 51 n.8, 51 n.13, 51 n.21, 51 n.27, 52 n.28, 52 n.30, 52 n.34, 67 n.6, 85, 91, 103 n.20, 104 n.31, 126 n.53, 163 n.38, 185, 188 n.17, 243 n.8
  Auson. *Caes.* 35–9, 47–50
  Auson. *Cento* 38–9, 49–50, 85, 91, 103 n.20, 104 n.31, 126 n.53
  Auson. *Epit.* 35–6, 39–50, 52 n.28, 52 n.30, 52 n.34
  Auson. *Ep. ad Symm.* 51 n.3, 51 n.21
  Auson. *Griph.* 37–8, 50, 185–6, 188 n.17
  Auson. *Lud.* 38
  Auson. *Mos.* 38, 50
  Auson. *Par.* I38, 39–41, 45, 47–8, 50, 51 n.24, 52 n.34
  Auson. *Prof.* 36, 38, 39–41, 45, 47–8, 50, 52 n.34
  Auson. *Techn.* 37, 50, 51 n.13
  Auson. *Urb.* 37–8

Bacchylides 107 n.107
Barron (historian), *see Suda*
Barthes, Roland 12, 13, 15 n.12, 116, 126 n.47, 129–37, 244 n.19
Basil of Caesarea 157, 168, 243 n.17
Benedict (saint) 159
Benjamin (monk) 157
Benjamin, Walter 24
Bessarion (monk) 145, 157, 162 n.18
Bible (New and Old Testament)
  Bible (Old Testament) 77, 116–17, 205, 206, 213, 215, 222 n.76
  Bible Ex ix, 213
  Bible Ez 174, 213
  Bible Gen 222 n.73
  Bible Is 174
  Bible Job 160, 213
  Bible Jon 206
  Bible Nr 213
  Bible Prov ix, 213
  Bible Ps 154, 155, 215–16,
  Bible (New Testament) 77, 205, 207, 213–14, 216
  Bible 1 Cor 152, 154, 163 n.34, 164 n.44
  Bible Eph 154
  Bible Heb 155
  Bible Joh 168
  Bible Lk 149, 215, 222 n.79
  Bible 2 Macc 116–17, 124 n.23
  Bible Mar 213–14
  Bible Mt 153, 145, 147, 161 n.16, 164 n.49, 213–14, 221 n.73
  Bible Sirach (*Ecclus.*) 216

Birt, Theodor 7, 15 n.22
Blin, Roger 196
Borges, Jorge Luis 4, 168–9, 174, 175 n.2
Bott, Heinrich 6, 7, 15 n.14, 15 n.15, 15 n.22
Breton, André 196

Caesar 36, 49, 69 n.45 90–1
Calvus 90–1
Carmen de figuris et schematibus 203
Carmina XII sapientum (*Twelve Wise Men*) 13, 233–46
Cato 55–71, 106 n.39, 106 n.41
 Cato *Agr.* 65, 68 n.21, 69 n.30
 Cato *Commentarii iuris ciuilis* 65
 Cato *De re militari* 65
 Cato *Or.* 63, 65, 66, 70 n.53
 Cato *Orig.* 56, 57, 59, 62–6, 67 n.2, 68 n.21, 70 n.58
Catullus 55, 67 n.2, 90–1, 107 n.44, 186
Charisius 102 n.10, 106 n.39
Cicero 57–9, 61, 63, 65, 67 n.6, 68 n.25, 69 n.35, 69 n.45, 70 n.50, 70 n.59, 88–9, 91, 105 n.36, 203, 234, 243 n.10, 269 n.8, 270 n.42
 Cic. *Arch.* 22 69 n.35
 Cic. *Att.* 68 n.18, 269 n.8, 270 n.42
 Cic. *Balb.* 59
 Cic. *Brut.* 59, 105 n.36
 Cic. *Cat.* 69 n.40, 70 n.50
 Cic. *Cato* 68 n.23, 68 n.25, 70 n.59
 Cic. *De consulatu suo* 62
 Cic. *De orat.* 203
 Cic. *Div.* 69 n.31
 Cic. *Fam.* 269 n.8,
 Cic. *Leg.* 57, 67–8 n.13
 Cic. *Nat. Deo.* 70
 Cic. *Off.* 69 n.45, 105 n.36
 Cic. *Orat.* 70, 203
 Cic. *Part.* 203
 Cic. *Phil.* 69, 89
 Cic. *Planc.* 70 n.57
 Cic. *Rep.* 69 n.46
 Cic. *Sen.*, *see* Cic. *Cato*
 Cic. *Tusc.* 58, 69 n.35, 70 n.59
Claudian 1, 184, 187,
 Claud. *carm. min.* 1, 184
 Claud. *carm. Gr.* 187
Clement of Alexandria 14, 115–26
 Clem. *Protr.* 119, 125 n.40, 126 n.46.
 Clem. *Strom.* 14, 115–26
Clement of Rome 123 n.11, 124 n.27
Cotton Genesis 77, 222 n.73
Croce, Benedetto 15 n.27

Dares Phrygius 51 n.27
Deleuze, Gilles 195, 197, 201 n.6, 244 n.20
Demosthenes 145
Derrida, Jacques 154, 164 n.54, 195, 197, 199, 201 n.5
Dictys Cretensis 51 n.27
Diderot, Denis 130
Dio Cassius 76, 218 n.11
Diomedes Grammaticus 97, 103 n.13
Dionysian Corpus (Pseudo-Dionysius Aeropagite) 14, 168–76, 181
Dionysios (author), *see Dionysian Corpus*
Dionysius of Halicarnassus 115, 118, 123 n.5
Disney, Walt 4
Donatus, Tiberius Claudius (*Inst. Verg.*) 245 n.38, 245 n.42
Dongshan Shouchu 155

Eco, Umberto 77, 79 n.22, 270 n.27
Empedocles 117, 125 n.30, 125 n.34
Ennius 56–7, 60–1, 69 n.35, 104 n.24
Esprit, Fléchier 24
Evagrius Ponticus 146, 148–9, 151, 159, 160 n.11, 162 n.22, 162 n.26, 163–3 n.30, 165 n.71
 Euagr. *De oratione* 162–3 n.30
 Euagr. *Gnostikos* 148, 165 n.71
 Euagr. *Praktikos* 146, 162 n.22, 165 n.71
Euripides 52 n.31, 100–1
 Eur. *Bacch.* 100–1
 Eur. *Hec.* 52 n.31
Excerpta rhetorica ex codice Parisino 7530 203–4, 219 n.23

Festus 14, 68 n.15, 86
Flaubert, Gustave 133–4
Foucault, Michel 160 n.7, 195, 196–7
Freud, Sigmund 29, 32 n.37, 130
Frontinus (*Strat.*) 69 n.44
Furius Antias 88–9, 105 n.34, 105 n.35, 105 n.36, 106 n.39

Galen 101 n.1, 107 n.46, 218 n.12
Galdi, Marco 6–7, 15 n.14, 15 n.17, 15 n.18, 15 n.19, 15 n.20, 15 n.21, 15 n.22
Gallimard, Gaston 194, 196
Gellius 59, 68 n.21, 70 n.49, 70 n.53, 83, 84, 86–94, 102 n.4, 102 n.11, 103 n.14, 103 n.16, 104 n.29, 104 n.30, 104 n.31, 104 n.32, 105 n.32, 105 n.36, 105 n.37, 105 n.39, 106 n.39, 106 n.41, 106 n.42, 106 n.43, 107 n.47, 107 n.48, 108 n.53
Genette, Gérard 9, 10, 16 n.35, 16 n.43, 74, 79 n.12, 243 n.5, 244 n.25, 246 n.51
Gide, André 129, 134, 196
Gneus Matius 106 n.39
Gregory of Nyssa 162 n.24
Gregory of Tours 78, 79 n.27
Guattari, Felix 195, 197, 201 n.6, 244 n.20

Hegel, Georg Wilhelm Friedrich 4, 11
Heraclitus 24, 117, 125 n.31
Herondas 107 n.48
Hierotheus 169, 172
Historia Augusta 51 n.7
Homer 35, 40–4, 46–7, 49, 52 n.28, 74, 187, 235, 243 n.8
Hom. *Iliad* 35, 40, 41–3, 46, 52 n.33, 74, 187, 212, 218 n.29, 235, 243 n.8
Hom. *Odyssey* 40, 45, 46–7, 235, 243 n.8
Horace 42, 43, 69 n.29, 79, 83, 180–1, 185, 186
Hor. *Ars* 79, 180
Hor. *Carm.* 42, 69 n.29, 181, 185, 186
Hor. *Epist.* 269 n.8,
Hyginus 70 n.58
Hyperechios (monk) 147, 158, 163
Hyperides 107 n.48

Ignace de Loyola 134
Ilioupersis 74
Irenaeus 161 n.15
Isaiah (monk) 151, 164 n.47
Isidore 104 n.23

James (monk) 141
Jason of Cyrene 117
Jerome 106 n.40
John Cassian 164 n.44
John Chrysostom 125 n.38
John III (Pope) 159 n.4
Joseph (monk) 155, 164 n.55
Julianus Toletanus 97
Julius Victor (*Rhet.*) 67 n.7, 203, 219 n.21
Justin (historian) 123 n.14

Kafka, Franz 1–2, 14 n.2, 24, 134
Keil, Heinrich 5, 15 n.16

La Bruyère, Jean 24
La Fontaine, Jean de 28
Laberius 92–3, 107 n.44, 107 n.48
Lactantius 68 n.17, 233
Lact. *Inst.* 68 n.17
Le Rochefoucauld, François de la 24
Lévi-Strauss 28, 32 n.36, 32 n.42
Life of Constantina 168
Life of Severus of Antioch 174
Little Iliad 74
Livius Andronicus 83
Livy 59–60, 69 n.29, 69 n.33, 69 n.44, 218 n.11, 245 n.35
Loeb, Pierre 196
Lot (monk) 155, 164 n.55
Lucilius 82, 92, 95, 98, 102 n.3, 105 n.36
Lucretius 24

Macrobius 105 n.35, 106 n.39, 243 n.10
Mallarmé, Stéphan 10, 133
Marcellus Empiricus 126 n.53
Marcus Aurelius 24
Marius Victorinus 203, 219 n.21
Marrou, Henri-Iréné 15 n.25
Martial 186–7, 188 n.25
Mazzarino, Santo 7, 16 n.28
Medicina Plinii 10–11
Merton, Thomas (mystic) 152
Michelstaedter, Carlo 24
Molière 131
Mommsen, Theodor 5, 15 n.16
Montaigne, Michel de 133
Moses ix, 120
Moses (monk) 151, 161 n.13, 164 n.46,

Nabokov, Vladimir 13, 248–55, 260–3, 267–8, 269 n.2, 269 n.17, 269 n.22, 269 n.23, 271 n.65
Naevius vii, 98–100
Nepos 13, 52 n.35, 55–66, 67 n.2, 67 n.3, 67 n.5, 67 n.6, 67 n.12, 68 n.14, 86, 69 n.31, 69 n.38, 70 n.55, 70 n.58, 71 n.62, 86
Nep. *Att.* 66, 67 n.1, 67 n.3, 67 n.10, 68 n.17, 68 n.20, 68 n.22, 69 n.46
Nep. *Cato* 13, 52 n.35, 55–66, 67 n.2, 67 n.9, 67 n.12, 68 n.20, 68 n.21, 68 n.24, 69 n.31, 69 n.38, 70 n.55, 70 n.58
Nep. *Hann.* 67 n.2
Nep. *Praef.* 67 n.2, 67 n.3
Newton, Isaac 250, 251, 254–5, 260, 263
Nicole, Pierre 24, 26, 32 n.19
Nietzsche 23, 134
Nilus of Ancyra 162–3 n.30
Nonius Marcellus vii, 14, 51 n.13, 82–109

Optatian 187
Ovid 52 n.31, 126 n.53, 180–1, 186, 188 n.8, 202, 218 n.4, 218 n.6, 271 n.67
Ovid *Met.* 52 n.31, 126 n.53, 181, 202, 218 n.6
Ovid *Trist.* 188 n.8

Pambo (monk) 161 n.14
Parmenides 117, 125 n.35
Pascal, Blaise 131–3
Paul the Deacon 86
Paulinus of Nola 34–5, 43, 49–50, 50 n.1
Paul. Nol. *Epist.* 34–5, 50 n.1
Paul. Nol. *Carm.* 51 n.3
Pelagius (Pope) 159 n.4
Perotti, Niccolò 102 n.7
Philo of Alexandria (*De somnis*) 125 n.38
Philo of Byzantium 124 n.27
Pi-yen chi (*Clue Cliff Collection*) 155, 165 n.61, 165 n.62, 165 n.64

Pindar 52 n.31
Plato 23, 27, 117, 125 n.32, 125 n.33, 125 n.39, 152, 160
Plat. *Crit.* 125 n.33
Plat. *Phaedr.* 125 n.33
Plat. *Symp.* 125 n.33, 125 n.39
Plat. *Thaeet* 125 n.33
Plat. *Tim.* 125 n.32
Plautus 98, 107 n.48
Plaut. *Vid.* 98
Pliny the Elder 4, 10, 11, 32 n.43, 57, 67 n.1, 68 n.16, 70 n.55, 104 n.23, 252, 270 n.27, 270 n.28
Pliny the Younger (*Epist.*) 13, 248–9, 252–61, 263–8, 269 n.8, 269 n.24, 270 n.26, 270 n. 28, 270 n.29, 270 n.31, 270 n.38, 270 n.43, 270 n.45, 270 n.48, 271 n.49, 271 n.54, 272 n.71, 272 n.76
Plotinus 163 n.38
Plutarch 58–60, 61–2, 68 n.25, 69 n.32, 69 n.44, 109 n.64, 119, 123 n.5, 124 n.27, 125 n.30, 126 n.45, 162 n.20
Plut. *Brut.* 123 n.5
Plut. *Cato Mai.* 58–60, 61–2, 69 n.32, 69 n.44
Plut. *Cato Min.* 125 n.30
Plut. *Demosth.* 162 n.20
Plut. *Is.* 119, 126 n.45
Plut. *Mor. (De fato)* 124 n.27
Poemen (monk) 147, 160 n.10, 161 n.13, 161 n.14, 163 n.31
Polybius 69 n.44, 123 n.5
Pompeius Trogus 123 n.14
Pomponius Mela 4, 104 n.23
Priscian 97
Proba 10, 85
Proclus 169
Proust, Marcel 129, 131–4, 136 n.76
Pseudo-Aristotle (*Peplos*) 41
Pseudo-Martyrius 125 n.38
Pseudo-Scymnos 115–16, 123 n.1, 123 n.2, 123 n.3, 123 n.10, 123 n.12
Publius Rutilius Lupus (rhetorician) 203
Pythagoras 120

Quenau, Raymond 10
Quignard Pascal 13, 14, 23–32, 51 n.6, 95
Quintilian (*Inst. Or.*) 103 n.13, 203, 264

Rhetorica ad Alexandrum 203–5, 212
Rhetorica ad Herennium 203, 219 n.24
Ribbeck, Otto 100–1
Riese, Alexander 5, 15 n.16
Rivière, Jacques 196
Rossano Gospels ix, 213–15, 221 n.63, 222 n.76
Rubens, Peter Paul 31 n.5

Sacerdos (grammarian) 97
Saint-Évremond, Charles de 24
Sallust 69, 70
Sall. *Cat.* 70 n.56
Sall. *Hist. frg.* 69 n.45
Seneca (*Epist.*) 69 n.33, 92, 107 n.45, 269 n.8, 270 n.42
Serenus Sammonicus (antiquarian) 95, 107 n.44, 108 n.57
Serenus Septimius (poet) 95, 108 n.57, 108 n.58
Servius 96–7, 102 n.10, 106 n.39, 212, 221 n.55, 245 n.40
Servius *ad Aen.* 96–7, 106 n.39, 245 n.40
Settis, Salvatore 73, 79 n.2
Simonides 52 n.32
Sisenna 88–9
Sisoes (monk) 160 n.10, 161 n.12
Solinus 4, 15 n.16, 104 n.23
Statius (*Silvae*) 187
Stesichorus (*Ilioupersis*) 76
Suda 115, 123 n.6
Suetonius 34–8, 47–50, 51 n.7, 91
Suet. *Caes.* 36, 37, 38, 47–8, 50, 51 n.7
Suet. *De regibus* 34–5, 50
Sulpicius Carthaginiensis 241
Sulpicius Severus (*Life of Saint Martin*) 168
Symmachus (*Epist.*) 51 n.21
Symphosius (*Aenigmata*) 14, 175 n.12, 177–88
Syncletica of Alexandria 146

Tabula Capitolina 74–6
Tabulae Iliacae vii, 74–5, 78, 187, 188 n.28, 219 n.29
Tacitus (*Hist. 5.11.*) 69 n.28
Terence 213
Terentius Vaticanus (*Vatican Terence*) viii, 213–15, 221 n.59
Theocritus 121, 126 n.51
Timotheus of Gaza 123 n.7
Tolstoi, Leon 129, 131, 132
Tryphon of Alexandria 203, 219 n.19

Varro 57, 67 n.1, 67 n.6, 70 n.58, 83, 90, 94–5, 103 n.13, 103 n.14, 104 n.29, 106 n.39, 107 n.48, 108 n.54, 108 n.59
Varro *Imagines* 67 n.1
Varro *L.L.* 104 n.29, 107 n.48
Varro *Men.* 106 n.39, 107 n.48
Vegetius (*Ep.*) 8–9, 14 n.5
Venantius Fortunatus (*carm.*) 188 n.22
Vergil vii–viii, 24, 35, 38, 42–6, 49, 83, 88, 91, 96–7, 104 n.32, 207–12, 217–18, 235, 272 n.79
Verg. *Aen.* viii, 43–6, 96–7, 184, 207, 209–12, 217, 220 n.46, 220 n.50, 233–42, 243 n.17, 244 n.28, 244 n.29, 255 n.31, 245 n.32, 245 n.33, 245 n.36, 245 n.37, 245 n.39,

245 n.41, 245 n.45, 246 n.46, 246 n.47, 246 n.49, 272 n.78, 272 n.79
Verg. *Ecl.* 207–12, 216–18, 220 n.50, 243 n.17
Verg. *Georg.* 70 n.51, 88, 97, 104 n.32, 188, 207, 209–12, 217–18, 220 n.46, 220 n.53, 243 n.17, 246 n.48
Vergilus Romanus (*Roman Vergil*) vii–viii, 207–16, 217–18, 220 n.43
Verrius Flaccus 86
Vienna Dioscorides 207
Vienna Genesis 77, 222 n.73
Virgil, *see* Vergil
Vita Antonii 149, 163 n.39, 163–4 n.44
Weil, Simone (mystic) 147, 163 n.32
Weitzmann, Kurt 74, 76, 79 n.13, 222 n.73, 222 n.74
Wittgenstein, Ludwig 73, 145, 152, 162 n.21
Wölffin, Eduard 6, 15 n.17
Wu-men kuan (*Gateless Barrier*) 141, 165 n.61, 165 n.64

Xiphilinus 76

Yushi Numura 165 n.65

Zoological Encyclopaedia of Constantine VII 115, 124 n.19

Figure 1 Wall painting of Ganymede (in the same form and posture as Endymion, Narcissus or Cyparissus) with Zeus as an Eagle led to him by a Cupid. From the Casa di Meleagro, Pompeii (VI.9.2); now Museo Archeologico Nazionale in Naples, no. 9547. Third quarter of the first century AD. Photo: Erich Lessing/Art Resource, NY.

Figure 2 Marble sarcophagus of Endymion asleep among winged putti; recut with a male portrait head from an earlier image of sleeping Ariadne. From Italy; now British Museum 1947,0714.8. Mid third century AD. Photo: The British Museum.

Figure 3 Marble sarcophagus showing Jonah and the whale, a female orant, a reading philosopher figure (these two figures with unfinished heads), the good shepherd, the baptism of Christ. End of the third century AD. Made in Italy; from the Church of Sta Maria Antiqua, Rome, Photograph: Boehringer, DAI Inst Neg: 52.421.

Figure 4 The Roman Vergil (BAV, MS Vat. lat. 3867) fol. 3v. Prefatory portrait to Vergil's Second Eclogue. Pigments on velum. Late fifth or sixth century, probably made in Italy. Now in the Vatican Library. Photo: Biblioteca Apostolica Vaticana.

Figure 5 The Roman Vergil (BAV, MS Vat. lat. 3867) fol. 14r. Prefatory portrait to Vergil's Sixth Eclogue. Pigments on velum. Late fifth or sixth century, probably made in Italy. Now in the Vatican Library. Photo: Biblioteca Apostolica Vaticana.

Figure 6 The Roman Vergil (BAV, MS Vat. lat. 3867) fol. 1r. Prefatory image to Vergil's First Eclogue, showing Tityrus playing his pipes to Meliboeus. Pigments on velum. Late fifth or sixth century, probably made in Italy. Now in the Vatican Library. Photo: Biblioteca Apostolica Vaticana.

Figure 7 The Roman Vergil (BAV, MS Vat. lat. 3867) fol. 16v. Prefatory image to Vergil's Seventh Eclogue, showing Meliboeus judging the poetic competition between Corydon and Thyrsis. Pigments on velum. Late fifth or sixth century, probably made in Italy. Now in the Vatican Library. Photo: Biblioteca Apostolica Vaticana.

Figure 8a and b The Roman Vergil (BAV, MS Vat. lat. 3867) fols. 44v. and 45r. Double-page frontispiece to Vergil's Third Georgic. Pigments on velum. Late fifth or sixth century, probably made in Italy. Now in the Vatican Library. Photo: Biblioteca Apostolica Vaticana.

Figure 9a and b The Roman Vergil (BAV, MS Vat. lat. 3867) fols. 100v. and 101r. Double-page frontispiece to the Second Book of Vergil's *Aeneid*. Pigments on velum. Late fifth or sixth century, probably made in Italy. Now in the Vatican Library. Photo: Biblioteca Apostolica Vaticana.

Figure 10 The Roman Vergil (BAV, MS Vat. lat. 3867) fol. 188v. Left-hand folio from a double-page frontispiece, perhaps to the Twelfth Book of Vergil's *Aeneid*, showing battle between the Trojans and the Rutulians. Pigments on velum. Late fifth or sixth century, probably made in Italy. Now in the Vatican Library. Photo: Biblioteca Apostolica Vaticana.

Figure 11 The Vatican Terence (BAV, MS Vat. lat. 3868) fol. 2r. Prefatory image for the whole codex with a portrait of the author in an imago clipeata held by two figures in actors' masks. Pigments on velum. Ninth-century copy (*c.* 825 AD) of an Italian original of the fifth century, perhaps made in Gaul. Now in the Vatican Library. Photo: Biblioteca Apostolica Vaticana.

Figure 12 The Vatican Terence (BAV, MS Vat. lat. 3868) fol. 77r. Prefatory image for the play *Phormio*, showing an arched aedicule with conch-filled tympanum flanked by vases holding ß actors' masks (for the speaking parts). Pigments on velum. Ninth-century copy (*c*. 825 AD) of an Italian original of the fifth century, perhaps made in Gaul. Now in the Vatican Library. Photo: Biblioteca Apostolica Vaticana.

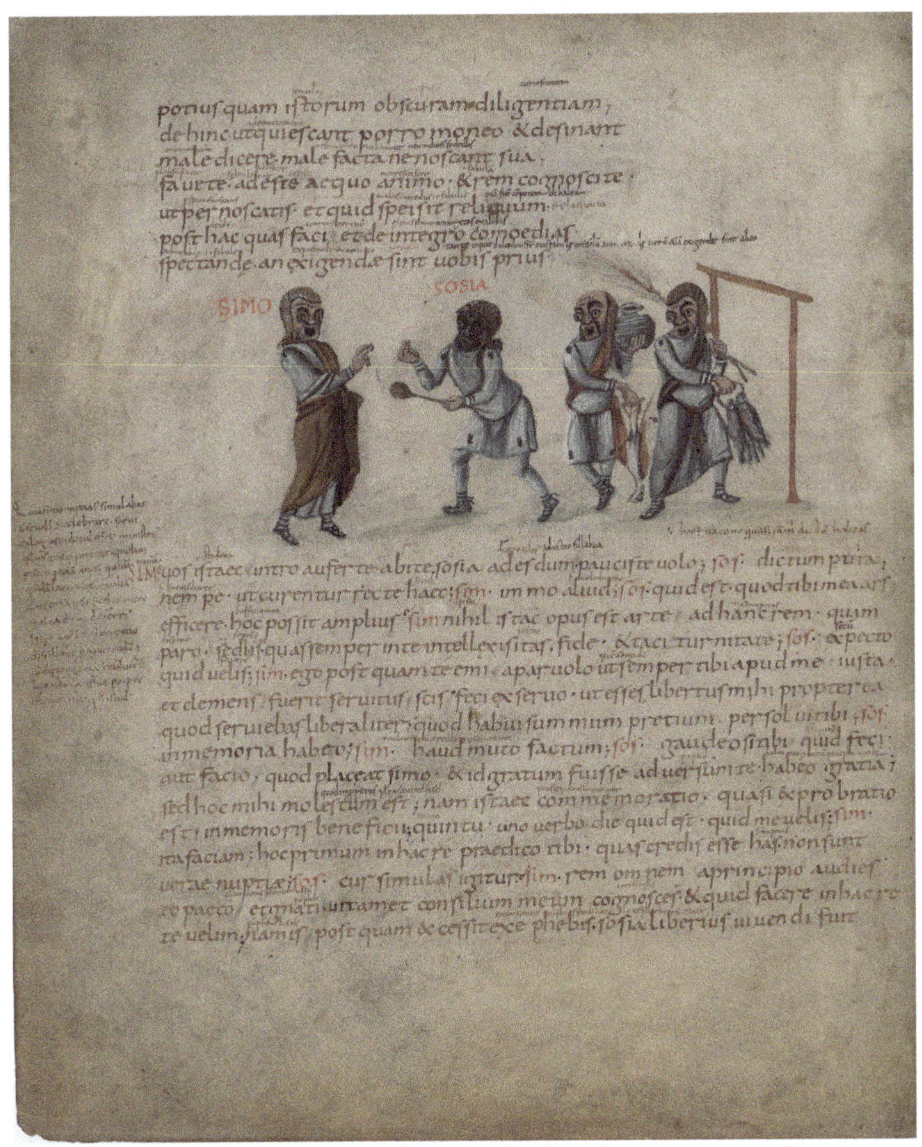

Figure 13 The Vatican Terence (BAV, MS Vat. lat. 3868) fol. 4v. Prefatory image for the first scene of Act 1 of *Andria* (from line 28), placed between this and the last lines of the prologue (21–27, at the top of the page). The illumination with all figures in actors' masks shows precisely the action of line 28, the first in the scene: Simo orders two unidentified slaves to take provisions into the house and addresses his freedman Sosia (both named characters are labelled in red). Pigments on velum. Ninth-century copy (*c.* 825 AD) of an Italian original of the fifth century, perhaps made in Gaul. Now in the Vatican Library. Photo: Biblioteca Apostolica Vaticana.

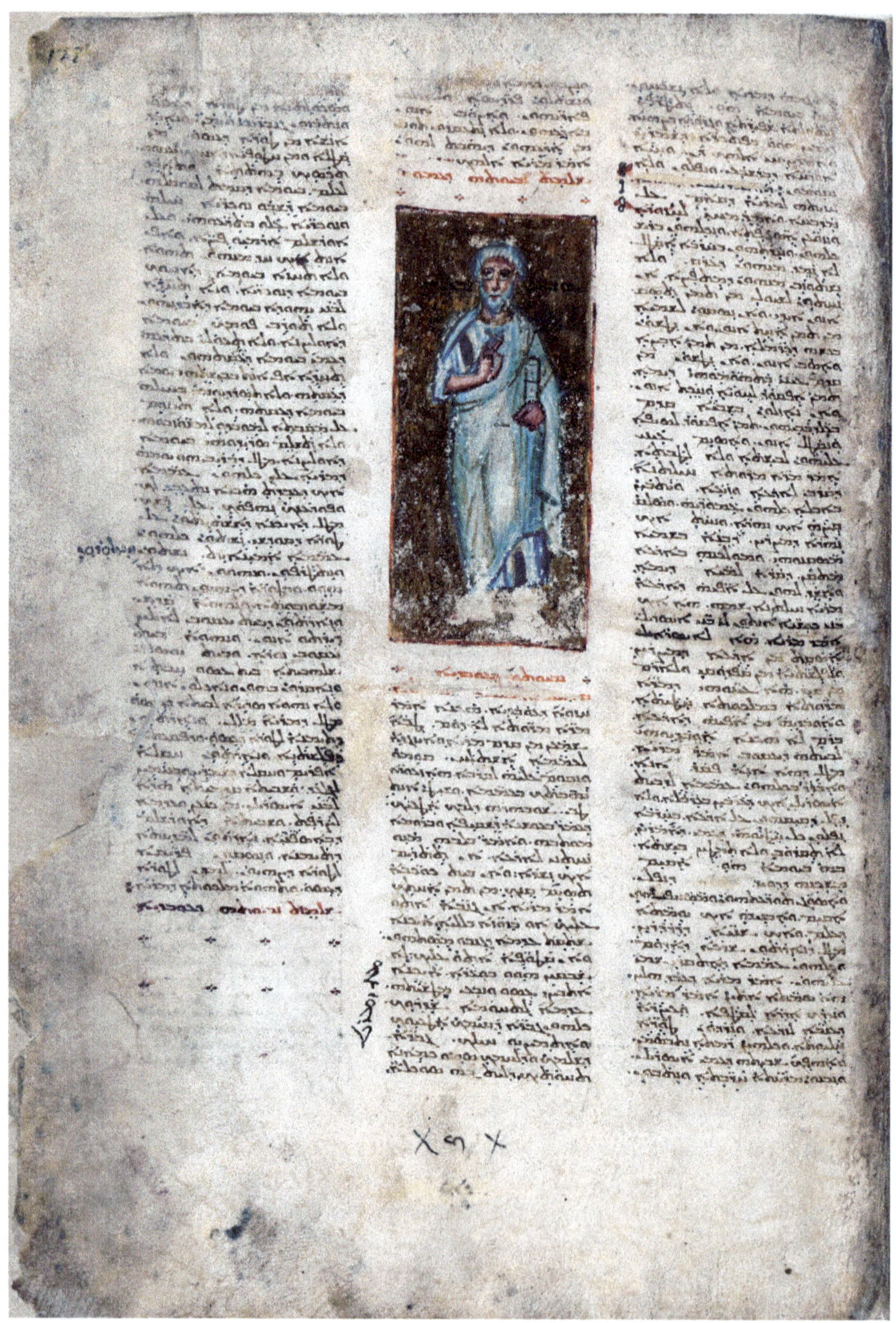

Figure 14 Syriac Bible in Paris (BnF, MS syr. 341) fol. 178r. Prefatory portrait to the Book of Obadiah. Pigments on velum. Sixth or early seventh century, made in Syria, now in the Bibliothèque nationale, Paris. Photo: gallica.bnf.fr / Bibliothèque nationale de France.

Figure 15 Syriac Bible in Paris (BnF, MS syr. 341) fol. 8r. Prefatory image to the Book of Exodus showing Moses and Aaron before Pharaoh and his attendants. Pigments on velum. Sixth or early seventh century, made in Syria, now in the Bibliothèque nationale, Paris. Photo: gallica.bnf.fr / Bibliothèque nationale de France.

Figure 16 Syriac Bible in Paris (BnF, MS syr. 341) fol. 118r. Prefatory image to the Book of Proverbs showing the Virgin and Child between Solomon and Ecclesia or perhaps a personification of Wisdom. Pigments on velum. Sixth or early seventh century, made in Syria, now in the Bibliothèque nationale, Paris. Photo: gallica.bnf.fr / Bibliothèque nationale de France.

Figure 17 The Rossano Gospels (Ms Σ, 042, Cathedral Library, Rossano, Italy) fol. 121r. Mark the Evangelist writing the gospel accompanied by a female figure with halo, perhaps a personification of Wisdom, perhaps the Virgin. His scroll bears the words in Greek 'the beginning of the Gospel of Jesus Christ, Son of God'. Pigments on purple-dyed velum. Sixth century, probably from the eastern Mediterranean, now in the Diocesan Museum, Rossano. Photo: Erich Lessing/Art Resource, NY.

Figure 18 The Rossano Gospels (Ms Σ, 042, Cathedral Library Rossano, Italy) fol. 7v. The Parable of the Good Samaritan. Pigments and silver ink on purple-dyed velum. Sixth century, probably from the eastern Mediterranean, now in the Diocesan Museum, Rossano. Photo: Erich Lessing/Art Resource, NY.

www.ingramcontent.com/pod-product-compliance
Lightning Source LLC
Chambersburg PA
CBHW060238100726
47907CB00003B/683

* 9 7 8 1 3 5 0 2 8 1 9 7 4 *